We at World Savings hope
that this unique collection of recipes
will provide you and
your family with many new
adventures into the
delicious world of food.

WORLD SAVINGS CALIFORNIA OFFICES

Antioch: Opening Soon
Arcadia: 1200 S. Baldwin Ave. at Duarte Rd. 91006 . . . . (213) 445-4311
Brentwood: 11601 Wilshire Blvd. at San Vicente 90025 . . . (213) 477-8004
Citrus Heights: 8477 Auburn Blvd. 95610 . . . . (916) 967-8274
Fountain Valley: 16123 Harbor Blvd. at Edinger 92708 . . . (714) 839-2851
Huntington Beach: 6952 Warner Ave. at Golden West 90247 (714) 842-9356
Irvine: 18100 Culver Dr. at Michelson Ave. 92664 . . . . . (714) 552-0200
Lafayette: 3557 Mt. Diablo Blvd. 94549 . . . . (415) 284-2323
Laguna Beach: 292 S. Coast Highway at Forest Ave. 92652 . (714) 494-9481
Lynwood: 11170 Long Beach Blvd. at Imperial 90262 . . . . (213) 636-0511
Northridge: 9036 Reseda Blvd. at Nordhoff 91324 . . . . . . (213) 886-4240
Ontario: 521 N. Euclid Ave. 91761 . . . . (714) 984-1225
Palo Alto: 700 Welch Rd. 94304 . . . . (415) 328-1831
Placerville: 1303 Broadway 95667 . . . . (916) 622-9200
Rancho Cordova: 10134 Coloma Rd. 95670 . . . . (916) 362-1321
Sacramento: 5500 Folsom Blvd. 95819 . . . . (916) 452-6151
Sacramento: 2119 Arden Way 95825 . . . . (916) 925-3592
Sacramento: 6300 Florin Rd. 95823 . . . . (916) 421-6980
San Bernardino: 1565 E. Highland at Del Rosa Ave. 92404 . (714) 886-4781
San Diego: 1170 Fifth Ave. at B Street 92101 . . . . (714) 239-2152
San Mateo: 97 Hillsdale Mall 94403 . . . . (415) 341-8751
San Ramon: 500 Alcosta Mall 94583 . . . . (415) 829-1670
So. San Francisco: 2234A Westborough Blvd. 94080 . . . . (415) 873-6181
Wilshire-Alvarado: 2033 Wilshire Blvd. at Alvarado 90057 . (213) 483-1016
Woodland Hills: 23325 Mulholland Dr.
      at Valley Circle Rd. 91364 . . . . (213) 888-8772

The World's Best Recipes COOKBOOK

The World's Best Recipes COOKBOOK

by

MARVIN SMALL

Hawthorn Books, Inc.   Publishers   New York

TO DORY, MY GOUR-MATE

CONTENTS

Even the most expert cook finds occasion to refer to a basic book, a dictionary of cooking, to jog the memory, clarify some terminology in a recipe, or verify a step in the procedure. Craig Claiborne, a celebrated chef and food editor, here describes the books he considers essential for fine home cooking. We print this with the special permission of Mr. Claiborne and Ford Motor Company's The Continental Magazine, *in which it first appeared.*

MY BASIC COOKBOOKS FOR HOME CUISINE
by Craig Claiborne

When I was asked recently to outline the books I would recommend for a basic cooking library, I remembered that my own career as a writer on food began in a brief and decisive moment when someone gave me the cookbook that I still consider the best.

The year was 1946 and it was Christmas. I was living in Chicago at the time on the small salary that came with my first job in the public relations office of a radio network.

Until then my cooking had consisted largely of grilling hamburgers, turning the crank for a freezer of Sunday ice cream, and basting the family barbecue at home in Mississippi.

I had gone home for the holidays and, as I recall, I grumbled considerably about the food in Chicago. Thus it must have been in the spirit of artfully conceived sympathy that my sister gave gifts that year. I returned to Chicago in the middle of a blinding snowstorm carrying under my arms two wild ducks, a new chafing dish, and a volume of Irma Rombauer's inspiring tome, *The Joy of Cooking*.

For the next several years the book was my kitchen Bible. I was soon whipping up a Hollandaise with considerable authority, making a béchamel sauce with even more dispatch, and turning out tortes with what I considered admirable élan. As I recall, I became rather famous in the neighborhood for my Koenigsberger Klops, Mrs. Rombauer's German meat balls.

Today I own three editions of *The Joy of Cooking*, each subsequent edition revised and enlarged, and I would rate any of the three as the finest basic cookbook available. My favorite, however, continues to be the first one, which, with the yellow pages and battered spine, still rests on my library shelves.

The more recent volumes, written in collaboration with Mrs. Rombauer's daughter, Marion Rombauer Becker, are far more detailed and comprehensive. But some of the home-spun charm is gone and, sentimentally perhaps, I miss it. For example, Mrs. Rombauer recounts a delightful anecdote told her by Konrad Bercovici: "Madame Schumann-Heink, the great opera singer, was sitting in front of an enormous steak. Caruso passed her table, and seeing the huge portion of meat before the singer, he said: 'Stina, you are not going to eat that alone!' 'No,' Schumann-Heink said, shaking her fine old head, 'No, not alone. With potatoes.'"

This cookbook is studded with anecdotes, cheer, and amusing observations. Many cookbooks approach food with solemnity, but this one lives up to its title completely. It has gusto. The very first chapter is on cocktails, and it starts as follows:

"The chief virtue of cocktails is their informal quality. They loosen tongues and unbutton the reserves of the socially diffident. Serve them by all means, preferably in the living room, and the sooner the better."

If there is a bride on your list or a bachelor with a lean and hungry look on his birthday, there could be no better gift than any available edition of *The Joy of Cooking*. These books are inspired, and for a neophyte's purposes, all-inclusive.

Wherever I've traveled in search of recipes—and it has involved several thousand miles gathering material for a book on an American regional cooking—people mention cookbooks to me. Some say they relish cookbooks while others declare they devour them. Many is the individual who avers that he or she uses them as bedside literature in lieu of a good mystery or fiction.

I am very much of a cookbook peruser both as a matter of professional and private interest. I can spend hours thumbing my way through odd volumes (to choose random examples) on Mediterranean cookery; Ada Boni's definitive book on Italian cooking, *Il Talismano della Felicita* (never properly translated into English); such staple works as Ali Bab's *Gastronomie Pratique;* and, of course, *Larousse Gastronomique.* One of the nicest books for perusing with pleasure is also one to which I would give high marks indeed for a basic in any cookbook collection. It is *The James Beard Cookbook* and happily it is available both in hard cover and paperback.

This book is written with great clarity and taste, and it is basic without being condescending. I have long enjoyed the author's recipe in his foreword for boiling water, and he may be the first and only authority to give such a recipe.

Then he gets down to the serious business of detailing recipes, and he can bring style to the kitchen without hitting the cook over the head with a wooden spoon and without boring him or her to death. To show the scope of the book: the recipes range from brownies to brioche and mashed potatoes to Anna potatoes. There are also such sophisticated and admirable dishes as coquilles St. Jacques (scallops in the shell) to an exceptionally good *navarin* or French lamb stew, lentil casserole, and chocolate mousse.

Let us call Mr. Beard's work volume number two on the basic list.

My third recommendation would be the one that I wish I myself had written. It is the superb *Mastering the Art of French Cooking* by Simone Beck, Louisette Bertholle, and Julia Child. Praising the volume at this late date, of course, is like rooting for motherhood, but it would be essential in my list of books for a serious library. The recipes of *Mastering the Art* are outlined in great detail and the volume as a whole is an incredible compendium of French cooking. Anyone who has truly mastered its details and put them into practice honestly has a good understanding of *la cuisine française,* classic style. This is by far the greatest book on French cooking ever written in English.

These, in sum, would be my choices for a basic library. Other than that the recommendations become random and specialized. For example, I would unhesitantly recommend any of Ann Seranne's books. Some of her best (she has many to her credit) are *The Complete Book of Desserts, The Complete Book of Home Baking,* and *The Complete Book of Home Preserving.* They are excellent. In the same specialized category I would place both of Paula Peck's estimable volumes, *The Art of Fine Baking,* and *The Art of Good Cooking.*

But keep Mrs. Rombauer in mind. If you cannot cook with her volume at hand it may be best to stick to the charcoal grill.

The World's Best Recipes COOKBOOK

APPETIZERS

ANTIPASTO

Antipasto is what its Italian name implies, an appetizer eaten in anticipation of the macaroni, spaghetti, or other pasta. Pastas, which are any type of paste or dough made from wheat flour, are an essential part of the Italian menu.

A real antipasto can be a zestful invitation to the meal, a rouser of the appetite and a stimulator of the digestive juices. Unfortunately, many Italian-American restaurants serve sad, second-rate antipastos—small plates of cole slaw with limp pieces of pimiento across the top, a salty anchovy or two, and a couple of olives.

The secret of a successful antipasto is in a combination of *opposites*. The coarse appetizer appears with the delicate, the abundant with the scant. Peasant salamis, sausage, and salt fish are offset by sophisticated delicacies such as artichoke hearts, Prosciutto (ham), and sautéed mushrooms. The celery and *finocchio* are cut big and bulky, while the meats are sliced paper-thin and spread out generously.

Here is the composition of an impressive yet simple antipasto served at the family restaurant of Signora Francesca Marchi, on East 31st Street in New York City.

This is a serving for two people and consists of three platters:

1 large platter with 2 whole tomatoes, 2 slices of melon, radishes, celery, and *finocchio* (also called fennel or "Italian celery")
1 large platter containing thinly sliced Italian salami
1 large platter with a special salad consisting of shredded red cabbage, large green olives, imported tuna fish, capers, parsley root (grated), chopped parsley, and diced celery, seasoned with salt, pepper, and oil

Italian bread is served with this antipasto. No butter with the bread. Signora Marchi says, "The butter is for the cooking, not the antipasto." The Marchis make a point of selecting the best vegetables for their antipasto: sweet melon to balance the acid tomatoes, piquant radishes to offset the bland taste of the celery. The salami is gently spiced, the salad blended harmoniously, with no one ingredient standing out, but still you are aware of each.

Here is another much-talked-about antipasto. Behind the Piazza San Marco in Venice there is one of the great restaurants of Italy, the internationally known Taverna La Fenice. Signor Alfredo Zoppi takes you into the kitchen if you wish, and you may select your own antipasto. I'd like to tell you about this antipasto selection, more to give you an idea of its scope than to expect you to copy it.

"In addition to the usual tinned food like sardines, salmon, olives, and so on," Signor Zoppi says, "here are some of the typical items on our Antipasto Buffet":

Smoked sweet Prosciutto (ham) cut as thin as possible (in Italy there is a special cutter for it, as well as for sausages)

Salame di Milano and *Mortadella*—two common Italian sausages

Granceole—crab meat served in its own shell

Gamberetti—very small shrimp, boiled and served cold

Aragosta—lobster

Cannocchie—sea cicadas (a type of crustacean)

Mazzarette—small hard-shelled crabs, boiled and seasoned with oil, pepper, salt, and lemon

Garusoli—sea snails

Ostriche—oysters

Capparozzoli—gray clams or mussels

Peoci—black mussels or clams

Cappa lunghe—special fingerlike mussels or clams

Pepperoni—yellow, red, green fresh sweet peppers

Sedano—white celery

Finocchio—fennel

Carciofi dell'Estuario—small, rather bitter artichokes

Fondi di carciofo—artichoke hearts

Asparagi di Bassano—white asparagus from Bassano

American travelers by the thousands have enjoyed the antipasto on the regular menu of the Daniele Restaurante in the conclusion that only a large metropolitan or native restaurant can serve an imaginative antipasto, here is the excellent antipasto on the regular menu of the Daniele Restaurant in the small town where I used to live, Millbrook, New York.

Jimmy Daniele says, "Our antipasto consists of eight separate platters":

1. A salad platter has a wedge of lettuce and slices of tomato; carrot sticks, topped with antipasto of eggplant; pepper ring with jumbo shrimps; a half-boiled egg with dressing; and a cucumber slice with a heart of artichoke; plus a slice of pizza rusticana
2. A platter of marinated trout, garnished with parsley and a thin-sliced onion decorated with pimientos—olive oil and vinegar added
3. A platter of imported Italian anchovies
4. A platter of Norwegian sardines

5. In the celery platter, dill pickles, radishes, scallions, and *finocchio*
6. Large green olives arranged on fresh lettuce leaves
7. Black olives arranged on fresh lettuce leaves
8. A platter of assorted cold cuts with cheese—salami, *capicola,* Canadian bacon, Italian Prosciutto (ham), plus Swiss and Provolona cheeses

HORS D'OEUVRES

The French word for "outside" is *hors* and the word for "work" is *oeuvre,* so *hors d'oeuvre* literally means "outside the work"—apart from the main part of the meal. Actually, hors d'oeuvres are elegant appetizers eaten at the table as a first course, with knife and fork, while canapés are eaten away from the table and held in the hand (with a cocktail or *apéritif* in the other).

Hors d'oeuvres should be considered either as part of a variety, or as a singleton. The mission of the *variés* or variety of appetizers is to give a blended excitement to the palate. The object of the individual hors d'oeuvre is to emphasize one flavor.

A slice of smoked salmon which is part of an assortment of hors d'oeuvres loses its identity, but contributes to the whole. The same salmon, served alone as *Saumon Fumé*, supplies an entirely different taste sensation. Here, no flavor detracts from that of the salmon, and a portion is usually three slices instead of one. By the addition of lemon juice, capers, and pepper freshly ground from a pepper mill, the full richness of the salmon is brought out and accentuated.

There used to be a small restaurant in Paris called the Relais de la Belle Aurore, which was particularly interesting because of its décor, including mementos of the French Revolution. It also earned some distinction by serving the finest champagne in pewter mugs. The hors d'oeuvres served here were especially notable. They were meats, salads, and "sea fruits" *(fruits de mer)*. Among the meats were twelve different styles of sausages, bolognas, and pâtés. The salad cart carried artichokes, celery *remoulade,* and a dozen other dishes. The "sea fruits" included several different kinds of crabs, shrimp, clams, sea urchins, and other varieties.

In innumerable other French restaurants, such appetizers as these are displayed on square white porcelain dishes on an hors d'oeuvres wagon:

Cooked ham	Anchovies
Smoked ham	Shrimps
Raw ham	Egg mayonnaise
Sausage—various kinds	Stuffed eggs
Liver pâté with truffles	Mushrooms in oil (mushrooms à la Grecque)
Pâté maison truffé (which is coarser)	Beetroot in oil and vinegar
Rillets (cubes of cooked, seasoned fresh pork)	Shredded celery in cream sauce
Smoked salmon	Green olives
Sardines	Black olives
Filets of herring in oil	Sliced pimiento
Bismarck herring or Rollmops	Tomato in oil and vinegar

Restaurant Voisin in New York City is considered by many to be one of the better French restaurants in America. Their usual variety of hors d'oeuvres consists of the following:

Sardines
Smoked salmon
Filets of anchovies
Smoked eel
Shrimps with Russian
  dressing
Stuffed eggs
Artichokes, vinaigrette
Eggplant à la Grecque
Salad of small onions

Mushroom salad
Pickled beets
Cole slaw salad
·Cucumber salad
Stuffed green peppers
Calf's brains, vinaigrette
Knob celery salad
Salade de boeuf
Bismarck herring in sour
  cream

PÂTÉ DE FOIE GRAS

No one with an appreciation of good food can deny the
gastronomic pleasures of real Strasbourg *pâté de fois gras*.
My wife is one of those who adores it, but American restaurants always bowled me over with the prices they charged

for it. One day when we were near Alsace-Lorraine, I suggested we drive over to Strasbourg, where she might eat her fill at a reasonable price. Eat she did, but the price was exactly the same as in the fanciest New York restaurant!

For all those who love pâté, we would like to quote some paragraphs from Waverley Root's *The Food of France*. Waverley Root is a cook supreme, and we say that from personal experience of one of his famous lobster meals, prepared for us when he was living on Cape Ann in Massachusetts. Always the francophile at heart, he now resides and writes in France.

"The invention of pâté de foie gras is often attributed to Jean Joseph Close (or Clause), an eighteenth-century Norman pastry cook who was brought to Alsace by his employer, the Marshal of Contades, who had been appointed governor of Alsace in 1762. There he was supposed to have created a dish in which he employed the goose liver along with chopped veal and lard, with a truffle in the center, the whole surrounded by a crust. It is obvious, however, that he could hardly have invented foie gras itself, which depends upon the manner of feeding the goose, but must have found this ingredient on hand when he arrived in Alsace. The dish became associated with him because he retired in Alsace and put his particular preparation of pâté de foie gras on the market there.

"Actually the use of artificially fattened goose livers goes much farther back than either Close or the producers of this dish in the Toulouse region. The Romans knew it, though apparently they did not employ the forcible feeding that makes foie gras nowadays. They waited until the bird was dead, but lost no time then; immediately the goose had been killed the liver was extracted and placed while still warm in milk. In this state it absorbed a great deal of the milk and became rich, succulent, and heavy—though probably not as heavy as the modern livers, which sometimes weigh as much as two and a quarter pounds, a large proportion for a bird whose top weight after fattening is about twenty-five pounds. The liver, in other words, accounts for one tenth the weight of the goose.

"The Alsatian fashion of roasting goose is to stuff it with sausage and serve it with sauerkraut soaked in the juice obtained from the goose as it cooks, further embellished with slices of fat pork and Strasbourg sausages—the sauerkraut sometimes being cooked with the goose. This is oie à l'alsacienne, and though à l'alsacienne guarantees nothing in particular, meaning only that the dish presented is cooked in the fashion Alsace has developed for that individual item, the chances are pretty good that a dish so designated will be accompanied by sauerkraut. The second best bet is that it will involve foie gras in one form or another. Aside from these two applications of the term, it will not be much of a guide to what you are getting unless you happen to know the particular dish to which it is applied."

The Food of France

PAULA PECK'S LIVER PÂTÉ

"To my mind," says Craig Claiborne, "Paula Peck is one of the most inventive, imaginative, and dedicated cooks of our time."

Mrs. Peck gives us this formula for a fine liver pâté that is delicate, rich, and delicious. It makes an excellent first course for a large gathering. Unfortunately, it does not keep for more than a few days, nor can it be canned, so make it shortly before it is needed.

Yields 3 quarts

1 teaspoon rendered chicken
   fat or rendered pork fat
2 pounds chicken livers
3 eggs
⅓ cup cognac
1½ cups heavy cream
⅔ cup diced fresh unrendered
   chicken fat or pork fat

1 onion, coarsely chopped
½ cup flour
5 teaspoons salt
1 teaspoon ground ginger
1 teaspoon monosodium
   glutamate
2 teaspoons white pepper
1 teaspoon allspice

1. Lightly grease a 3-quart mold with rendered fat.
2. In an electric blender, make a fine purée of the livers, eggs, cognac, and cream. From time to time add a little diced fat, onion, and flour. (It will not be possible to do the entire mixture at one time. Three or 4 separate blendings will be needed.)

3. Add the seasonings to the purée and mix well. Pour into the mold and cover the top with a double thickness of aluminum foil.
4. Place in a pan of water and bake in a 325° oven for 1 hour. Cool the pâté, then store it in the refrigerator. If desired, the top may be decorated with slices of truffle and a clear aspic poured over, after the pâté has been chilled.

Paula Peck's Art of Good Cooking

ROBERT CARRIER'S BRANDADE (PÂTÉ) OF SMOKED TROUT

Tradition-breakers and taste-makers come along only once in a long while. For example, there was a French silversmith named Paul de Lamerie, who emigrated to England in the early 1700's, adapted the rococo manner of Louis XV furniture to silver, and set a completely new decorative style. Also in the 1700's, Josiah Wedgwood, an English potter, combined new materials and a new technique to produce his famous white-on-blue and white-on-black Jasperware. In the 1800's there was an Irish author named George Moore, who wrote *The Mummer's Wife,* the first novel to be printed in a popular edition and circulated widely so that millions could read it instead of a privileged few. And in more recent times—1892—in this country, Charles K. Harris wrote a song called "After the Ball," which was the first ballad to have a tremendous sale in sheet music, and helped bring pianos and music into homes all over America.

Well, this is a long way around to saying that Robert Carrier has been a taste-maker—a man who went to England from America, by way of France, and helped change English tastes in food so that a million or more English housewives now cook by Carrier recipe books and Cooking Cards and enjoy the finest food. When I first met Bob Carrier, he was Food Editor of the London *Times,* after having been a brilliant success in the same capacity for the British editions of *Harper's Bazaar* and *Vogue.* We shall never forget the evening we spent at his London home with a group of his friends. I have forgotten the actual food he served, since there were *apéritifs,* four fine wines served with dinner, and brandy afterward. Dory recalls that at three A.M. we were still doing the "Twist," which was then popular, and that Bob's literary friend Oliver Lawson-Dick suggested in a polite English manner that he thought it was time we said goodbye. We did go then, only to return to more Carrier wizardry in his restaurant in Islington. Islington used to be a run-down section of London, and so Carrier was again a tradition-breaker by opening up there. This potted smoked trout is one of the unique fish dishes created by Robert Carrier and served in his gourmet restaurant. It can also be made with cod or kippers.

Makes 4 servings

4 smoked trout	salt
4 to 6 tablespoons heavy cream	freshly ground black pepper
	parsley, finely chopped
2 tablespoons olive oil	hot toast triangles
juice of ½ lemon	

1. Remove skin and bones from trout. In a mortar, pound fillets into a smooth paste with cream and olive oil.
2. Add the lemon juice and season to taste with salt and fresh black pepper. Chill.
3. Just before serving, turn mixture out into 1 large soufflé dish or individual dishes. Sprinkle with a little parsley. Serve hot toast triangles along with it.

SHRIMP OR LOBSTER "TITUS"

This is a simple yet highly successful first course, originated by Otto Horcher of Restaurante Horcher in Madrid.

Rival restaurateur Vernon Jarratt feels that Horcher tends to use pineapple where it doesn't fit, but we can report that it does fit in here.

Makes 1 serving

1 slice canned pineapple	paprika cream sauce*
3 shrimps or 3 lumps of lobster meat	herb garnishing: parsley or dill

* A medium-thin white sauce flavored with sweet paprika.

Just place the shrimp or lobster around the slice of pineapple, pour the paprika cream sauce generously over, and garnish with the finely chopped parsley or dill.

GLAZED SHRIMP HORS D'OEUVRES

1 pound fresh prepared
  shrimp, chilled
1 cup canned tomatoes
6 tablespoons water
2 tablespoons chopped celery
1 carrot, sliced
1 tablespoon chopped green
  pepper

1 whole clove
¼ teaspoon salt
⅛ teaspoon pepper
¾ tablespoon plain gelatin
1½ teaspoons lemon juice
  potato chips

1. Put tomatoes and 4 tablespoons water in saucepan. Add vegetables and seasoning and bring to boiling point on high heat. Reduce heat and cook 15 minutes; strain.
2. Soften gelatin in 2 tablespoons cold water 5 minutes. Add to hot tomato juice and stir until gelatin is dissolved. Stir in lemon juice. Chill in refrigerator until of syrupy consistency.
3. Dip cold shrimp in gelatin mixture. Drain on cake rack and chill. Repeat several times to build up heavy coating of aspic on shrimp.
4. To serve, place a glazed shrimp on a potato chip.

Cocktails and Snacks
ROBERT AND ANNE LONDON

SEVICHE

(MARINATED FISH)

If you have been to Acapulco on the West Coast of Mexico seviche is no newcomer to your palate, for here the vendors on the beach sell it to bathers, and the hotels serve it as an appetizer.

Why Acapulco is the romantic place it is (or was), I never exactly knew until one night in February when Hank Scheuttauff brought his portable phonograph onto the terrace of his cottage and played the sensuous Brazilian music of Villa-Lobos. Far beneath us were the shimmering waters of the Pacific. The palm trees swayed against a background of majestic cliffs, and, above, all the stars in the universe shone in their glory.

It would be a little too much to expect romance in every serving of seviche, but from it you will at least catch a bit of the zestful flavor of Acapulco. Once I asked Isabella for her seviche recipe. Isabella is the Madonna-like creature who presided over the dining room of El Mirador, the hotel built over the rocks where the diving boys pirouette into the inlet below. Isabella began her recipe with "First, you take a small barracuda"—which would be as simple as taking a small cobra or a small tarantula. Here is an easier—and safer—recipe for a hearty seviche.

1 pound boneless fish,
    uncooked
3 bay leaves
    lime juice, enough to cover
1 clove garlic, finely minced
4 tablespoons white vinegar
1 large sweet onion,
    sliced thin
2 small dry red Jap peppers,
    chopped
2 lemons, sliced and
    quartered
4 sprigs of watercress
½ teaspoon salt

1. Cut the fillets of uncooked fish into small thin strips. Use any white meat fish, such as red snapper, corbina, fresh tuna or sea bass. Place in suitable porcelain container. Add the bay leaves, salt to taste, and enough lime juice to cover. Lift the fish so that the lime juice will cover all sides. Place in the refrigerator to marinate over night.
2. Then add the minced garlic, thinly sliced onion, and chopped red peppers that have all been soaked in the vinegar.
3. Decorate with slices of lemon and sprigs of watercress. Chill well and serve as an appetizer.

The Spanish-Mexican Cook Book
DON CARLOS

SMOKED SALMON IN SOUR CREAM-HORSERADISH SAUCE

Good new combinations for hors d'oeuvres are not easy to come by, so we are especially thankful to Mrs. Peck, whose sophistication extends to the simple things in cookery. Your guests will enjoy this one.

Makes 6 servings

½ pound smoked salmon, shredded
½ cup finely minced shallots, red onions, or scallions
2 teaspoons fresh chopped dill
¾ cup sour cream

2 tablespoons horseradish (approximately)
1 tablespoon mayonnaise
salt and pepper
red cabbage leaves

1. Add shallots and dill to smoked salmon.
2. In a separate bowl, combine sour cream, horseradish, and mayonnaise. Season with salt and pepper. Taste, and add additional horseradish if necessary.
3. Add dressing to salmon mixture. Toss gently. Serve in red cabbage leaf cups, using about 2 tablespoons of salmon mixture for each leaf. Garnish with additional chopped dill. Serve with thinly sliced buttered rye or pumpernickel.

Paula Peck's Art of Good Cooking

ESCARGOTS AU VIN XERBES

This is a specialty of Jacques' French Restaurant on North Michigan Avenue in Chicago. One of the delights of eating at Jacques' is its garden with a slide-away glass roof, so that, whatever the weather, the garden atmosphere remains the same.

4 dozen cooked snails, with shells
1 pound butter
2 ounces shallots, chopped fine
2 cloves garlic, chopped fine
¼ ounce parsley, chopped

2 teaspoons Worcestershire sauce
1 teaspoon salt
⅛ teaspoon white pepper
¼ cup dry white wine

1. Drain cooked meat of snails and set aside. To make butter stuffing, mix together all ingredients except wine. Put a little of this prepared stuffing into each shell.
2. Put 1 cooked snail into each shell. Close the openings with a little more prepared butter stuffing. Place snails in snail dish or shallow baking pan.
3. Add wine and bake in moderate oven until butter in shells starts to boil. Serve at once.

CHOPPED CHICKEN LIVERS

The French take very seriously their pâté de fois gras and other liver pâtés—and Jewish people also take seriously their *gehakte leber,* chopped liver. Sam Levenson says his mother made *gehakte leber* mostly out of cuts even the cow never used. It was sometimes made from the spleen, cheek, lung, or heart . . . with a touch of liver for flavor. In today's more affluent society, Mama uses liver all the way through, and usually chicken liver. On special occasions, such as bar mitzvahs, birthdays, and weddings, the chopped chicken liver might appear molded in the shape of a heart, with the initials of the honored person or persons appearing via olive slivers or radishes embedded in the chopped liver. They say you haven't lived until you've visited the Stage Delicatessen on Seventh Avenue in New York, and eaten a triple-decker sandwich of chopped liver, turkey, and pastrami—or a "just plain" sandwich of chopped liver and hot corned beef.

¾ pound chicken livers
6 tablespoons chicken fat
1 or 2 hard-boiled eggs
1 large or 2 small onions, chopped fine

diced celery, if desired
diced green pepper, if desired
salt and pepper to taste

1. Cook the chicken livers in the chicken fat over a moderate flame until they are firm, but not well done.
2. Along with the hard-boiled eggs, put through food chopper, using the finest blade.
3. Blend well with the onions, green pepper and celery if

desired, and enough additional chicken fat to make smooth paste. Season to taste.

4. Serve cold.

NOTE:

The onions and green pepper may be sautéed with the chicken livers, if preferred.

MUSHROOMS STUFFED WITH WALNUTS AND PISTACHIOS, GLAZED

Bill Tarr was one of the best-paid advertising copywriters in the business when he decided to give it up to become a sculptor . . . and a dynamic sculptor he has indeed become. His beautiful wife has a remarkable talent of another sort, that of preparing gourmet meals in almost no time and seemingly without effort. More than one hundred of her tested recipes are now in a book, *The 10 Minute Gourmet Cookbook*, and this is one of the unique hors d'oeuvres from that book. If you seek a first course both daringly different and filled with flavors all will enjoy, by all means try this.

4 tablespoons butter	¼ cup shelled pistachios
8 mushrooms, large	¼ cup shelled walnuts
½ cup chutney	

1. Light broiler and set on high flame. Melt butter in skillet over medium flame.
2. Peel mushrooms and chop stems. Add mushroom caps and chopped-up stems to skillet and sauté for 2 minutes. Turn and fry 1 minute more. Remove mushroom caps from pan.
3. Add chutney to butter in skillet. With paring knife, cut any large pieces into smaller ones, the size of your thumbnail.
4. Add pistachios to skillet. Chop walnuts to the same size as the chutney and stir into skillet mixture. Cook for 1 minute. Stuff mushrooms with skillet mixture. Place in heatproof dish and set under broiler for a few minutes until browned. Serve hot.

NOTE:

Garnish (optional): Top each mushroom with 1 small bit candied cherry and 2 green halves of pistachio nut, set like a flower with 2 green leaves. Decorate plate with sprigs of watercress.

The 10 Minute Gourmet Cookbook
YVONNE YOUNG TARR

HOT CHEESE SOUFFLÉ
HORS D'OEUVRES

American cheese	1 medium-sized egg,
day-old bread	separated
soft butter or margarine	¼ teaspoon salt

1. With a 2-inch round cutter, cut out 12 to 14 rounds of day-old bread. Spread very lightly with soft butter or margarine.

2. Grate firm American cheese, and measure 2 cupfuls. Do not pack cheese into cup, and do not grate it more than a few minutes before it is to be used.
3. Separate the egg. Place white in a 6-inch bowl and beat until very stiff peaks form. Add the whole egg yolk and beat until blended.
4. Add salt and fold in the grated American cheese, mixing with a fork until thoroughly mixed.
5. Shape 1 slightly rounded *ordinary* teaspoonful (*not* a measuring spoon) of cheese mixture into a ball, flatten slightly and place on center of each bread round, leaving outer edge of the bread, about ¼ inch, free of cheese to prevent dripping on sides of bread.
6. Place on a flat baking sheet about 2 inches from flame, and broil about 5 minutes, or until brown and puffy, in a preheated 400° F. broiler. Watch closely that they do not burn. Serve at once as hot hors d'oeuvres, or as accompaniments to soups and salads.

NOTE:

Cheese mixture may be placed on bread rounds several hours before they are to be broiled. In this case, store them covered in refrigerator or a cold place to prevent topping from spreading.

Antoinette Pope School Cookbook
ANTOINETTE AND FRANÇOIS POPE

SWISS FLAN

The word flan means different things in different countries: In Spain it is a plain caramel custard; in France, a fruit tart in pastry; in Switzerland, a cheese custard in pastry. And sometimes Swiss Flan is made with onions and cheese in custard, and is similar to a Quiche Lorraine. Betty Wason gives us this recipe along with many other excellent cheese recipes in an interesting book, *A Salute to Cheese.*

Makes 10 to 12 hors d'oeuvres

PASTRY:

1 cup biscuit mix	¼ cup light cream
3 tablespoons butter	

1. To make pastry, chop butter into the biscuit mix, work in cream, and roll out on lightly floured board; or press into a 9-inch pie pan, fluting the edges.
2. Chill while preparing filling.

FILLING:

1 large onion, sliced or chopped	2 cups (½ pound) natural Gruyère, shredded
2 tablespoons butter	¼ teaspoon salt
2 eggs, beaten	

1. Cook onion in butter until golden; cool slightly. Add eggs, cheese, and salt.
2. Pour this mixture into pastry, and bake in oven preheated to 425° F. (hot), and continue baking 25 to 30 minutes or until a knife inserted in the center comes out clean.
3. Serve warm as a luncheon entree to 4 to 6 persons, or cut into small wedges for appetizers.

NOTE:

Instead of this pastry, regular pie crust may be used. Or make pastry with 1 cup flour, 1 teaspoon baking powder, ¼ teaspoon salt, ⅓ cup butter, and 1 beaten egg. Do not attempt to roll out this butter-rich pastry; press it with your fingers into pie pan, fluting the edges.

A Salute to Cheese
BETTY WASON

STUFFED EGGS IN TOMATO CREAM SAUCE

Makes 6 to 12 servings

12 hard-boiled eggs	1 cup concentrated tomato purée
3 tablespoons butter	
6 tablespoons concentrated tomato purée	2 cups hot Béchamel Sauce (see page 255)
1 teaspoon salt	1 hard-boiled egg
dash of pepper	chopped parsley
	chervil

1. Cut hard-boiled eggs in half lengthwise. Mash the yolks with the butter, concentrated tomato purée, salt, and pepper.
2. Stuff the egg whites with this mixture. Arrange them in a shallow buttered casserole and put the casserole in a moderate oven (350° F.) until the eggs are heated through but not browned.
3. Combine 1 cup concentrated tomato purée with the hot Béchamel Sauce and coat the eggs with this mixture.
4. Sprinkle with chopped hard-boiled egg and with parsley and chervil.

The Gourmet Cookbook, Vol. II

HERRING SALAD

Herring is an important item in the food fare of all the Scandinavian peoples—and of Netherlanders, too. In Sweden you get the *strömming,* a dwarf herring from the Baltic Sea. The Swedish cook serves this herring in every imaginable way, even as a herring sandwich—two herring fillets with parsley between. There are as many variations in herring salads as there are in chicken soup. This one calls for cooked meat, potatoes, apples, and other ingredients not usually expected in such a salad.

Makes 8 servings

2 salt herring	5 tablespoons vinegar
1½ cups cooked meat	(or sherry)
(any kind)	2 tablespoons sugar
1½ cups cooked beets	¼ teaspoon pepper
2 cups cooked potatoes	garnish of 2 hard-boiled
3 raw apples	eggs, 3 to 4 boiled beets,
2 pickled cucumbers	parsley, whipped cream

1. Clean and soak herring overnight. Skin, bone, and fillet. If still too salty, soak in milk for a couple of hours. Wipe dry on napkin.
2. Now cut in ⅓-inch cubes, or smaller, herring, meat, beets, potatoes, apples, and cucumbers. Mix all together in large bowl.

3. Add vinegar (or sherry), sugar, and pepper. Season to taste. It should be pleasantly sharp. If it is too dry, add a couple of tablespoons sour cream or mayonnaise.
4. Pack tightly on serving platter, either in a mound or oblong fashion, or chill in a mold which has been rinsed in cold water.
5. For the garnish, separate the yolks and whites and rub each through sieve. Mince the beets very fine.
6. Make alternate red, white, and yellow strips diagonally across the mold. Place a lavish wreath of green parsley around the salad. Serve with whipped cream tinted pink with beet juice.

The Smörgåsbord Cookbook
ANNA OLSSON COOMBS

MUSHROOMS À LA GRECQUE

Here is a delicious mushroom and onion dish, a favorite at Robert Carrier's London restaurant. It is a fine, easy hors d'oeuvre or first course.

Makes 4 to 6 servings

2 carrots	bouquet garni made of
1 Spanish onion	2 sprigs parsley, 2 sprigs
4 tablespoons olive oil	thyme, 2 bay leaves, and
2 tablespoons corn oil	1 stalk celery, tied
¼ pint dry white wine	together
salt	1 fat clove garlic
freshly ground pepper	1 pound button mushrooms
	½ pound tomatoes

1. Chop carrots and onion coarsely. Sauté in 2 tablespoons olive oil and the corn oil until they are soft and golden.
2. Just moisten with white wine. Add salt and pepper to taste. Add the bouquet garni and garlic clove.
3. Wash mushrooms well. Trim stems and add mushrooms to vegetables. Add peeled and seeded tomatoes and a little more wine if necessary. There should not be too much liquid at this stage, as the mushrooms will add liquid in cooking.

4. Cook, uncovered, for about 15 to 20 minutes. Remove from heat. Allow to cool. Remove herbs and add remaining 2 tablespoons olive oil. Sprinkle with freshly chopped parsley and serve cold.

ROBERT CARRIER

PICKLED CUCUMBERS

2 to 3 cucumbers	pinch of salt and pepper
1 cup sugar	1 to 2 tablespoons parsley,
1 to 1½ cups vinegar	finely chopped

1. Peel the cucumbers and groove them neatly with a silver fork. Slice thinly.
2. Make a brine of sugar, vinegar, and condiments and stir until sugar melts.
3. Pour it over the cucumbers and chill in refrigerator a couple of hours before serving.
4. Then sprinkle generously with the parsley and serve crisp and cold.

NOTE:

This is a succulent complement to fish and meat dishes, a refreshing ingredient in other green salads, and wonderful with just plain bread and butter.

The Smörgåsbord Cookbook
ANNA OLSSON COOMBS

MARINATED CARROTS

"Hors d'oeuvres, as I remember them in my mother's home," says Louis Diat, who was for many years chef of the famous old Ritz-Carlton Hotel in New York, "were usually served on special occasions like holidays, and at company meals, or in summertime for Sunday dinner. Not little snacks made by spreading fish and cheese pastes on tiny crackers, but real food served at the table either for the first course of dinner or the main course of luncheon. They were good, filling food and if eaten for the first course could be depended upon to make the more expensive main dish go farther. At luncheon, when served with a salad or preceded by our favorite onion soup, a generous platter of hors d'oeuvres was hearty enough for the main part of the meal.

"There was food economy in the French fashion, for hors d'oeuvres used up small amounts of leftover vegetables, meat, and fish. And when there was a sudden abundance of some vegetable in the garden, my mother was not long in fixing up the surplus in a spicy, cold sauce for hors d'oeuvres."

1 pound new spring carrots	bouquet garni made of
1 glass white wine	2 sprigs parsley, a little
1 cup water	thyme, 1 bay leaf, and
1 clove garlic, crushed	2 stalks chervil (or about
½ tablespoon salt	½ teaspoon chopped
1 tablespoon sugar	chervil)
5 tablespoons salad oil or	
olive oil	

1. Scrape carrots and cut in quarters. Put remaining ingredients in saucepan and boil 5 minutes. Add carrots and cook until medium done. (They should be a little firm.)
2. When cool, moisten with a little of the cooking liquor and serve from a small bowl. Sprinkle top with chopped chervil and parsley. One-half teaspoon of dry mustard may be added to the cooking liquor if the flavor is liked.

French Cooking for Americans
LOUIS DIAT

SWEDISH MEAT BALLS

There is an old story about the six Scandinavians, strangers to one another, who found themselves together on a small boat. The two Danes soon began to toast each other in aquavit, the two Norwegians soon began to fight . . . but the two Swedes stood aloof from each other because they hadn't been introduced. The Swedes are, or have been, more formal than many other people (dinner clothes in Stockholm can mean, for men, swallowtails, and not just tuxedos), but when you get to know them the Swedish people are very warm and friendly. In the performances at the Drottingholm Court Theatre, about five miles outside of Stockholm, the musicians still wear powdered wigs, and the beginning of an act is announced by the staccato clop of the beadle's staff on the stage floor. The Stockholm City Hall is one of the most beautiful modern buildings to be seen anywhere . . . and the food at such restaurants as the Riche and the Operakallären is superb.

Köttbullar, or meat balls with gravy, is as Swedish as their blond-haired children, and equally honest and hearty. *Köttbullar* can be part of the smörgåsbord, or may be extended into a main course.

2 pounds hamburger (preferably 1½ pounds beef and ½ pound pork)
2 slices bread
2 cups water
1 onion, minced and sautéed

2 potatoes (boiled and mashed)
3 teaspoons salt
⅛ teaspoon pepper
2 eggs
butter (or other fat) for frying

1. Have the butcher grind the meat a couple of times. Soak bread in water. Mince and sauté onion. Mash the potatoes.
2. Now mix all ingredients in a large bowl and keep on working it until you have a smooth, spongy mass. It is easiest to achieve this by using your hand.
3. Heat butter (or fat) in frying pan. Shape the balls by using spoon and palm of your hand, both wet.
4. Brown evenly in butter (or fat), shaking pan during the process to keep the round shape. Remove to kettle. Repeat until mixture is used up.

GRAVY

3 to 4 tablespoons butter (or other fat)
½ cup flour

3 cups stock (use beef cubes)
1 cup cream
salt, pepper to taste

1. Make gravy in the same frying pan by heating butter (or fat) and adding flour. Heat and stir to a golden paste.

2. Add stock gradually, stirring briskly to avoid lumps. If you prefer a darker gravy add a few drops of Kitchen Bouquet or brown some sugar for the purpose.
3. Add cream and season to taste. Simmer sauce 4 to 5 minutes.
4. Then pour it over meat balls and let them cook on low flame 40 to 60 minutes. Neither overcooking nor reheating will harm this wonderful concoction.

NOTE:

The use of pork in the meat balls cuts down on the quantity of fat needed in the frying process besides adding a nice, sweet flavor to the meat. For special occasions it is very nice to add ¼ to ½ pound of chopped and sautéed mushrooms to the gravy and let them simmer with the meat balls.

The Smörgåsbord Cookbook
ANNA OLSSON COOMBS

CANAPÉS

Canapés are appetizers served on thin slices of bread or some other edible base so they can be eaten away from the dinner table, without a plate or cutlery.

Canapés have a long history. The Chinese originated the idea of serving before-dinner delicacies. Then, according to top gourmet Crosby Gaige, the Russians "improved" on Chinese simplicity, and made a Chinese puzzle of the simple canapé by combining all manner of tidbits.

Canapés must never be large or heavy or too plentiful before dinner. They should, through their spiciness and piquancy, rouse the gastric juices and sharpen the appetite. A leading New York caterer says, "When we cater for an important dinner or banquet, we keep the canapés very small and the selection limited, so that the appetite is not dulled." Good servers do not loiter with the canapé tray—the guest is not given a chance to take more than one canapé at a time. The servers are courteous, but quick on the getaway.

The bread for canapés can be toasted or left plain. Toasted bread is usually used by leading chefs, who toast one side only . . . most often the untoasted side is used for the spread, but for some canapés it's better to have the toasted side up. Besides white, rye, pumpernickel or other bread or toast, you can use little cocktail puffs, potato chips, tiny biscuits, small crêpes or blinis, melba toast, timbale cases, slices of pickle and crackers. A pastry bag equipped with an assortment of fancy tubes is very useful in making appealing canapés.

Fannie Farmer's "Cocktail Checkerboard" is an interesting way to serve canapés: "Make perfectly square canapés (measured with a ruler) of two sorts in contrasting colors, such as mushroom and smoked salmon or caviar and egg, etc. Arrange like a checkerboard on a large tray. Along the edge place pastry sticks brushed with melted butter and sprinkled with chopped parsley and minced onion."

A popular canapé among many hostesses is this tangy tidbit:

½ pint sour cream
1 package Lipton's Onion
   Soup Mix—dry, right
out of the envelope, no
  water added

Mix these ingredients and serve on Melba rounds or pumpernickel crackers. Some hostesses place the canapés under the broiler for a few minutes.

CANAPÉ BUTTERS

Canapé butters are often the secret of the tastiest canapés. They give lift and life to the garnishings over them . . . and lengthen the freshness of the bread beneath. Here are some favorite canapé butters. Chill well before using. Store in a covered container. If butter is too stiff when needed, cream it enough to soften.

Anchovy Butter:—Cream together ¼ pound unsalted butter with 1 to 2 tablespoons anchovy or sardellen paste. Add a dash or two of paprika in the process. Or use 8 to 10 anchovy fillets, well-pounded, and the yolks of 2 hard-boiled eggs. Cream the butter and mix in the mashed anchovies, egg yolks and a little lemon juice. Press through a fine sieve with the back of a wooden spoon.

Caper Butter:—Mash to a paste about 2 tablespoons of

finest capers without the juice. Mix into ¼ pound creamed salt butter. Rub through sieve to remove caper skins.

Caviar Butter:—Mix 2 teaspoons caviar, ¼ teaspoon grated onion, few drops of lemon juice. Add to ¼ cup (⅛ pound) creamed unsalted butter. For red caviar butter, whip together 1 part red caviar to 2 parts creamed butter, crushing the caviar in the process.

Cheese Butter:—Add ¼ cup soft snappy cheese to ¼ cup creamed butter.

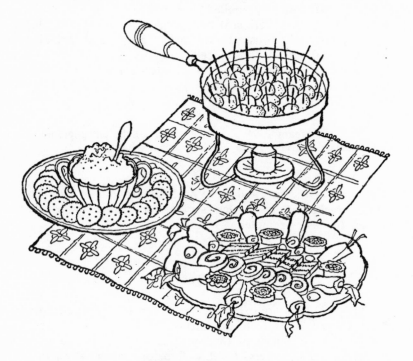

Chivry Butter:—Combine ½ teaspoon each of finely chopped parsley, chives, chervil, tarragon, shallots, or watercress. Cream with 2 tablespoons salt butter.

Chutney Butter:—Mix 1 tablespoon imported chutney into ¼ cup creamed butter.

Deviled Butter:—Set out 3 tablespoons butter, 5 teaspoons Worcestershire sauce, 3 teaspoons Tabasco sauce, 1 teaspoon dry mustard, 1 teaspoon finely chopped chives and 1 teaspoon grated onion. Cream the butter until very airy, then blend all ingredients thoroughly.

Garlic Butter:*—Your guests' (and your own) tolerance for garlic governs the strength of this spread. Start with 1 clove garlic to each tablespoon salt butter then adjust as you see fit. Thoroughly mash or pound the garlic, which should be balanced and dried. Cream into the butter, stirring in a pinch of cayenne. Press through a fine sieve.

Herring Butter:—In a mortar, pound together ¼ pound fillets of dried red herring and ¼ pound unsalted butter. Rub through sieve.

Horseradish Butter:—Season 1 teaspoon freshly grated horseradish with salt and lemon juice. Add a little beet juice for coloring if you prefer (it's nice to make some canapés with white and some with colored horseradish butter). If prepared horseradish is used, squeeze out the juice. In a mortar pound the horseradish with 1 tablespoon butter. Or, cream the horseradish and butter together and pass through a sieve.

Lobster Butter:—Use any of the coral or red parts inside the cooked lobster, including the creamy foam. Pound in a mortar with unsalted butter, 1 teaspoon of the "lobster coral" to 2 tablespoons butter.

---

* The subject of garlic leads to endless arguments among cooks. Some declare you can't cook without it, others insist it's a cover-up for lack of skill or for poor quality food. Nobody here wants to believe that in Northern Italy the cooking is *without* garlic. It is true, however, that in Rome and the north, you will not habitually find garlic in any food. In Harry's Bar in Venice, for example, you have to ask for garlic to get it—and this identifies you as a Southern Italian—or an American.

The writer Ford Madox Ford tells of an English fashion model who loved garlic so much she went home on a Friday before Bank Holiday and made herself a *Poulet Bernaise,* the main garniture of which is *two pounds* of garlic per chicken. To her great surprise, she found that there wasn't a trace of garlic on her breath at the end of the holiday—whereas before, even a little garlic used to start an outcry among her associates and family. What had happened was that the absorption of so immense a quantity of garlic had schooled her body in assimilating it.

Cora, Rose, and Bob Brown claim that, if you like garlic butter but it doesn't like you, if you first fry the garlic cloves in olive oil, you get the garlic zest without becoming a garlic pest. They say to let the garlic pop and skip in the frying pan until before it gets brown; then drain and cool a little and mash into 4, 5 or 6 times as much sweet butter.

Mustard Butter:—Soften ¼ pound butter and cream with 1 teaspoon prepared mustard. Chill particularly well before using. If a hotter butter is desired, use a mixture of regular prepared mustard with dry mustard.

Paprika Butter:—Cream ¼ pound butter with 1 teaspoon paprika until soft and light. Mix in ½ teaspoon white wine and ½ teaspoon lemon juice.

Smoked Fish Butter:—Pound smoked salmon, sturgeon, white fish, carp or other smoked fish. Or use salmon paste if available. Knead 2 tablespoons of butter with 1 teaspoon of the mashed fish or fish paste.

Shrimp Butter:—Pound well 6 cooked, shelled shrimp. Blend with 2 tablespoons salted butter, dash of paprika and few drops of lemon juice.

Watercress Butter:—Use only the watercress leaves, no stalks. Chop very fine, tie in cloth and dip into ice-cold water few times. Squeeze dry and cream together with sweet butter and either salt and pepper or a tiny amount of anchovy paste. If a dark green butter is desired, use equal parts chopped watercress and butter. If light green, use 1 part watercress to 3 parts butter.

SHRIMP CANAPÉ À LA IRMA

Germaine Wells inherited Arnaud's Restaurant (in New Orleans) in 1948 from her father, Count Arnaud Cazenave. Mrs. Wells continued to preserve the famous recipes of the establishment and originated many dishes in the true Arnaud tradition. Canapé Irma is named for her mother.

Makes about 3 dozen

1 pound shrimp, boiled	2 tablespoons flour
½ bunch shallots	2 tablespoons butter
small clove garlic	toast cut in desired forms
fish broth	2 hard-boiled eggs
parsley	grated cheese
½ wine glass claret wine	bread crumbs
2 egg yolks	

1. Mince shallots with garlic and fry in butter until browned. Add flour to make a roux.

2. Add enough fish broth to make a thick sauce. Slice shrimp fine, pour into sauce. Cook about 20 minutes.
3. Add wine mixed with beaten egg yolks to tighten dressing. Season to taste.
4. Spread on toast forms; border with hard-boiled eggs and parsley, minced fine. Top with bread crumbs and cheese.
5. Bake in moderate (350° F.) oven until golden brown.

The Southern Cook Book
MARION BROWN

NOTE:
A roux, as you undoubtedly know, is a combination of butter and flour in equal parts and is used as the basis of sauces, soups, etc. The butter and flour should be cooked over very low flame and should be stirred constantly until nearly dry, and until it becomes the desired shade of brown. Brown roux is used for highly seasoned dark sauces; a pale roux for the more delicate sauces.

OYSTER CANAPÉS

small circles of white bread, toasted on one side	mayonnaise
mustard butter	hard-boiled egg yolks
raw oyster	chives, finely chopped

1. Spread the mustard butter on the untoasted side of the bread circles.
2. Dip raw chilled oysters in mayonnaise and place on bread circles, one to a canapé.
3. Mix the egg yolks, which have been put through a sieve, with the chopped chives and use as a garnish.

CANAPÉS MICHELINE

squares of thinly sliced dark bread	small oysters
horseradish butter	white wine, heated
caviar	mayonnaise, flavored with mustard

1. Spread the horseradish butter evenly on each bread square.
2. Border each canapé with the caviar.
3. In the center, place a small oyster which has been dipped in the heated white wine and drained.
4. Use fancy tube of a pastry bag to cover all with the mustard flavored mayonnaise.

HOT OYSTER BALLS

1 pint oysters	dash of Tabasco sauce or
1 teaspoon grated onion	pinch of cayenne
1 teaspoon minced parsley	pinch of mace
1 cup soft breadcrumbs	2 eggs
about ¼ teaspoon salt	2 tablespoons butter
about ¼ teaspoon pepper	cornmeal or fine dry
	breadcrumbs

1. Pour boiling water over drained oysters. Drain well and chop fine. Add onion, parsley, and soft breadcrumbs. Season to taste and mix to stiff paste with 1 beaten egg and the butter.
2. Form into small balls. Roll in beaten egg, then in cornmeal or dry crumbs.
3. Fry in deep fat (360° F.) until browned. Drain on absorbent paper. Serve hot on picks.

Cocktails and Snacks
ROBERT AND ANNE LONDON

CHEESE SPREAD CORNELL

Katherine Cornell is remembered as one of the greatest actresses of the century. I can still close my eyes and see her at the Empire Theatre, with Brian Aherne, in "The Barretts of Wimpole Street." Only the top performers played at the Empire Theatre in New York—Ethel Barrymore, Lynn Fontanne, Alfred Lunt, Ethel Waters, Julie Harris, and others of their stature—and Katherine Cornell was a star among them. This recipe came from her father, Dr. Cornell. Miss

Cornell fills small earthenware bowls and crocks with this spread, to give as gifts to her friends.

1½ pounds Cheddar cheese
¼ teaspoon salt
¾ teaspoon dry mustard
¼ cup chopped parsley
¼ cup chopped onion
2 tablespoons soft butter

dash of Tabasco sauce
dash of Worcestershire
   sauce
¼ cup tomato catsup
⅓ cup good sherry wine

1. Grate Cheddar cheese. Add salt, dry mustard, chopped parsley and chopped onion. Chop these as fine as possible.
2. Work in butter. Add a dash of Tabasco, a dash of Worcestershire sauce, tomato catsup, and sherry. Work together until all the lumps are eliminated and the mixture is smooth and creamy. Set in any small serving dish or bowl. An earthenware crock makes a very attractive receptacle for this spread.

The Perfect Hostess Cook Book
MILDRED O. KNOPF

HOT MUSHROOM MERINGUES

Makes 10 to 12 appetizers

1 cup fresh mushrooms or
   ½ cup best quality
   canned mushrooms
2 tablespoons butter
¼ teaspoon salt
⅛ teaspoon garlic salt
   pinch of pepper

2 slightly beaten egg yolks
2 tablespoons coffee cream
1½ inch rounds of untoasted
   bread
Parmesan cheese
2 egg whites

1. Wash the fresh mushrooms and dry well (or use canned mushrooms). Chop fine and sauté in butter. Season with salt, garlic salt and pepper.
2. Combine the beaten egg yolks with the coffee cream and add to hot cooked mushrooms. Continue to cook over very low flame until thickened, about 5 minutes.
3. Spread on rounds of untoasted bread (in baking, bread will toast at bottom), sprinkle with a little Parmesan cheese.

4. Beat the leftover egg whites until very stiff. With a small spatula, spread them on entire surface of mushroom mixture.
5. Bake at 400° F. on a lightly greased baking sheet 10 to 15 minutes, or until whites are delicately brown. Do not broil, as meringue will toughen.

NOTE:

These appetizers may be prepared in advance, but egg white must not be beaten and spread until ready to be baked and served.

Antoinette Pope School Cookbook
ANTOINETTE AND FRANÇOIS POPE

LIVERWURST CANAPÉ

rounds or ovals of bread
butter
mustard

liver sausage
grated onion
stuffed green olives

1. Spread the bread rounds with butter and a thin layer of mustard.
2. Blend the grated onion into the mashed liverwurst and spread thickly on top of the mustard.
3. Broil close to the flame of a hot (400° F.) oven for about 10 minutes until puffy.
4. Garnish with slice of green olive and serve hot.

HOT HAM BOUCHÉES

Makes about 30 canapés

2 tablespoons butter or
other shortening
1 medium-sized peeled
tomato cut very fine
2 tablespoons finely chopped
green onions and tops

½ cup finely chopped ham
2 whole eggs, slightly beaten
small round or oval
bread cases
grated Parmesan or
American cheese

1. In butter or other shortening, sauté tomatoes for 5 minutes. Add chopped green onions and tops and chopped ham. Add the eggs and cook over low flame until thick. Let cool.
2. Fill small round or oval bread cases with this mixture and sprinkle top with Parmesan or American cheese.
3. Broil before serving.

NOTE:
May be prepared hours in advance, kept covered with wax paper in a cool place, and baked at 400° F. about 12 minutes just before serving.

BREAD CASES

With 2-inch cutter, prepare rounds or oval-shaped pieces from sliced bread (60 for this recipe). From half of them remove centers, using top of No. 3 star tube. Put together with a little butter.

Antoinette Pope School Cookbook
ANTOINETTE AND FRANÇOIS POPE

PASTRY SNAILS AND FILLINGS

Use any pie crust. The following method is joyously acclaimed by many.

2 cups all-purpose flour	¼ cup water
1 teaspoon salt	⅔ cup shortening

1. Sift flour, then measure. Resift it into a bowl with salt.
2. Measure ⅓ cupful of this mixture and place it in a small bowl or cup. Stir into it to form a smooth paste ¼ cup water. Cut shortening into the flour mixture in the first bowl until it is the size of small peas. To do this use 2 knives or a pastry blender.
3. Stir the flour paste into the dough. Work it with your hand until it is well incorporated and the dough may be gath-

ered into a ball. Treat the dough as you would any pie crust. It may be chilled before it is rolled.

4. Roll the dough into very thin oblongs. Spread them with fillings as given below. Roll oblongs like a jelly roll. Chill the rolls; cut them in ½-inch slices and bake them on a greased pan in a hot oven (425° F.).

FILLINGS FOR PASTRY SNAILS

1. Two parts of soft cream cheese and 1 part anchovy paste or Roquefort.
2. Grated American cheese seasoned with cayenne, curry or mustard.
3. Soft cream cheese seasoned with catsup, salt and paprika.
4. Roquefort cheese, cream cheese and sherry.
5. Deviled ham thinned with a very little cream, seasoned with mustard.
6. Deviled ham sprinkled with grated American cheese, seasoned with a dash of mustard, salt and paprika.
7. Braunschweiger sausage thinned with tomato soup, seasoned with Worcestershire sauce.
8. Mock pâté de foie gras spread. Remove the skin from ½ pound liver sausage. Mash with a fork. Beat into it 1 tablespoon mayonnaise, 1½ tablespoons lemon juice, ½ teaspoon salt and ⅛ teaspoon white pepper.

The New Joy of Cooking
IRMA S. ROMBAUER AND
MARION ROMBAUER BECKER

DIPS, WHIPS, AND OTHER APPETIZERS

In addition to Italian Antipasto, French Hors d'Oeuvres, Scandinavian *Smörgåsbord* and Chino-Russian Canapés, a new group of appetite-provoking foods has come into vogue. It is the result of a trend to informality—and is strictly American.

This modern group of appetizers consists of dunks, dips, whips, "noshes," wrap-arounds and other similar, easily handled cocktail accompaniments.

CLAM DIP

Makes about 20 servings

1 small can chopped clams	2 (3-ounce) packages
4 tablespoons mayonnaise	cream cheese
1 tablespoon lemon juice	1 tablespoon chives, chopped
salt	1 tablespoon olives
Tabasco sauce	

1. Drain the clams.
2. Mix the mayonnaise and lemon juice; season with salt and Tabasco.
3. Mash cheese with a fork, then mix thoroughly with mayonnaise.
4. Add the chives, olives, and clams to the mayonnaise and cheese and beat until well blended.
5. Chill before serving. Serve with thin fingers of toast or potato chips.

Delicious Seafood Recipes
LOUIS GARRISON

SMÖRGÅSBORD

Here in America, we think of *Smörgåsbord* as an exclusively Swedish creation. Certainly most Americans have been introduced to it through Swedish restaurants. Actually, the *Smörgåsbord* belongs to all the Scandinavian countries. Literally it means "spread for bread," but most of us think of a *Smörgåsbord* as a long buffet table stacked with fish, meat, cheese and other delicacies.

From the Swedish-American restaurants the *Smörgåsbord* idea spread to country clubs, where it frequently became standard fare on Thursday, which was once "the maid's day off." Today there is hardly a resort hotel or a tour ship which does not recognize the popularity of the buffet table which sprang from the *Smörgåsbord*.

There are no set rules for what should go on this table;

it depends on whether it will serve as the forerunner of a dinner as is the custom in Scandinavia, or whether it constitutes almost the entire meal, as it often does here.

Anna Olsson Coombs offers this suggestion for a suitable *Smörgåsbord* meal. You must remember this cardinal rule of the *Smörgåsbord:* On the first round, you eat only fish; on the second, cold meats; and on the third, the hot dishes.

Bread (loaf and hardtack)   Varieties of cheese
Butter   Pickled herring
Jars of Swedish caviar
Cold boiled smoked tongue
(lavishly decorated with beets and kale)
Steamed spareribs (cut in attractive pieces and served in
a mound surrounded by heaps of prunes and apples)
Herring salad
(served with whipped cream tinted with beet juice)
Mackerel in aspic   Omelet or soufflé
Swedish meat balls   Anchovy or herring temptation
Small boiled potatoes
Coffee and cookies (for dessert)

The revolving *Smörgåsbord* table at the Three Crowns Swedish restaurant in New York City contains platters of such cold dishes as:

Pickled herring

Herring in cream

Herring in wine sauce

Salt herring—skinned and
cut in thin pieces in a
cream and dill sauce

Baked mackerel fillet

Jellied eel

Fresh shrimp

Baked fresh sardines

Swedish anchovies—the
whole fish, not the usual
rolled fillets

Pickles

Olives

Relishes

Celery

Bleu cheese

Caraway cheese

Swiss cheese

Gold cheese

Cottage cheese

Various cheese spreads

Liver paste

Head cheese—pigs' heads
and shoulder of pork and
veal

Veal in aspic

Ham
Roast beef
Corned beef
Smoked tongue
Potato salad
Cole slaw

Ham salad
Macaroni salad
Fish salad (usually cod)
Roast breast of veal—cooked
   with dill, spices, back fat
Fruit gelatin

The hot dishes, called *Smårvarmt* and kept warm in chafing dishes, can be chosen from the following variety:

Omelets—baked ham,
   smoked salmon, chives,
   cheese, lobster, mush-
   room, asparagus
Beef stew
Swedish meat balls
Fish balls
Barley hash—made of left-
   over meats, ground with
   barley, potatoes and spices
Kidney stew
Small boiled potatoes in their
   jackets, cooked with dill
Stuffed cabbage

Cabbage pudding
Herring and meat cakes with
   raisin sauce
Swedish hash—browned
   diced corned beef
Chopped veal cutlet
Pork and boiled potato
   sausage
Boiled lamb in dill sauce
Fish pudding
Liver and rice cakes, sliced
   and served with drawn
   butter

The Swedish custom is to choose your herring and other cold fish first, then the jellied and other cold meats and salads, and then the *Smårvarmt*. Herring is almost always eaten with boiled potatoes and a glass of aquavit or beer.

No story about *Smörgåsbord* is complete without mention of Oskar Davidsen's on the banks of the Peblingesøen Lake, in Copenhagen. It is the birthplace of the Danish sandwich and has the longest bill of fare in the world . . . with 177 kinds of open sandwiches, each available on rye, white, sour or crisp bread. Among Davidsen's sandwich combinations are:

Sliced potato with fried egg on toast
Hans Andersen's Favorite (crisp bacon, tomato, liver paste
   with truffles, meat-jelly and horseradish)
Lobster with asparagus in mayonnaise
Ham with Camembert, raw egg yolk and chives

Crisp bacon with fried onions
"Union Jack Sandwich" (raw, scraped fillet of beef with
   shrimps and raw egg yolk)
Tongue with fried egg
Parboiled egg with smoked eel
Hot scrambled egg with smoked salmon on toast
Grated carrot with raw egg yolk and sliced lemon
Bombay toast (macaroni, chicken giblets in curry-mayon-
   naise with egg and smoked salmon)

On and on goes the list—better send to Oskar Davidsen's for
a complete copy . . . or for some of the sandwiches themselves, by airmail.

EXOTIC HORS D'OEUVRES

For those who are interested in exotic hors d'oeuvres, we give
you here lists of three styles—the Dutch *Rijsttafel* or "rice
table," the Chinese "cold dishes," and the hors d'oeuvre specialties of Greece.

RIJSTTAFEL

Rijsttafel, or "rice table," is a style of eating the Dutch
discovered during the days of their Dutch East Indies empire,
now Indonesia. It consists of a central, large dish of rice surrounded by as many as twenty smaller dishes, particularly of
spicy meats and vegetables.

One or two at a time you transfer the contents of the little
dishes onto the big pile of rice, eat the rice and its condiments together and in between cool off with generous
draughts of cold Dutch beer. Among the Rijsttafel dishes
served in such Amsterdam restaurants as Bali are: pork in
soya sauce, meat in Madeira sauce, steamed meat, liver in a
special sauce, eggs in sauce, sweet potatoes, bean sprouts,
roast pork on sticks, fried bananas, stuffed omelet, vegetables
in peanut sauce, cucumber in sour sauce, mixed sour vegetables, fruit in a sweet and sour sauce and fried grated
coconut.

CHINESE HORS D'OEUVRES

Chinese hors d'oeuvres, called in Chinese "cold dishes," have in recent years become a fascinating attraction to Western epicures who frequent the best Chinese restaurants. When ordering dinner at a good Chinese restaurant, call ahead and insist on having these dishes as a starter: Sliced, semi-pickled vegetables, herb-aromatized liver and kidneys, "drunken chicken," fish smoked in the Chinese manner. At your restaurant, follow these cold dishes with quick-fried wine-sipping dishes, to be brought to the table at 10-minute intervals. Suggestions: toasted prawns sprinkled with sesame seeds (a Peking dish), diced chicken cubes fried in soya jam (another Peking dish), thin-sliced steak in oyster sauce (Cantonese), deep-fried paper-wrapped chicken (Cantonese).

GREEK HORS D'OEUVRES

In the lovely Taverna Ta Nissia of the Athens Hilton Hotel this is a typical hors d'oeuvre list:

Taramasalata (spread made
  with roe of gray mullet)
Kalamata olives
"Louza" ham from Mykonos
Anchovies in olive oil
Kotopitta (creamed chicken)
Dolmadakia (stuffed vine
  leaves)
Marides friture (fried white-
  bait with lemon)
Stuffed tomato with rice and
  pignolia nuts
Sardines in oil-and-lemon
  dressing

Squid in red wine sauce
Fried baby squash
Messolonghi boutarge
Artichokes and fennel,
  Grecian style
Beans plaki
Spanakopitta (spinach)
Hot souzoukakia with tomato
  sauce
Lakerda with pickled
  vegetables
Tyropitta (cheese)
Miniature yarpakia with
  avgolemono sauce

SOUPS AND CHOWDERS

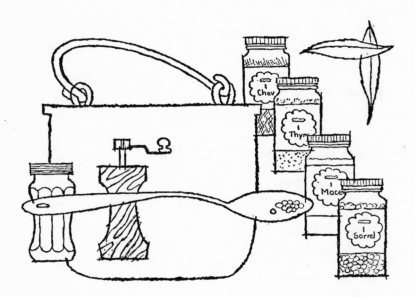

IRMA ROMBAUER'S FAVORITE SOUP

Mrs. Irma S. Rombauer's *Joy of Cooking* is one of the most successful cookbooks ever published. For years now, considerably more than a million families have been enjoying foods prepared in accordance with its directions. It is as much to honor her achievement as to give you its benefits, that we here publish the recipe for her favorite soup.

The first *Joy,* a modest volume, was published privately in 1931. It was written at the request of Irma Rombauer's children, who, on leaving home, asked for a record of "what mother used to cook." In 1936 The Bobbs-Merrill Company brought out an enlarged and revised edition of the timidly launched maiden effort and this was followed by a second enlarged and revised edition in 1943, and the book has had several subsequent editions.

Mrs. Rombauer says: "My roots are Victorian but I have been modernized by life and my children. My book reflects my life, and, as you may see by its timely contents, I have not stood still. Every effort has been made to encourage the cook in her daily grind by lifting everyday food out of the commonplace."

Makes about 15 cupfuls

1 gallon water	1 whole stalk celery with
1 2-pound beef bone	leaves
1 2-pound veal bone	1 bunch parsley
2 pounds brisket of beef	3 or 4 carrots
1 large onion	½ pound snap beans
1 No. 2 can tomatoes	1¼ cups fine noodles, broken
2 teaspoons salt	

1. Place in a soup kettle the water, beef bone, veal bone, brisket of beef, onion, tomatoes and salt. Cover the pot closely. Simmer the soup for about 3½ hours.
2. Cut up and add celery with leaves, parsley, carrots and snap beans. Simmer the soup ½ hour longer.
3. Remove the meat. Put the soup through a puree strainer. Chill it. Remove the fat.
4. Reheat the soup. Add noodles. Simmer for about 10 minutes or until tender.

The New Joy of Cooking
IRMA S. ROMBAUER AND
MARION ROMBAUER BECKER

JAMES BEARD'S POT AU FEU

This is a classic dish of the French countryside and is prepared in many ways in different regions of the country. Basically it is a combination of beef, chicken and vegetables. The broth is usually served first, and after that the boiled beef and the chicken with the vegetables from the pot. Horseradish sauce is sometimes served with it, or mustard.

Makes 8 servings

2 pounds lean beef, brisket, round or rump	5 or 6 carrots
	2 or 3 turnips
whole fowl or 2 pounds wings and backs	4 or 5 leeks
	4 quarts water
1½ pounds shin bone with marrow	parsley
	thyme
2 onions	1 clove garlic
cloves	1½ tablespoons salt

1. Place in 8-quart kettle beef, fowl, shin bone with marrow. Add onions stuck with cloves, carrots, turnips and leeks with the green cut away.
2. Cover with water and bring to a boil very slowly. Boil for 5 minutes and skim off the scum from the top. Add 1 or 2 sprigs parsley, a sprig of thyme, and a clove of garlic. Reduce the heat, cover the kettle, and allow to simmer 4 hours. After 1 hour's cooking add salt.
3. Remove the meat and the chicken from the kettle and keep warm. Strain the broth, remove some of the vegetables from the strainer, and add them to the dish with the meat. Skim off the fat from the broth.
4. Serve bowls of the broth with pieces of well-dried French bread. Serve the meat and—if you have used a whole bird —the chicken with the vegetables, and pass either mustard or horseradish sauce. A good green salad with this, and perhaps some excellent cheese, make a hearty meal.

The Fireside Cook Book
JAMES A. BEARD

MULLIGATAWNY

This substantial curry soup is for those many souls who have developed a crush on food with a tang to it. Mulligatawny is like a page right out of Rudyard Kipling—"from India's sunny clime, where I used to spend my time, a serving of Her Majesty the Queen."

The source of this particular mulligatawny recipe is the little book called *Soup!* by Evelyn Gendel, a treasury of sixty super soups.

Makes 4 to 6 servings

1 onion	6 cups light chicken bouillon
1 carrot	(or bouillon and water,
½ white turnip	half and half)
4 tablespoons butter	1 bay leaf
1 pound lean lamb	pinch of thyme
1 teaspoon curry powder	1 teaspoon lemon juice
1 tart apple	1 cup cooked rice (about)

1. Thinly slice the onion, chop the carrot and turnip, and sauté them all in butter until golden brown.
2. Remove lamb fat and skin, cut lamb in small pieces, add to the pot and sear. Stir in curry powder.
3. Mix well, cook for a few minutes more. Stir in hot chicken bouillon. Bring to a boil, skim, add a peeled and cored apple, cut up, and season with bay leaf and thyme. Lower the fire and simmer, covered, for at least 2 hours. If liquid cooks down, add more water. Strain.
4. Return the meat pieces to the strained soup, bring to a boil again, add lemon juice, and simmer a few minutes more. Serve with plain boiled (hot) rice in a separate dish.

Soup!
EVELYN GENDEL

SCOTCH LAMB AND BARLEY BROTH

For more than twenty-five winters, the sole "main dish" of the chic Lord & Taylor Soup Bar has been a single soup—

this Scotch Broth. The thousands of sophisticated New Yorkers who visit the Soup Bar attest to the superiority of this recipe.

Makes 6 servings

2 pound neck of lamb	1 onion
2 tablespoons barley	2 stalks celery
1 small turnip	2 teaspoons chopped parsley
1 carrot	salt and pepper

1. Wipe meat, cut into small pieces, and put in saucepan with 2 quarts cold water.
2. Bring to a slow boil, then simmer for 1 hour, skimming well several times.
3. Dice all the vegetables and add to the broth; also add barley, salt and pepper. Continue cooking until vegetables are tender, about 1½ hours longer.
4. Skim again. Sprinkle with chopped parsley just before serving.

Soup Bar
Lord & Taylor
New York City

MINESTRONE MILANO

Milan, Italy, is the home of many wonderful things. The world's most renowned opera house, La Scala, stands not far from one of the most beautiful of all cathedrals, a marvel of white marble bristling with belfries, gables, pinnacles and statues. And not far away is the Brera Palace and Picture Gallery which houses several of the world's greatest paintings, including the Dead Christ by Mantegna (a great study in the foreshortening of a figure), as well as a famous Pietà by Giovanni Bellini and, if memory serves me, a great Sacre Conversasione by Piero della Francesca. Milan is today a lively, businesslike city with modern buildings going up so fast they overshadow the gracious old ones. In Milan you can eat well, and this minestrone or vegetable soup is one of the Milanese specialties (see also Osso-Buco and Rizotto).

Makes 6 servings

4 tablespoons olive oil
1 cup shredded cabbage
½ cup julienne-cut green
  beans
½ cup julienne-cut celery
1 clove garlic, mashed
8 green onions, cut into
  3-inch strips
4 stalks Swiss chard,
  shredded
1 cup strained tomatoes

1 tablespoon chopped
  parsley
6 cups warm veal, chicken,
  or beef stock
1 cup cooked pea beans
⅛ teaspoon thyme
2 teaspoons salt
½ teaspoon pepper
½ cup macaroni, broken
  into pieces
grated Parmesan cheese

1. Casserole in the making: Heat oil slowly in a 4-quart marmite. Place marmite on an asbestos pad.
2. Add all the vegetables but tomatoes and pea beans. Cook, stirring occasionally, until the vegetables begin to brown.
3. Add warm stock, tomatoes, beans, thyme, salt and pepper. Cover and simmer 45 minutes.
4. Add macaroni and cook 15 minutes longer. Serve in warm individual casseroles with grated cheese.

The Casserole Cookbook
JOHN AND MARIE ROBERSON

TURTLE SOUP

Everybody knows the famous turtle soup song from *Alice in Wonderland* that goes:

> Beautiful soup, so rich and green,
> Waiting in a hot tureen!
> Who for such dainties would not stoop?
> Soup of the evening, beautiful soup!
> Soup of the evening, beautiful soup!
>   Beau-ootiful Soo-oop!
>   Beau-ootiful Soo-oop!
> Soo-oop of the e-e-evening,
>   Beautiful, beautiful soup!

One of the oldest and most gracious dining places in America is Shoyer's, located in the heart of historic Philadelphia.

On its walls are many interesting items of Americana, including a silk engraving of George Washington, dated 1780; an 1862 parole issued by the Confederate authorities to a captured Union lieutenant; an antique poster headed, "Mothers, look out for your children"; and other memorabilia. Shoyer's Turtle Soup is famous, and if you can get some good fresh turtle meat from your fish dealer, by all means try it. You'll have to make quite a batch at one time, but it keeps and even gets better on reheating.

Makes about 15 servings

3 pounds turtle meat	1 cup canned tomatoes
1 cup chopped onions	½ lemon (juice of)
1 clove garlic	3 hard-boiled eggs
2 tablespoons minced parsley	2 teaspoons salt
2 tablespoons butter	½ teaspoon pepper
2 tablespoons flour	1 pint cooking sherry

1. Put turtle meat in a saucepan with 1 gallon of water and boil for 10 minutes.
2. Brown onions, garlic, parsley, and flour in the butter, stirring constantly, then add turtle meat that has been cut into 1-inch pieces, cook for 5 minutes and add tomatoes.
3. Add water in which turtle meat was parboiled. Cook for 1 hour or until turtle meat is tender. Season with salt and pepper, add lemon juice.
4. Remove from heat and add finely chopped hard-boiled eggs. Lace in 1 pint of cooking sherry.

Shoyer's Restaurant
Philadelphia, Pa.

JEWISH CHICKEN SOUP

In the Jewish home, chicken soup is associated with Sabbaths and holidays. Specially rich clear chicken soup is commonly called *Gilderne* and is served as a "must" at wedding anniversaries, especially the twenty-fifth and fiftieth.

Fowl that has had the fatty portions removed is best for soup. Sections of chicken should include the gizzard, heart, neck and feet.

Makes 8 to 10 servings

4½- to 5-pound fowl (remove fatty portions)	2 stalks celery including leaves
1 large onion	1 bay leaf
1 large carrot, diced, sliced or strips	6 peppercorns (optional)
	1 quart of boiled water per pound of chicken

1. Prepare chicken parts (including gizzard, heart, neck, and feet) for cooking. Cook in water slowly after bringing to a quick boil. Skim carefully.
2. Add seasoning and vegetables after 30 minutes of simmering. Cooking time depends on tenderness of fowl.
3. Strain soup while hot just before serving.

Jewish Cookery
LEAH W. LEONARD

CALIFORNIA CHICKEN GUMBO

California cooks, like good cooks of all the other forty-nine states, make and enjoy all kinds of soups. There are the excellent canned and dehydrated soups; there are the old family recipes for soups, brought from New England, or down South, or the Middle West, or Mexico, or China, or wherever. And then there are some special soups that seem to fit in especially well with California ways of doing things.

This recipe makes one of the best soups ever.

Makes about 2½ quarts, or 10 generous servings

4 tablespoons butter	1 cup sliced okra (fresh or canned)
¼ cup diced smoked ham	1 cup chopped fresh or solid-pack canned tomatoes
½ cup diced celery	
1 green pepper, chopped	
1 large onion, chopped	
¼ cup raw rice	2 tablespoons chopped pimiento
1 tablespoon flour	
2 quarts strong chicken broth	½ cup coarsely diced cooked or canned chicken

1. Fry the ham, celery, green pepper, and onion in the butter until soft. Add rice and cook, stirring, 5 minutes.
2. Add flour, blend, then stir in broth and heat.
3. Add remaining ingredients, season to taste with salt and pepper, cover and let simmer 40 minutes.

The California Cook Book
GENEVIEVE CALLAHAN

CREAM OF TOMATO SOUP

With all due respect to the wonderful Mr. Campbell and other makers of ready-made soups, good homemade cream of tomato soup has a flavor which eludes the can. It is a little more expensive, but so packed full of essential foods that it can well be the basis of a meal.

If for any reason the serving is delayed, keep the two mixtures warm in their separate pans because they may curdle if actually cooked together. Some cooks use a pinch of soda to prevent curdling. But baking soda destroys vitamins and has an unpleasant taste. If you follow these directions, the soup should not curdle.

Makes 6 servings

3 cups canned or fresh
   tomatoes
1 onion stuck with cloves
   sprig of parsley
3 tablespoons butter
3 tablespoons flour

3 cups milk
salt
pepper
croutons or popcorn
   (optional)

1. Put tomatoes into a saucepan, add peeled onion stuck with cloves, and a sprig of fresh parsley. If the tomatoes are fresh, cut them up and add ½ cup water. Simmer for 15 minutes, then strain and put the sieved pulp back on the fire to become thoroughly heated again.
2. While the tomatoes are cooking, prepare the cream sauce. Melt butter in a saucepan, blend in flour and when that is smooth slowly add milk. Bring to a boil, stirring all the while, then simmer for 5 minutes to cook the flour.

3. Just before serving, combine the cream and tomato pulp, season, stir briskly and serve at once. Nicely browned croutons or toasted popcorn go well with this soup.

100 Summer and Winter Soups
ANN ROE ROBBINS

THOMAS E. DEWEY'S BERKSHIRE SOUP

Makes 4 servings

1 onion, finely chopped	1 teaspoon salt
¼ cup butter	½ teaspoon pepper
½ bay leaf	2 cups water (boiling)
12 peppercorns	1 cup corn
2 tablespoons flour	½ cup cream
1 can tomatoes	2 egg yolks
2 tablespoons sugar	

1. Cook onion and butter 5 minutes, stirring constantly.
2. Add bay leaf, peppercorns and flour. Cook 2 minutes.
3. Then add tomatoes, sugar, salt, pepper, boiling water and simmer 20 minutes.
4. Add corn, cook 10 minutes and force through purée strainer.
5. Just before serving, add egg yolks slightly beaten and diluted with cream.

Stars in Your Kitchen
MARTA MICHEL

PURÉE MONGOLE

Purée Mongole is simply a combination of cream of tomato and cream of pea soup—and can be made with canned soups if you wish. The canned soups should be diluted with milk rather than water, and the seasoning should be liberal. But it takes very little time to make your own, and there is no comparison in the results. Excellent in winter or summer, for luncheon or supper.

Makes about 8 servings

1 cup split peas	pepper
5 cups water	1 cup cream
2 cups tomato juice	croutons
1 onion	about 1 cup flaked fish
2 tablespoons butter	(optional)
salt	

1. Soak split peas overnight in plenty of water to cover.
2. The next day drain them, add 5 cups of water, tomato juice, salt, and pepper.
3. Fry a minced onion in butter until the onion is soft and yellow (which takes about 10 minutes), and add that also. Bring to a boil, season with salt and pepper, and simmer about 45 minutes or until the peas are very soft.
4. Then strain the soup to remove the pea husks, add cream, bring to a boil again and it is ready to be served. Croutons are delicious with this soup. And it can be turned into a real meal by adding some fresh or canned flaked crab meat, lobster, salmon, or canned tuna to the soup.

100 Summer and Winter Soups
ANN ROE ROBBINS

POTAGE ST. GERMAIN

Pea Soup was seldom called *Potage de Pois* but usually *Potage St. Germain*. The reason is that exceptionally good green peas grow abundantly in St. Germain, a place not very far from Paris and the French like to honor a town that has some special virtue by naming a dish for it.

You will find the flavor and color of this soup made of dried peas greatly improved if a cup of fresh green peas (or the pods of very young tender peas) which have been cooked until soft and then rubbed through a sieve are added to the soup after it has been strained. The pods, if young and tender, are particularly good. In some French families this soup would be served the day before or after they had Leek-and-Potato Soup, because it uses up the green part of the leeks that are left.

Makes 6 servings

2 cups split peas	1 medium carrot, chopped
5 cups water	2 leeks, green part
1 teaspoon salt	1 bay leaf
2 tablespoons butter	a little thyme
½ cup fat salt pork,	1 cup spinach leaves or
finely chopped	green lettuce leaves
1 medium onion, chopped	bread croutons

1. Soak peas in water to cover about 1 hour. Drain, put in a saucepan with 4 cups of water and salt. Bring to a boil, skim, cover and cook slowly.
2. Melt 1 tablespoon butter in a saucepan, add salt pork and onion and cook until it melts and starts to brown. Add carrot, leeks, spinach or lettuce leaves, bay leaf and thyme and cook for a few minutes.
3. Add to the split peas. Continue cooking all together for about 1 hour or until peas are soft.
4. Rub through a sieve, add remaining cup of water (or a cup of bouillon or stock) if the soup is very thick. Bring to a boil, skim, correct the seasoning, adding a little sugar if desired. Add remaining tablespoon of butter. Serve with croutons.

French Cooking for Americans
LOUIS DIAT

BOULA-BOULA

Boula-Boula is a sophisticated soup which may have (but probably didn't) originate at Yale University. Nonetheless, a Harvard graduate, John F. Kennedy, enjoyed it and his wife Jacqueline often served it. Whether "boula" originated from the word "boule," an aristocratic advisory body of ancient Greece, or whether it came from the French word for ball, deponent knoweth not. I do remember running all over Paris for a "boule pour le riz," a ball in which to cook rice, which my wife had seen in somebody's kitchen. At any rate give Boula-Boula "the old college try."

Makes 4 servings

2 cups freshly shelled green peas	2 cups canned green turtle soup
1 tablespoon sweet butter	1 cup sherry
salt and pepper	½ cup heavy cream, whipped

1. Make a green pea purée by cooking the peas in boiling salted water until tender and straining through a fine sieve or whipping in a blender.
2. Reheat the purée and add the butter. Add salt and pepper to taste.
3. Mix in the turtle soup and sherry and heat to just under the boiling point.
4. Place soup in serving cups, cover each cup with whipped cream and put the cups under the broiler to brown the topping. Serve immediately.

GAZPACHO

Gazpacho, the popular iced Spanish soup, was described, somewhat disparagingly, by Theophile Gautier after a journey to Spain in 1840; like all good Frenchmen he was apt to be suspicious of foreign food.

"Our supper was of the simplest kind; all the serving men and maids of the hostelry had gone to the dance, and we had to be content with a mere Gazpacho," he wrote. "It is the favorite dish of the Andalusians, and the prettiest women do not shrink from swallowing bowlfuls of this hell-broth of an evening. Gazpacho is considered highly refreshing, an opinion which strikes me as rather rash, but, strange as it may seem the first time one tastes it, one ends by getting used to it and even liking it. As a most providential compensation we had a decanter of an excellent dry white Malaga wine to wash down this meager repast, and drained it conscientiously to the last drop, thus restoring our strength, exhausted by a nine hours' spell upon indescribable roads at a temperature like that of a kiln." (From *A Romantic in Spain*, published by Alfred A. Knopf.)

Here is a rather sophisticated version of Gazpacho. It is by Elizabeth David, one of England's greatests gifts to cooking.

Makes 4 to 5 servings

½ pound onions	3 cloves garlic
2 pounds fresh tomatoes or	1 tablespoon paprika
1 large can tomatoes	2 or 3 tablespoons olive oil
pepper	1 cucumber
salt	12 black pitted olives
sugar (small amount)	ice cubes
½ glass red wine	chopped parsley

1. Make a fairly thick tomato soup with onions, tomatoes, salt, pepper, a little sugar, and red wine. Put them through a sieve.
2. In a mortar pound garlic cloves, add salt, pepper and paprika, and olive oil, drop by drop. When this mixture has the consistency of mayonnaise stir in gradually the cold tomato soup.
3. Put in a cucumber cut in small cubes and a dozen pitted black olives. Stand in the refrigerator, and before serving put a cube of ice and a handful of chopped parsley into each plate.

The Book of Mediterranean Food
ELIZABETH DAVID

KENTUCKY BLACK BEAN SOUP

They tell a story here about a certain Louisville host who gave his annual Derby breakfast, a celebrated affair where business and professional men, dowagers and debutantes rubbed elbows with horse trainers, politicians and farmers. At this gathering, after plying his guests with that particular "sippage" which has made Kentucky immortal (mint juleps to the uninitiated), the host finally led them into the dining room where, as they say in Victorian novels, "a truly sumptuous repast had been spread."

The guests began to cram themselves with the tempting morsels—that is, all but one. Alone in a corner, the host spied a local farmer holding an empty plate. Asked if he were ill or if anything were wrong, the old man shook his head. "You know I got to admit all these here vittals," pointing to the table, "look mighty pretty. But now that I done seen these fancibles, I'm a-wondering whar's the fillables."

Here is a "fillable," a Kentucky culinary masterpiece from pre-Civil War days.

MARION FLEXNER

Makes 12 servings

1 pound black beans, soaked
   overnight in water
1 pound lean veal
1 lemon (cut in eighths)
½ teaspoon nutmeg
3 tablespoons salt, or
   more to taste
2 tablespoons Worcester-
   shire sauce
3 quarts water
1 veal knucklebone with
   meat

4 cloves stuck in lemon
   pieces
¼ teaspoon allspice
¼ teaspoon black pepper
1 cup sherry
3 onions, chopped
2 tablespoons butter
lemons
hard-boiled eggs for
   garnishing

1. Cover beans with water and soak overnight. Drain.
2. Next morning put 3 quarts of water in a soup kettle. Add veal, knucklebone, lemon, beans, salt, pepper, Worcestershire sauce, and spices and boil slowly until beans are mushy (3 to 4 hours).
3. Remove meat and set aside. Remove lemon and cloves and discard.
4. Press beans through a strainer or food mill. As this is hard to do, it may be necessary to add a bit more water to dissolve strained soup.
5. Fry onions until brown in butter and add to the soup. Add sherry and more salt and pepper if necessary. Heat to the boiling point.
6. Serve 1 slice of lemon and 1 slice of hard-boiled egg in each plate or cup.

Out of Kentucky Kitchens
MARION FLEXNER

VEGETARIAN MUSHROOM AND BARLEY SOUP

Among New York's so-called "dairy" restaurants, and there are quite a few such places where they cook without meat or meat products, a favorite soup is mushroom and barley. Properly prepared, it is thick and hearty—a meal in itself.

Makes 8 servings

10 fresh mushrooms, thinly sliced	¼ cup diced onions
4 tablespoons large pearl barley	3 tablespoons butter
	2 teaspoons salt
½ cup dried lima beans	¼ teaspoon pepper
2 quarts water	½ cup milk
¼ cup diced celery	2 tablespoons flour
¼ cup diced carrots	chopped dill

1. Wash mushrooms, barley and lima beans.
2. To boiling water, add the mushrooms, barley, beans, salt, pepper, 1½ tablespoons butter, celery, and carrots.
3. Cook for 1 hour, until barley is tender. While soup is simmering, stir slowly every 20 minutes.
4. In a saucepan, melt remaining butter over low heat, and sauté onions. Add flour, stir to fine consistency. Add milk, making a smooth white sauce.
5. When soup is done, add white sauce and mix well. Adjust seasoning to taste. Serve hot, garnished with chopped dill.

VIRGINIA PEANUT SOUP

Peanut soup is to Virginia what white bean soup is to Boston. Here is a recipe that originated in the Hotel Roanoke, deep in the heart of Virginny.

Makes 15 servings

2 quarts chicken broth	3 tablespoons flour
1 small onion, diced	⅓ teaspoon celery salt
¼ pound butter	1 teaspoon salt
1 pint peanut butter	1 tablespoon lemon juice
2 stalks celery, diced	ground peanuts

1. Melt butter in cooking vessel and add onion and celery. Sauté for 5 minutes, but do not brown.
2. Add flour and mix well. Add hot chicken broth and cook ½ hour.
3. Remove from stove, strain and add peanut butter, celery salt, and lemon juice.
4. Just before serving, sprinkle with ground peanuts.

The Southern Cook Book
MARION BROWN

FRENCH ONION SOUP

Makes 4 servings

2 large onions, sliced thin and sautéed in butter until brown	1 teaspoon Worcestershire sauce
2 cups stock	salt and pepper to taste
½ cup cream	toast
	grated Parmesan cheese

1. Boil the sautéed onions in stock for 10 minutes.
2. Add cream, salt, and pepper to taste.
3. Just before serving add 1 teaspoon Worcestershire sauce.
4. In each bowl of soup place a thin slice of toast covered with grated Parmesan cheese.

Stars in Your Kitchen
MARTA MICHEL

CARRIER'S ONION SOUFFLÉ SOUP

Bob Carrier is one of the most colorful characters in present-day cookery. His real name is Robert Carrier MacMahon, and he grew up on the banks of the Hudson River, near

Sleepy Hollow, where Rip Van Winkle slept for twenty years.
Now Robert Carrier is the patron of one of the finest gourmet
restaurants in the world, the author of numerous best-seller
cookbooks, and the creator of the Carrier Cooking Cards,
which I urge you to run out and buy if you do not already
own them.

Makes 4 to 6 servings

2½ pints well-flavored French onion soup	6 tablespoons freshly grated Gruyère (Swiss) cheese
4-6 slices well-toasted French bread, buttered	2 egg whites, stiffly beaten salt
¾ pint thick Béchamel Sauce (see page 255)	freshly ground black pepper nutmeg

1. Prepare the thick Béchamel Sauce, remove from the heat
   and stir in the freshly grated cheese. Meanwhile preheat
   oven to 450°.
2. Allow cheese mixture to cool and fold in the stiffly beaten
   egg whites. Season to taste with salt, pepper and nutmeg.
3. Pour the onion soup into individual ovenproof bowls (or
   one large one), top with buttered rounds of toast and
   spoon the cheese mixture over this. Bake in preheated hot
   oven for 8 to 10 minutes or until soufflé has risen and is
   golden.

ROBERT CARRIER

CHESTNUT SOUP OF THE AUVERGNE

William I. Kaufman is one of the world's most published
food authorities. He is the author or co-author of more than
twenty-five books, including *The Art of Creole Cookery, The
Art of India's Cookery, The Coffee Cookbook* and others, including *Cooking in a Castle,* from which comes this recipe,
Potage de Châtaignes à l'Auvergnate. Cooking in a Castle
shares some of the secrets of Old France with the modern
American housewife. In past centuries, the prestige of a
castle often was based upon the culinary specialties and abili- .

ties of the chef. The lord of the manor's social standing frequently depended upon the quality of the cuisine served in his château. As a result, the demand for new exciting dishes was great, and the competition keen for the reputation of setting a *bonne table.* "In the more deluxe châteaux," says Mr. Kaufman, "the range of foods is wider—the more sumptuous the environment, the greater the stress on *haute cuisine.* The smaller châteaux feature the more regional cuisine." Today, following the pattern of Stately Homes of England, many of the châteaux of France are also hostelries where you can stay, enjoy the luxuries of the peaceful surroundings, and partake of fine food. You can start your trip now, with this Chestnut Soup, easily made in your kitchen.

Makes 8 servings

1¾ pounds chestnuts	¼ teaspoon dry mustard
1 bouquet garni made of	dash of baking soda
sprigs of fresh parsley,	⅓ cup sherry
tarragon, etc.	2 egg whites
1 quart chicken stock	dash of salt
1 cup heavy cream	3 tablespoons ground nuts

1. Make slits in the chestnuts; spread in a shallow pan. Bake in 450° oven, 15 minutes; cool. Shell and skin chestnuts. Place in a deep saucepan, with the bouquet garni.
2. Add enough water to cover; bring to a boil. Cover; reduce heat and simmer 20 to 25 minutes, or until chestnuts are tender. Drain and force chestnuts through a sieve into deep saucepan.
3. Add the chicken stock and bring to a boil. Add heavy cream, mustard and baking soda. Again bring to a boil. Remove from heat, stir in the sherry; keep warm.
4. Beat egg whites until stiff, but not dry. Gradually add salt and beat until very stiff. Fold in ground nuts. Drop by spoonfuls on brown paper on a baking sheet; place this under broiler until meringues are lightly browned.
5. Spoon the soup into bouillon cups and top each with a meringue.

Cooking in a Castle
WILLIAM I. KAUFMAN

WATERCRESS SOUP

(SOUPE AU CRESSON)

Watercress soup, created in France and popularized by Mapie, Countess de Toulouse-Lautrec, makes a dashing start to almost any kind of meal—formal or informal, fancy or peasant. And it is so easy to prepare.

If fresh chervil is not available, use fresh parsley.

Makes 4 servings

1 pound (3-4) potatoes
2 cups scalded milk
   salt
1 bunch watercress

4 tablespoons butter
4 tablespoons chopped fresh
   chervil

1. Peel the potatoes and cut them into small pieces. Boil in a quart of water. Do not strain but mash them in the water in the saucepan. Add the milk and season with salt.
2. Trim the stems from the watercress and wash well. Add the leaves to the soup and cook for 10 minutes. Just before serving, add the butter and chopped chervil.

La Cuisine de France

GREEK AVGOLEMONO SOUP

This is an elegant, delicious soup and so easy to make. I use canned chicken soup with rice instead of the chicken stock and raw rice called for in the following standard Greek recipe, and because the rice in the canned soup has already been cooked, I remove it before heating the soup and replace it after the soup has come to a boil. One more point: since the ready-made soup is already salted, omit the salt called for in the recipe. While the broth may be canned, you must use fresh lemon juice.

Last summer we served Avgolemono Soup in mugs as a preliminary to a buffet supper, and it was a huge success. You can also use it as an excellent medium-thick sauce for meats, fish or vegetables, by simply cutting the amount of the chicken broth in the recipe.

Makes 6 servings

6 cups chicken broth	1 teaspoon salt
¼ cup raw rice	3 eggs
¼ cup fresh lemon juice	1 lemon, thinly sliced

1. In large saucepan, combine the chicken broth, raw rice and salt and bring to a boil.
2. Reduce the heat, cover and let simmer until the rice is just tender. Remove pot from stove. (If you have used canned chicken soup with rice, you will add the cooked rice after the soup has come to a boil and is simmering.)
3. In a bowl, beat eggs until pale yellow and fluffy. Beat in the lemon juice.
4. Slowly stir 2 cups of the hot broth into the egg-and-lemon mixture and whisk vigorously. Then pour this back into the pot of soup and whisk until it thickens slightly.
5. Cool to room temperature, then refrigerate until very cold. Stir before serving. Garnish with lemon slices.

RUSSIAN TEA ROOM BORSCHT

New York's famous Russian Tea Room retains a name which smacks of watercress sandwiches and petits fours. But as any knowing New Yorker is aware, the Russian Tea Room near the old Carnegie Hall has long been the mecca of local and visiting musicians who are hardly the delicate fingertip-sandwich type. Here the meal begins with a good hearty borscht, plus piroshke (meat-filled pastry) on the side. Then a good Russian meat dish, vegetables, dessert and the inevitable tea (served in a glass to warm the hands, Russian-style). For after the concert the fare is often a stack of blini with red caviar and sour cream. I do not know whether Faith Kaye, the owner, makes any money in the place because its habitués spend many long hours in discussion over their food . . . and where else in America can a restaurant patron bask in the musical sunshine of so many present and future Stokowskis, Bernsteins, or Ormandys?

Makes 6 servings

1½ quarts beef stock	1 small can tomatoes
1 pound fresh beets	1 small can tomato paste
2 carrots	2 tablespoons sugar
1 large onion	½ head fresh cabbage
2 stalks celery	2 tablespoons Ac'cent (MSG)
1 parsnip	6 tablespoons sour cream
2 tablespoons salt	2 tablespoons fresh dill

1. All vegetables must be brushed, washed, and peeled. Cut beets, carrots, and parsnip in julienne slivers. Dice the celery and cube the other vegetables.
2. Bring the beef stock to a boil and add beets, carrots, onion, celery and parsnip. Add salt to boiling soup.
3. At the very end, when these vegetables are cooked, add the tomatoes, tomato paste, cabbage, sugar, and Ac'cent. Cabbage, in any event, should not cook for more than 10 to 15 minutes.
4. Stir well, allow to simmer until ready to serve. Just before serving in individual plates, top with tablespoon of sour cream and sprinkle with fresh dill.

Russian Tea Room, New York City

COLD SOUP INDIENNE

"You haven't lived until you've had a cup of this soup on a hot day," declares Lilian MacKendrick, a leading painter. "This recipe is my treasure—and my glory. The ritziest cold vichyssoise or borscht seem merely ordinary in comparison. It is a soup which dazzles even the most demanding gourmet."

Makes 4 servings

2 medium-sized onions, minced	1 tablespoon flour
½ teaspoon curry powder	1 sour green apple, chopped fine
1 quart real chicken broth (not cubes)	2 tablespoons grated coconut
2 fresh tomatoes	clove of garlic
1 slice lemon	sweet cream
1 tablespoon butter (not margarine)	

1. Lightly brown onion in butter and add garlic, curry powder and flour. Cook a few minutes.
2. Add chicken broth. Add apple, tomatoes, coconut, lemon. Cover and simmer 1½ hours.
3. Strain and cool. Add ½ as much sweet cream as soup. Serve cold.

LILIAN MAC KENDRICK

CHEDDAR CHEESE SOUP

Old Drovers Inn is a pleasant little hide-away from care and cooking, located in Dover Plains, just two hours away from New York via the beautiful Taconic Parkway. Breakfast is served in the Federal Room, and you feel very Colonial when you eat there. Dinner is by candlelight in the truly inn-like dining room . . . and Cheddar Cheese Soup is a specialty of the house. In fact, it is possible that this cheese soup was invented here.

Makes about 2 quarts

4 tablespoons butter	2 tablespoons flour
½ cup diced carrots	6 ounces young Cheddar
½ cup diced green pepper	cheese, grated
½ cup minced onion	6 ounces well-cured Cheddar
½ cup diced celery	cheese, grated
1 quart well-seasoned chicken	salt
stock (or chicken bouillon	white pepper
cubes and water)	milk

1. Melt the butter in the upper part of a a double boiler. Add the vegetables and braise till tender. Do not let them brown.
2. Blend in the flour and cook for 1 minute, stirring constantly.
3. Pour in the stock and stir till thickened.
4. Put the pan into the lower part of the double boiler, in which the water is boiling. Add the cheeses and stir until the cheese has melted.

5. Thin to cream consistency with milk. Season to taste with salt and pepper, and then strain.
6. Reheat in double boiler and serve hot.

NOTE:
In warm weather chill and serve very cold.

Old Drovers Inn
Dover Plains, N.Y.

PLUM OR APPLE SOUP

The collecting of all sorts of objets d'art is a universal trait. Some people go in for collecting old English silver, others collect Meissen porcelain, and there are people who favor buttons, belt buckles, or bottles. In recent times, primitive sculpture has become a favorite among collectors. A leading dealer in this fascinating art is Julius Carlebach, whose Carlebach Gallery is located in the new art center in New York on Madison Avenue and 79th Street. An outstanding cook as well as art dealer, Julius Carlebach's fruit soup is made this way:

Makes 8 to 12 servings

1 pound plums, pitted and halved	10 cups water
	4 tablespoons sugar
peel of ½ lemon	4 to 6 whole cloves

1. Put all ingredients in saucepan and cook over medium flame until fruit is soft and mushy.
2. Purée fruit.
3. Add to liquid and put in refrigerator until cold.
4. Serve with tiny soup macaroons, rice krispies, or little bits of pastry meringue.

NOTE:
Apple soup can be made by substituting apples for plums.

Carlebach Gallery, New York City
JULIUS CARLEBACH

CORN CHOWDER

The corn chowder connoisseur will recognize the significance of the word "chowder" when he knows that it comes from a French word meaning kettle, or pot. Only the initiated realize that the sole genuine, history-proved, traditionally accepted method of making real corn chowder is to cook it in an old iron kettle, which sits in a hole ordinarily occupied by one of the stove covers. They know, too, that a good, big, wood-burning kitchen stove has three rows of stove lids of two each. To make corn chowder that's something more than a mess of potatoes, onions, and corn in a quart or two of liquid, these stove lids are essential; for to reach the heights of which it is capable, chowder must be started slowly and permitted to gather momentum in flavorful lusciousness as the hours tick by.

1. Try out 2 or 3 slices of salt pork, with a few streaks of lean marbling the white goodness; cut the nut-brown, crisp slices into small cubes and place them, with the tried-out fat, in the bottom of the kettle sitting in one of the middle-row holes.
2. Cut up 2 or 3 onions and fuse them with the pork scraps. Add some half-boiled potatoes and mix the 3 ingredients.
3. After ½ hour or so, add 2 quarts of whole milk and 1 or 2 cans of cream-style corn. Little by little, the chowder warms.
4. When all is blended, move the kettle to a front hole over the crackling fire. Stir it constantly, tasting frequently. Never let corn chowder boil. When it is piping hot, place the kettle in one of the rear holes to keep warm. Then, and only then, add salt and pepper to suit.
5. Corn chowder should not entirely cool before the final re-heating. Made right after dinner, it is in its prime for supper. Served with plenty of crackers to crumble into the savory bowlful, where a good pat of butter floats on top, it's a supper dish that the countryman looks forward to, after the day's chores are done.

Country Flavor
HAYDN S. PEARSON

NEW ENGLAND CLAM CHOWDER

There was a time when many members of the Art Colony of America—particularly those artists, writers, and playwrights who lived in New York—spent their summers in Provincetown, Massachusetts. Eugene O'Neill had many of his plays tried out at the Wharf Playhouse there. Norman Mailer first made himself heard speaking at the meetings in the art museum of Provincetown. Hans Hofmann, that great old man of modern painting, conducted a famous art school in Provincetown. Harry Kemp, the poet, held forth on the dunes, as did Chaim Gross, the sculptor, Sol Wilson, the painter, and many others who felt they had something to say and contribute.

Among the better known permanent residents of Provincetown was Peter Hunt. Peter was famous on many scores, but mostly for his ability to take an old run-down kitchen chair and redecorate it to make it into an article of beauty. He was also an excellent chef, and among his best dishes was a steaming bowl of New England Clam Chowder.

"My father could never cook anything except clam chowder," he wrote. "He always made it in our house and he won a little fame for it. His secret, I believe, was the addition of a few bay leaves, which I wonder if other people use in their chowder."

Makes 6 servings

1 quart soft-shell clams, ground in meat chopper	4 potatoes, sliced
3 ounces salt pork, diced	1 pint milk
1 onion, sliced	salt and pepper
	butter

1. Try out (slowly sauté) the pork. Add the onion and fry until golden brown.
2. Add the potatoes and the juice from the clams; cover with boiling water and let simmer until the potatoes are done.
3. Add the clams and cook for 10 minutes.
4. Just before serving add the milk, heated, then the seasoning and a good-sized lump of butter.

Peter Hunt's Cape Cod Cookbook

MANHATTAN CLAM CHOWDER

Makes about 8 servings

2 dozen hard-shell clams in their juice	1½ pints boiling water
1 small cube salt pork	1 cup chopped fresh tomatoes (or drained canned tomatoes)
1 garlic clove, crushed	
½ cup thinly sliced leeks	1 teaspoon thyme
½ cup minced onion	bay leaf
¼ cup chopped celery	dash of pepper
½ cup chopped green pepper	few cloves
½ cup cubed carrots	4 tablespoons tomato catsup
3 cups cubed potatoes	1 tablespoon flour
2 teaspoons salt, or to taste	1 tablespoon butter

1. Drain the clams and set aside the juice. (You will need about 3 cups.) Chop the hard parts of the clams fine, the soft parts coarsely. Keep separate.
2. Try out (slowly sauté) the salt pork, then add garlic, onions, and leeks and cook gently until they are soft.
3. Add all the vegetables except the tomatoes and pour the boiling water over all.
4. Add the salt and cook covered over a high fire and allow to come to a boil. Lower the flame and cook gently for another 8–10 minutes.
5. Now add the hard part of the clams and cook for 10 minutes more. Add the tomatoes, herbs, pepper, catsup, the rest of the clams, and the clam liquor.
6. In another pan, melt the butter, blend in the flour and add this to the chowder, mixing thoroughly. Allow to simmer for 20 minutes and serve piping hot.

MAINE LOBSTER STEW

The preparation of the perfect Maine Lobster Stew is simple but it does not allow for short cuts. Stirring is most important, otherwise the stew will curdle. The steps to success are (1) partial cooling before gently adding the hot milk, a mere trickle at a time, (2) constant stirring until the stew reaches a rich salmon color under your spoon, and finally (3) "aging" to improve the flavor. Two days are prescribed by masters of the Maine Lobster Stew for aging, with a minimum of five to six hours. Aging should take place in a cool room for the first few hours, followed by refrigeration until it is time to reheat it for serving.

Makes 4 servings

Meat of 4 boiled lobsters, cut in fairly large chunks —keep the green tomalley and the coral separate	½ cup butter 1 quart rich milk or half-and-half salt and pepper

1. Simmer the tomalley and coral in the butter for 7 or 8 minutes, using a heavy kettle.
2. Add the lobster meat and cook 10 minutes over low heat. Remove from heat and cool slightly.
3. Slowly, very slowly, add the milk, stirring constantly. Add salt and pepper to taste.
4. Allow the stew to "age" at least 5 to 6 hours before reheating.

OYSTER STEW

This is the best known oyster stew in America. To enjoy its goodness, travelers from all the world visit The Oyster Bar in New York's Grand Central Terminal. There are many "oyster bars," but when one speaks of "The Oyster Bar," it is taken for granted that the Grand Central bar is intended.

A secret of The Oyster Bar's oyster stew is that clam liquor is used instead of oyster liquor. The Oyster Bar management doesn't usually reveal this because it feels most people won't bother to get the extra clam liquor. Freeman ("Doc") Lewis was the first to tell me that it *does* make a difference. While you'll get a fine stew using the liquor of the oysters, you will hit the heights by substituting the juice of clams.

Makes 1 serving

7 freshly opened oysters	celery salt
½ cup clam liquor	2 pats of butter
Worcestershire sauce	1 cup milk
paprika	

1. In deep pan, place a dash of Worcestershire sauce, paprika, celery salt and 1 pat of butter and bring to boiling point.
2. Add oysters and clam liquor and cook until edges of oysters curl.
3. Add milk and bring to a boil.
4. Pour in bowl and top with paprika and a pat of butter.

The Oyster Bar, Grand Central Terminal
New York City

SHRIMP GUMBO

On the pathway to the Mayo Clinic in Minnesota, Grandma Anderson bought herself a hotel and established her now famous Dutch Kitchens. Today the Hotel Anderson is run by the grandchildren, but is still dominated by the spirit of this woman who loved to cook and loved to have people "eat hearty."

Most of the choice dishes of the Hotel Anderson are of Pennsylvania Dutch origin, but this one is the result of granddaughter Jeanne Hall's stay in the South. Specifically it comes from Dr. R. R. Russ's fabulous cook Ben, in Biloxi, Mississippi.

Makes 6 to 8 servings

3½ cups canned tomatoes	3 strips bacon
2 cups tomato juice	3 tablespoons flour
4 cups water	1 large onion, minced
10 bay leaves	1 clove garlic, minced
salt and pepper	2 cups cooked shrimp
2 tablespoons Worcestershire sauce	1 tablespoon gumbo filé (optional)
2 pounds fresh okra, sliced	2 cups hot boiled rice

1. Combine the tomatoes, tomato juice, water, seasonings, and okra in a kettle.
2. Fry the bacon crisp, chop it, and lay it aside.
3. Add the flour to the bacon fat in the pan, make a thick paste, and simmer until brown. Add the garlic and onion to this, fry until light brown, and combine with the tomato mixture.
4. Add the shrimp. Simmer for about 1 hour and 20 minutes.
5. Add the filé and serve on mounds of hot boiled rice in deep soup dishes. (This constitutes a whole meal.)

NOTE:
Two cups of cooked crab meat may be substituted for the shrimp, if desired, or the meat from 12 hard-shelled crabs.

500 Recipes by Request
JEANNE M. HALL AND
BELLE ANDERSON EBNER

BOUILLABAISSE

Bouillabaisse is a product of Marseilles, France, where it is made heavily infused with garlic. At Louis Marino's place near New York's Fulton Fish Market, you can get an excellent bouillabaisse with just a modest garlicky flavoring. In making yours, add more or less, as you like. Someone has said that garlic in food is like insanity in art. To be a great artist it doesn't hurt to have a little touch of insanity; to have a great bouillabaisse it doesn't hurt to have a little touch of garlic.

Makes 6 to 8 servings

1 medium carrot, sliced
2 medium onions, sliced
1 clove garlic
4 tablespoons olive oil
3 pounds fish in season, cooked and boned (cod, haddock, whiting, etc.)
1 cup tomatoes
1 bay leaf

2 cups fish stock or water
1 dozen oysters, clams, or scallops
1 cup shrimp or crab
2 teaspoons salt
½ teaspoon pepper
2 tablespoons lemon juice
¼ cup sherry

1. Brown the carrot, onion, and garlic together in hot oil. Remove the garlic clove.
2. Add the fish, tomatoes, bay leaf, and stock. Allow to simmer for 15 minutes.
3. Remove the bay leaf and add the remaining ingredients, all but the sherry. Allow to cook for another 5 minutes.
4. Add the sherry and serve immediately.

Sloppy Louie's Restaurant
New York City

FISH CHOWDER

There are a number of well-known fish restaurants in New York—among them Gage & Tollner in downtown Brooklyn, Lundy's in Sheepshead Bay, and, of course, the famous Sweet's on Fulton Street. This is a notable fish chowder created by Peter Cheuces, long-time chef at Sweet's.

Makes 4 to 6 generous servings

¾ pound fish (halibut or any other white fish)	2 tablespoons butter
¼ pound potatoes	¼ teaspoon curry powder
¼ cup finely chopped onions	1¼ tablespoons flour
¼ cup finely chopped celery	1 cup hot milk
	salt and white pepper

1. Boil the fish, bones and all, in enough water to cover. Save the liquid. Flake the fish and set aside.
2. Dice and boil the potatoes and set aside.
3. Braise onions and celery in the butter until they are soft, but not too brown. While cooking, add the curry powder and flour, stirring all the while. When mixture becomes thick, remove from flame.
4. Add at once the liquid in which the fish was cooked, and keep stirring.
5. Gradually add the hot milk, salt and pepper, and let come to a boil until the chowder reaches the consistency you want.
6. Add chunks of fish and the diced boiled potatoes and serve.

Sweet's Restaurant
New York City

BREADS AND ROLLS

FRENCH BREAD

Makes 2 medium-sized loaves

1 cake or envelope of yeast
    dissolved in ¼ cup
    warm water
½ cup milk, scalded
1 tablespoon butter

1 tablespoon sugar
1½ teaspoons salt
1¼ cups warm water
5 cups sifted flour

1. Add butter, sugar, and salt to the scalded milk and let
   stand. When barely warm add the water and the softened
   yeast.

2. To this mixture add the flour, sifting in gradually. The dough should be just slightly sticky.
3. When thoroughly blended turn out the dough onto a lightly floured pastry board and knead for about 10 minutes. The dough should then be smooth and stretchy.
4. Set the dough in a buttered bowl, cover and keep in a warm place until it has doubled in quantity. (This should take about 2 hours.) Make 2 deep indentations in the dough—if they remain, the dough has risen sufficiently.
5. Break down the dough and let stand again until it doubles in bulk. Knead for about a minute.
6. Make 2 long loaves. Place on a buttered baking pan, cover and again allow to rise until double in quantity. When the loaves have risen part way, make small, deep slits diagonally across the tops. Brush tops with a little milk.
7. Place a pie tin filled with boiling water on bottom of the oven, to make a crusty loaf. Bake in hot oven (400° F.) for 50 minutes.

SALLY LUNN

The Cowan family figured prominently in the history of Salisbury, North Carolina. The following recipe for Sally Lunn, a bread that was often eaten in the past, was first used by Mrs. Thomas L. Cowan, and has been handed down for five generations in that family. Our contributor is the great-great-granddaughter of Mrs. Cowan.

1 quart flour (4 cups)
3 large eggs, or 4 small, separated
1 cup lard and butter mixed

1 cup milk, tepid
3 tablespoons sugar
2 teaspoons salt
1 yeast cake dissolved in ½ cup lukewarm water

1. Beat yolks and whites separately.
2. Add the sugar and salt to the flour.
3. Melt the shortening and pour into the beaten egg yolks. Add the milk, yeast, flour, and stiffly beaten egg whites.

4. Beat thoroughly and set aside in a warm place until risen to double in size (about 3 hours). Then beat, beat, beat.
5. Pour into a greased cake pan (funnel), and let rise again (1½ to 2 hours).
6. Bake in a moderate oven about 45 minutes and serve with melted butter. (Start oven at 325° F. and, when half-done, increase to 375° F.)

The Southern Cook Book
MARION BROWN

SANDWICH LOAF

loaf of white or whole-wheat bread
chicken or shrimp salad
drained crushed pineapple and cream cheese
drained sliced tomatoes, lettuce, or watercress
softened cream cheese, cottage cheese or 1 cupful mayonnaise to which ½ teaspoon gelatin soaked in 1 tablespoon water has been added
hard-cooked eggs
stuffed olives
red caviar
parsley, watercress, pimiento

1. Cut the crusts from the bread. Cut the loaf into 3 or 4 lengthwise slices.
2. Butter the inner sides of the slices and spread them with a layer of chicken or shrimp salad, a layer of crushed pineapple and cream cheese, a layer of drained sliced tomatoes, lettuce or watercress, or with any good combination of salad or sandwich ingredients. Be sure to cut the bread thin enough or spread the fillings thick enough to keep the bread from dominating.
3. Wrap the loaf firmly in a moist towel, chill it well, unwrap it and place it on a platter. Cover it with softened cream cheese, smooth cottage cheese, or with mayonnaise to which gelatin soaked in water and dissolved over heat has been added and which is ready to set. If it fits with your fillings, add 2 tablespoonfuls anchovy paste to the cream or cottage cheese.
4. Garnish the loaf with eggs, olives, caviar, parsley, watercress, and pimiento. To serve cut it into slices.

NOTE:
If you want festive individual servings, cut the bread into rounds or squares, fill the layers as described above, cover them with the cream cheese which has been put on in decorative patterns and then serve topped with a lighted birthday candle.

The New Joy of Cooking
IRMA S. ROMBAUER AND
MARION ROMBAUER BECKER

PUMPERNICKEL

This recipe comes from the members of a Danish church in the robust city of Seattle, Washington. It calls for the use of *surdejg* or sourdough, which is made the day before. Take 1 cup of any kind of yeast dough and blend it with ½ cup rye meal and 2½ cups lukewarm water. Let this stand at room temperature until the next day when you are ready to make your pumpernickel.

Makes 3 (2½-pound) loaves

1 yeast cake
4 cups white flour or rye
    graham flour
    sour dough

¼ cup salt
12 cups rye meal
1½ quarts water (6 cups)

1. Dissolve yeast in ¼ cup lukewarm water. Mix the yeast, sour dough, salt, lukewarm water, and the rye and white flour. Mix well.
2. Let rise 2 hours, then knead this down; let stand 15 minutes.
3. Form into loaves, let rise again about 20 minutes.
4. Bake at 375° F. for 1½ to 1¾ hours.

From Danish Kitchens

JENNIE GROSSINGER'S CHALLAH

One day when I was very young, my mother dispatched me to a local travel agent to inquire the way to get to a town called Luzon. The only Luzon the travel agent had ever heard of was in the Philippines so he rubbed his hands in expectation of a large commission and gave me a brightly illustrated brochure of these islands far away. But all my mother sought was the route, by railroad, of course, to a Luzon in the Catskill Mountains, where she had heard of a small farm which took in summer boarders. Today, most everybody knows that the Catskills harbor many giant resort hotels, where eating is a major function. And it is widely known that they, the Catskills, are the heart, if not the entire body, of the famous "Borscht Circuit," where innumerable TV comedians first saw the light of day and pay.

In this haven of eaters, actors, honeymooners, and those who hope to be honeymooners, Grossinger's has long stood at the top, largely through the warm personality of its founder, Jennie Grossinger. If all the rye bread served by Jennie Grossinger were laid end to end, it would circle the world not once, but many times. Not to mention an ocean of chicken-and-matzo-ball soup and a Mt. Everest of sour cream on blintzes.

The challah is the traditional Sabbath and holiday bread of Jews throughout the world, and Jennie Grossinger's recipe is well worth following.

Makes 1 very large loaf

1 cake or package yeast	2 eggs
2 teaspoons sugar	2 tablespoons salad oil
1¼ cups lukewarm water	1 egg yolk
4½ cups sifted flour	4 teaspoons poppy seeds
2 teaspoons salt	

1. Combine the yeast, sugar and ¼ cup lukewarm water. Let stand 5 minutes. NOTE: ⅛ teaspoon saffron can be dissolved in the water if you like additional flavor and color.
2. Sift the flour and salt into a bowl. Make a well in the center and drop the eggs, oil, remaining water and the

yeast mixture into it. Work into the flour. Knead on a floured surface until smooth and elastic. Place in a bowl and, brush the top with a little oil.

3. Cover with a towel, set in a warm place and let rise 1 hour. Punch down, cover again and let rise until double in bulk. Divide the dough into 3 equal parts.

4. Between lightly floured hands roll the dough into 3 strips of even length.

5. Braid them together and place in a baking pan. Cover with a towel and let rise until double in bulk. Brush with the egg yolk and sprinkle with the poppy seeds.

6. Bake in a 375° oven 50 minutes or until browned.

NOTE:

If you wish, divide the dough into 6 parts and make 2 large loaves, or make 1 loaf and many small rolls. You may also bake the bread in a loaf pan.

The Art of Jewish Cooking

BRIOCHE

Start this at least a day before you plan to use it.

Makes 6 servings

1 cake yeast, or 1 package granular yeast	1½ cups butter
4 cups flour	8 eggs
½ teaspoon salt	¼ cup cream
2 tablespoons sugar	2 egg yolks, beaten

1. Crumble the yeast cake (or pour the granular yeast) into ¼ cup lukewarm water. Stir, and add enough of the flour (1 to 1½ cups) to make a very soft ball of paste. Drop this into about 3 quarts of warm water (80° F.), cover, and set to one side in a warm place.

2. Sift the remaining flour into a bowl and add the salt and sugar. Cream the butter and add the eggs to the butter 1 at a time, beating well after each addition. Make a hollow in the center of the flour-and-sugar mixture and gradually add the butter mixture, beating thoroughly after each addition.

3. When the 2 mixtures are combined, beat the batter hard until it is no longer sticky and does not cling to the sides of the bowl or to the spoon. (Some recipes say this must be mixed with the hand, but I find that a spoon is perfectly satisfactory. It is hard work, whichever way you choose.)

4. When the yeast mixture rises to the top of the water (in about ¾ hour), remove it from the water and add it to the flour-and-egg mixture. Knead the 2 together and beat for at least 5 minutes—the longer you beat, the finer will be the grain of the brioche. Let the mixture rise until it has doubled in bulk. Punch it down in the middle, and pull it down from the sides of the bowl, but do not pummel. Place it in the refrigerator overnight. (It may be kept in the refrigerator for a week, if desired.)

5. Brioche dough is usually baked in what is called a brioche head or crown. Make ⅔ of the dough into a ball and place in a round pan. The pan should be large enough so that it is only ½ filled by the ball of dough. Make an incision in the shape of a cross on the top of the ball, form the remaining ⅓ of the dough into a ball, and insert it in the center of the cross. Let this rise until doubled in bulk.

6. Mix the cream and egg yolks, brush over the top of the brioche, and bake in a 350° F. oven until brown (1 hour for a large brioche, 20 to 25 minutes for individual ones).

The Christmas Cookbook
ZELLA BOUTELL

SOUTHERN CORN BREAD

In Indian usage throughout the Americas, the name for corn by whatever tribe spoken, meant "our life," or "our mother," or "she who sustains us." It was the cultivation of corn that turned our Indians from nomadic to agrarian habits. The very putting of seed corn into earth, the giving of it to the Earth Mother who nourished it so it grew strong enough to bring forth seeds of its own—here was the beginning of the Indians' cult of worship, out of which in turn grew the songs, dances, ceremonials and traditions derived from the principle of life, of survival itself.

Corn has a taste and a mind of its own, as its admirers know. But it has, nevertheless, a willingness to combine gladly with other ingredients. Yet through all these numberless combinations it is never submerged, and in fact manages to give some new virtue to each fellow-ingredient.

2 cups white cornmeal	½ teaspoon soda
1 cup boiling water	1 teaspoon baking powder
2 egg yolks, beaten	¾ cup buttermilk
1 tablespoon butter or lard, melted	2 egg whites, beaten

1. Scald the cornmeal with the boiling water and add all the other ingredients, beating well.
2. Fold in the beaten whites last.
3. Pour into a greased pan and bake in moderate oven 25 or 30 minutes.

Whole Grain Cookery
STELLA STANDARD

CHEESE BREAD

People who can remember back to the days when Tuesday was always baking day at home are fortunate indeed. "That was the day I first learned which day was Tuesday," says Marye Dahnke. No perfume can compete with the fragrance of new-made bread cooling in the pantry. And even if most homemakers these days devote less time than they used to to bread baking, all good cooks like to have one special yeast bread at the tips of their fingers. For a real triumph in bread baking, a specialty well worth cultivating, try this cheese bread recipe. The loaf is fragrant, it's luscious, and it's easy to do—a reputation-maker for any hostess.

Toast made with this cheese bread is delicious.

1¼ cups milk
1 tablespoon sugar
1 teaspoon salt
½ tablespoon butter or margarine
½ cake compressed yeast, or ½ package dry granular yeast
1 tablespoon lukewarm water
2¾ cups flour
1½ cups shredded American Cheddar cheese
melted butter or margarine

1. Scald the milk; add the sugar, salt, and ½ tablespoon of butter or margarine. Cool to lukewarm. Crumble the yeast into the water, let soften a few minutes, and add to the milk mixture.
2. Add 2 cups flour and mix well. Add the cheese and the remaining flour, and mix again.
3. Knead on a floured board for 10 minutes.
4. Place the dough in a greased bowl, brush with melted butter or margarine, cover, and let rise in a warm place until double in bulk.
5. Knead, shape into a loaf, place in a greased 4 x 8-inch loaf pan, and brush with melted butter or margarine. Cover with a fresh towel and let rise until double in bulk.
6. Bake in a moderately hot oven, 375° F., 50 minutes.

The Cheese Cook Book
MARYE DAHNKE

McCALL'S BEST NUT BREAD

A good basic cooking book is *McCall's Cook Book*. You won't find Beef Wellington or Blanquette of Veal, but the elementaries like how to coddle an egg are all there, as well as a surprising number of international dishes—the popular Japanese Tempura, for example, which appears on page 285.

2½ cups sifted all-purpose flour
3 teaspoons baking powder
½ teaspoon salt
1 egg, beaten
1 teaspoon vanilla extract
¾ cup sugar
¼ cup butter or margarine, melted, or salad oil
1¼ cups milk
1 cup finely chopped walnuts or pecans

1. Preheat oven to 350° F. Grease a loaf pan 9 x 5 x 3 inches.
2. Sift flour with baking powder and salt.
3. In large bowl, combine egg, vanilla, sugar, and butter. Using wooden spoon or portable electric mixer, beat until well blended. Add milk, blending well.
4. Add flour mixture, beating until smooth. Stir in nuts.
5. Pour batter into prepared pan; bake 60 to 65 minutes, or until cake tester inserted in center comes out clean.
6. Let cool in pan 10 minutes. Remove from pan; cool completely on wire rack. To serve, cut into thin slices.

SHAPE VARIATIONS:

1. Divide batter evenly among 4 greased 5½ x 3¼-inch pans; bake at 375° F., 25 minutes, till cake tester inserted in center comes out clean. Let cool in pans 10 minutes. Remove from pans; cool completely on wire rack. To serve, cut into thin slices.
2. Divide batter evenly among 6 greased 10½-ounce cans, filling half full. Bake at 375° F., 35 minutes, till cake tester inserted in center comes out clean. Cool in cans 10 minutes. Remove from cans; cool completely on wire rack. To serve, cut into thin slices.
3. Divide batter evenly among 4 greased, 1¼-pound cans, filling half full. Bake at 375° F., 40 minutes, till cake tester inserted in center comes out clean. Cool in cans 10 minutes. Remove from cans; cool completely on wire rack. To serve, cut into thin slices.

FLAVOR VARIATIONS:

1. Kumquat-Pecan Nut Bread: Use pecans, reducing amount to ½ cup. Add ½ cup finely chopped preserved kumquats to batter, along with nuts in Best Nut Bread recipe. Bake as directed.
2. Lemon-Prune Nut Bread: Omit milk in Best Nut Bread recipe. Combine ½ cup chopped, pitted, dried prunes with 1¼ cups boiling unsweetened prune juice; let cool. Use in place of milk. Add 1 tablespoon grated lemon peel along with nuts. Bake as directed.
3. Candied Fruit Nut Bread: Instead of walnuts or pecans, add 1 cup finely chopped mixed candied fruit and ½ cup

sliced Brazil nuts to Best Nut Bread recipe. Bake as directed.

4. Cherry-Raisin Nut Bread: Use walnuts reducing amount in Best Nut Bread recipe to ½ cup. Combine ¼ cup finely chopped, drained maraschino cherries, ½ cup seedless raisins, and ½ teaspoon almond extract with vanilla. Add to batter along with nuts. Bake as directed.

McCall's Cook Book

BANANA TEA BREAD

Makes 1 loaf

1¾ cups sifted flour	⅔ cup sugar
2 teaspoons baking powder	2 eggs, well beaten
¼ teaspoon soda	1 cup mashed bananas
½ teaspoon salt	(2 to 3 bananas)
⅓ cup shortening	

1. Sift together flour, baking powder, soda, and salt.
2. Beat shortening until creamy. Add sugar gradually and continue beating until light and fluffy. Add eggs and beat well.
3. Add flour mixture alternately with bananas, a small amount at a time, beating after each addition until smooth.
4. Turn into a well-greased bread pan (8½ x 4½ x 3 inches) and bake in a moderate oven (350° F.) about 1 hour 10 minutes.

Recipe favorite from
The New York Times

ORANGE BREAD

American women are emancipated from the bread tray and rolling board to an extent not enjoyed anywhere else in the world, yet the best cooks in our own country take pride and delight in turning out, occasionally, if not regularly, bread to be proud of.

Good bread tastes sweet and nutty, like the grain from which the flour has been milled.

State Fair judges score bread on seven points: shape, crust, and volume (size of loaf) usually rate ten points each; texture, grain and color rate twenty, ten, and ten points, respectively; and flavor stands alone for thirty points.

2 cups all-purpose flour	2 eggs
3 teaspoons baking powder	3 tablespoons orange rind
½ teaspoon salt	2 tablespoons orange juice
½ cup butter or other shortening	¾ cup milk
	½ cup cut nut meats
1 cup sugar	½ cup cut raisins

1. Sift flour, then measure and sift 3 times with salt and baking powder.
2. Cream butter. Add sugar gradually, and cream until smooth. Beat in eggs, 1 at a time. Add orange rind and juice.
3. Add flour mixture alternately with milk and juice, ending with flour. Add chopped nuts and raisins sprinkled with a little flour.
4. Bake in loaf pan (9 x 4½ x 2½ inches) at 350° F. for 1 hour.

Blue Ribbon Prizewinner: Mrs. Frank Pellman

The State Fair Cook Book
LOIS J. HURLEY AND
ISABELLE J. GROETZINGER

NORWEGIAN CHRISTMAS BREAD

There is nothing fancy about Norwegian *Julekake*. In fact, it is so good as coffee cake or for breakfast, just because it is plain.

Hanna Winsnes, who wrote a pioneer Norwegian cookbook back in 1888, says the hands should be greased when kneading Christmas bread, to use as little extra flour as possible. She also advises using powdered sugar. The baking of Christmas bread was naturally a rite not to be compared with everyday cooking. For this reason, only the finest flour, imported from Hungary, was traditionally used in making the Christmas bread. Leftovers make a delicious bread pudding.

Makes 1 sizable loaf

¾ cup sugar (scant)
½ pound butter
2 eggs
2 egg yolks
2 teaspoons ground
 cardamom

2 yeast cakes
1 cup milk
4½ cups flour (scant)
1 cup chopped citron
1 cup seedless raisins

1. Beat sugar and butter until white, add the whipped eggs, egg yolks, and the cardamom.
2. Dissolve yeast cakes in lukewarm milk, and add this to egg mixture, alternately with the sifted flour.
3. Work dough well, let stand in warm place for 3 hours. Knead with citron and raisins, place in well-greased loaf pan and let rise for 2 more hours.
4. Bake in warm oven for about 1 hour. Can be served with or without butter.

Cook Book of Norwegian Recipes
HANNA WINSNES

POPOVERS

Makes 1 dozen popovers

1 cup flour, sifted
½ teaspoon salt

2 eggs, lightly beaten
1 cup milk

1. Sift the flour together with the salt once again.
2. Combine the lightly beaten eggs with the milk, then mix with the dry ingredients. (The batter will be thin.)
3. Heat iron gem pans till very hot, then butter well. Pour in batter till cups are half filled.
4. Bake for 20 minutes in a hot (450° F.) oven. Then decrease heat to 375° F. and bake for another 20 to 30 minutes.
5. Serve piping hot.

PARKER HOUSE ROLLS

In Boston, the word "park" is softly bleated, like the call of a sheep. (Bostonians don't seem particularly sensitive about it, and certainly no offense is intended.) One doesn't say "park the car," but pa-a-a-a-k the c-a-a-a-r. Accordingly, a soft, folded-over roll is referred to as a Pa-a-a-aker House roll. But just as a rose smells sweet no matter what you call it, a Parker House roll is good if you merely flatten out the name. Here is the Parker House's own recipe for a batch of about two dozen perfect, well-risen Parker House rolls.

½ cup scalded milk
½ cup boiling water
1 teaspoon salt
1 teaspoon sugar
1 tablespoon butter

½ yeast cake dissolved in
  ¼ cup lukewarm water
3 cups bread flour, or
  enough to knead

1. Put milk, water, salt, butter, and sugar into mixing bowl and mix well. Add yeast. Then add flour until it is stiff enough to knead. Cover and let it rise to double its bulk.
2. Shape into balls, put into buttered pan and cover. Let it rise in a warm place again to double its bulk.
3. With the floured handle of a wooden spoon press the balls through the center almost cutting in half. Brush ½ with butter, fold other half over and press together like a pocketbook.
4. Let rise again and bake in a hot oven (400° F.) for 15 minutes.
5. Brush the tops with butter after baking.

Parker House Hotel
Boston, Mass.

CROISSANTS

Makes 6 servings

2 cakes or envelopes of
    yeast
¼ cup warm water
4 cups flour
1_ teaspoon salt

1 tablespoon sugar
1½ cups milk
¾ pound butter
    egg yolk beaten in a little
    cold milk

1. Soften the yeast in the warm water in a mixing bowl. Add 1 cup of the flour and blend until smooth and form into a ball. Cut a few indentations in the top of the ball. Cover with a cloth and keep in a warm place until quantity has doubled.
2. Mix the remaining flour (3 cups) with the salt and sugar and sift onto a pastry board. Stir in the milk gradually until the dough is smooth.
3. Add to first mixture, mixing well. Cover with a cloth and let stand for about 10 minutes.
4. Roll the dough out onto pastry board and form a long strip about ½ inch in thickness. Form the butter into a flat rectangle and put in the center of the strip. Then fold the right end over the center of the strip and the left end over the right, forming 3 layers of dough.
5. Roll out the dough again until it is ½-inch thick and forms a long strip and refold as in step 4. Cover and chill in the refrigerator for several hours.
6. Remove from refrigerator, roll out and refold again. Repeat the rolling and refolding twice more. Chill in the refrigerator again, this time for about 1 hour.
7. Roll out the dough to ⅛ inch in thickness and cut into 6-inch squares. Cut each square in half diagonally. Beginning with the wide side of the triangle, stretch slightly as you roll toward the point. Form the rolls into crescents and place on a lightly floured baking tin.
8. Cover with a towel and let rise in a warm place until they are double in bulk. Brush with egg yolk beaten with a little milk and bake in a hot oven (400° F.) for 5 minutes. Lower the temperature to 350° F. and let bake until croissants are golden brown. This should take about 15 to 20 minutes.

MUFFINS

INGREDIENTS	Plain Muffins	Corn-meal	Bran	Whole-Wheat	Berry	Nut or Raisin
Flour White	2 cups	1 cup	1 cup	1 cup	2 cups	2 cups
Cornmeal		1 cup				
Bran			1 cup			
Whole-Wheat				1 cup		
Sugar	2 tbs.	2 tbs.	2 tbs.	2 tbs.	2 tbs.	2 tbs.
Baking powder	4 tsp.	4 tsp.	4 tsp.	5 tsp.	4 tsp.	4 tsp.
Salt	1 tsp.	1 tsp.	1 tsp.	1 tsp.	1 tsp.	1 tsp.
Egg, beaten	1	1	1	1	1	1
Milk	1 cup	1 cup	1 cup	¾ cup	1 cup	1 cup
Shortening, melted	3 tbs.	3 tbs.	3 tbs.	3 tbs.	3 tbs.	3 tbs.
Berries					1 cup	
Nuts or raisins						¾ cup

Makes about 14 muffins

1. Combine and sift together the flour ingredients, sugar, baking powder, and salt. Add the beaten egg and milk. Mix well. Add the melted shortening.
2. Dredge in flour all dry or well-drained berries, nuts and raisins and add to the mixed batter.
3. Fill well-greased muffin tins about ⅔ full.
4. Bake in a hot oven (400° F.) for 20 to 25 minutes. After 20 minutes, test with a cake tester. If no dough adheres to the tester, the muffins are done. Serve hot.

You Can Cook If You Can Read
MURIEL AND CORTLAND FITZSIMMONS

BAGELS

The bagel is as New Yorkese as Broadway. Once, when the city's flags were at half-mast for a leading citizen, the wits of Tin Pan Alley claimed it was really because the bagel makers were on strike. Cream cheese and lox (smoked salmon— preferably from Nova Scotia) on bagel is supper fare to make the eyes roll in ecstatic delight. The standard definition of a bagel is "a doughnut dipped in cement." They sure can harden up fast, so eat 'em while they're fresh—or toast them.

Makes 12

3 cups flour (plus 3 table-spoons for kneading board)	3 tablespoons salad oil (or shortening)
1½ teaspoons salt	1 egg
2 tablespoons sugar	4 quarts boiling water
1 package yeast	2 tablespoons sugar (to be added to boiling water)
⅔ cup lukewarm water	

1. Sift dry ingredients together into a deep mixing bowl.
2. Dissolve yeast in ⅓ of the lukewarm water. Add oil or melted shortening to remainder of warm water and stir into dissolved yeast.
3. Make a well in the center of flour mixture and stir in the liquid, adding slightly beaten egg when half the liquid has been used. Stir briskly to form a ball of dough and knead on a lightly floured board 2 minutes.
4. Return dough to mixing bowl, smooth side up, and punch down 3 times. Cover and let rise at room temperature 15 to 20 minutes, or until the dough has come to top of bowl.
5. Knead again on board till smooth and elastic as for rolls. Divide dough into 12 equal portions. Form into lengths not more than ¾ inch thick, pinching ends together. Place these crullerlike shapes of dough on a floured cookie sheet and slip under broiler flame 3 minutes.
6. Drop each bagel into rapidly boiling water in a deep kettle and cook over moderate heat 15 to 20 minutes. Skim out and place on a cookie sheet. Bake at 375° F. for 10 min-

utes, then increase heat to 400° F. for 5 to 6 minutes or till bagels are browned and crust golden brown and crisp, approximately 15 minutes.

Jewish Cookery
LEAH W. LEONARD

ZELMA'S ICE BOX ROLLS

Millions of people remember Marjorie Kinnan Rawlings as the author of *Cross Creek* and *The Yearling*. She was also a great cook and wrote a cookery book featuring many of the recipes of her own southern locale.

"This recipe," she said, "comes from my friend Zelma, the local census-taker. It came into my life along with my friendship with her at a time when the delights of Florida woods and streams were fresh and new. It is as simple a recipe as I know for raised rolls, as delicious, as convenient. The mixture may be kept in the ice box as long as ten days, ready at hand for serving hot rolls on an hour's notice. It reaches perfection when baked out of doors in a Dutch oven. Cast iron has never been improved on for cooking.

"Let no modern cook feel pity for our foremothers who baked their breads and their meats in a Dutch oven on an open hearth. The Dutch oven is of varying sizes, made with three legs for sitting evenly over hot coals, a long handle for lifting, and a tight lid indented to a depth of about an inch and a half. On this lid are scattered hot hardwood coals. Only practice can determine the amount of coals and the degree of heat necessary under and on the oven. The inexpert might safely bake cornbread in a Dutch oven. Only the expert dare attempt the baking of Zelma's rolls. They must bake neither too fast nor too slow. They must emerge oak-brown of crust on all sides, meltingly light and fluffy and thoroughly done within. An ordinary oven will serve if necessary. The heat in this case should be 375° F. for 30 minutes, increasing the last 10 minutes if needed for good browning."

Makes 4 servings

1 cup hot mashed potatoes	1 egg
1 cup sugar	1 teaspoon salt
1 cup hot potato water	⅓ cup melted shortening
1 cup cold water	2 cups flour, sifted
1 yeast cake dissolved in	
½ cup lukewarm water	

1. Stir gar into hot mashed potatoes until smooth.
2. Add 1 cup of the hot potato water, and 1 cup cold water. Cool until lukewarm. Add yeast cake dissolved in water.
3. Let mixture stand 5 hours, covered. Then place in the ice box, and rolls may be made from it on short notice. The basic mixture keeps well about a week.
4. To make the rolls, beat 1 egg into a measuring cup. Fill the cup with basic mixture. Turn into mixing bowl and add salt, melted shortening, and flour.
5. The rolls may be shaped by hand directly from the bowl, without kneading. Or the dough may be rolled out on a floured board and made into Parker House Rolls. More flour will be necessary in handling.

Cross Creek Cookery
MARJORIE KINNAN RAWLINGS

DUNCAN HINES FAMILY'S
BUTTER HORN ROLLS

Many men make their living by cooking, but in all America probably only one has earned his by eating. Duncan Hines first became famous through his *Adventures in Good Eating,* a travelers' guidebook to the best eating places in this country. The response to this book demonstrated that Americans will go miles out of their way to get a superior meal. Its success led Duncan Hines to dedicate himself to the cause of good victuals. Hines is like the old lady in his own story. On her one hundredth birthday this lady was asked if there was any one thing to which she attributed her age. She thought a moment and answered, "Yes I think there is—vittles." Duncan Hines has collected recipes from everywhere. Here is one right from the Hines kitchen in Bowling Green, Kentucky.

¾ cup butter
½ cup sugar
4 cups flour
1½ teaspoons salt

1 cake yeast
1 cup scalded milk
3 eggs, beaten

1. Cream butter and sugar together.
2. Sift flour and salt and add to creamed mixture.
3. Mix yeast and milk and add. Stir beaten eggs into mixture. Let rise light—high and airy. Put the dough on a towel, fold over and knead.
4. Cover top of dough with butter and cover with wax paper. Set in refrigerator overnight.
5. Roll out the size of large pie and cut in 6 or 8 pieces. Grease top with butter, then roll.
6. Let get very light and bake in 425° F. oven for 15 minutes.

Adventures in Good Cooking
DUNCAN HINES

HUSH-PUPPIES

Hush-puppies are in a class by themselves. They are a concomitant of the hunt, above all of the fishing trip. Fresh-caught fried fish without hush-puppies are as man without woman, a beautiful woman without kindness, law without policemen. The story goes that they derived their name from old fishing and hunting expeditions, when the white folks and the Negro help ate to repletion, and the hunting dogs, already fed, smelled the delectable odors of human rations and howled for the things they scented. Negro cook or white sportsman tossed the remaining cornmeal patties to the dogs, calling "Hush, puppies!"—and the dogs, devouring them, could ask no more of life, and hushed.

Makes 3 to 4 servings

1 cup cornmeal
2 teaspoons baking powder
½ teaspoon salt
1 small to medium onion,
   minced

1 egg
¼ cup milk or water

1. Mix together the dry ingredients and the finely cut onion.
2. Break in the egg and beat vigorously. Add the liquid.
3. Form into small patties, round or finger-shaped. Drop in deep smoking fat in which fish has been fried, until they are a deep brown. Serve hot and at once.

Cross Creek Cookery
MARJORIE KINNAN RAWLINGS

CHEESE CUSHIONS

Cooking with cheese can be easy and great fun. After twenty-five years of applying this conviction to the subject professionally, I find the truth more profound every day and practice its precepts continuously in my own home kitchen. Cheese under fire shows highly individual quirks of character, but do not let this discourage you. Proceed firmly but cautiously. Spare the heat; it spoils the cheese dish. Easy does it, that's the discipline for cheese cookery, and to that treatment you will find cheese dishes responding like biddable children.

These puffy little morsels are an ideal accompaniment to salads, or simple luncheon or supper dishes. Handsome on well-spread buffet tables.

MARYE DAHNKE

Makes 62 squares

⅔ cup shredded sharp Ameri-   2 cups flour
    can Cheddar cheese   ½ teaspoon salt
½ cup butter or margarine   ⅛ teaspoon red pepper

1. Blend the cheese and butter or margarine thoroughly. Work in the flour sifted with the salt and red pepper. No water should be added; the mixture will be crumbly.
2. Place in waxed paper and chill several hours.
3. Roll to ½-inch thickness, folding the crumbs over and over until the mixture is firm. Cut into ¾-inch squares.
4. Place on a cookie sheet, leaving space between the squares. Bake in a moderate oven, 350° F., 20 minutes.

The Cheese Cook Book
MARYE DAHNKE

EGG AND CHEESE DISHES

OMELET

For omelets it is necessary to have a cast-iron or aluminum pan. The metal must be of a porous nature; so copper, tin-lined or stainless steel pans are of no use for this purpose.

When the pan is new, rub over the surface with a piece of dry steel wool. Then clean pan thoroughly with oil. Never touch the pan with water at any time. When thoroughly clean fill with oil and leave for about forty-eight hours. Pour off the oil, which, of course, can be used again, and wipe the pan thoroughly. Get it very hot and then the pan is seasoned for use.

Eggs should be strictly fresh for all purposes *except* the omelet. For this dish they should be at least two or three days old, for new-laid eggs curdle in the pan.

Makes 4 servings

1 teaspoon butter	1 teaspoon cold water
3 eggs	salt and pepper

1. Test the heat of the pan by trying it with a small piece of butter. If the butter sizzles briskly without browning when it dissolves, the pan has reached the right temperature.
2. Drop in at once butter and eggs, which have been beaten with 1 teaspoon cold water, salt and pepper until they mix without being frothy.
3. Stir quickly with a fork and shake the pan until the eggs begin to set. Then stir more slowly on the top of the set eggs for a minute or two.
4. Leave for a second. Fold over the omelet to the edge of the pan. Turn out at once onto a hot serving dish.

The Cordon Bleu Cook Book
DIONE LUCAS

MIMI SHERATON'S SEDUCTIVE CAVIAR OMELET WITH SOUR CREAM

I had never met Mimi Sheraton before she brought to my home the roast beef for Wally and Irene Reiss's wedding party. But the moment we tasted the beef, I said I had to find out more about this luscious dish (Mimi, not the roast beef). Mimi Sheraton made her big hit with *The Seducer's Cookbook* in which she wrote about the seductive lure of food.

Says she: "Ever since I was fifteen and was persuaded to neck with a boy who gave me a frozen Milky Way, I have been aware of the seductive powers of food. It was, of course, too heady a combination to resist—a double portion of forbidden fruit—since my mother had forbidden candy because it would ruin my teeth, and necking because it would, sooner or later, ruin everything else.

"In that simple adolescent experience one can find all the reasons why food succeeds as a seductive lure when other measures fail:

1. It is, as already stated, disarming in its wholesome innocence.
2. It arouses the senses and awakens the appetite.
3. It is the symbol of physical temptation.
4. It leaves one with a sense of ease and well-being.
5. It fosters intimacy between two people sharing the same physical sensation; with luck, only the first of many.
6. Good food, be it pâté or a pizza, candy or caviar, breakfast or a banquet, conveys a sense of luxury and license, an aura of sybaritic indulgence.
7. Most people feel like lying down after a good meal anyway."

Mimi Sheraton's book is lots of fun, so we heartily recommend that you read it. Meanwhile make this seductive caviar omelet:

Makes 2 servings, naturally

6 eggs
2 tablespoons cold water
2 tablespoons butter
  salt

2 tablespoons caviar, black or red, but with as little salt as possible
4 teaspoons sour cream
1 teaspoon minced dill

1. Make each omelet separately and keep the first on a heated platter until the second is ready. For each, break 3 eggs into a bowl, add 1 tablespoon cold water and just the merest dash of salt.
2. Put 1 tablespoon butter in a 9-inch or 10-inch skillet (if you have a real omelet pan on hand, of course use it).
3. When butter is almost turning brown, pour eggs in, swirl once with a fork and keep tilting the pan toward and away from you so that the cooked portion of the eggs slides to the center and the uncooked portion flows onto the pan. This is done on a moderately high flame and eggs should be sufficiently cooked in 3 or 4 minutes.
4. Fold omelet in half or in thirds and turn onto heated plate.

5. Make second omelet. When both are ready, cut a slit in the top, place 1 tablespoon caviar in each, top with 2 teaspoons sour cream, and sprinkle with dill.

The Seducer's Cookbook
MIMI SHERATON

EGGS FLORENTINE

Makes 4 servings

1 pound fresh spinach or 1 package frozen spinach salt and pepper to taste 8 eggs	Mornay Sauce (see page 256) grated Parmesan cheese

1. Cook the spinach and season to taste. Chop it fine.
2. Line a large shallow baking dish, or 4 individual dishes with the chopped and seasoned spinach.
3. Poach the eggs and place on top of the spinach, allowing 2 for each serving.
4. Top with Mornay Sauce and sprinkle generously with grated Parmesan cheese.
5. Place under the broiler to brown.

EGGS BENEDICT

Makes 1 serving

1 English muffin 2 thin slices of sautéed or broiled ham, or Canadian bacon	butter 2 poached eggs Hollandaise Sauce (see page 258)

1. Split the English muffin and toast it. Butter lightly.
2. On each half of muffin place a slice of ham or Canadian bacon.
3. Place a poached egg on top of each ham slice.
4. Spoon generous quantity of Hollandaise Sauce over all. Serve hot.

EGGS FOO YOUNG

Makes 4 servings

8 eggs	2 scallions or an onion
1 teaspoon salt	3 heaping tablespoons
½ pound of meat in strips	peanut oil
¼ bunch celery	2 tablespoons soy sauce
¼ pound bean sprouts	2 teaspoons sugar

1. Beat the eggs together with the salt.
2. Slice the scallions or onion and celery diagonally into thin strips about 1 inch long.
3. Heat 1 tablespoon of the peanut oil in a skillet, add the meat and stir for 1 minute. Add scallions, celery, and bean sprouts and stir for another minute.
4. Add the soy sauce and sugar, stir, cook 1 minute and then remove all from the pan.
5. In the same skillet, heat 2 tablespoons peanut oil. Turn heat to medium and pour in all the eggs. Leave them whole—do not stir or break. Lift the bottom occasionally to avoid sticking or burning.
6. After 1 minute and while the eggs are still partly liquid, add the strips of meat, celery, scallions, and bean sprouts. Pour off the juice and save to make sauce. Fold the eggs over like an omelet, and cook 1½ minutes on each side.

SAUCE

Juice from cooked vegetables	1 tablespoon cornstarch dissolved in 2 tablespoons water

1. Heat the juice. Pour the dissolved cornstarch into it and heat till translucent.
2. Pour over the eggs.

Chinese Rathskeller, New York City

EGGS IN HELL

(UOVA IN PURGATORIO, OEUFS D'EN BAS, ETC.)

Makes 4 servings

4 tablespoons olive oil
  (substitute will do,
  dadblast it)
1 clove garlic
1 onion, minced
2 cups tomato sauce (Italian
  kind is best, but even
  catsup will do if you cut
  down on spices)

1 teaspoon minced mixed
  herbs (basil, thyme)
1 teaspoon minced parsley
  salt and pepper
8 eggs
  slices of French bread,
  thin, toasted

1. Heat the oil in a saucepan that has a tight cover.
2. Split garlic lengthwise, run a toothpick through each half, and brown slowly in oil. . . . Add the onion and cook until golden. Then add the tomato sauce and the seasonings and herbs. Cook about 15 minutes, stirring often, and then take out the garlic.
3. Into this sauce break the eggs. Spoon the sauce over them, cover closely, and cook very slowly until eggs are done, or about 15 minutes. (If the skillet is a heavy one, you can turn off the heat and cook in 15 minutes with what is stored in the metal.)
4. When done, put the eggs carefully on the slices of dry toast, and cover with sauce. (Grated Parmesan cheese is good on this, if you can get any.)

How to Cook a Wolf
M. F. K. FISHER

EGG ROLLS

Makes 16 rolls

EGG ROLL SKIN:

6 eggs
⅔ cup flour

1 cup water

1. Mix together.
2. Use a 10-inch pan, slightly greased, and make thin pan-cakes, heated on one side only.

FILLING:

1 pound pork (chop) shreds (less commonly, beef shreds)
½ pound fresh shrimps, chopped
3 scallions cut into shreds
1 pound pea sprouts

2 tablespoons soy sauce
1 teaspoon sugar
1 teaspoon salt
3 heaping tablespoons lard enough vegetable oil for deep frying

1. Wash the pea sprouts.
2. Heat the lard in a skillet over big fire and stir-fry the meat shreds and the shrimps for 1 minute. Add scallions and pea sprouts and stir for 2 more minutes, adding sauce, sugar, and salt toward the end.
3. Take out and divide into 16 portions. Place each portion on a sheet of the egg roll skin and fold up slantwise like a Chinese package. Only do not tuck in the last corner. Just roll over and paste it on with a little water. The frying will make it stay put.
4. Heat the deep-frying oil over medium fire, turn to low if it has a tendency to smoke. Deep-fry the rolls for 6 minutes. Turn each so as to have each side immersed, since the upperside tends to float outside of the oil. The rolls are done when they are golden brown. Cut up into small sections before serving.

How to Cook and Eat in Chinese
BUWEI YANG CHAO

EGG WITH A HAT

Almost three million copies of *Fannie Farmer's Cook Book* have been printed since its inception. As this best seller has wended its way through seventy-five printings, various changes have been required, yet these lines from the first edition have remained:

But for life the universe were nothing;
And all that has life requires nourishment.

Makes 1 serving

1 slice of bread	salt and pepper
1 egg	butter for sautéing

1. Cut round out of slice of bread with 2½-inch cookie cutter.
2. Melt butter in heavy pan, sauté both pieces of bread on one side. When beginning to brown, break egg into center of hole, sprinkle with salt and pepper, and continue cooking.
3. When brown, turn and brown other side, adding butter as needed.
4. Serve with cut-out piece on top.

The New Fannie Farmer
Boston Cooking School Cook Book

TORTILLA POMPOSO

"When I was so fortunate as to inherit from a departing friend the services of Berta Herrera," says General Frank Dorn, "I soon discovered that though her cuisine was tops, her English was decidedly less than adequate. We quickly solved our language problems, to everyone else's confusion, by devising a mixed lingo of Spanish, Chinese, and English in which we carried on long involved conversations, principally about food and the lax manners of young girls who had not been educated in a convent. Berta was an artist who accepted nothing short of perfection. Once she was insulted when a well-meaning woman guest asked her what brand of chili powder she used. Berta carefully ground a blend of five different varieties of whole dried chilis on her own metates, and scorned any brands. Her great contribution to Sunday mornings was Tortilla Pomposo. With all the flourish that her five-foot height and ample figure would permit, she would plump down the Pomposo on the table and step back with her hands on her hips, and demand, 'How you like?' To which I could only reply, 'Perfect, Berta, like all your dishes.' "

Makes 4 or 5 servings

SAUCE:

4 strips finely chopped
 bacon
2 green peppers, finely
 chopped
2 onions, finely chopped
6 bay leaves
½ cup Mexican (or unsweetened) chocolate, ground
 and made into a paste

2 tablespoons chili powder
 salt and Tabasco sauce
 to taste
½ teaspoon whole pepper-
 corns
½ teaspoon sage
1 cup dry claret
2 cups sliced small mush-
 rooms

1. Brown, but do not cook to crispness, the bacon, peppers, onions, and bay leaves in a deep skillet or saucepan.
2. Add chili powder, chocolate, salt, Tabasco, peppercorns, sage, and claret, and cook for 5 minutes after mixture comes to a boil, stirring constantly.
3. Add a little cornstarch and stir into mixture until it thickens slightly. Add mushrooms, and allow the sauce to simmer for 5 minutes under a cover.

OMELET*:

8 eggs
 water
 cornstarch

dry strips of toast
almond paste

1. Prepare a fluffy omelet, using 8 eggs, beating whites separately from yolks, and adding a little water and cornstarch to the whites after they have hardened. Fold in the yolks.
2. Raise on top of stove. Place in a slow oven for about 15 minutes.
3. Pour half the sauce over ½ of the surface of the omelet. Fold the other half over, and pour on the rest of the sauce.
4. Serve with dry strips of toast spread with almond paste.

The Dorn Cookbook
GENERAL FRANK DORN

---

* Tasty tortillas are canned by Ashley's Inc. at 6590 Montana Avenue, El Paso, Texas. Many fine food shops carry these prepared tortillas—as well as Ashley's enchilada sauce.

EGGS OX EYES

The French word *formidable* takes the place of the English "wonderful," but with a little extra "oomph" to it. "The *formidable* Monsieur Smith" would be saying Mr. Smith is quite a man!

Well anyway, here is a *formidable* egg dish, the recipe of the Hotel of the Old Mill of Dijon, France.

Makes 6 servings

6 slices stale bread, ¾ of an inch thick	1 generous teaspoon rich, sweet milk
sour cream	tomato sauce
6 eggs	mushrooms cooked in butter
salt and white pepper, mixed	

1. Toast stale bread on both sides and stamp into rounds about 3 inches in diameter, then remove the middle of each round with a 1½-inch cutter.
2. Place the rings in a generously buttered baking dish; spread over them gradually as much sour cream as they will absorb without becoming sodden; then break a fresh egg carefully into each ring.
3. Sprinkle lightly with salt and pepper; cover each egg with milk; place in a slow oven (300° F.), and bake until eggs are set but not hard.
4. Serve on hot, individual plates, surrounding each egg with a ribbon of tomato sauce to which has been added thinly sliced fresh mushrooms cooked in butter.

The Gold Cook Book
LOUIS P. DE GOUY

EGGS GELATIN

Louise Holt, of Greensboro, was intrigued in Paris by the inimitable French cuisine. A special luncheon dish (which in similar form has long been served in the South) is Eggs Gelatin, simply a soft-boiled egg in clear aspic. The secret of the dish is in the boiling of the eggs to attain, but not pass, the perfect congealed stage. After much experimenting she finds that the eggs should be boiled about five minutes, then plunged into cold water, taken out and peeled. Perhaps this stage does not suit you, so boil the egg to suit your taste; then proceed as follows:

Makes 3 servings

6 boiled eggs	mayonnaise seasoned with
2 cups beef, or any tasty	spices and herbs to suit
bouillon or consommé	taste, or French dress-
1 envelope plain gelatin	ing

1. Soak the gelatin in ¼ cup of the cold bouillon. Heat the remainder of the bouillon, add gelatin and stir until dissolved.
2. Pour into 1 large mold or 3 individual molds. Let chill until it begins to set, then place eggs in the gelatin.
3. Allow to congeal thoroughly,. and serve, 2 eggs for each serving. If in individual molds, have molds large enough to hold 2 eggs. Serve on watercress and garnish with mayonnaise or French dressing.

NOTE:
The eggs may be stuffed, if desired. If egg is allowed to cool in shell, it is more congealed; large eggs should boil 1 minute longer than small ones. Peel carefully.

The Southern Cook Book
MARION BROWN

POACHED EGGS IN RED WINE

Makes 4 servings

1 pint red Burgundy wine	pinch of thyme leaves or
1 onion, sliced	1 bay leaf
1 carrot, sliced	4 eggs
1 lump of sugar	marrow
pinch of salt	toasted English muffins
	cornstarch (small amount)

1. Put the wine in a deep saucepan. Then add the onion, carrots, sugar, salt and thyme or bay leaf. Let this boil for about 10 minutes.
2. Remove the vegetables and strain.
3. Slide the eggs into the boiling wine and poach. Remove the eggs and thicken wine with cornstarch to make a sauce.
4. Place the eggs on the toasted English muffins. Pour the sauce over the eggs and on top place very neatly sliced marrow.
5. Put the platter with the eggs and sauce and marrow under the broiler for about ½ minute and then serve.

La Crémaillère
Banksville, New York

EGGS EVA

Eva is the breathtakingly beautiful sister of glamorous Zsa Zsa Gabor. Her name is pronounced not Eva, like Uncle Tom's, but Ava, like Ava Gardner's. Sister Eva does fancy dishes for after-theater suppers. She cooks everything with green peppers, an old Hungarian touch.

Makes 4 servings

8 small sausages	salt and pepper
4 eggs, slightly beaten	green pepper, chopped
½ cup cream	butter for frying

1. Fry sausages and put aside. Drain off fat.
2. To slightly beaten eggs, add cream, salt and pepper.
3. Melt butter in pan, add eggs, and scramble lightly. Fold in sausage and chopped green pepper and serve.

Look Magazine

HUEVOS RANCHEROS

Texas, more than four centuries after white men and Indians first met hereabouts, has evolved through adoption, adaptation, and mutation a cuisine that has come to be pretty much its own.

Even in a meat-eating state like Texas, the egg is one of man's best friends. No range count of Texas egg recipes would be representative without *huevos rancheros.* Like most egg and Mexican recipes, *ranchero* versions are numerous and most are simple. This one is neither particularly simple nor especially complicated. The flavor "secret" in it came from José who was and may still be operating a little pink stucco café which he called Taxco, in Dallas. That secret is to use leaf orégano.

Makes 4 servings

4 eggs
3 tablespoons onion, chopped
1 clove garlic, minced
2 tablespoons butter
2 tablespoons chopped bell pepper

pulp of 2 green pod peppers (chilis)
¼ teaspoon leaf orégano
1 large tomato, peeled and chopped
salt and pepper
½ cup meat stock or water

1. Cook the onion and garlic in the melted butter until golden.
2. Add the bell pepper, pod peppers, orégano, tomato, salt, and pepper.
3. When well mixed, add the meat stock or water, and cook until the vegetables are tender and the sauce has thickened.
4. Fry or scramble 4 eggs. When cooked, pour the sauce over them.

NOTE:

All *huevos rancheros* and other Mexican dishes should be served with tortillas, either soft or crisp. They can be bought from Mexican stores or restaurants, or made.

The Texas Cookbook
ARTHUR AND BOBBIE COLEMAN

CHARCOAL DEALER'S OMELET

This is a dish for men of virility. Its vigor reminds me of a book called *Two Eggs on My Plate* by Oluf Reed Olsen.

Olsen was a young Norwegian full of despair at seeing his country occupied and destroyed during World War II. He joined the quiet undercover fight against the Nazi foe.

All during the training period the young men were fed on rationed fare. But one day they would find two fried eggs on their breakfast plates. This was the notice that today was their day to take off—the day for action.

Makes 4 servings

1 cup chopped onion   4 eggs
2 tablespoons butter or fat

1. Fry chopped onion with butter or fat until golden brown. Drain the fried onions and set aside.
2. Beat 4 eggs and make an omelet in the same fat, adding salt and pepper to taste.
3. Serve the omelet with the fried onions on top.

Greek Cookery
NICHOLAS TSELEMENTES

SCOTCH WOODCOCK

Makes 4 servings

rounds of hot buttered   4 eggs
   toast   4 tablespoons light cream
anchovy paste   1 tablespoon minced parsley
2 tablespoons butter or   salt and pepper
   substitute   paprika

1. Spread toast lightly with anchovy paste and keep hot.
2. Melt butter or substitute, add eggs beaten with cream, then add seasonings and flavorings.

3. Cook gently as for scrambled eggs, stirring constantly until thickened, preferably using a double boiler.
4. Pour over toast and dust with paprika.

Egg Cookery
LILY HAXWORTH WALLACE

SWEET AND SOUR EGGS

Makes 6 servings

1 tablespoon butter	2 bay leaves
1 small onion, minced	2 tablespoons vinegar
1 teaspoon flour	¼ teaspoon salt
½ cup water	1 tablespoon sugar
3 or 4 cloves	12 eggs

1. Melt butter in a saucepan, add onion and cook slowly. Do not brown.
2. Add flour and brown slightly. Add water, cloves, and bay leaves and cook until smooth, stirring constantly. Simmer 15 minutes longer.
3. Add vinegar, salt, and sugar and, as soon as sauce comes to a rapid boil, add eggs 1 at a time, breaking each into a saucer and then slipping it into boiling liquid.
4. Cover and cook a few minutes as preferred.

United States Regional Cook Book
RUTH BEROLZHEIMER

HAM AND EGGS JERSEY

For many years Ann Batchelder was the food editor of the *Ladies' Home Journal.* She was known and loved in millions of homes because what she said came right from the heart. Her love for food was tied to her love for people.

"The food offered one's guests," said Ann Batchelder, "should be . . . beautiful to the eye, enchanting to the imagination, satisfying to the palate, and never-to-be-forgotten by the guest. The simplest dishes may fulfill all these requirements. Indeed, it is in the preparation, dressing, and serving of simple dishes that the cook's highest art is required. Like the simple Paris frock, the simple dish shows the greatest finesse."

cold cooked ham   raw potatoes
pure cream   fat for frying
2 eggs for each serving   salt and pepper

1. Slice ham very thin. Have as many shallow ramekins as there are people to be served, for this dish must be served in individual baking dishes which are fairly shallow. A deep casserole won't do. Now cover the bottom of your ramekins with a little pure cream. Over this place slices of cooked ham, then cover the ham with cream, season with salt and pepper.
2. Put the ramekins into the oven.
3. When the cream is very hot, break 2 eggs carefully into each ramekin and set back in the oven until the eggs are done as you like them. You know as well as I that some folks like eggs almost as they come from the shell, and some prefer them a little this side of well done. But that is up to you.
4. Before you start your ham and eggs, have on the range a frying pan with about 1½ inches of fat in it. Let this get pretty hot. Into it slice quite thick raw potatoes and let them fry, turning occasionally, until they are brown and tender.
5. By the time your ham and eggs are ready, if you started your potatoes first, everything will be done at once, for these fried raw potatoes are part and parcel of this elegant dish.

Ann Batchelder's Cookbook

BRENNAN'S EGGS HUSSARDE

New Orleans is a city of restaurant *aficionados* who have a high and rigid criterion in judging food. Brennan's has consistently met the standards of local people and visitors alike. This family-run establishment was founded by Owen Brennan who was about the least likely of New Orleans' citizens to open a restaurant devoted to *haute cuisine*. He had at various times peddled candy bars from door to door, operated a gas station and worked at numerous other activities foreign to fine eating. But in 1943 he bought the historic Old Absinthe House and across from it thought to open a glorified hamburger stand where he could send customers in need of sobering up.

It was a friend, "Count" Arnaud Cazenave, owner of another famous restaurant, Arnaud's, who goaded him into culinary stardom by declaring that while the Irish were a nation of poets, they could do little more in the way of cooking than boil potatoes. He might have gone as far as to suggest that even at that they weren't so hot. "I'll show you," shouted Owen Brennan, "that an Irishman, this Irishman, can run the best French restaurant in New Orleans." And with that he brought in Paul Blange, the chef who made good on Brennan's promise.

Here is one of the *spécialités* of the Maison Brennan. While a Hollandaise sauce is given elsewhere, we also give you Brennan's recipe, which is a bit different, so that you'll have your Eggs Hussarde just as he serves them.

Makes 1 serving

2 large thin slices ham,
   grilled
2 Holland rusks
¼ cup Marchand de
   Vin Sauce

2 slices tomato, grilled
2 eggs, soft poached
¾ cup Hollandaise Sauce

1. Lay a large slice of ham across each rusk and cover with Marchand de Vin Sauce. Cover next with tomato and then egg.
2. Top with Hollandaise Sauce. Garnish with sprinkling of paprika.

MARCHAND DE VIN SAUCE

Yields 2 cups

¾ cup butter
⅓ cup finely chopped
   mushrooms
½ cup minced ham
⅓ cup finely chopped shallots
½ cup finely chopped onion
2 tablespoons garlic, minced

2 tablespoons flour
½ teaspoon salt
⅛ teaspoon pepper
   dash cayenne
¾ cup beef stock
½ cup red wine

1. In a 9-inch skillet melt butter and lightly sauté the mushrooms, ham, shallots, onion, and garlic. When the onion is golden brown, add the flour, salt, pepper, and cayenne.
2. Brown well, about 7 to 10 minutes. Blend in the stock and the wine and simmer over low heat for 35, to 45 minutes.

HOLLANDAISE SAUCE

Yields 1 cup

4 egg yolks
2 tablespoons lemon juice

½ pound butter, melted
¼ teaspoon salt

1. In top half of double boiler, beat egg yolks and stir in lemon juice. Cook very slowly in double boiler over low heat, never allowing water in bottom pan to come to a boil.
2. Add butter a little at a time, stirring constantly with a wooden spoon. Add salt and pepper. Continue cooking slowly until thickened.

Maison Brennan
New Orleans, La.

FONDUE NEUCHÂTELOISE

Makes 2 servings

½ pound Switzerland Swiss cheese, shredded, or finely cut
1½ tablespoons flour
1 clove fresh garlic
1 cup Neuchâtel wine (or any light dry wine of the Rhine, Riesling or Chablis types)
salt, pepper, nutmeg to taste

1 loaf French or other white bread with a hard crust (or at least four hard rolls), cut into bite-size pieces, each of which must have at least one side of crust
3 tablespoons Kirschwasser or 2 tablespoons of any nonsweetened fruit brandy such as apple jack, slivowitz, cognac, etc., or light rum (optional)

1. Dredge cheese with flour.
2. Rub the cooking utensil well with garlic. (You will need an earthenware casserole holding about 4 cups, or a chafing dish or similarly shaped cooking utensil with a handle.)
3. Pour in the wine and set over very slow fire. (This fondue is best made over an alcohol stove, the flame of which is easily adjustable; or any electric plate, with an asbestos pad, that will hold the cooking utensil securely.) When the wine is heated to the point at which air bubbles rise to the surface (*never* boiling point), stir with a fork and add the cheese by handfuls, each handful to be completely dissolved before another one is added.
4. Keep stirring until the mixture starts bubbling lightly. At this point add a little salt and pepper and a dash of nutmeg (optional). Finally add and thoroughly stir in the Kirschwasser (or other brandy).
5. Remove the bubbling fondue from the fire and set immediately onto your preheated table heating element.
6. Spear a piece of bread with a fork, going through the soft part first and securing the points in the crust. The idea is not to lose your bread when you dip it into the fondue. Dunk the bread in the fondue in a stirring motion until

your neighbor takes over to give you a chance to enjoy your morsel. While each one takes his leisurely turn in rotation, the stirring will help maintain the proper consistency of the fondue and will assure that each piece is thoroughly coated with melted cheese.

7, Care should be taken that the fondue keeps bubbling lightly. This is done by regulating the heat, or by turning it off or on. If the fondue becomes a little too thick at any time, the defect can be rectified by stirring in a little preheated (never cold) wine. Toward the end, some of the melted cheese will form a brown crust at the bottom of the utensil. When that happens, keep the heat low in order to prevent the utensil from cracking. The crust can easily be lifted out with a fork and is considered to be a delicacy.

Switzerland Cheese Association

PIPERADE

Piperade is the best known of all Basque dishes, and various recipes for it have appeared in English cookery books. It is a mixture of pimientos, tomatoes, and onions, with eggs added at the end; the final result is a creamy scrambled-egg effect deliciously blended with the vegetables in which the pimiento flavor slightly dominates. Sometimes one meets it with the purée of onions, tomatoes, and pimientos topped with fried eggs, sometimes in the form of an omelette; the scrambled-egg version is the most characteristically Basque.

There is a small restaurant in Paris called Louisette. You may have difficulty spotting it, but it is near Quay San Michel —and here you will get a really fine Piperade. Order with it a bottle of Louisette's special rosé wine.

Makes 6 servings

pork or bacon fat	6 eggs
1 pound onions	salt, pepper
1 pound tomatoes	marjoram
3 fairly large red peppers or about 6 of the small green ones	

1. In a heavy frying or sauté pan melt some pork fat (sometimes olive oil is used for this dish, but pork, or even bacon fat, suits it better).
2. Put in the sliced onions, and let them cook slowly, turning golden but not brown; then put in the pimiento, cut into strips; let this cook until it is soft, then add the chopped tomatoes, with a seasoning of salt, ground black pepper and a little marjoram. Cook with the cover on the pan.
3. When the whole mixture has become almost the consistency of a purée, pour in the beaten eggs, and stir gently, exactly as for ordinary scrambled eggs. Take care not to let them get overcooked.

French Country Cooking
ELIZABETH DAVID

WELSH RABBIT

The Welsh Rabbit is thought to be the oldest cooked cheese dish in the world. Years ago in Wales, when meat was scarce, the men of the family went hunting for rabbits. If they came home empty-handed, it was up to the womenfolk to provide a hearty substitute for the meat they didn't catch.

The housewife would cut a chunk of cheese into small bits and place it in an iron pan on the hearth, before the huge fire that was the house's only source of heat. She then hung strips of bacon on the cranes above the pan. As the bacon cooked the fat dripped into the melting cheese.

When the dish was ready it was eaten with bread. As a joke at the expense of the unsuccessful hunters it was named Welsh Rabbit. So, don't call it "rarebit."

The oldest Welsh Rabbit recipes almost always call for stale ale. Marye Dahnke says, "I've tried ale both fresh and stale and can't see what differences it makes. Tired beer does just as well as stale ale. In fact a Welsh Rabbit doesn't really need the benefit of either beer or ale."

Makes 4 to 6 servings

½ tablespoon Worcester-
    shire sauce
⅛ teaspoon paprika
½· teaspoon dry mustard
    dash of cayenne

salt to taste
½ cup ale or beer
1 pound sharp American
    Cheddar cheese
    crisp toast

1. Mix all the seasonings to a smooth paste. Add the ale or beer, put into a skillet, and let stand over very, very low heat until the ale or beer is hot.
2. Add the cheese, crumbling it as you add it. Then stir in the same direction until the cheese is melted.
3. Serve piping hot over fresh, crisp toast. (Use wilted ale if you like, but don't use wilted bread.)

NOTE:
Cream or evaporated milk may be substituted for the ale or beer if desired. If you prefer a rabbit with more "bite," add a little extra Worcestershire sauce and cayenne.

The Cheese Cook Book
MARYE DAHNKE

CHEESE SOUFFLÉ

Out where I live in East Hampton, the town fire siren announces noon, as it does in many another small town. On lazy summer days that's our signal to gather under the lawn umbrella and enjoy a cheese soufflé and a simple salad made with greens right out of the garden. There's something pompous and show-offy about a successful cheese soufflé. But you know that pride goeth before a fall, and there's nothing to prick one's culinary pride faster than a fallen soufflé. So serve yours at once, very hot.

Makes 4 to 6 servings

3 tablespoons grated
    Parmesan cheese
2 sections Camembert cheese
2 tablespoons butter
¾ cup milk
3 tablespoons flour

4 egg yolks
5 egg whites
1 teaspoon dry mustard
    cayenne pepper
    salt

1. Put cheese through a strainer. Beat egg whites to stiffness. Set aside both these ingredients.
2. Melt butter in a pan. Stir in flour, cayenne pepper and salt.
3. Pour on the milk and stir over fire until mixture thickens. Do not allow to boil.
4. Remove and stir in strained cheese. Add mustard, egg yolks and beaten egg whites.
5. Grease the soufflé dish, tie a band of wax paper on outside. Pour in the mixture and bake for 30 minutes at 375° F. Serve immediately!

FISH AND SEA FOOD

FILLET OF SOLE BONNE FEMME

Two of the best restaurateurs in the world are undoubtedly Fred Decré and Robert Meyzen, both of whom grew up in the business under the famous Henri Soulé of Le Pavillon, and now are the directing geniuses of La Caravelle in New York which is today probably the leading French restaurant in America. They also operate La Crémaillère in Banksville, Westchester County, New York. They recently started another interesting New York restaurant—Le Poulailler (meaning chicken coop), which applies the gourmet concept, but has moderate prices.

This recipe, supervised by La Caravelle's great chef, Roger Fessaguet, is one of the dreamiest, although one of the creamiest, fish dishes you can ask for. But considering that it is a dish rich in nutrition as well, the five hundred calories per portion might be permissible even on a weight-maintenance diet. We hate to be so technical about so gorgeous a repast, but it's better thus than to have you pass up this piscatorial achievement. Rather serve your reducers a little smaller portions than to deny them this pleasure.

Makes 8 servings

6 large fillets of sole (or fillets of flounder)	2 sprigs of parsley, chopped
	juice of 1 lemon
1 pound of fresh white mushrooms	salt and white pepper to taste
1 chopped onion	½ cup butter
2 glasses dry white wine	2 tablespoons flour
1 cup bouillon or chicken broth	½ cup heavy cream
	1 egg yolk

1. Place half the sliced mushrooms in the bottom of a buttered shallow pan, add half of the chopped onion, half of the parsley, salt, and pepper.
2. Put the fillets over this and place the rest of the mushrooms, onion, parsley, and seasoning over them. Add the wine and dot with butter.
3. Cover with oiled wax paper and cook on top of the stove until the liquid reaches the boiling point. Then place in a moderate oven (350° F.) for 10 minutes.
4. Remove the liquid to a saucepan and let simmer until it is reduced to half the original quantity.
5. Blend ½ cup of butter with 2 tablespoons of flour and add to the liquid, stirring slowly. This will thicken it to the consistency of a sauce. Add ½ cup of cream mixed with the egg yolk.
6. Make sure the fillets are thoroughly dry, then pour the sauce over them and place under the broiler until well browned.

La Caravelle
New York City

FILLET DE SOLE SCHEVENINGEN

This special dish is dedicated to the well-known fishing port of Scheveningen near The Hague, the birthplace of its creator. For it we have to thank Chef Hollaar of the Hotel Lauswolt in Beetsterzwaag, Holland. From its inception the recipe was a success, and people came from all over Holland to enjoy it.

Makes 4 servings

8 fillets of sole	Hollandaise Sauce
8 scrambled eggs	(see page 258)
16 asparagus tips	4 king-size prawns (shrimp)

1. Salt the fillets and dredge them with flour. Fry slowly in butter until they have a nice gold-brown color. Arrange the fillets neatly (one next to the other) and cover them with the scrambled eggs, so that only the middle part is covered.
2. Now put the asparagus tips on the top. The Hollandaise Sauce goes partly over the tips and one prawn is served with each portion.
3. Mashed potatoes are normally served with Fillet de Sole Scheveningen. For decoration use lettuce and tomatoes.

Hotel Lauswolt
Beetsterzwaag, Holland

SOLE FOUQUET

A fish dish which I recommend especially to you is wonderful Sole Fouquet. At the famous New England Toll House, Ruth Wakefield and her assistants spent a lot of time working out this recipe for fish connoisseurs since the Fouquet Restaurant in Paris did not care to part with its secrets.

Makes 4 servings

4 fillets lemon sole	2 bay leaves
2 cups water	pinch of thyme
1 small onion, sliced	salt and pepper

1. Place fillets in shallow baking dish. Add water, sliced onion, bay leaves, thyme, salt, and pepper. Simmer a few minutes until fish is done.
2. Pour off liquor and strain.

SAUCE

½ cup sliced mushrooms	½ cup chopped peeled tomato
4 tablespoons butter	(use only outside firm
4 tablespoons flour	shell)
liquor in which fish has	1 tablespoon Parmesan
been cooked	cheese
	white wine

1. Cook mushrooms in butter. Blend in flour. Add hot liquor (in which fish has been cooked), stirring until thick. Add chopped tomato, Parmesan cheese, white wine, salt and pepper to taste.
2. Pour sauce over fish in baking dish, place under broiler flame and brown. Serve at table from baking dish.

The Toll House Cook Book
RUTH WAKEFIELD

FISH SAUTÉED IN ANCHOVY BUTTER

Until recently Dr. Burt Aginsky was professor of anthropology at the College of the City of New York, and Dr. Ethel Aginsky held the same post at New York's Hunter College. A more delightful, youthfully alive couple you would be hard put to find. Since they have a taste and a "feeling" for food and are world travelers, at home alike in Hong Kong, Dublin, or with the Pomo Indians, we sought their *one* best recipe. This is it—gleaned from a marine radio operator in Honolulu. It's very simple.

Makes 4 servings

4 fillets of fish (sole, haddock, flounder or other favorite fish)
2 tablespoons butter

2 ordinary slender cans of anchovy fillets (the flat, not the rolled anchovies)
3 tablespoons olive oil

1. Make a mixture of the butter, olive oil, and anchovies, working up a paste or butter.
2. Heat in skillet until warm, not hot.
3. Add the fish fillets and increase the heat.
4. Sauté the fish in the anchovy mixture until both sides are golden brown.
5. Place fish on a warm platter, and pour the sauce over the fish.

Drs. Ethel and Burt Aginsky

BAKED FISH

(BASS, BLUEFISH, COD, OR HADDOCK)

1. Stuff a good-sized fish with either of the following dressings, sew the opening with needle and thread.
2. Cut 3 or 4 gashes through the skin on each side. This keeps the fish in shape during the cooking.
3. Lay 6 good-sized strips of salt pork over the top.
4. Bake in very hot oven (550° F.) for the first 15 minutes, then reduce the heat to 425° F. and continue baking for 30 to 45 minutes according to the size of the fish. Allow ¾ to 1 pound of fish per person.

NEW ENGLAND STUFFING

3 cups bread crumbs
2 small onions, chopped fine
sprinkle of thyme

1 beaten egg
½ teaspoon salt
⅛ teaspoon pepper

Mix well and moisten with water.

OYSTER STUFFING
(*Wonderful with Codfish*)

2 cups cracker crumbs
¼ cup melted butter
¼ teaspoon salt
1½ teaspoons lemon juice
⅛ teaspoon pepper

¼ teaspoon poultry seasoning
1½ tablespoons chopped onion
2 cups washed oysters
1½ tablespoons parsley,
   chopped fine

Mix ingredients lightly with fork.

Peter Hunt's Cape Cod Cookbook

PIERRE FRANEY'S STUFFED STRIPED BASS

Pierre Franey is undoubtedly one of the greatest chefs in the world. It was his kitchen that helped make the reputation for New York's Le Pavillon restaurant.

Pierre Franey's stuffed striped bass, in the words of Craig Claiborne, "is one of the most delectable dishes ever created. The preparation takes considerable time since it necessitates boning the fish and making the stuffing and the white-wine sauce, but the result makes the effort well worth it."

Makes 6 to 8 servings

2 striped bass (2½ pounds)
   or 1 bass (5 pounds)
   salt and freshly ground
   black pepper
¾ cup butter
½ pound mushrooms, finely
   chopped
½ lemon
¼ cup finely chopped onion
½ teaspoon minced garlic
¼ teaspoon ground thyme

½ teaspoon ground sage
¼ teaspoon finely chopped
   bay leaf
¼ cup finely chopped shallots
   or green onions
1 cup dry white wine
1½ cups soft fresh bread crumbs
1 egg yolk
2 tablespoons finely chopped
   parsley
White Wine Sauce

1. Preheat oven to moderate (350° F.).
2. Bone the fish or have it boned, but without splitting fish

in two. To do this, carefully trim around rib bones and back bones to, but not through, the back section. Pull out remaining bones with tweezers. Reserve the bones for sauce recipe (below). Sprinkle inside of fish with salt and pepper.

3. Melt half of the butter in a skillet. Add mushrooms to the butter and immediately sprinkle with lemon juice. Cook until mushrooms are wilted. Add the onion, garlic, thyme, sage, bay leaf, half of the shallots, and salt and pepper to taste.

4. Stuff fish with mushroom and herb mixture. Cover the opening with a neat length of aluminum foil and tie with string.

5. Rub a baking dish with 2 tablespoons butter and sprinkle with salt, pepper and the remaining shallots. Place the stuffed fish in the baking dish and dot it with remaining butter. Pour the wine over the fish and cover with aluminum foil.

6. If small fish are used, bake for 40 minutes; if large fish is used, bake for 1 hour. In any event, bake until fish flakes easily when tested with a fork.

7. Transfer fish to a warm serving platter and remove foil and string. Use pan liquid as indicated in sauce recipe (below). Serve the fish with the White Wine Sauce and with boiled whole small potatoes buttered and sprinkled with parsley.

WHITE WINE SAUCE

Makes about 2 cups

bones from fish	¼ cup butter
⅓ cup dry white wine	3 tablespoons all-purpose flour
2 cups water	pan liquid from baking fish
1 garlic clove, peeled	(see above)
2 parsley sprigs	¼ teaspoon cayenne pepper
1 small white onion, peeled	¾ cup heavy cream
salt	1 teaspoon lemon juice
10 peppercorns	

1. Place the fish bones in a small saucepan and add the wine, water, garlic, parsley, onion, salt to taste and peppercorns. Bring to a boil and simmer for 20 minutes to make stock.

2. Melt half of the butter in a saucepan and stir in the flour, using a wire whisk. Add 1½ cups of the stock, stirring vigorously until the mixture is thickened and smooth. Simmer for 30 minutes over very low heat, stirring occasionally.
3. When fish is cooked, add the pan liquid from the baking dish. Stir in the cayenne. Put sauce through a sieve.
4. Reheat the strained sauce. Stir in the cream, the remaining butter and the lemon juice. Stir briefly and serve immediately with the fish.

The New York Times Cook Book
CRAIG CLAIBORNE

BAKED BASS CREOLE

Many cooks—not just inexperienced ones—feel that cooking fish and shellfish in any but the familiar ways is something only a chef can do. However, bearing a few things in mind, anyone, whether novice or expert, can prepare delicious, interesting, and varied fish dishes.

The most important thing to remember in cooking fish is: Don't cook it too long. Overcooking draws out the natural juices and causes the flesh to shrink and dry out. Almost any kind of fish can be baked. If you put the fish in a hot oven first, the surface is quickly done and the moisture and flavor sealed in. Then reduce the temperature in two or three minutes and cook until the flesh flakes easily when tested with a fork. Only oily or fat fish, such as whitefish, swordfish, red snapper, salmon, and pompano should be broiled. Small fish, such as Virginia spots, butterfish, and small trout should be sautéed in butter or oil.

LOUIS GARRISON

Makes 4 servings

4- pound bass	½ cup chopped celery
1 tablespoon lemon juice	1 tablespoon chopped
salt and pepper	parsley
6 tablespoons butter	1 cup bread crumbs
1 tablespoon chopped peeled onion	

1. Have fish cleaned and boned. Wipe with a damp cloth. Sprinkle with lemon juice, salt, and pepper.
2. Melt the butter in a heavy frying pan. Sauté the onion, celery, and parsley; add the bread crumbs and mix thoroughly.
3. Place the stuffing in the fish and sew opening together or fasten with skewers. Place in a well-buttered baking dish.

SAUCE

3 tablespoons butter	2 cups canned tomatoes
4 tablespoons chopped peeled onion	2 tablespoons lemon juice
	1 sprig thyme
2 tablespoons chopped green pepper, seeds and fibers removed	½ bay leaf
	salt and cayenne
	1 tablespoon Worcestershire sauce
2 tablespoons chopped parsley	1 small can mushrooms

1. Melt the butter and add the remaining sauce ingredients except the mushrooms; bring to boil, lower heat and simmer 10 minutes. Correct seasoning.
2. Pour sauce over the fish and bake in a preheated moderate (350° F.) oven 1 hour; baste with the sauce every 10 minutes.
3. Strain liquid off the mushrooms. Just before removing fish from oven scatter the mushrooms on top; let mushrooms heat through. Serve very hot.

Delicious Seafood Recipes
LOUIS GARRISON

PAPRIKA FISH

Friday was the fish day in Vienna, although fish was available every day of the week and was sold in various fish specialty stores. On Fridays these fish stores moved to the market place, among the produce stalls, and displayed their choice live fish in large wooden troughs, much to the delight of the children, who would try to catch them.

Of all the ways to prepare just any kind of fish, this is undoubtedly the one best liked in Vienna. Although it is suitable for any fish, it is preferable to use one of the larger varieties, such as bass, small haddock, scrod, mackerel, larger porgies, snappers, or kingfish. All may be cooked in this manner. If you prefer, you may have the fish cut in fairly thick steaks. If fillets are used, they should be rolled and secured with toothpicks.

Makes 8 servings

8 portions of fish or 1 whole fish weighing about 4 pounds	1 cup cream
	2 tablespoons paprika
	½ teaspoon pepper
¼ to ½ cup butter	1 teaspoon salt
2 large onions, sliced	

1. Use either a roasting or a baking pan, depending on the size of the fish. Melt butter, add onions, and sauté until light yellow.
2. Place the fish on top of the onions. Beat the cream lightly with the paprika, salt, and pepper and pour it over the fish.
3. Place in a moderate oven (375° F.) and bake, basting frequently. For a 4-pound fish the baking time is 30 to 35 minutes. For a fish steak 1½ inches thick, 25 minutes is sufficient. If the steak is thicker than 1½ inches, it should be baked a few more minutes. A rolled fillet will need only 15 minutes.
4. Remove fish to a serving platter and strain sauce over the fish. Serve with plain boiled potatoes or with noodles.

The Viennese Cookbook
IRMA RHODE

BROILED SALMON

Whether this is done over charcoal or under gas or electric flame, the procedure is the same. The fish should be about two inches from the heat unit.

salmon steaks or fillets	rosemary, dill, or tarragon
oil	salt and pepper
lemon juice	

1. Brush the steaks or fillets well with oil and squirt with a little lemon juice. If you like herb flavors, you will find that rosemary, dill, or tarragon are all delicious when cooked with salmon. Rub in a little of the herbs before you oil the fish.
2. Place the fish in an oiled broiling pan which has been pre-heated and broil for approximately 5 minutes.
3. Baste the fish with the oil in the pan and turn and broil for approximately 5 minutes more or until the fish flakes easily with a fork. Salt and pepper and remove to a hot platter.
4. Serve with plenty of lemon, plain boiled potatoes, and a cucumber salad.*

NOTE:
Variation: If you prefer a rich sauce with the already rich salmon, serve a Hollandaise (page 258) or a Béarnaise (page 251).

James Beard's Fish Cookery

SALMON MOUSSE

(WITH SOUR CREAM CUCUMBER SAUCE)

3 cups cooked salmon	1½ tablespoons melted butter
½ tablespoon salt	¾ cup milk
1½ tablespoons sugar	¼ cup vinegar
½ tablespoon flour	¾ tablespoon granulated gel-
1 teaspoon dry mustard	atin soaked in 2 table-
few grains of cayenne	spoons cold water
2 egg yolks	

1. Separate salmon into flakes.
2. Mix dry ingredients, add egg yolks, butter, milk and vinegar.
3. Cook over boiling water, stirring constantly until mixture

---

* Gillian Sandlands, New York painter, has done a fine book *Salads for the Gourmet*. With broiled salmon she suggests a salad of Boston lettuce, cucumber, pimiento, chicory, and chervil or parsley—plus correctly made French dressing prepared with tarragon vinegar.

thickens. Add soaked gelatin. Add entire mixture to salmon.

4. Mold, chill and serve with Sour Cream Cucumber Sauce.

SOUR CREAM CUCUMBER SAUCE

1 cup sour cream
1 tablespoon vinegar
1½ tablespoons lemon juice
½ to 1 teaspoon sugar
  few grains of pepper

½ onion passed over grater
  2 to 3 times
1 cucumber, seeded, peeled,
  and diced

Blend ingredients and chill.

Food as Famous Folks Like It
ROBERT NATHAN

MACKEREL WITH OLIVES

And I went to the stall where
  they sold fresh mackerel
("Now then! Tuppence for a fresh caught
  mackerel!")
Have you got a rabbit, 'cos I don't like
  mackerel?
But they hadn't got a rabbit, not anywhere there.

When We Were Very Young
A. A. MILNE

This simple recipe comes from the eminent Dr. Edouard de Pomiane, and it transforms the humble mackerel into something aromatic and delicious.

  small fresh mackerel
6 pitted green olives for
  each fish

salt, pepper
pitted black olives
olive oil

1. Clean small fresh mackerel. Stuff each fish with a half-dozen pitted green olives.
2. Place in a baking dish, preferably of earthenware, add salt and pepper and cover the bottom of the dish with olive

oil. Surround the fish with a generous quantity of pitted black or so-called "Greek" olives.

3. Bake in a hot oven for 30 minutes, basting frequently, and serve in the baking dish. Serve with steamed potatoes.

NOTE:

Bulk olives should be used, preferably the Greek or Italian type. The conventional stuffed and bottled olives don't work nearly as well.

Clementine in the Kitchen
PHINEAS BECK

SWEET AND PUNGENT FISH

You will note that in this recipe there is no reference as to the number of persons it will serve. That is because the Chinese do not plan a meal as we do. They usually figure a soup and two dishes for two people, a soup and four dishes for four people, and so on. They strive to obtain variety and contrast in each meal. The dessert course is very simple, usually canned fruit such as *lichee* nuts or dragon eyes, or Chinese preserved mixed fruit or almond cakes. However, most of our American cakes, pies, and puddings go well after a Chinese meal if variety is desired.

HENRY LOW

1 pound boned pike
2 slices canned pineapple
1 large green pepper
1 cup sugar
1 cup vinegar
1 teaspoon salt
1 teaspoon black sauce
 (gee yeou)

½ teaspoon gourmet powder
 (mei jing)
1 egg
4 tablespoons flour
½ cup stock or water
3 teaspoons cornstarch

1. Clean and cut pepper and pineapple into 8 pieces each.
2. Mix egg and flour together, stir until smooth.
3. Cut fish into 1-inch pieces. Dip fish in egg and flour, fry in deep fat until brown.
4. Bring vinegar and stock or water to a boil. Add pineapple, pepper, sugar, salt and gourmet powder; bring to a boil.

5. Add the fried pieces of fish and black sauce, then add cornstarch which has been made into a smooth paste. Stir constantly and cook 2 minutes more.

Cook At Home in Chinese
HENRY LOW

POMPANO EN PAPILLOTE

Pompano en Papillote is the brain child of Jules Alciatore of Antoine's Restaurant in New Orleans. He baked pompano fillets in paper hearts to celebrate the visit to New Orleans of Alberto Santos-Dumont, the Brazilian balloonist, in the early 1900's.

Antoine's pompano-in-a-bag is one of the most widely used methods of baking fish (meat or fowl), especially the tender pompano. The procedure may be a simple one. The fish is prepared as for ordinary baking, slipped into a heavy brown paper bag (or a bag made of waxed paper), tied tightly, and whisked into the oven to stew in its own rich juices. Mackerel, speckled trout, bass, fresh salmon, or any other baking fish can be done in this manner.

Makes 6 servings

3 medium-sized pompano	salt, pepper
3 cups water	½ clove garlic, minced
1 chopped shallot, or 2 tablespoons chopped onion	1½ cups chopped onions (extra)
	pinch of thyme
6 tablespoons butter	1 bay leaf
2¼ cups white wine	2 cups fish stock
1 cup crab meat	2 tablespoons flour
1 cup diced cooked shrimp	2 egg yolks

1. Clean pompano; cut into 6 fillets, removing head and backbone.
2. Simmer head, bones, and water (to cover) until there are 2 cups stock.
3. Sauté shallots and fillets in 2 tablespoons butter; add 2 cups wine. Cover and simmer gently 5 to 8 minutes—until fillets are tender.

4. Sauté crab meat, shrimp, and ¼ garlic clove in 1 table-spoon butter. Add onions, remaining ¼ garlic clove; cook 10 minutes. Add thyme, bay leaf, and 1¾ cups fish stock. Simmer 10 minutes.
5. Blend the flour and butter, gradually add remaining ¼ cup fish stock. Add to crab meat mixture with wine stock drained from fillets. Cook, stirring constantly, until thickened.
6. Beat egg yolks; add hot sauce and ¼ cup wine. Mix thoroughly. Place in refrigerator to chill until firm.

The Southern Cook Book
MARION BROWN

GEFILTE FISH

Gefilte is from the German *gefüllte* (stuffed), hence stuffed fish. The techniques for preparing Gefilte Fish have changed since the invention of the food chopper. In the old days all Jewish grandmothers used a wooden bowl and chopping knife to reduce the filleted fish to a smooth pulp. Today the latest model chopper makes short shrift of what was a customary Friday morning kitchen ceremonial.

Gefilte Fish is served chilled, with beet-juice flavored horse-radish. Carrot slices cooked with the fish are usually used for garnish. It is the first course of Sabbath eve meals and occupies first place on holiday menus as well.

LEAH W. LEONARD

Makes 4 to 6 servings

3 pounds fish (any firm-fleshed fish, preferably yellow pike, carp, buffalo, or any combination of these)
salt (as required)
2 large onions, 1 diced

2 eggs
pepper to taste (optional)
1 large carrot, sliced
2 stalks celery, diced
2 slices white bread, soaked and squeezed
parsley

1. Skin and bone the fish, leaving skin attached to bones of each part or cut. After the whole fish has been dressed and sectioned, salt evenly skin-bone cuts to be stuffed. Let

stand in a covered glass bowl in the refrigerator while chopping the filleted parts or flesh.

2. Grate in 1 onion, add eggs, salt and pepper to taste, and soaked bread if desired as a "stretcher." If no bread is used, add 2 tablespoons cold water and combine thoroughly.

3. Wet the hands and return pulp to bones, covering with the attached skin. Place the head bones and diced vegetables in the bottom of a deep pot. Place filled fish sections neatly on top, add cold water to cover. Cover pot.

4. Bring to a quick boil, remove cover and turn down heat, keeping the fish at a slow boil 1½ to 2 hours. The liquid should be reduced by half.

5. When cool, remove to a platter carefully, to retain shape of each section. Strain the liquid over the fish or into a separate bowl. Chill thoroughly before serving, using the carrot for garnish.

6. The jelled sauce may be cut and served separately or as an additional garnish.

Jewish Cookery
LEAH W. LEONARD

KIPPERED HERRING OR BLOATER
CREAMED WITH EGGS

Through all the ages the story of the symbolism of fish is found in one legend after another. Paganism, Christianity, idolatry, romance, prophecy, hieroglyphics, language, astrology, and architecture are all themes conjured up by the one word: fish. In our alphabet and in the zodiacal signs we have first the waters of the sea and then the fish. Our *M* is *mu* in Greek and *mem* in the Hebrew and Phoenician. The words *Mu* and *mem* in these languages mean "the sea." Our letter *N* follows and is *nu* in Greek and *nun* in Hebrew and Phoenician. These words in these languages mean "the fish." The letters *M* and *N*, therefore, as they follow each other, read: *M*, the sea; *N*, the fish. The two signs of the zodiac, Aquarius and Pisces, follow each other in the same sequence. Aquarius, the symbol of water and waves; Pisces, the symbol of the two fishes, or double fish, with its qualities of love and wisdom.

In one manifestation or another the romance, the legends,

and the symbolism of fish that have been ours through all the ages are still with us. We have our "sacred cod" in the State House in Boston; and there is the traditional blessing of the fishing fleet at Gloucester before it goes to sea. Annually at St. Dunstan's in London the catches of many thousands of pounds of fish are blessed before they are distributed to the markets.

Fish is still a festival food in practically every country in the world; and it continues to have special significance on the menus of all holy days.

MILO MILORADOVICH

Makes 4 to 6 servings

6 soft-smoked kippers or bloaters	4 hard-boiled eggs, cubed
1 cup milk	2 boiled potatoes, diced
1 cup water	2 cups white sauce (p. 254)
pepper to taste	6 sweet pickles, chopped
	6 slices buttered toast

1. Place kippers in saucepan over medium flame; cover with milk and water; bring to boiling point; simmer 10 minutes; remove from liquid; take all bones and skin from fish; flake with fork.
2. To white sauce in top section of double boiler (over lower section half-filled with boiling water), add flaked kippers, cubed hard-boiled eggs and potatoes; season with pepper to taste; heat gently 3 minutes.
3. Serve piping hot over buttered toast placed on preheated individual plates. Garnish with chopped sweet pickles.

NOTE:
Any variety smoked fish may be prepared in the same manner. *Do not boil smoked salmon, carp, chub, garfish, or sturgeon.* Simply flake fish and heat thoroughly in white sauce.

The Art of Fish Cookery
MILO MILORADOVICH

SHAD ROE AND BACON

Shad roe can be a succulent delicacy or a sorry disappointment. To avoid the latter and insure the former, we went to

Louis Morino, who operates Sloppy Louie's, eating place of the fishmen from New York's famed Fulton Fish Market.

As the name implies, there's nothing fancy about Louie's place and there's nothing fancy about Louie's talk. He gives it to you straight. "If you cook shad roe too fast," he says "them damn little eggs split out of the skin and be all over the place." Louie says the trick to making really good shad roe is to parboil or steam it—gently. Shad roe is in season only from April to September, after that you get frozen roe— and Louie's set against that.

Here is Louis Morino's way of preparing Shad Roe and Bacon.

Makes 4 servings

2 pairs of shad roe	1 bay leaf
twist of lemon peel or	dash of garlic powder or a
¼ of a lemon	clove of garlic (optional)
tablespoon or more of	1 teaspoon chopped parsley
butter	grilled bacon

1. Place shad roe in a saucepan and barely cover with cold water. Add the lemon and bay leaf.
2. Cook over very low flame (you can cover the pan if you like). It should take 20 to 25 minutes of very slow cooking before the water comes to a boil. This process toughens the skin of the roe.
3. Remove roe from the pan and drain on absorbent paper.
4. Meanwhile, melt the butter in a frying pan, add garlic and a teaspoon of chopped parsley. Sauté the roe until golden brown. Remove roe and place on a heated serving dish.
5. Strain the butter in which the roe was cooked and pour over. Place strips of bacon over all and serve hot.

Sloppy Louie's Restaurant
New York City

EMILY POST'S EXQUISITE SHRIMP

"Exquisite Shrimp," says Emily Post, "is an almost revolutionary way of cooking shrimp, and is, oh, so much better

than the usual recipe, which almost invariably starts out with
'boil the shrimp.'

"This recipe is a little complicated, but anyone who once
tries it will almost certainly never boil shrimp again."

Makes 4 servings (as the main course of a dinner)

2 pounds raw fresh shrimps (about 32 shrimps)
2 cups liquid (½ water and ½ wine; or water and chicken stock, or all water)
6 peppercorns
1 bay leaf
½ teaspoon salt (scant)
6 to 7 tablespoons butter (fresh, unsalted if possible)
3 tablespoons flour

1. Remove shells and black veins which run under the surface of the shrimp the length of the back. This is most easily done with a pair of scissors. Throw away the veins, but keep all the shells.
2. Put shells in a saucepan together with liquid, which may be half water and half white wine, or water and chicken stock, or even all water. Add the peppercorns, bay leaf, and salt and bring to a boil. Lower flame and simmer 15 minutes. Strain through a sieve, pressing the shells to extract all the liquid. Discard the shells, and if there is more than 1½ cups of liquid, boil it till it is reduced to that volume.
3. Melt 3 tablespoons of the butter in the top of a double boiler over a flame. Blend in the flour and add slowly the 1½ cups of the liquid the shells were cooked in, stirring constantly. Continue stirring at simmering temperature until sauce thickens. Place over simmering water and cover.
4. Heat 3 to 4 tablespoons of the butter in a skillet and add the peeled shrimps, which have been rinsed in water, drained, and dried. Turn them over and about till pink and white all over. Do not overcook! About 4½ or 5 minutes will be enough. Turn the shrimps and the butter and juices in the skillet into the sauce in the top of the double boiler, stir all together, and serve on rice.

NOTE:
For the rice try using 3 tablespoons butter, 1¾ cups chicken stock, 1⅓ cups long-grain rice, and ½ teaspoon salt, and cook.

The Emily Post Cookbook

SHRIMP CURRY

Makes about 12 servings

4 large onions, chopped
3 large cloves garlic, chopped
4 tablespoons butter
3 cups water or coconut milk
3 large tomatoes, peeled and chopped
2 large apples, chopped
1 cup chopped celery
1 tablespoon shredded coconut
1 piece fresh ginger root or ¾ teaspoon powdered ginger
1 tablespoon sugar
1½ tablespoons curry powder (or more according to taste)
1½ tablespoons flour
1½ teaspoons salt
¼ teaspoon pepper
1½ pounds cleaned raw shrimp

1. Sauté onions and garlic in butter till lightly browned. Add water and bring to a boil.
2. Add tomatoes, apples, celery, coconut, and fresh ginger root, if available.
3. If powdered ginger is used, blend it with sugar, curry powder, flour, salt and pepper. Add cold water to moisten to a paste and add, stirring, to boiling mixture. Simmer, stirring occasionally, till vegetables are very tender, or about 40 minutes.
4. Add shrimp and cook 5 minutes. Serve on rice.

The New York Times

GRILLED SHRIMP LOUISIANA

A veteran traveler stopped for a snack at a little lunch counter outside Charleston, South Carolina. As he was eating, his eye fell on a shelf of canned shrimp. "Tell me," he said to the proprietor, a venerable man, "how is it that here in the very heart of the shrimp country, you have all those cans of shrimp?" "Oh, them," smiled the owner, "they's for folks what don't like shrimp so much."

Here, on the other hand, is something for folks what *does* like shrimp so much. It comes from one of the finest restaurants in America, Whyte's, in downtown New York. Many of the country's top-bracket business men and political leaders patronize Whyte's. At lunch time, particularly, it has a hearty masculine air. Among Whyte's clientele of bankers, brokers, lawyers, judges and other important people, Grilled Shrimp Louisiana is perennially popular.

Incidentally, I owe this recipe to Walter Caron, captain of waiters, who is one of New York's opera buffs—no opera is unknown to him; all opera singers are correctly appraised by him.

Makes 2 servings

1 pound extra large raw shrimps	1 teaspoon dry mustard
1 teaspoon Worcestershire sauce	1 tablespoon milk
1 teaspoon lemon juice	few grains pepper
	dry bread crumbs
	melted butter

1. Remove shells from raw green shrimps and with a small knife carefully remove black intestinal vein. Rinse shrimps in cold water, place in bowl and drain off surplus water. Sprinkle Worcestershire sauce and lemon juice over them, sift dry mustard on top and let stand at least 30 minutes.
2. Now, take a spoon and fork and toss the shrimps, adding milk, a few drops at a time, until shrimps are saturated and seasonings are thoroughly absorbed.
3. Dip each shrimp in dry bread crumbs and place on broiler. (If you have an old-fashioned hand broiler that clamps together, so much the better, as this facilitates the turning. Otherwise shrimps have to be turned individually.) Drip a little melted butter over the shrimps and broil in hot oven until lightly browned. Both sides of shrimp must be exposed to broiler flame.

4. Serve 7 to 8 shrimps to a portion, arranging them in a row on a long strip of freshly made toast. Garnish each plate with a small timbale of boiled rice and pour Sauce à la Whyte around the rice and over the shrimps.

SAUCE À LA WHYTE

1 pound fish (any inexpensive kind)	2 tablespoons butter
1 onion, chopped fine	2 tablespoons flour
1 carrot, chopped fine	1 teaspoon paprika
1 pint water	few grains cayenne
1 teaspoon salt	1 cup milk
1 stalk celery, chopped fine	½ cup heavy cream

1. Cover fish and chopped vegetables with water, add salt and boil together about 30 minutes in a covered saucepan, until a good fish broth is obtained.
2. Uncover saucepan and boil until broth is reduced to a cupful and strain.
3. Melt butter, blend in flour, paprika, and cayenne. Gradually add the cup of strained fish stock and milk, stirring until perfectly smooth and the boiling point is reached. Add cream and let boil 2 minutes.
4. Strain again for perfect smoothness and serve piping hot.

Whyte's Restaurant
New York City

BUTTERFLY SHRIMPS

1 pound jumbo shrimps	flour
½ pound sliced bacon	oil for frying

1. Clean and shell shrimps and remove black vein. Split each shrimp down the back almost to the tail. Leave on tail. Make 3 slits on inside of shrimp.
2. Slip ½ strip of bacon into slits, weaving in and out. Roll shrimps in flour.
3. Put small amount of oil into frying pan. When hot, fry shrimps for 5 minutes on each side.
4. Serve with Chinese Barbecue Sauce.

BARBECUE SAUCE

4 tablespoons soy sauce
1½ tablespoons honey
1 teaspoon salt

½ teaspoon pepper
1 clove garlic, crushed
½ jigger whisky or brandy

Mix all ingredients together.

Oriental Cookbook
ALICE MILLER MITCHELL

KETTLE CLAMBAKE

When Marjorie Mosser embarked on the compilation of *Good Maine Food,* her uncle, Kenneth Roberts, who wrote many fine novels, said he stood up every good cook he knew at the point of a gun to get their recipes for her. Among the hundreds he "stood up" were John P. Marquand, Trader Vic, George Rector, and the Duchess of Windsor. This collaboration has resulted in a book as delightful as it is useful and devoid of frills.

A favorite aunt of mine used to tell about her happy girlhood days at Old Orchard Beach, near Portland, Maine. The gayest times always centered around the clambake. No longer need old-fashioned clambakes be confined to the Eastern Coast. With fast freight and air shipments, anyone can enjoy this Kettle Clambake right in his own backyard.

Makes 8 servings

8 live lobsters
    washed seaweed
    green corn

clams
melted butter
salt

1. Assemble 8 people around an outdoor fireplace. Put a layer of washed seaweed in the bottom of a large kettle, and on the seaweed put 8 live lobsters. Cover with a layer of seaweed, and on it place a layer of green corn in the husks. Add another layer of seaweed, top with clams and add another layer of seaweed.
2. Place a cover on the kettle, and put kettle over fire. The

steaming time will vary, according to your fire, but 1½ hours will usually elapse before clams are shucked.

3. Supply each participant with melted butter into which to dip clams. When the clams have been consumed, the corn will be ready to eat. Serve with butter and salt.

4. The lobsters will then be done, and should also be served with melted butter. The conventional accompaniment is a large pot of boiled coffee.

Good Maine Food
MARJORIE MOSSER

CLAM FRITTERS

"Cherrystones" and "littlenecks" are quahaug clams. They have hard shells and are delicious when eaten raw without "cocktail-sauce." Quahaugs can be cooked in an infinite number of ways. Here is a popular favorite.

Makes 4 servings

1 cup sifted flour	1 teaspoon baking powder
1 quart finely chopped clams	1 beaten egg

1. Mix flour and baking powder together. Add the clams and the egg.
2. Drop tablespoonfuls into hot fat in a deep skillet and fry until brown.

Peter Hunt's Cape Cod Cookbook

OYSTERS ROCKEFELLER

"O Oysters," said the Carpenter,
"You've had a pleasant run!
Shall we be trotting home again?"
But answer came there none—
And this was scarcely odd, because
They'd eaten every one.

"The Walrus and the Carpenter"
Alice Through the Looking Glass

Makes 1 serving

6 oysters on the half shell	1 tablespoon butter
1 cup raw spinach, put through meat chopper	3 cloves garlic salt
¾ cup sour cream	pepper
3 tablespoons grated cheese	bread crumbs
½ cup whipped cream	

1. Mix ¼ cup sour cream with a little crushed garlic, salt, pepper.
2. Remove oysters from shells and place a teaspoon of this mixture in the bottom of each shell.
3. Return oysters to shells, over the mixture.
4. Mix the remaining sour cream with the ground spinach and add a little garlic, salt, and pepper. Cover the oysters with this mixture.
5. Sprinkle with the grated cheese and just a few bread crumbs. Dot with butter.
6. Brown under broiler. Remove and top each oyster with a tablespoon of whipped cream. Again brown under broiler, and serve.

COQUILLES ST. JACQUES AU GRATIN

"Scallops are a favorite stand-by in New England, where I'll wager that not one in fifty escapes being fried in deep fat," says Phineas Beck. "A few are doubtless broiled on skewers between squares of bacon and served with a Maître d'Hôtel sauce. Those are the 50-to-1 shots. Yet Madame Prunier lists fifteen other ways to cook them. Clementine was impressed when Mr. Stacy delivered a pound of scallops all cleaned and removed from their shells. But she missed the flat shells, which are essential to her method of cooking them. We rescued a dozen or more shells from the Stacy shack by the sea, and Clementine proceeded with her old familiar Coquilles St. Jacques au Gratin, the classic French way of preparing scallops."

Makes 4 servings

sea scallops	salt, pepper
dry white wine	fine bread crumbs
6 shallots	grated Swiss cheese
¼ pound thinly sliced mushrooms	

1. Wash scallops in cold water and cut each in 4 pieces. Place them in a casserole and cover with dry white wine.
2. Add finely chopped shallots and thinly sliced mushrooms. Allow to boil for 10 minutes. Salt slightly and add pepper.
3. Place the scallops in 4 scallop shells, powder with fine bread crumbs and grated Swiss cheese. Brown in the oven and serve in the shell, very hot.

Clementine in the Kitchen
PHINEAS BECK

In this Sea Food section, we must find room for this pelican poem:

A wonderful bird is the pelican,
His bill will hold more than his bellican.
He can take in his beak
Enough food for a week,
But I'm darned if I know how
the hellican.

—Dixon Merritt (1879–1954)

MUSSELS À LA MARINIÈRE

In giving us this peasant version of Mussels à la Marinière, Phineas Beck, the biographer of that delightful character Clementine, tells this amusing story: "On Sunday afternoons Clementine was in the habit of taking long bicycle rides to satisfy her curiosity about this strange new land (America). The Sunday motorists often stuck their heads out of their car windows and laughed at her, for reasons which mystified her, but she didn't mind.

"She returned from one such expedition livid with excitement, and called excitedly to my wife, *'Madame! J'ai trouvé des moules! Des quantités des moules!'* . . . We all rushed into the kitchen. Wrapped up in somebody's Sunday newspaper were great clusters of small, purplish-black mussels. Clementine had pedaled far that day, to a rocky promontory jutting out into the Atlantic. Seated on the rocks and watching the waves break at low tide, she suddenly saw something to thrill her thrifty Burgundian soul—great patches of perfectly good mussels, the very kind of mussels they serve in Prunier's in Paris. Clementine could conceive of only one course of conduct—to gather several handfuls of these toothsome mollusks at once, wondering in the meantime why they were ignored by all the other Sunday trippers. When the Beck family sat down to great heaping soup plates full of Moules à la Marinière the next day, we wondered too."

Makes 3 or 4 servings

2 quarts of mussels	freshly ground pepper
4 or 5 sections garlic	2 ounces butter
minced parsley	

1. Brush and scrape the mussel shells, and wash in several waters, clipping the "beard" with a knife. (Maybe this laborious procedure is the reason mussels aren't popular.)
2. Place mussels in a pan, add garlic chopped fine, a good fistful of minced parsley, a little freshly ground pepper, and butter. Salt is not needed.
3. Cover the pan, place over a brisk fire and cook for 5 or 6 minutes, shaking the pan 2 or 3 times. Remove the lid.
4. The mussels are open, ready to be served with the sauce in soup plates.

Clementine in the Kitchen
PHINEAS BECK

CRAB MEAT NORFOLK

The Greeks held crab meat in high regard for its aphrodisiac or amatory effect. But then, they considered all shellfish, and many other types of fish, to have a similar potency. The Greeks were not alone in this belief. Traditionally, fish has been considered a powerful and unfailing aid to amour, particularly because of its phosphates and iodine. The Roman poets sang paeans of praise to fish of the rivers and seas. In Egypt, the aphrodisiac attributes of fish were so generally "recognized" that priests were forbidden to eat it. In Russia, Catherine II, whose husband was the grandson of Peter the Great, was childless and the Empire craved an heir . . . so with infinite realism, she ordered a meal of caviar and sturgeon, invited one Saltikoff, an officer of the guard—and presto, in due time a son was born. The fish may have been incidental to the result, but it was given the credit.

Whether Crab Meat Norfolk is named for the virgin queen Elizabeth's Earl of Norfolk or for the State of Virginia's city of Norfolk, is not known, but we rather think the latter.

Makes 4 servings

1 pound lump crab meat ⅔ cup butter
3 teaspoons cider vinegar

1. Place crab meat in casserole, pour the vinegar over, add melted butter and place in oven at 400° until sizzling hot.
2. Serve at once with rice and a creamy cole slaw. Before you cook the rice, sauté it a few minutes in butter.
3. For an interesting combination, julienne pieces (slivers) of Virginia ham can be added to the crab just before baking.

Helen Corbitt's Cookbook

DEVILED CRABS

Makes 6 servings

2 cups crab meat
¼ cup sherry
1 teaspoon Worcester-
   shire sauce
3 egg yolks, beaten
3 tablespoons butter
2 tablespoons flour

½ teaspoon salt
1 teaspoon dry mustard
   white pepper
2 cups milk
½ cup buttered bread crumbs
   crab shells

1. Mix the crab meat with the sherry, Worcestershire sauce, and egg yolks.
2. Melt the butter, stir in the flour mixed with the seasonings. Add the milk, and stir over the heat until thick.
3. Add the crab meat, and blend well.
4. Fill the crab shells with the mixture, sprinkle with the buttered crumbs, and bake in a moderate oven, 375° F., for 10 minutes until brown.

NOTE:
Some recipes call for minced hard-boiled eggs, minced parsley, lemon juice, and horseradish. Their use depends on whether you like highly seasoned dishes. For the above recipe, ½ teaspoon horseradish and 2 tablespoons lemon juice would be sufficient, and 2 hard-boiled eggs minced fine.

Secrets of New England Cooking
ELLA SHANNON BOWLES AND
DOROTHY S. TOWLE

LOBSTER

Unless you can get good fresh lobsters, pass by these lobster recipes . . . there's nothing more disappointing than a tough, dried-out lobster. But if you can buy newly caught lobsters, read on. Down East, in Cushing, Maine, we join in an annual lobster feast with our loving friends, Ben and Lillian Mild-woff, who live next to the farm where Andrew Wyeth painted his famous "Christina's World," reproductions of which now hang in homes all over America. Here are Ben and Lillian's several different lobster recipes—all great. Remember, Maine or Long Island lobster meat is entirely edible except for the small crop or craw behind the eyes, and the dark vein running down the back. The green substance is the liver or "tomalley" and is excellent eating. So is the red or "coral" which is the lobster's undeveloped spawn. A chicken lobster weighs 1 pound, a large lobster 2 pounds or over. In between there are heavy chickens (1⅛ pounds), quarters (1¼ pounds) and selects (1½ to 1¾ pounds).

BOILED LOBSTER

This is the way many *cognoscenti* prefer their lobster—neat, with no trimmings except a side dish of melted butter in which to dunk the lobster meat.

Place the live lobsters in a large kettle containing about 3 inches of briskly boiling salted water. Cover immediately. From the time the water boils again, allow 18 to 20 minutes. Serve the whole lobster, either hot or cold.

LOBSTER SALAD

For each cup of boiled and chilled lobster meat, cut in small pieces, allow 1 tablespoon mayonnaise. Mix thoroughly and chill again. Place on crisp lettuce leaves and sprinkle with paprika. Top with the unbroken meat of a whole lobster claw.

LOBSTER ROLL

Makes 4 servings

2 cups chilled cooked lobster
    meat
2 tablespoons mayonnaise

¼ cup finely diced celery
4 hamburger rolls
melted butter

1. Thoroughly mix the lobster meat, mayonnaise, and celery. Place in refrigerator until ready to use.
2. Split and toast the hamburger rolls, spread with melted butter, fill rolls with lobster meat and serve.

LOBSTER COCKTAIL

Makes 1 serving

¼ cup lobster meat, cut in
    pieces
2 tablespoons catsup

2 tablespoons sherry
1 teaspoon lemon juice
6 drops Tabasco sauce

Blend well, chill thoroughly and serve in cocktail glasses.

LOBSTER CASSEROLE

Makes 4 servings

2 tablespoons butter
2 tablespoons flour
½ teaspoon dry mustard
    salt and paprika
3 chicken lobsters, boiled
5 slices bread, crusts removed,
    broken into pieces (not
    too small)

1 cup thin cream or
    half-and-half
½ cup milk
    bread crumbs or cornflakes
2 tablespoons melted butter

1. Melt butter in double boiler. Add flour, mustard and dashes of salt and paprika.
2. To this paste, slowly add the cream and milk. Stir constantly to make smooth and continue to stir and cook until thickened.
3. Add lobster meat, and when this has been absorbed, add bread. Mix well and pour into casserole.
4. Top with bread crumbs or cornflakes, dribble or brush on melted butter. Bake in 350° F. oven just long enough to reheat mixture and lightly toast topping.

BROILED LOBSTER

Use live lobsters. Don't be afraid . . . handled right, they don't pinch. For each serving, split 1 live lobster. To do this, use a sharp, pointed knife. Cross the large claws and hold firmly with the left hand, make a deep incision with the knife at a point between the 2 large claws, and quickly draw the knife through the entire length, including the tail. Remove the dark vein and the craw or sac in the head.

Makes 4 servings

1½ cups cracker crumbs, or cracker meal
½ teaspoon salt

2 tablespoons Worcestershire sauce
8 large lettuce leaves
1 cup melted butter

1. Make a dressing by mixing the cracker crumbs, salt, and Worcestershire sauce.
2. Spread this generously over each lobster half. For eye-appeal, cut off 4 of the small claws and press into the dressing. To preserve moistness, place a lettuce leaf over each dressed lobster half.
3. Place lobsters on broiler, 8 to 10 inches from the flame, and broil for 25 to 30 minutes. Remove the charred lettuce leaves and serve lobster with melted butter.

BAKED LOBSTER

Makes 4 servings

4 live lobsters
16 old-fashioned unsalted
    crackers (Uneeda Bis-
    cuits)
    salt and pepper
¼ cup melted butter

3 to 4 tablespoons sherry
    additional melted butter
    grated Parmesan cheese
    paprika
4 large lettuce leaves

1. Slit lobsters as directed in Broiled Lobster recipe. Remove craw and vein, but preserve the tomalley and juice.
2. Roll or grind the crackers into fine crumbs, season with salt and pepper. Mix crumbs with melted butter, milk, and sherry. Stuff lobsters as full as possible with this dressing.
3. Dribble or brush on additional melted butter, sprinkle liberally with grated cheese and paprika. To preserve moistness, place lettuce leaves over the dressing.
4. Bake in hot oven (350° to 400° F.) for 30 to 40 minutes. Remove lettuce leaves and serve at once.

LOBSTER NEWBURG

Makes 3 or 4 servings

2 egg yolks, slightly beaten
½ cup heavy cream
¼ cup butter
3 tablespoons sherry
½ teaspoon salt
    nutmeg

    cayenne
¾ pound lobster meat, in
    chunks about size of
    small walnut
    fresh triangles of buttered
    toast

1. Combine eggs and cream. Over low heat, melt butter in medium saucepan.
2. Stir in egg-cream mixture and sherry. Cook, stirring constantly, until mixture thickens.
3. Remove from heat. Mix in a dash of salt, dash of nutmeg, and few grains of cayenne. Add the lobster and gently reheat.
4. Serve hot over toast triangles.

LOBSTER CANTONESE

General Frank Dorn spent many years in China and became an expert on all types of Chinese cooking—Cantonese, Mandarin, and others. This recipe may seem a little difficult, but it really isn't.

Makes 6 servings

2 tablespoons peanut oil (olive oil can be substituted)
1 clove garlic
½ teaspoon salt
   pepper to taste
½ pound raw ground pork
1 tablespoon bamboo shoots, chopped small
1 tablespoon water chestnuts, chopped fine

2 tablespoons finely chopped green onions
2 lobsters, about 2 pounds each
1 cup chicken stock, or broth
1 teaspoon sugar
2 eggs, slightly beaten
1 tablespoon cornstarch
1 tablespoon soy sauce
¼ cup water

1. Mix ground pork, bamboo shoots, water chestnuts, chopped green onions, a little salt, and pepper in a mixing bowl.
2. Drop the live whole lobsters in boiling water, and boil for 5 minutes. Remove the lobsters, and when they have cooled sufficiently to handle, split them lengthwise. Remove the dark veins, or intestinal tracts, and corals, if the latter are found, and throw them away.
3. A Chinese cook then cuts the lobster halves crosswise into pieces from 1 to 1½ inches long. He cuts off the legs, cutting them to about the same length pieces, and cracks open the claws. The Chinese do not remove the meat from the shells, claws, or legs, maintaining that the shells add to the flavor of this dish.
4. However, for American consumption, when chopsticks probably will not be used, the meat can be removed from the shells and cut into chunks about 1 to 1½ inches long. Similarly the meat can be removed from the claws, and the legs if the latter are large enough. The directons are the same in either case.

5. Mix the ground pork combination with the lobster chunks. In a large skillet heat the peanut oil over a low flame. Add the garlic clove, salt and pepper. Allow to sizzle for 2 minutes. Remove the garlic clove. Add lobster chunks and pork combination. Pour in stock and add the sugar. Cover the skillet and cook over a low flame for 10 minutes. Stir in the slightly beaten eggs, and cook for 2 more minutes.
6. While the above is cooking, blend cornstarch, soy sauce, and ¼ cup of water into a smooth paste. When the eggs have cooked for 2 minutes, add the cornstarch paste. Stir to mix thoroughly with other ingredients, and cook until the sauce thickens, about 2 or 3 minutes.
7. To serve, place the lobster chunks with the thick sauce on a platter, and garnish with watercress. As is the case with all Chinese food, it is better to eat this with chopsticks.

The Dorn Cookbook
GENERAL FRANK DORN

LOBSTER CARDINAL

This is the lobster dish of stateliness and beauty, like the bird bearing the same name. Of all the feathered friends who patronize the gourmet feeders outside my window, none is more brilliant, nor has more grace, than the flaming red male cardinal with his distinct crest and patch of black from eye to throat. And with him, or nearby, you'll always see the Missus in her more modest plumage of cinnamon-yellow, but with the same characteristic elegance. For a dish of elegance, proceed with Lobster Cardinal.

Makes 6 servings

3 live lobsters, 1½ pounds each	1 cup milk
	¼ cup tomato paste
3 tablespoons salt	1½ tablespoons minced shallots
1 large bay leaf	¼ teaspoon cayenne pepper
2 sprigs thyme or ½ teaspoon dried thyme	4 tablespoons cognac
	¼ cup heavy cream
12 peppercorns	1 beaten egg yolk
6 tablespoons butter	6 teaspoons grated Parmesan cheese
4 tablespoons flour	

1. In a large kettle, bring to a boil enough water to cover the lobsters (but do not put in lobsters yet). Add the salt, bay leaf, thyme, and peppercorns. Simmer, covered, for about 5 minutes.
2. Plunge the lobsters into the boiling water. Cover and simmer for exactly 20 minutes, drain, and let lobsters cool.
3. When cool enough to handle, split the lobsters lengthwise; remove and discard the tough sac near the eyes. Remove the body meat and the green or yellow "coral." Set aside meat and shells.
4. Remove the claw meat, discarding claw shells, and chop together the claw and body meat. Meanwhile, preheat the oven to 400°.
5. Melt ⅔ of the butter (4 tablespoons) and stir in the flour until blended and smooth. Add the milk, stirring rapidly with a whisk until a thick sauce results. Then cook about 5 minutes, stirring constantly, and add the tomato paste.
6. Melt the remaining butter in a frying pan and add the shallots. Sauté briefly and add the lobster meat, coral, cayenne pepper, and some shakings of salt. Cook briefly, stirring, and sprinkle in 2 tablespoons of the cognac.
7. Stir in the tomato paste sauce and then the cream and bring to a boil. Remove from the heat. Arrange the lobster shells on a large baking dish and sprinkle the insides gently with the remaining 2 tablespoons of the cognac.
8. Fill the shells with all except half a cup of the lobster mixture. Take this remaining ½ cup mixture, combine it with the beaten egg yolk and spoon this lightly over the tops of the filled shells.
9. Sprinkle with Parmesan cheese and bake till bubbling. Run the dish under broiler just briefly enough to give a brown glaze and serve at once.

LOBSTER ALLA DIAVOLO

In Italy, Ada Boni's *Talismano della Felicita* has been recognized for a quarter of a century as the standard cookbook. More than a quarter million copies have been sold—an extraordinary record in a country where the art of cooking is handed down from mother to daughter and written recipes are generally viewed with suspicion and derision. Signora Boni's recipe for delectable Lobster Diavolo is most simple.

Makes 2 to 4 servings

2 medium lobsters (boiled)
2 tablespoons olive oil
2 tablespoons butter, melted
½ cup vinegar
½ teaspoon pepper
5 red pepper seeds
    (optional)

1 teaspoon meat extract,
    dissolved in 1 cup boiling
    water
1 teaspoon tomato paste
1 tablespoon butter
1 teaspoon flour
½ tablespoon prepared mustard

1. Cut lobsters in halves lengthwise and place shell side down in baking dish. Sprinkle with oil and melted butter and bake in hot oven 20 minutes.
2. Place vinegar, pepper, and red pepper seeds together in saucepan and simmer until vinegar is reduced to half quantity.
3. Add meat extract in hot water and tomato paste to vinegar and cook 10 minutes.
4. Mix together butter and flour, blending well, and add slowly to sauce. Mix well, add mustard and pour over baked lobsters.

The Talisman Italian Cook Book
ADA BONI

MIXED SEAFOOD COQUILLE

This interesting combination comes from Vivienne Marquis who, with Patricia Haskell, has written a most informative book on the cheeses of the world—how they are made, how they taste, how to choose and use them. You would do well to add *The Cheese Book* to your library.

Makes 4 to 6 servings

2 cups white sauce (see page 254)	3 tablespoons dry white wine
chives	½ cup scallops, raw
parsley	½ cup crab meat (fresh, frozen, or canned)
½ cup shrimp, half-cooked	½ cup lobster meat, cooked
2 ounces butter	pinch of dry mustard
a few mushrooms	salt and pepper
2 shallots or 1 small onion	grated Parmesan cheese

1. Make 2 cups of white sauce. Chop chives and parsley and set aside.
2. Half-cook the shrimp by dropping them, in their shells, into boiling water for 1½ minutes. Drain; shell and devein shrimp.
3. Heat 2 ounces butter in frying pan over a moderate flame. When hot, add a few mushrooms cut into pieces and sauté mushrooms until golden brown.
4. Add chopped shallots or onion and the white wine. Add the raw scallops, the half-cooked shrimp, the crab meat, and cooked lobster meat; cover pan and cook for about 2 minutes over medium flame. Add the white sauce and cook uncovered for 5 minutes more.
5. Remove from fire and add dry mustard, salt, and pepper to taste, and a scant handful of chopped chives and parsley mixed. Stir all together.
6. Spoon the mixture into individual buttered coquille shells (or small ramekins or a large baking dish) and cover generously with the Parmesan. Broil under medium flame only as long as needed to brown.

The Cheese Book

FROGS' LEGS SAUTÉ PROVENÇALE

Don't forget that Provençale means garlic and plenty of it. Near that handsome old church in Paris, the Val de Grace, there is a little bistro which specializes in dishes Provençale, including Frogs' Legs. In a moment of weakness I ordered them . . . and there followed numerous other moments of weakness. In New York, one naturally goes to La Grenouille for Frogs' Legs, or prepares them at home with James Beard's recipe. "Frogs' legs come in many sizes," notes Mr. Beard, "and for my taste the small ones are by far the best. They are delicately flavored, tender and cook very quickly. About six pairs of the small sort are a good portion. Frogs' legs are better if soaked in milk for an hour or more before cooking."

frogs' legs	garlic—1 clove per
milk	portion
flour	parsley
olive oil	salt and pepper

1. Soak the frogs' legs in milk, dry, and roll them in flour.
2. Sauté them very quickly in olive oil. When nicely browned, add chopped garlic and parsley and blend well. (Use about 1 clove of garlic for each portion. Plenty of parsley, of course.) Salt and pepper to taste.

James Beard's Fish Cookery

MEATS

CHARCOAL BROILED STEAK

Of the many ways of cooking steak this one is best suited to the outdoor charcoal fire. Sirloin, porterhouse, flank, or blade chuck are the best cuts. Steak should be about 3 inches thick, with all the fat left on.

FIRES

Charcoal fires must be made in such a way that all the wood burns evenly, making hot coals at one time. This is done by first selecting the place for the fire where the draft will feed from the front. In rocky country, build a wall on 3 sides leaving front open. In flat lands, dig a pit 6 inches to 1 foot deep. Use dry shredded bark, abandoned bird nests, dry grass, or paper loosely crumpled. Build a wigwam of small twigs over the tinder, then lay logs in log-cabin formation on top. Leave 1 inch for air space between sticks. Remember, a fire needs plenty of air, so avoid packing too tightly. Once started, leave it alone until all the pieces are going well. Then bunch it together with a stick until bed is a flat even mass of hot coals.

CHARCOAL

Most important part of charcoal broiling a steak is the fire. If a supply of well-seasoned wood such as hickory, oak or maple is on hand, you're in real luck for nothing can equal them for putting the right flavor into the meat. The secret is to have a deep bed of coals, 5 or 6 inches at least. When all the flame has gone leaving the coals a glowing red, lay the steak directly on top of the coals. This will smother the fire that will flame up from the melting fat. A little blaze around the edges will do no harm, but the main thing is to keep flames away from the surface of the meat. It's the heat from the coals that does the cooking, not the flames.

TIMING

Broil about 2 minutes, then turn the steak over so both sides are quickly sealed, holding in the juices. For a steak to be at the point where it is the most tender, tasty and juicy, the meat should be broiled to a crisp on the outside, well done for about ½ inch on both sides and then pink turning to red in the very center. The usual time for medium-rare with this method is about 10 minutes on each side. If you're not sure, it is better to make a small cut near the bone for a test rather than to overcook.

The Outdoor Picture Cookbook
BOB JONES

STEAK NINO

This chafing dish *spécialité* is named for a maître d' of New York's Drake Hotel, who made it popular. It is now widely served in better restaurants, usually under the name of Steak Diane, but nowhere is it better prepared than in the Drake Room.

Makes 1 serving

1 14-ounce sirloin steak	salt
2 tablespoons butter	freshly ground pepper
½ teaspoon dry mustard	olive oil
1 teaspoon chopped chives	juice of ¼ lemon
1 teaspoon chopped parsley	
1 teaspoon Worcestershire sauce	

1. Have the butcher trim the meat well and pound it very thin with a mallet. Heat 1 tablespoon of butter together with a few drops of olive oil, the dry mustard, and the chives in a large skillet or chafing dish.
2. Use a low flame, being careful not to scorch the chives. Season the steak with salt and pepper to taste and brush it lightly all over with olive oil.
3. Add steak to the sizzling butter mixture; cook quickly, about 1½ minutes on each side. Remove steak to a warm platter.
4. To the remaining butter mixture in the skillet, add lemon juice, Worcestershire sauce, 1 tablespoon of butter and the parsley. Blend quickly over low flame; pour over steak and serve.

Drake Room, Drake Hotel
New York City

TOURNEDOS NICOISE

Tournedos are slices of beef cut from the heart of the fillet. These de luxe morsels of meat may be prepared as Tournedos

Rossini, Tournedos Melba, Tournedos Béarnaise and in several other styles. All are elegant, as is this—Tournedos Niçoise.

tournedos
peeled, pressed and chopped
   tomatoes, tossed in butter
crushed garlic
chopped tarragon

cooked string beans mixed
   with butter
small potatoes cooked in
   butter

1. Sauté the tournedos in butter, and arrange them in the form of a crown.
2. In the center of each tournedo set a small heap, consisting of ½ tablespoon of peeled, pressed, and chopped tomatoes, tossed in butter, together with a little crushed garlic and chopped tarragon.
3. Surround with small heaps of string beans mixed with butter, and also heaps of small potatoes, cooked in butter, alternating the 2 garnishes.

The Escoffier Cook Book
A. ESCOFFIER

BOEUF À LA MODE

Makes 8 servings

4 pounds round of beef
1 clove garlic
2 onions
2 small carrots
1 cup celery stalks, diced
¼ cup suet or salt pork
   or butter

2 cups tomato purée
2 cups red wine
1 teaspoon salt
10 peppercorns
2 bay leaves

1. Sear the meat.
2. Cook the garlic, onions, carrots, celery in the suet fat, the salt pork, or the butter for 5 minutes using a low flame.
3. Add to the meat. Add wine, tomato purée, salt, peppercorns, and bay leaves.
4. Set over a low fire. Let the meat cook slowly, approximately 3 hours, until tender. The cooking pot should be

of heavy metal so that the heat is spread and there is little danger of burning. There should not be much liquid in the cooking pot at any time but if there seems to be danger of the meat burning add a small amount of hot water.

NOTE:

If desired, young carrots may be added during the last hour of cooking. These are used to garnish the meat platter.

Cooking With a Foreign Flavor
FLORENCE LA GANKE HARRIS

FILLETS OF BEEF RAPALLO

Coming down from the hills, on the road from Genoa to the Mediterranean, one suddenly spies the little town of Santa Margherita nestled in the sheltered bay of the Gulf of Rapallo. The air is scented from the fragrance of camellias and oleander mingled with the salt of the azure sea ahead. Soft breezes rise to greet the visitor to this·dreamy fairyland. The region is known for its fine cuisine. Mildred Knopf's recipe for Fillets of Beef is well named in its honor.

Makes 6 servings

2 ounces butter
1 small onion
1 box fresh mushrooms
6 center slices, 1 inch thick, from a whole tenderloin of beef
salt, pepper, paprika

6 slices bread, 1 inch thick
butter
sage, thyme, and/or marjoram leaves
6 cold boiled potatoes
melted butter, flavored with herbs

1. Preheat broiler for 20 minutes.
2. Render butter in a skillet and slightly brown minced onion. When onion is brown, add box of mushrooms, turn down flame, and allow to simmer slowly.
3. Cut 6 even slices, 1 inch thick, from center of a whole tenderloin and rub each slice with salt, pepper, and paprika. Cut 6 1 inch slices of bread from a loaf of white bread and shape with a sharp kitchen knife to exact shape

of tenderloin slices, then butter thickly on each side. Press a leaf of any preferred fresh herb (thyme, sage, or marjoram) on to each buttered slice of bread. Arrange tenderloin and bread slices alternately on a skewer long enough to handle the whole and long enough to balance ends on the rims of a well-buttered dripping pan.

4. Take boiled potatoes, cut into slices, and drop into dripping pan. Pour additional butter over them and balance the skewer with the alternate slices of meat and bread on the ends of the dripping pan. Place under a very hot broiler and broil for 15 minutes, basting now and again with melted butter flavored with mixed herbs of the variety used on the bread slices.

5. When meat is done, remove the potatoes with a broad spatula to a hot platter, pour a little melted butter over them, then hold the skewer over the potatoes and carefully push the meat and bread off on the top of the potatoes. Empty the mushrooms and contents of skillet over all. Replace under broiler to reheat for 1 minute. Serve quickly.

NOTE:

A skewer long enough to accommodate the slices of tenderloin and bread and at the same time long enough to permit its ends to rest on either end of a dripping pan is not the simplest thing in the world to find. I know because I spent the better part of a week, darting in and out of hardware stores, looking. My search came to an end when a bright young man in one of the stores suggested I buy a 10-cent length (the exact length required) of heavy wire and allow him to straighten it and file one end to a point. This particular wire is the approximate circumference of a #8 knitting needle.

The Perfect Hostess Cook Book
MILDRED O. KNOPF

DAVE CHASEN'S HOBO STEAK

Of Dave Chasen, whose Chasen's Restaurant is a justifiably famous Hollywood landmark and a national institution (like the National Gallery of Art in Washington, D. C.—but with much better food), it can be said that he prepared for his role as chief caterer to the Hollywood gourmet by eating, and whipping up for his friends such delectations that twenty years later they still remember the special flavor of the beef or the piquancy of the dressing.

I wish I had time to tell you about the Hobo Steak. It's Dave's invention and for my money I'd much rather have it around than heavy water or any of these other new-fangled ideas. There's a 1½-inch crust of salt that keeps the natural juices of the steak from seeping out and it's absolutely the most—I mean when you even think about it it's—well, go try it yourself one of these days. I see it's time for dinner and I've just written myself into one hell of an appetite.

BUDD SCHULBERG

Makes 4 to 6 servings

2 sirloin steaks, cut 2 inches thick	4 cups salt
	1 cup water (about)
1 teaspoon freshly ground black pepper	½ pound butter
	3 to 12 bread slices, thinly cut

1. Season steaks with black pepper. Place side by side in large skillet or deep broiler pan with fat edges toward perimeter of pan. Slip two lengths of cotton string under each steak (crosswise of steak and dividing steak roughly into thirds lengthwise); tie up steaks.
2. Combine salt and water to make soft mush; spread half the mush about 1½ inches thick over tops of steaks.
3. Place skillet or pan on broiler rack with top of steaks about 3 inches below unit or tip of flame. Broil 15 to 20 minutes, or until layer of salt begins to separate from meat. With broad spatula or pancake turner, lift off salt; turn steaks.
4. Using remaining salt mush, cover uncooked surface of meat. Continue broiling 15 to 20 minutes, or until salt begins to separate or rise from meat.
5. During last few minutes of broiling period, toast bread; keep it warm.
6. In another skillet or heavy frying pan, melt butter, allowing it to sizzle but not brown. At end of broiling period, remove salt from steaks; cut steaks in ¼-inch slices. Add

slices to butter in pan; sauté ½ minute or less on each side. Place on toast; serve immediately.

Holiday Book of Food and Drink

ROAST BEEF AND YORKSHIRE PUDDING

While Lawry's of Los Angeles may dispute this, there is probably no roast beef like that of Simpson's of London. Unfortunately for our readers, their beefs run a bit (!) larger than home cooking permits. Simpson's says, "Best roasting joints are sirloins and ribs—the only way to roast is on the spit or roasting jack. Sirloins of about thirty-five pounds need about two hours and foreribs of about twenty-four pounds need about three and a half hours."

There is "A Song in Praise of Old English Roast Beef," written about three hundred years ago by Richard Leveridge.

The captain of an American naval vessel recently had his men sing this song before meals because he felt it started their digestive juices working. Here are a few stanzas.

When mighty Roast Beef was the Englishman's *Food,*
It enobled our Veins and enriched our Blood,
Our Soldiers were brave and our Courtiers were good.
 Oh the Roast Beef *of Old England,*
 And *Old English* Roast Beef.

But since we have learn'd from all-conquering France
To eat their Ragouts as well as to dance,
We are fed up with nothing but vain Complaisance.
 Oh the Roast Beef, *etc.*

Our Fathers of old were robust, stout and strong,
And kept open House with good Cheer all Day long,
Which made their plump Tenants rejoice in this song,
 Oh the Roast Beef, *etc.*

Oh then they had Stomachs to eat and to fight,
And when Wrongs were a-cooking to do themselves
 right!
 Oh the Roast Beef *of Old England,*
 And *Old English* Roast Beef.

Here is a practical recipe for a standing rib roast or rolled rib roast:

Heat oven to 325° F. (slow moderate). Season meat with salt and pepper. Place fat side up, in open pan. Do not add water; do not cover; do not baste.
Roast:
Rare: 18 to 20 minutes per pound
Medium: 22 to 25 minutes per pound
Well done: 27 to 30 minutes per pound
Add 10 minutes per pound for rolled roast.

SIMPSON'S RECIPE FOR YORKSHIRE PUDDING

4 eggs	salt
1 quart milk	drippings from roast
½ pound flour	

1. Put flour and a good pinch of salt into basin.
2. Break in eggs and add half of the milk, stir gradually and add to remainder of the milk by degrees until a smooth batter is formed.
3. Beat well for 10 minutes, allow to stand for 1 hour, beat again for a few minutes.
4. Place dish and drippings in oven to get hot, then pour in batter and cook for 25 minutes, then place under meat in front of open fire for about 15 minutes.

Simpson's Restaurant
London, England

BEEF WELLINGTON

Here is one of the smartest-looking beef dishes to appear on a dinner table . . . roast fillet of beef, spread with pâté de fois gras and encrusted with pastry! The famous Twenty-One Restaurant in New York serves a fine Beef Wellington which you should try.

Makes 6 servings

4- pound fillet of beef
1 stick of butter
salt
freshly ground pepper
1 cup sliced carrots
½ cup sliced celery
½ cup sliced onion
⅓ cup chopped parsley
1½ teaspoons chopped fresh
rosemary

½ teaspoon crushed rosemary
1 bay leaf
pâté de fois gras, approximately ¾ pound
pie or puff pastry
milk or egg yolk
1 cup veal stock
1 truffle, or ¼ cup mush-
rooms, chopped

1. Spread the butter over the meat. Sprinkle with salt and pepper. Preheat the oven to very hot (450° F.).
2. Spread the vegetables, parsley, rosemary, and bay leaf in a shallow baking pan and set the roast on them.
3. Cook at 450° F. for 40 to 50 minutes and remove the roast. Allow to cool completely. Then spread pâté over the entire surface, reserving ½ cup pâté for sauce.
4. Make a pie pastry or puff pastry, roll it to ⅛-inch thickness and wrap around the pâtéed roast. Trim the pastry edges and moisten with water; press edges together to seal. If you wish, decorate the top with a ½-inch lattice strip of pastry.
5. Place in a baking pan, seam side down and brush the crust with milk or with egg yolk beaten with a teaspoon of milk. Prick the crust in several spots to allow the steam to escape.
6. Bake in preheated hot oven (425° F.) for 15 to 20 minutes or until brown. Transfer to warm platter and keep warm. Add to the roasting pan the veal stock, ¼ cup pâté de fois gras and chopped mushrooms (or truffle). Simmer 10 to 15 minutes or until a sauce forms.
7. Slice the crust-and-beef. Serve the sauce separately.

MUNICH BEEF

At eleven A.M. each day, thousands of people from all over gather in front of the Munich City Hall, to await the appearance of the glöckenspiel, a pageant of figures which move, carousel-like, around the clock tower.

This is but one of Munich's many attractions. Munich is one of the most interesting cities in Europe. It is the home of the fabulous *Deutsches Museum* where you go down into a replica of a coal mine, see all sorts of motors and contraptions at work, and find a thousand other fascinations. The *Alte Pinocotek* in Munich is one of the truly great art museums containing some of the best paintings in the world (particularly Rubens'). The Munich opera house is a gem of rare beauty. There are also many church interiors beautifully decorated in the white baroque style, particularly one called The Church in the Meadow, located in a nearby town called Weis. The surrounding area abounds in unique castles, lovely lakes and magnificent scenery. For me, Munich holds an added attraction because it is the place where the famous Nymphenburg figures are made. Designed by an artist named Bustelli, these porcelain figurines compare favorably with the best of Meissen.

Each year, Munich holds an *Oktoberfest,* or harvest festival, and then everyone, young and old, has a happy time drinking good Munich beer, singing and making merry.

Berneita Tolson and Edith McCaig have collected a number of excellent recipes using beer, and Munich, the biggest beer-drinking city, would naturally have a special meat-and-beer dish. You can prepare it the day before serving, if you wish; it can be reheated and tastes even better than when first made.

Makes 6 servings

3 pounds lean beef, cut into 2-inch cubes	2 12-ounce cans beer
3 tablespoons fat	1 tablespoon lemon juice
1 cup minced onion	¼ cup currant jelly
1 cup sliced carrots	1 teaspoon dehydrated orange rind
1½ teaspoons salt	2 tablespoons flour
½ teaspoon black pepper	canned or cooked new potatoes (optional)
2 teaspoons monosodium glutamate (MSG)	chopped parsley

1. In a heavy kettle, melt the fat and brown the meat well on all sides. Add the onions and cook a few minutes longer. Then add the carrots, salt and pepper, MSG, and beer.

2. Cover and cook over low heat for 3 hours, adding more water if needed. Then add the lemon juice, jelly, and orange rind.
3. Mix the flour with a little water and stir into the kettle to thicken the gravy. Cook, stirring, for 5 more minutes.
4. You may add small canned or cooked new potatoes near the end of the cooking time if you wish. Garnish dish with chopped parsley and serve.

The Beer Cookbook
BERNEITA TOLSON AND
EDITH MC CAIG

HUNGARIAN BEEF PAPRIKASH

You may wonder why the word paprikash is sometimes spelled without the "h"—namely, paprikas. It's because in Hungarian, a final "s" becomes "sh." Either way—paprikas or paprikash, it turns out to be pronounced the same in English . . . which reminds me of an amusing experience when I owned a farm in Ulster County, up near the art colony of Woodstock in New York State. A boarding house nearby catered to Hungarians and one day I was introduced to a group of new boarders. Shortly after, I met them at the General Store and in unison they said, "Hello Mr. Kish!" Gently I remonstrated that my name is "Small," not "Kish," when I realized that in Hungarian Small is *Kish,* but spelled, if you please, "Kiss."

Beef Paprikash usually calls for hot paprika powder, but for his recipe Joseph Pasternak prefers a mixture of the very hot kind with the mild, sweetish paprika, to give it a more delicate flavor. You may have to do a little searching for a source of supply, but you'll be well repaid to do so.

Makes 6 to 8 servings

3 pounds rump or sirloin tip
3 tablespoons shortening
1 large onion, minced
1 clove garlic, minced
1 tomato, peeled and minced
1 green pepper, peeled and minced

1 tablespoon paprika, sweet and hot mixed
salt, pepper, if needed
green pepper rings for garnish

1. Trim the excess fat from the meat. Wipe with a damp paper towel and cut the meat into 1½-inch pieces. Sear them on all sides in the shortening.
2. Add the minced vegetables and garlic and cover. Cook slowly for 2 hours, adding ½ cup water if necessary to prevent sticking and burning.
3. When almost done, remove from the heat and stir in the paprika. Continue cooking slowly, adding a little more water if necessary to make plenty of gravy.
4. When the meat is tender, taste and add salt and pepper if needed. Garnish with green pepper rings and serve very hot with egg barley, rice, potatoes, or noodles.

Cooking with Love and Paprika
JOSEPH PASTERNAK

BEEF STROGANOFF

Since man is never satisfied, even with the best, I decided to improve on Beef Stroganoff—a 'purpose which might seem almost impertinent. But what could be better than to combine the Russian with the strange combination of flavors from the Javanese Shrimp Sauce for shellfish and meats. . . . The combination itself is simple enough, but the preparation of the two dishes takes time and patience. I believe the result is tops for all meat dishes I know, but you should judge for yourself. If desired, you can omit the sour cream in the recipe for Beef Stroganoff.

GENERAL FRANK DORN

Makes 4 servings

1½ pounds lean beef (best meat for this dish is tenderloin, but sirloin will do well if you take the time to cut out *all* fat)	½ pound fresh mushrooms 2 tablespoons butter ½ pint sour cream 1 tablespoon flour salt and paprika to taste

1. Cut beef across the grain into strips about ¼ inch thick. Then cut strips into pieces about 1 inch long. Place butter

in a deep skillet. When hot add the beef and cook for 15 minutes under a cover, turning the meat over occasionally.

2. Cut the mushrooms into small pieces, and add to the beef in the skillet. Cook with the meat for 10 minutes. If the pan becomes dry, add a small quantity of butter.

3. Place the meat and mushrooms in the top of a double boiler, leaving the juices in the skillet.

4. Add 1 tablespoon of butter and 1 tablespoon of flour to the juices in the skillet. Melt over a slow flame and stir until the mixture is smooth. Add sour cream. Stir over a low flame until cream and other ingredients are thoroughly mixed.

5. Pour the contents of the skillet into the top of the double boiler with the meat and mushrooms. Stir and cook for 10 minutes.

6. Place Beef Stroganoff inside a large rice ring on a platform or round serving dish. Pour Javanese Shrimp Sauce over it, and serve.

JAVANESE SHRIMP SAUCE

6 strips bacon, chopped small
2 bell peppers, chopped fine
2 large onions, chopped fine
12 bay leaves
¼ pound butter
¼ teaspoon Tabasco sauce
1 teaspoon peppercorns
½ teaspoon salt
1 teaspoon whole cloves
1 teaspoon crushed cinnamon sticks
½ teaspoon celery salt
½ teaspoon sage
½ teaspoon paprika

1 teaspoon dry mustard
2 tablespoons sugar
½ teaspoon ground ginger
2 cups dry red wine
½ cup brandy
juice of 2 oranges
juice of 2 lemons
peel or rind of ½ an orange, cut up very small
peel or rind of ½ a lemon, cut up very small
1½ pounds shrimps, cleaned, cooked, and shelled

1. Sauté bacon, onions, bell peppers, and bay leaves in a skillet. Add butter and stir until melted.

2. Add all seasonings and ingredients—except shrimps—and stir constantly over a low flame. Add wine and brandy, and cover the pan.

3. Allow to simmer under cover for about 15 minutes.

4. Add shrimps, and stir until shrimps are broken up and

more or less dissolved. Simmer under cover for 10 minutes.
5. Pour over prepared Beef Stroganoff.

The Dorn Cookbook

BOILED BEEF AND COTECHINO

Few Americans think of boiled beef as the gastronomic treat it is known for in Central Europe. In Vienna there was a restaurant that was held in high esteem for its boiled beef—twenty-four different varieties of it, to be exact. The restaurant was Meissl & Schadn, an eating-place of international reputation.

In Vienna a person who couldn't talk learnedly about at least a dozen different cuts of boiled beef, didn't belong, no matter how much money he'd made, or whether the Kaiser had awarded him the title of *Hofrat* (court councillor) or *Kommerzialrat.*

JOSEPH WECHSBERG

Makes 6 servings

4 pounds bottom round (a piece that is almost solid meat)
1 1-to-1¼-pound *cotechino* (Italian fresh sausage)
1 knuckle of veal
4 medium-sized onions
2 leeks
bunch of parsley
bunch of carrots
1 parsnip

outer stalks and leaves of 1 large or 2 small bunches of celery
1 green pepper, cut into pieces
2 cans Campbell's Condensed Consommé
6 cans water
1 teaspoon thyme
2 bay leaves
salt, pepper
1 medium-sized cabbage

1. Sear all sides of meat, which has been rubbed with flour, by placing in a very hot (550° F.) oven for 20 minutes.
2. Tie into a single bunch the leeks, parsley, 1 carrot, parsnip, and celery. Place this and the meat, onions, and seasoning, together with the soup and water, in large pressure cooker (pressure canner). Add the knuckle of veal, close the cooker, but place over a *very* low flame.
3. After 4½ hours, open cooker. (If flame has been low enough, the pressure in the cooker will be practically at

that of the atmosphere and the weight can be lifted without cooling; there will be only a wisp of steam escaping.)

4. Remove the bunch of parsley, celery, etc., and skim off any grease. Add cabbage cut into 6 segments with the stem and inner core removed, rest of bunch of carrots, sliced, the rest of celery, chopped, and the sliced green pepper. Close cooker and bring up to 15 pounds pressure. Remove from flame and open when pressure drops.

5. One hour before meal is to be served, make numerous small holes in the skin of the *cotechino* with a sharp fork and boil it slowly in water to cover for 1 hour. Cut into 6 slices and serve 1 with each portion of boiled beef and Chives Sauce.

6. Serve 6 cups of bouillon from the liquid. Then serve the meat with Chives Sauce, and the cabbage, carrots, and celery. Return unused meat and vegetables to the liquid, remove veal knuckle, place in bowl, cover, and put in refrigerator. Chick peas go well with this dish.

NOTE:

If you serve 4 instead of 6, you will be very grateful the next day when you taste the marvelous aspic you will have. This can be served with a piece of the meat and the vegetables left over, or a 3½-minute boiled egg (cold and with the shell carefully removed to leave the egg unbroken) may be added for each person.

Blue Trout and Black Truffles
JOSEPH WECHSBERG

CHIVES SAUCE

Makes 2 cups sauce

3 tablespoons butter	3 tablespoons chopped chives
3 tablespoons flour	1 cup sour cream
1 cup meat stock	salt and pepper

1. In a double boiler, melt the butter and blend the flour into it. Add the meat stock. Stir.
2. Add the chopped chives, stir and cook until sauce thickens.
3. Stir in sour cream, add salt and pepper, and serve when heated. If ready too soon, turn off flame and cover tightly to prevent skin forming.

The Emily Post Cookbook

SAUERBRATEN MIT KARTOFFEL KLÖSSE

(POT ROAST WITH POTATO DUMPLINGS)

Luchow's, on East 14th Street in New York City, is America's most famous German restaurant and from his upstairs art-decorated office, Jan Mitchell runs it with efficiency and love. Luchow's has an interesting background which he tells about.

"Luchow's is more than a restaurant; it is a way of life. August Guido Luchow, who created it, and whose mirror and portrait are now the only visible reminders of his expansive, happy personality, is still present in the spirit of the restaurant he founded, in its devotion to good living and good friends.

"In acquiring Luchow's it was my object to bring back the splendor of the old days, as well as to preserve what remained of them. Especially I wanted to bring back the festivals—the Venison Festival, the Goose Feast, the Bock Beer Festival, and the May Wine Festival, with beer served in the old beer mugs, replicas of the menus of 1900, German bands playing, and all the rest that memory recalls. One of my rewards has been the heartwarming appreciation of the patrons who have thanked me for preserving one of the few New York landmarks that survive.

"But a more personal satisfaction comes especially at Christmas time, when the largest indoor tree in the city towers twenty-five feet or more in the Café, aglow with five hundred electric candles and original nineteenth-century toys imported from Germany. The holy village is beneath, with the church bells chiming hymns and the Apostles revolving in the tower, all hand-carved by famous woodcarvers in Oberammergau, Bavaria, and the orchestra plays carols while the diners sing. Some of these diners have been coming for a half-century, and the waiters who serve them did so when they both were young. Nor has the Christmas menu changed, with its oxtail soup, boiled carp, roast goose with chestnut stuffing, creamed onions, pumpernickel, plum pudding with brandy sauce, and ice cream Santa Clauses.

"And when the lights are turned down at six o'clock on Christmas Eve, the orchestra plays 'Silent Night,' and the tree blazes suddenly with its own special glory, the true reward comes to me. The old friends of August Luchow shake my hand, often with the tears on their cheeks, and they say to me, 'If August should come in tonight, he would feel at home. Nothing has been changed.' "

Makes 6 or more servings

3 pounds round steak	1 pint red wine vinegar
1 tablespoon salt	2 bay leaves
½ teaspoon pepper	2 tablespoons kidney fat
2 onions, sliced	6 tablespoons butter
1 carrot, sliced	5 tablespoons flour
1 stalk celery, chopped	1½ cups sugar
4 cloves	8 or 10 gingersnaps, crushed
4 peppercorns	

1. Wipe steak with damp cloth; season with salt and pepper. Place in earthen, glass, or enamelware bowl. Combine onions, carrot, celery, cloves, peppercorns, vinegar, and bay leaves and pour over meat. Cover and put in refrigerator 4 days.
2. On fifth day remove from refrigerator, drain meat, sauté in kidney fat and 1 tablespoon butter in enamelware, glass or earthenware utensil, until seared on all sides. Add marinade liquid and bring to boil, then lower heat and let simmer about 3 hours.
3. Melt remaining 5 tablespoons butter in a pan. Stir flour smoothly into it. Add sugar, blend, and let brown to nice dark color. Add to simmering meat mixture. Cover and continue cooking until meat is tender, about 1 hour longer.
4. Remove meat to a warmed serving platter. Stir crushed gingersnaps into the pot juices and cook until thickened. Pour this special sauerbraten gravy over meat.
5. Serve with potato or bread dumplings. A fine full-bodied red wine is a fitting complement to this well-known dish.

Luchow's German Cookbook

POTATO DUMPLINGS

Here is a recipe by an authority on German cooking and a noted cookbook author.

Makes 5 servings

6 medium-sized potatoes (about 2 pounds) 3 eggs	6 tablespoons of flour buttered crumbs

1. Boil the potatoes and let stand for a few hours or overnight, still in their jackets.
2. Peel the potatoes and mash them or put through a ricer. Then add the eggs and the flour and roll the mixture into little balls.
3. Chill in the refrigerator for about an hour before cooking.
4. Cook in lightly salted water that is just under the boiling point. When the dumplings are finished they will rise to the top.
5. Serve hot with melted brown butter and crumbs.

NOTE:

To make sure your mixture is of the right consistency, you can test by making a single dumpling and cooking. If this doesn't hold together, add a little more flour.

An original recipe
by HELMUT RIPPERGER

BOEUF BOURGUIGNON

This is one of the noblest stand-bys of *la cuisine française.* The French housewife's genius in making a commonplace stew into something exotic and supremely flavorful is demonstrated in this aromatic dish. Wander over the hillsides of Nuits-St. Georges or Vosne-Romanée on an autumn evening in peaceful days and peer into the kitchen of the wine grower's house. This is the dish that is likely to be simmering on the back of the stove: a peasant dish, if you wish, but fit for any patrician palate. At the risk of repeating a well-known recipe, we would like to give you a Burgundian's own version of this dish, straight from her own notebook.

Dry boiled rice is a good companion piece, and so is a vigorous red wine, such as a Corton, Pommard, or California Pinot Noir. A cold winter's night can be brightened in many ways, but rarely in a more earthy and satisfying manner than this.

PHINEAS BECK

Makes 6 servings

2 tablespoons butter
2 pounds lean stewing beef
1 tablespoon flour
  salt, pepper
1½ cups dry red wine
½ pound small onions
1 carrot
½ cup mushrooms

clove of garlic
6 shallots
  bouquet garni of parsley,
    thyme and bay leaf
  veal knuckle
½ cup Madeira
  liqueur glass of brandy

1. In an iron casserole, bubbling with butter, brown lean stewing beef, cut in 1½-inch cubes, until the meat is "closed." Remove the meat, add flour and make a *roux brun*. Add salt, pepper, and dry red wine.
2. Slice onions, carrot, mushrooms, garlic, and shallots. Brown ⅔ of your onions apart in butter.
3. Return the meat to the casserole, add the sliced vegetables, the browned onions, and bouquet garni. Add a veal knuckle, if one is obtainable. Add also Madeira if you have some, and enough water to bring the liquid level with the meat.
4. Put the lid on this poetic ensemble and allow it to simmer very gently from 3 to 4 hours, until the meat is tender. Half an hour before serving add a liqueur glass of brandy. Strain the vegetables from the dark, russet-red sauce before serving.

Clementine in the Kitchen
PHINEAS BECK

ESTERHÁZY ROSTBRATEN

The Esterházy family was one of the oldest and the richest of the Hungarian nobility. They played an important role in Vienna. This elaborate way of preparing a steak was named in their honor and is one of the best-known Viennese dishes, second only to *schnitzel* in popularity.

Makes 8 servings

3 pounds round steak, cut
    1½ inches thick
4 carrots, coarsely chopped
2 onions, coarsely chopped
2 parsnips, coarsely chopped
2 stalks celery, coarsely
    chopped
3 to 4 tablespoons fat
1½ tablespoons flour

¼ cup sour cream
1 cup meat stock (or bouillon
    cube)
2 tablespoons thick brown
    butter sauce
2 teaspoons capers
1 teaspoon paprika
    salt and pepper
¼ cup Madeira wine

1. Prepare sauce by sautéing the chopped vegetables lightly in hot fat. When they are soft, sprinkle them with flour and blend in well the sour cream, meat stock, brown sauce, capers and paprika.
2. Sear the meat on both sides in hot fat quickly and well, in a frying pan, or dot with melted butter and slide under the broiler for 1 minute or 2 for each side. Season the steak with salt and pepper.
3. Place in a large casserole with a tight-fitting cover and add the sauce. Adjust the cover and bake in a moderate oven (325-350° F.) for 25 minutes.
4. Remove cover and add Madeira. Replace cover and bake an additional 5 minutes. Serve in the casserole.

The Viennese Cookbook
IRMA RHODE

HUNGARIAN GOULASH

There are plenty of stories about Hungarians and their foibles. This one you'll like. George Lang of the Four Seasons Restaurant in New York tells of the parlor game he once played with his Budapest-raised colleagues. They took a Hungarian love poem and translated it into German. They translated the German into French, the French into English, the English into Italian, and finally the Italian back into Hungarian. This final translation emerged not as a love poem but as a recipe for goulash! Like most Hungarian stories, this one can be believed, or not.

The Hungarians are an interesting people: the peasants are colorful, the intellectuals sit by the hour in coffee houses—or at least they used to—and argue on either side of any question, while they listen with passion to *Zigeiner* (Gypsy) music. They place the leader of the Gypsy orchestra on a pedestal, referring to him with great respect as *Primash*— number one. A number of leading American scientists are of Hungarian birth or extraction, among them Edward Teller, the Nobel physicist, and Albert Szent-Györgyi, who discovered vitamin C. My maternal grandparents were Hungarians and it was because I had heard so much about the beauties of Budapest, that we traveled there a few years ago, only to run into one of those unscheduled experiences one prefers to forget: being quarantined inside our hotel for two solid weeks because some chambermaid was suspected of having smallpox. But despite our predicament and that of three hundred others, I must say the Hungarian Government treated us well—filled us with good food, good music and a quite acceptable wine called Bull's Blood. It is available in America and is reasonably priced. Have your dealer order it and try it with your goulash.

Makes 8 to 10 servings

4 pounds beef (chuck or rump), cut in 2-inch pieces	6 onions, coarsely chopped
	3 tablespoons paprika
	1½ teaspoons salt
2 strips bacon or salt pork or 2 tablespoons bacon fat	2 green peppers, coarsely chopped

1. Brown half the beef in its own fat in a large skillet; transfer to a kettle or Dutch oven and repeat with other half.
2. Rinse the skillet with a cup of water and add the liquid to the meat. Cover and cook slowly over low heat.
3. Chop the bacon and fry in skillet; add the onions and brown lightly.
4. Stir in the paprika and salt; then combine with the simmering meat. Stir in the uncooked green peppers and continue cooking slowly for about 2 hours or until the meat is tender—not soft.

5. Serve piping hot from an earthenware casserole. Serve with noodles, a green salad and dark bread.

> *The Art of Hungarian Cooking*
> PAULA POGANY BENNETT AND
> VELMA R. CLARK

BEEF STEW

For more years than many of our readers are old, Haydn S. Pearson has been writing flavorsome inspirational essays on country life. *Life* Magazine considers Pearson's pieces as "among the most delightful bits of nature writing now being done in the United States." Any attempt to conform this essay on beef stew to the style of our other recipes would be giving it a presumptuous city-slicker treatment. This recipe is therefore printed just as it appeared in *The New York Times* and in Haydn Pearson's book, *Country Flavor*. Other Pearson recipes are Red Flannel Hash (page 249) and Corn Chowder (page 64).

Philosophers have long pondered the problem of rise and fall among nations. Ingenious and logical hypotheses have been promulgated. There are those who believe that a nation's eating habits and its position among its peers have a direct correlation. We view with perturbation the decline of beef stew.

We do not refer to quantity. A dish allegedly beef stew is commonly offered on menus. A concoction with that label is tossed together in many a home. It is the quality that needs attention. Beef stew, humble and plebeian by reputation, can be one of life's gastronomical experiences. But it isn't a dish to be mixed in casual nonchalance.

First of all, one's attitude must be right. The making of a beef stew should be approached in a leisurely manner and with full concentration. If one is disquieted about the stock market, if he's wondering whether he should be putting on the storm windows or paying the month's bills, he cannot receive all that beef stew has to offer.

A proper stew should always be made in the morning. After the chunks of beef are half cooked, the vegetables should be added and cooked right in the beef-flavored water. It is rankest heresy to cook the vegetables separately. A stew should contain white potatoes, carrots, onions, turnips, just a bit of cabbage, and plenty of sweet potatoes. It's unthinkable to rate a beef stew triple-A priority that doesn't include sweet potatoes. After the stew is cooked, it should be set aside to cool. It is the reheating that brings out all the subtle nuances, the utterly delicious and the completely satisfying flavor. There's no proof that Jupiter served beef stew at the Olympian meals; but, if he had known about it, ambrosia would not have received so much publicity.

Country Flavor
HAYDN S. PEARSON

PLANKED HAMBURGER CLUB STEAKS

I like one man's dream of "the perfect balanced menu"—sparkling Burgundy balanced with hamburgers.

Here is a hamburger recipe that certainly calls for something special to go with it . . . like sparkling Burgundy. Well, beer, then.

Makes 4 servings

2 pounds ground beef, round or chuck	2 cups cooked vegetables (such as peas, green beans, carrots, asparagus, baby beets, green lima beans, Brussels sprouts, or whole kernel corn)
1 tablespoon melted butter	
1 teaspoon salt	
¼ teaspoon pepper	
3 cups hot mashed potatoes	
1 egg yolk	
1 tablespoon milk	

1. Preheat broiler and rack at full heat for 15 minutes.
2. Prepare mashed potatoes.
3. Shape meat into 4 large oval-shaped steaks about ¾-inch thick.
4. Place oiled plank or greased ovenproof platter in oven to heat.
5. Grease broiler rack lightly and place steaks on rack so that top of meat is 2 inches from the tip of the flame. Broil at full heat for 2 minutes on each side or just long

enough to sear. Transfer to heated plank or ovenproof platter. Spread with melted butter and season with salt and pepper.

6. Outline edge of plank with a border of mashed potatoes (use a pastry bag for an attractive design). Brush with beaten egg yolk mixed with milk.

7. Place in a hot oven (450° F.) for 7 to 10 minutes or until potatoes are lightly browned. Arrange seasoned hot vegetables in the spaces around the meat. Serve directly from the plank or platter.

The Hamburger Cook Book
ESTHER K. SCHWARTZ AND RUTH KOOPERMAN

AL CAPP'S NEW ENGLAND BOILED DINNER

Al Capp is known for his creation of Li'l Abner and other wry characters. Being a New Englander, his favorite recipe is naturally New England Boiled Dinner, and Al Capp declares that the following directions are authentic and taken from a family cookbook.

Makes 4 to 6 servings

5 pounds corned beef	3 large yellow turnips
6 peppercorns	8 small onions
½ clove of garlic (optional)	6 medium-sized potatoes
3 small parsnips	1 head of cabbage
6 large carrots	parsley

1. Wipe 5-pound piece of corned beef with a damp cloth and tie to keep in shape. Place it in cold water to cover. Add peppercorns and garlic.

2. After meat has cooked for 4 hours, remove it from the pot.

3. Peel, quarter and simmer in the stock for 30 minutes, the parsnips, carrots and turnips. Skin and add the onions.

4. Peel, quarter and simmer the potatoes in the stock for 15 minutes longer.

5. Cut head of cabbage into wedges, add, and simmer until tender (for about 10 to 15 minutes).

6. Reheat the meat in the stock. Serve it on a platter surrounded by the vegetables, garnished with parsley.

NOTE:
You may, of course, follow the old-fashioned method of cooking the cabbage much longer, in fact, for several hours. A
piece of salt pork, about 2 pounds, is sometimes added for
the last 2 hours.

Stars in Your Kitchen
MARTA MICHEL

ZÜRICH LEBERSPIESSLI

Zürich, in Switzerland, is a city dominated by banking. They
say that if a Swiss banker jumps out of a window, follow him,
because there's 6 percent in it. But the Swiss banker can be
as friendly as anyone else, the countryside around Zürich is
most beautiful, and the Swiss do love good food. One of the
specialties of Zürich is Leberspiessli, or liver-on-skewers, and
this is the way it's made:

Makes 2 to 3 servings

1 pound calves' liver   salt and pepper to taste
  sage leaves   butter for frying
  bacon strips

1. Skin the liver and cut it into strips about 1½ inches long
   and ¼ inch thick. Season with salt and crushed sage
   leaves. (Or, if you prefer, wrap the whole sage leaves
   around the pieces of liver.)
2. Wrap the liver in the bacon strips and spear on wooden or
   metal skewers. Five or 6 pieces on each skewer will make
   1 portion.
3. Brown on both sides in a generous amount of butter.

NOTE:
This can be varied by broiling on both sides until brown.
Leberspiessli is usually served on a layer of green beans.

Gusti Egli's Columna-Treu Restaurant
Zürich, Switzerland

BEEF TONGUE WITH RAISINS, PRUNES, AND ALMONDS

Makes 6 servings

1 fresh beef tongue	½ cup tarragon or cider
2 onions, sliced	vinegar
2 bay leaves	¼ cup red wine
3 sprigs parsley	½ cup sugar
½ lemon, sliced	¼ teaspoon ground cloves
6 whole peppercorns	¼ teaspoon cinnamon
1 tablespoon salt	¼ teaspoon mixed spices
1 teaspoon black pepper	½ cup seedless raisins
1 tablespoon butter	1 cup soaked prunes
1 teaspoon flour	¼ cup blanched almonds

1. Wipe fresh tongue with a damp cloth. Place in a good-sized pot and cover with cold water. Add sliced onions, bay leaves, parsley, lemon, whole peppercorns, salt, and black pepper.
2. Bring to a gentle boil, then simmer between 2 and 3 hours, depending on size and tenderness of tongue. Test with a fork. As long as it feels hard, it is *not* done. When tender, remove from liquid, pull off skin, and return to pot to cool in its own water.
3. Melt butter. Rub in flour and gradually add tarragon or cider vinegar and red wine, stirring constantly until thickened. Add sugar, stir once more, then add the following spices: ground cloves, cinnamon, and mixed spices.
4. Warm raisins, prunes, and almonds in this sauce. Place tongue in an iron pot or large, deep skillet and pour sauce over the tongue. Simmer very slowly for ½ hour, turning tongue occasionally and basting every few minutes with the sauce. Serve, carved into even slices, on a hot platter surrounded and strewn with the raisins, prunes, and almonds.

NOTE:
If you have a little extra time, remove the prune pits and stuff the prunes with additional blanched almonds.

The Perfect Hostess Cook Book
MILDRED O. KNOPF

SWEETBREADS EN BROCHETTE

Makes 6 servings

2 pairs sweetbreads	butter
18 to 20 mushrooms	salt and pepper
4 or 5 rashers bacon	chopped parsley

1. Soak sweetbreads in cold water for ½ hour, then simmer in salted water for 20 minutes. Cool in cold water and remove membrane, tubes and excess fat.
2. Cut prepared sweetbreads in 1-inch squares. Wash and remove stems from mushrooms.
3. Cut bacon in 1-inch pieces and sauté for a few minutes until partially cooked. Drain on absorbent paper.
4. Alternate pieces of sweetbread, mushroom caps, and squares of bacon on medium-sized skewers, allowing one skewer for each serving.
5. Brush well with butter, sprinkle with salt and pepper, and broil, turning frequently until the sweetbreads are nicely browned and the mushrooms cooked.
6. Sprinkle with chopped parsley and pour a little melted butter over each skewer before serving.

VARIATIONS:
You may use small cubes of ham with the sweetbreads, or use the tiny plum or cherry tomatoes for a change of flavor.

The Fireside Cook Book
JAMES A. BEARD

CERVELLES AU BEURRE NOIRE

It is said that New York moves uptown at the rate of an inch a day. Whether or not this is so, the section of Manhattan known as Yorkville—beginning at 85th Street and Park Avenue and roughly ending at the Mayor's residence in Carl Schurz Park—appears now to be blossoming as an eating area. There are all standards of German restaurants, as of old, but along with them now are French, Greek, American, and others, including a four-star Casa Brazil and an ever-busy Brochetteria where only skewered dishes are available. Among this polyglot mixture, there is Un Coin de Paris, a family-run bistro that could be right out of rue de Seine, rue Jacob, or any other Left Bank street. The menu is limited but the fare is good . . . and in summer there is a pleasant garden for outdoor eating. Papa Camille Blois's *Diplome Culinaire* hangs on the wall, Mama busies herself everywhere, son Guy is *sommellier,* and even the Japanese wife is active as a waitress. One favorite there is Calf's Brains in Brown Butter Sauce, and this is the way they prepare it:

1 fresh calf's brain	capers
2 ounces wine vinegar	butter
salt	lemon juice
pepper	

1. Boil brain with 2 tablespoons of vinegar for about 10 minutes until cooked.
2. Strain on paper towel, cut in half and slice each half lengthwise.
3. Arrange on plate with vegetables.
4. Burn about 2 tablespoons of butter until color is hazelnut. Do not let it foam.
5. Pour butter on brain and sprinkle capers over all. Can be served with 2 ounces of vinegar or the juice of half a lemon.

NOTE:

Special instructions: Fresh brain should be washed under *cold water* and all red membrane removed. In order to keep brain from breaking, cradle it in your left hand under running water and remove veins and membranes very gently with the right hand. Make sure none are left, or when cooked those membranes will shrink and become tough.

OXTAIL PARISIENNE

In making Oxtail Parisienne *(Queue de Boef)* or any oxtail ragoût, I always prefer to start the cooking a day ahead and then to let it stand overnight in the refrigerator after the first four hours of cooking. This gives the fat a chance to rise to the surface and congeal and every single bit of it can be easily removed. An oxtail ragoût that has not been thoroughly skimmed is apt to be overrich in fat and too heavy for some digestions. Remember, however, that there must be enough liquid to cover the oxtails. If they poke up through the surface, it is almost impossible to get off all the fat.

LOUIS DIAT

Makes 3 servings

1 oxtail (about 2 pounds), cut in sections
1 teaspoon salt
a little pepper
3 tablespoons beef fat
3 carrots, cut in large dices
6 small onions
2 tablespoons flour
1 clove garlic, crushed
bouquet garni made of 3-4 sprigs parsley, 1-2 stalks celery, ½ bay leaf, pinch of dry thyme, or 1-2 sprigs fresh thyme, 1 leek—tied together in small bundle
½ glass white wine or sherry (optional)
1 cup canned tomatoes
stock or water to cover meat
½ cup sautéed mushrooms
3 medium potatoes, cut in pieces
chopped parsley

1. Season oxtail with salt and pepper. Put fat in saucepan and when hot, add oxtail. Cook until all the pieces are golden brown all over. Add onions and carrots and let them brown.
2. Pour off all the fat from the pan, add flour and garlic and mix well. Add bouquet garni, wine, tomatoes, and stock (or water), using enough liquid to cover the meat well. Bring to a boil, cover and cook slowly 4 hours.
3. Skim off all the fat, then add mushrooms and continue cooking 35 to 40 minutes longer or until meat is tender.
4. Meanwhile boil potatoes until done, drain and add. Correct the seasoning and serve sprinkled with chopped parsley.

French Cooking for Americans
LOUIS DIAT

OSSO-BUCO

In Milan, Italy, the number one restaurant is Giannino's, run with loving care by the family. Right past the entrance you see a large glass-encased kitchen where buxom white-aproned women and white-hatted chefs prepare the notable dishes of this outstanding restaurant. Osso-Buco is a Milanese creation, a specialty of Giannino's—and with it goes another specialty— Risotto alla Milanese. (See page 305.)

Osso-Buco means "bone with a hole." This typical North Italian dish is made with 1½-inch-thick slices cut from the very young calf's lower leg—any Italian butcher should know how to cut them. The bone is surrounded by tender meat while the center is filled with marrow which must be scooped out—in Italy there are special gadgets sold for this purpose— and eaten together with the rest of the meat. Osso-Buco is a main meat course and can be served with either risotto, mashed potatoes, and/or spinach or other green vegetables.

Makes 6 servings

6 osso-bucos
1 small onion, chopped fine
1 small carrot, chopped fine
  half stalk of celery,
    chopped fine
4 ounces butter
1 tablespoon flour

1 small can tomato sauce
  (like Del Monte Span-
  ish Style)
½ cup stock bouillon
  peel of half a lemon
1 tablespoon parsley,
  chopped fine
  salt and pepper to taste

1. Brown the chopped vegetables slightly in 2 ounces of the butter; add the osso-bucos and brown on all sides. Then add salt and pepper and the rest of the butter into which the flour has been worked.
2. Add the tomato sauce mixed with the stock and cover saucepan, cooking very slowly for about 1½ hours.
3. About 10 minutes before cooking time is up, add the lemon peel (in 1 piece or 2 or 3 large ones) and the chopped parsley.
4. Remove lemon peel before serving. The osso-bucos should be served in the gravy, like a stew.

Giannino's Restaurant
Milan, Italy

COSTOLETTE DI VITELLO
ALLA BOLOGNESE

I write this after a week of scouting the restaurants of Rome, and I am glad to report that George's Restaurant on Via Marche is still tops. The dining room is run with grace by the mustachioed Englishman Vernon Jarratt, and the kitchen is gently but firmly supervised by the slim, alert Italian-born Signora Jarratt. Together they produce an atmosphere of refinement and culinary perfection. One of their specialties is Costolette di Vitello alla Bolognese, for which the recipe follows.

Only a few rare souls make this dish correctly, so please follow the Jarratt directions carefully.

Makes 6 servings

6 veal cutlets, ½ inch thick, with the bone
2 eggs
bread crumbs
2 ounces of butter
4 tablespoons peanut oil or sesame oil—*not* olive oil

salt
6 slices of Prosciutto crudo (Italian raw, dried Parma ham), machine-sliced very thin
6 heaping tablespoons of freshly grated Parmesan cheese

1. Make cuts around the edges of the cutlets; this is to prevent them from curling during the cooking.
2. Beat the 2 eggs—*no salt*. At the last moment just before placing in frying pan, roll the cutlets first in the beaten egg and then in the breadcrumbs.
3. Put all the butter, together with the oil, in a large frying pan with a thick bottom. This must be big enough to take the cutlets without their overlapping. When the butter and oil mixture is foaming, slide in the cutlets, using a certain delicacy in this operation. Immediately reduce the heat to the lowest possible point.
4. Continue cooking for 6 to 7 minutes. Do not move the cutlets during this time; do not prick them with a fork. Using tongs, turn the cutlets in the pan, and cook the other side for about 5 minutes.

5. Remove the cutlets from the pan 1 at a time, holding each up long enough for the melted fat to drip off. Lay them in an ovenproof dish big enough to hold them without overlapping. Sprinkle them with salt, and put a slice of ham, folded to size, on each cutlet. Spread 1 heaping tablespoon of the grated Parmesan on each cutlet.
6. Put the dish under the grill until the Parmesan is melted. Transfer them to a heated serving dish. The classical way of finishing these cutlets is to lay a thread of glace de viande (reduced Sauce Espagnole) over each cutlet. However, this is not an essential.

SIGNORA JARRATT'S VARIATIONS:

Veal Cutlet Valdostana: Slit a pocket horizontally in the cutlet and insert the slice of ham therein. Use Fontina cheese for this variation if you can. (Fontina is also a great cheese for eating with fruit so it's worthwhile seeking out a source of supply.)

Veal Cutlet Cordon Bleu: Slit the veal cutlet and use cooked ham in the center instead of raw ham. Place foie gras atop the cutlet and use grated Gruyère cheese instead of Parmesan.

NOTE:

P.S. *Re* garlic: I love Signora Jarratt particularly for agreeing with my views on garlic. Garlic, we both say, is for peasant dishes, where cheap cuts of meat were habitually used and required doctoring, or for pasta dishes which were considered too bland. Not for delicate cosmopolitan-type food, not for gentle salads, not for anything where the flavor of the food is in itself distinctive.

George's Restaurant
Rome, Italy

BLANQUETTE OF VEAL

This is becoming a highly popular veal dish. It is not too difficult to prepare, and though rich, it isn't too rich.

Makes 6 servings

2¼ pounds shoulder or breast of veal	4 carrots, peeled and quartered
1 large onion	2 tablespoons flour
6 peppercorns	4 tablespoons butter
2 teaspoons salt	2 egg yolks
1 clove garlic	½ cup heavy cream
2 stalks parsley	½ pound small mushroom
12 small white onions, peeled	caps

1. Cut the veal into 2-inch pieces. Parboil for 5 minutes in a saucepan with water to cover. Drain.
2. Add to the saucepan the large onion, peppercorns, salt, garlic, and parsley, with about 4 cups water, to cover. Bring to a boil, let simmer for 1 hour. Add the small onions and the carrots; then let simmer an additional 30 minutes, or until veal is tender.
3. Transfer meat, carrots, and onions to a hot serving dish and keep hot. Strain the stock and reduce to about ⅔.
4. Blend the flour with 2 tablespoons butter, add to the broth, bring to a boil and cook for a minute. Beat the egg yolks lightly with the cream, and stir into the broth. Stir over the flame until sauce thickens, but do not let boil. Adjust the seasonings and pour the sauce over the meat, carrots, and onions. Sauté the mushrooms in the remaining butter and use as a garnish. Serve with rice or boiled (or mashed) potatoes.

VEAL PAPRIKASH

Joseph Pasternak, who made more than one hundred movies, including *Destry Rides Again, One Hundred Men and a Girl, Please Don't Eat the Daisies,* is also noted for his culinary artistry. Born in Hungary, he came to America a penniless immigrant and seven years later became a successful motion picture producer. From his native Budapest, Mr. Pasternak brings us good humor as well as good recipes. "Life for my friends in Budapest," he says, "was always one long struggle to avoid work. Ideally they rose around five in the afternoon and went to bed in the early morning when the cafés were at long last closed. But I had to make pictures from nine A.M. to six P.M. and their habits combined with my schedules, made for the sleepiest collection of actors and technicians ever assembled. Nowadays, I never make a *paprikash* without thinking of those times and what fun they were. I hope that this simple but delicately flavored *paprikash* will convey to you some of the magic of the Budapest I remember."

Makes 4 to 6 servings

2 pounds veal shoulder	1 fresh tomato, chopped
2 tablespoons shortening	salt, pepper, paprika to taste
1 large onion, chopped	1 cup water
¼ clove garlic	green pepper rings for
¼ green pepper, chopped	garnish

1. Cut the meat into 1-inch cubes. Sauté in the shortening over low heat with the chopped onion, garlic, and green pepper for 5 minutes.
2. Add the tomato and the seasonings, then stir in the 1 cup water.
3. Cover and continue cooking gently until the meat is tender, about 1 hour. If you want more gravy, add a little more water as it cooks.
4. Serve garnished with green pepper rings.

Cooking with Love and Paprika
JOSEPH PASTERNAK

SCHNITZEL À LA BUDAPEST

When my daughter Claire was a little girl we traveled through Germany, and, though she couldn't read the restaurant menus she put on a bluff to the waiters and made believe she could. After due pondering, it always came out the same. With great pomposity she declared, "I think I'll have a schnitzel." Everywhere we went, it was schnitzel, until we thought it would come out of her ears. One of my fond memories of that trip was having our photos taken in the Berlin Zoo, holding real lion cubs. Years later, when Dory and I visited Berlin after World War II, the Zoo photographer was still photographing visitors holding lion cubs; try it sometime—they have the softest fur and a great sense of play. But in the meantime, try Joe Pasternak's notable schnitzel, a recipe which he says will always remind him of the happy days in Budapest when it was a city full of Gypsy music, love, and laughter—and when his friends kept him up all night and borrowed money from him in an endless variety of irresistible ways.

Makes 6 servings

6 veal slices, pounded thin	½ pound mushrooms, minced
salt	or sliced
pepper	1 tablespoon catsup
paprika	1 cup chicken broth
cayenne pepper	¼ cup sherry
flour	finely minced parsley for
butter	garnish
1 tablespoon finely minced onion	

1. Season the schnitzels with salt, pepper, paprika, and cayenne pepper, and dredge lightly with flour. Brown them gently in butter over moderate heat, until golden on each side.
2. Add the rest of the ingredients, except the parsley, and cover. Simmer for 15 minutes, or until the veal is tender. Remove the schnitzels and keep warm.
3. To make a gravy, thicken the pan liquid with about 1 tablespoon flour. Boil, stirring constantly, until slightly reduced, and pour over the meat.
4. Sprinkle with parsley and paprika before serving.

Cooking with Love and Paprika
JOSEPH PASTERNAK

WIENER SCHNITZEL

Of all the popular Viennese dishes which are internationally known, the most famous is schnitzel. What steak is to the American, schnitzel is to the Austrian. But although a schnitzel is cut from a leg of veal, it is not a veal steak.

For a true schnitzel, the meat should not be cut straight across the grain, but on a slight slant, half with and half against the grain, and the slices should be from one eighth to one quarter inch thick. After the slices are cut and trimmed, they should be placed between several thicknesses of waxed paper and pounded gently with a flat-faced wooden mallet, or with the flat side of a cleaver, until they are one sixteenth to one eighth inch thick. The purpose of the pounding is to partially break down but not mash the fibers of the meat. An old rule is that a schnitzel should be pounded so thin that a newspaper can be read through it. Although this is an exaggeration, the schnitzel must be thin enough so that it will cook through in about a minute. The pounded slices are marinated in lemon juice for an hour and should be turned frequently while they are marinating.

IRMA RHODE

Makes 8 servings

2 pounds veal, prepared for schnitzel
lemon juice to cover meat
½ pound butter, melted
12 anchovy fillets, mashed
pinch of paprika

2 whole eggs
8 tablespoons water
1 cup fine dry bread crumbs mixed with ¼ cup flour

1. Marinate the schnitzel cuts in lemon juice for 1 hour. Just before sautéing the schnitzel, prepare the sauce by melting the butter and adding the mashed anchovies and paprika. Keep hot.
2. Beat the eggs lightly in a bowl. Add water and dip the schnitzel into the mixture. Dredge with mixed bread crumbs and flour and allow to stand for 15 to 20 minutes.
3. In a good-sized skillet, melt the butter and let it foam well. Reduce the heat. Add schnitzel and sauté 1 to 1½ minutes for both sides. The slices are done as soon as the coating turns a golden brown.
4. Sprinkle lightly with lemon juice at once and pour the hot sauce over them. Serve immediately with quartered lemons on the side as a garnish.

The Viennese Cookbook
IRMA RHODE

SCALOPPINE AL MARSALA

The great French author, Anatole France, once said, "Hunger and love are the pivots on which the world turns. Mankind is entirely determined by love and hunger." Why this quotation comes to mind in thinking of Scaloppine al Marsala I can't tell you, but there seems to be something about this dish that is so light and gay, so soul satisfying that the quotation is apt.

Makes 3 or 4 servings

1 pound leg of veal, all lean, sliced and beaten as thin as possible
3 ounces butter
¼ cup flour

1 teaspoon salt
1 wine glass (about two jiggers) Marsala wine or sherry

1. Mix flour and salt and dip veal slices in mixture.
2. Melt butter in frying pan and brown veal on 1 side for about 3 minutes. Turn and brown the other side about 3 minutes.
3. Add the Marsala and cook for another minute or two.
4. Serve very hot, placing scaloppine on warmed serving dish. Cover with sauce from the pan.

NOTE:
For good results meat must be very thin and cooking time very short.

VEAL CHOPS PARMIGIANA

Makes 6 servings

6 veal chops
2 eggs, slightly beaten
1 teaspoon salt
⅛ teaspoon pepper
¾ cup fine dry bread crumbs
½ cup olive oil
1½ cups tomato sauce
¼ teaspoon basil

dash of Worcestershire sauce
⅛ teaspoon garlic powder
1 tablespoon butter
¼ cup freshly grated Parmesan cheese
½ pound Mozzarella cheese, sliced

1. Casserole in the making: Wipe chops with a damp cloth and dip into eggs which have been mixed with salt and pepper. Dip into bread crumbs, taking care to coat chops on all sides.
2. Heat oil until sizzling. Brown chops on all sides in oil.
3. Place in a large greased Paris-style casserole.
4. Cook tomato sauce with basil, Worcestershire sauce, and garlic powder until thickened. Add butter. Stir until melted. Pour over chops and sprinkle with Parmesan cheese. Cover and bake in a moderate oven (350° F.) 25 to 30 minutes, or until chops are tender.
5. Remove the cover and place slices of Mozzarella cheese over chops.
6. Return to the oven and bake until the cheese is melted and lightly browned.

The Casserole Cookbook
JOHN AND MARIE ROBERSON

VEAL BIRDS

Makes 4 to 6 servings

1½ pounds lean veal cutlets (cut ¼ to ⅓ inch thick)	1 teaspoon poultry seasoning
¼ cup flour	1 small onion, chopped fine
¾ cup bread crumbs	5 tablespoons butter
¾ cup chopped celery	¼ cup stock or water
1 cup chopped veal trim- mings, with sausage meat added (about ½ cup of each)	1 egg, beaten ½ cup stock ½ cup cream salt and pepper

1. Cut veal into pieces about 3 x 4 inches and pound with wooden mallet. Dredge 1 side with seasoned flour.
2. Melt 2 tablespoons of the butter and lightly brown chopped onion and remove from the fire. Add bread crumbs, celery, chopped veal, sausage meat, seasoning, stock or water, and beaten egg. Mix together well and let stand 10 minutes.
3. Divide stuffing so that each piece of veal will have its share. Wrap each piece around its portion of stuffing, having the dredged side of the veal outside. Fasten each roll with small metal skewers or wooden toothpicks or tie them with string.

4. Brown each bird well on all sides in the remaining 3 table-spoons of butter. Add the stock and the cream, cover tightly, and simmer for 35 or 40 minutes. Thicken gravy with a little flour or add more cream if necessary.

The Emily Post Cookbook
EMILY POST

VEAL CUTLETS IN SHERRY

If you love good food, you can cook good food. There is no reason to fear any recipe, no matter how elaborate the finished product. For in *all* cooking there are just a certain number of things that you do—processes that are called by name: to stir, to beat, to fold, to baste, to fry, to broil, to sift, to measure, to blend, to simmer, to peel. The average plain cook has heard of these. It is the manner in which they are used that makes all the difference between fine food and dull, uninteresting food.

Makes 6 servings

2 pounds very thin veal cutlets
salt, pepper, paprika
1½ cups freshly grated Parmesan cheese
¼ cup olive oil

1 mashed clove garlic
1 cup very dry sherry
2 cups freshly cooked and buttered peas
little additional grated Parmesan cheese

1. Order veal cutlets and have the butcher pound them very, very thin with the flat side of his cleaver. Cut them into individual portions, add salt, pepper, and paprika. Then scatter each portion with an equal share of grated Parmesan cheese. Pound the cheese gently into both sides of the meat with a wooden meat-pounder.
2. Heat olive oil and garlic in a large skillet. Quickly fry the cutlets on both sides until appetizingly brown. Cover with dry sherry, rapidly bringing to a boil.
3. Remove to a hot platter, drain the sauce over them, and cover with freshly cooked and buttered peas. Sprinkle the peas with a little added grated Parmesan cheese.

NOTE:

Be certain that the cutlets remain juicy! Fried and buttered noodles make a nice bed on which to place these cutlets.

The Perfect Hostess Cook Book
MILDRED O. KNOPF

VEAL ROAST WITH ANCHOVIES

There was once a restaurant in Louisville famous all over the country for its gourmet Viennese recipes. It was called the Old Vienna, and closed soon after I came to Louisville to live. Someone told me about this Veal Roast recipe (one of their specialties) and when I talked to my butcher about it he said, "You don't have to tell me how to prepare that—I used to do it for the Old Vienna!" Don't let the ingredients put you off— the stuffing completely disintegrates while cooking and there is left only a solid piece of the most deliciously flavored meat you will taste in a long time. This is just as good cold as hot. Slice very thin. It makes wonderful sandwiches, too. You had better not try to prepare this yourself for roasting—let your butcher do it, sewing or tying the anchovies and kidneys into the roll. That's what I do.

MARION W. FLEXNER

Makes 8 to 10 servings

4- or 5-pound veal roast, cut from the leg
1 whole can anchovy fillets (12 to 18)
1 or 2 veal kidneys, depending on size of the roast. (Be sure the pelvis or white part in the center has been removed. You must use only the outside lumps of meat, free from fat.)
2 tablespoons olive oil, bacon fat, or butter

1 pod garlic
2 onions, 1 peeled, 1 charred*
2 cups white wine, or more if this cooks down
2 carrots
pepper to taste
(Do not add salt until meat is half-done—the anchovies are very salty and added salt may not be necessary.)
2 tablespoons chopped parsley

* To char onion: wipe with a dry cloth but do not wash. Leave on the outer skin; do not peel. Set in a container in a moderate oven (375° F.). Let onion roast until dark brown outside and soft inside—it will not matter if it burns a little on the outside.

1, The anchovies and kidneys should be tied securely in the meat before it is rolled.

2. Rub the meat with pepper and oil and braise in the roasting pan in which it is to be cooked. The garlic browns with the roast. When meat is brown all over, add wine and let get hot, then add carrots and 1 whole onion, peeled, and put the top on the pan.

3. Set in a moderate oven (375° F.) and let cook 30 to 40 minutes per pound, or until veal is done enough to cut with a fork. Taste every now and then to see whether or not the gravy is properly seasoned. Add the charred onion as soon as it is brown on the outside and soft inside. Mash into the gravy with the back of a spoon.

4. When the meat is about half-done and the juices have had time to blend, I add the salt. Also, I never let the gravy cook away entirely. Add more wine from time to time if necessary. There should be about a cup of gravy when the meat is ready to serve, and sometimes I pour this off and add a little more wine to the meat, keeping the rich brown gravy to reheat when needed. This gravy thickens itself and is without a doubt one of the most delicious I have ever tasted. Add the chopped parsley to it before sending it to the table.

Out of Kentucky Kitchens
MARION W. FLEXNER

KIDNEY FLAMBÉS BOURGUIGNON

When New York's famous Ritz-Carlton Hotel moved uptown, two notable eating places were lost—the famous Ritz Gardens, which were part of the old hotel, and La Crémaillère, an exclusive restaurant in an old brownstone house that gave way to the new Carlton. But, unlike an old soldier, who merely fades away, La Crémaillère happily sprang up again in the fashionable town of Banksville in suburban Westchester County. There Antoine Gilly once more put to good use his deft cooking hand. And a good thing too, for Gilly's life was wrapped up in La Crémaillère. It wasn't long before the Cadillacs and Rolls Royces began arriving at the new restaurant . . . and this famous Burgundy dish is one of the reasons for the attraction. (Not long ago M. and Mme. Gilly retired to France and those other two great French restaurateurs, Fred Decré and Robert Meygen, have taken over La Crémaillère and its tradition.)

Makes 4 servings

2 pounds of lamb or veal kidneys	2 shallots
olive oil	pony of Cognac or Armagnac
butter	

1. Remove the skin, fat and nerve particles from the kidneys.
2. Cut into small pieces and fry in a pan with a little olive oil over a very high fire for 2 minutes.
3. Drain and put them back into the pan with a little butter. Sauté the kidney pieces for 1 minute and then add 2 chopped shallots.
4. Pour over them the flaming Cognac and the Burgundy Wine Sauce given below, and serve hot.

RED WINE SAUCE

4 pounds of veal bones	1 bay leaf
2 carrots	1 sprig of celery
1 onion	1 bunch of parsley
1 clove of garlic	12 black peppercorns
red Burgundy wine	pinch of salt
pinch of thyme	

1. Brown the veal bones in a moderate oven with the carrots, onion and garlic.
2. Place them in a skillet, cover with half water and half red Burgundy. Add thyme, bay leaf, celery, parsley, peppercorns and salt. Let cook for 10 hours.
3. Strain and return to stove and let simmer until the liquid becomes thick enough to use as a sauce.

La Crémaillère
Banksville, New York

CROWN OF LAMB CHOPS

rib rack of ½ lamb   strips of salt pork
chicken fat or butter   salt

1. Take the entire rib rack of half a lamb that is not too heavy, and separate the bones between each rib, but do not chop all the way through, leaving the chops attached. Scrape the ribs clean, just as for French chops. Chop them off to an even length, salt the meat and turn it inward, fastening it so that it forms a ring and all the ribs are visible from the outside.
2. Place this crown of chops in a roasting pan with some chicken fat or butter, tie a strip of salt pork around each of the ribs, so that they will not burn.
3. Roast in a hot oven for 35 minutes, basting frequently and occasionally adding a drop of water.
4. When serving, remove the salt pork and leave the chops in their crown-like shape, cutting through between each rib and letting the ribs stand up.
5. Fill the center with any desired vegetable or potatoes.
6. Serve the chops with their gravy from which all fat has been removed and with some currant jelly.

The Continental Cook Book
JOSEPHINE BONNÉ

ABBACCHIO AL FORNO

Maria Lo Pinto is a lawyer by profession and a cook by love. Her book, *The Art of Italian Cooking,* stamped her as an outstanding creator and reporter of notable Italian recipes, of which this Abbacchio al Forno is an outstanding example. Following Miss Lo Pinto's first cookbook came two others, *The Art of Making Italian Desserts,* and *The New York Cookbook.*

When she was a little girl, Maria used to ask her grandmother endless questions about cooking, to which "Nonni" replied with that typical Old World attitude toward New World patterns, *Americani non Cucinano*—Americans don't cook, so you don't need to know anything about it. But learn Maria did, and today many Americans are grateful for her Americanization of Italian recipes.

Abbacchio al Forno is a specialty of Rome, and no restaurant does it better than Giggi Fazi, a place which combines zany-ness with good old-fashioned family-ness. Mr. Fazi says the lamb must be not over seven weeks old.

Makes 6 servings

1 leg of lamb (4 to 5 pounds)	½ teaspoon sage or 8 fresh
5 tablespoons olive oil	sage leaves
4 cloves	salt and pepper to taste
2 strips of bacon	2 large ripe tomatoes or 1 cup
1 large onion, sliced	canned tomatoes
1 teaspoon rosemary	1 cup hot broth or water

1. Wash lamb in cold water and wipe dry with absorbent paper. Rub with oil. Insert cloves on top of lamb. Place lamb in oval baking pan.
2. Cut bacon into small pieces. Add to bottom of pan with balance of oil and onion. Sprinkle over lamb rosemary, sage, salt and pepper.
3. Brown in preheated hot oven (450° F.) about 20 minutes. Turn and brown other side for 30 minutes.
4. Chop tomatoes, combine with broth or hot water and pour in bottom of pan. Cover and cook about 30 minutes longer or until meat is tender.
5. Serve very hot with pan gravy.

The New York Cookbook
MARIA LO PINTO

LAMB PILAF

(PILÂV KUZULU)

Makes 4 servings

2 cups of rice	1 ounce of sugar
4 cups of meat stock or	1 teaspoon of black pepper
water	1 dessert spoon of salt
½ pound lamb	2 ounces of pine nuts
3 medium onions, finely	2 ounces of currants
chopped	chopped sage and parsley
4 ounces of fat	½ teaspoon mixed spice
1 large tomato	

1. Melt the fat in a saucepan, cut the lamb into strips and lightly fry. Drain off but keep hot.
2. In the same fat, fry the chopped onion, but do not on any account brown it. Now add the pine nuts and then the rice; fry for 5 minutes more, stirring almost continuously to prevent sticking.
3. Add the seasonings, currants, chopped tomato, and the boiling stock. Stir again and cook very gently covered with a cloth as well as the lid until the liquid is absorbed.
4. Return the lamb, add a little chopped sage and parsley. Re-cover and allow to stand in a warm place without further cooking for 15 or 20 minutes.

Sultan's Pleasure
ROBIN HOWE AND PAULINE ESPIR

SHISH KEBAB

Shish Kebab has become a greater and greater favorite over the years. In New York there is a small restaurant called the Brochetteria which serves only skewered dishes, principally shish kebab—and there are long lines waiting to get in. Marinating is an important part of the success of a shish kebab, but aside from the fact that there should be an overnight marinade, shish kebab is easy to prepare and most satisfactory, served either on a bed of rice or with vegetables. No one makes better Shish Kebab than the famous Omar Khayyam restaurant in San Francisco, and here is their recipe.

Makes 8 to 10 servings

1 leg of lamb (about 5 to 6 pounds)
½ pound of onions (sliced)
1 tablespoon salt
½ teaspoon pepper
⅓ cup sherry wine
2 tablespoons oil
1 teaspoon regoni or orégano

1. Remove all fat and gristle from leg of lamb. Bone it and cut into inch squares.
2. Mix meat with sliced onions, seasonings, and other ingredients.

3. Let mixture stand at least a few hours; overnight preferably.
4. Put on skewers and broil on charcoal fire or gas broiler.
5. Serve with rice pilaf as side dish or serve on a bed of rice.

Omar Khayyam's
San Francisco, Calif.

SNITZ AND KNEPP

Most typical of our Pennsylvania Dutch meat dishes today are the beef and chicken potpie, ponhaus and scrapple, pickled pigs' feet (souse), and roast pig stomach (Dutch goose). And one must not forget the *schnitz un knepp.* If it is prepared by cooking a ham bone and then adding the dried apple snitz, we may list it with the meat dishes. Family appetites differ, however, on how this old-fashioned favorite should be prepared. Many prefer only the flavor of the fruit and dumplings and do not use meat.

MARY EMMA SHOWALTER

Makes 8 servings

1½ pounds cured ham or
    1 ham hock

2 cups dried apples
2 tablespoons brown sugar

1. Wash dried apples, cover with water and soak overnight.
2. In the morning, cover ham with cold water and cook slowly for 3 hours.
3. Add apples and water in which they soaked. Add brown sugar and cook 1 hour longer.

KNEPP
(*Dumplings*)

2 cups flour
3½ teaspoons baking powder
½ teaspoon salt

1 egg, beaten
2 tablespoons butter
⅓ to ½ cup milk

1. Sift together dry ingredients. Stir in beaten egg and melted butter. Add milk to make a batter stiff enough to drop from a spoon.

2. Drop batter by spoonfuls onto boiling ham and apples. Cover pan tightly and cook dumplings 10 to 12 minutes. Do not lift cover until ready to serve.

The Mennonite Community Cookbook
MARY EMMA SHOWALTER

STUFFED PORK CHOPS

Helen Corbitt, whose recipe this is, is a truly creative cook and expert party-giver. She is Yankee-born, but Earl Wilson, the columnist, calls her "the greatest cook in Texas." The Duke of Windsor and other notables have praised her fare and demanded her recipes. Miss Corbitt's stuffed pork chops are a superb dish when company's coming. Please do these; they are so good!

Makes 8 servings

2 cups frozen corn, chopped	1 cup chopped fresh apple
2 cups white bread crumbs	¼ cup cream
1 teaspoon salt	1 teaspoon poultry seasoning
¼ teaspoon pepper	8 2-rib pork chops (try to
1 tablespoon chopped onion	have the butcher cut the
2 tablespoons chopped parsley	pocket for the stuffing)
1 tablespoon butter	salt and pepper
1 egg, beaten	1 cup stock or water

1. Mix corn, crumbs, teaspoon salt, ¼ teaspoon pepper. Sauté onion and parsley in butter, add to corn mixture with the beaten egg and apple.
2. Stir in the cream with a light touch; add the poultry seasoning, stuff the pockets of the pork chops, and brown on both sides in a heavy skillet.
3. Sprinkle with salt and pepper, pour 1 cup stock or water in the pan, cover, and bake at 350° F. for 1½ to 2 hours. Add more liquid if necessary.

Helen Corbitt's Cookbook

BAKED PORK CHOPS CHARCUTIÈRE

Beef, lamb, mutton, pork, and veal are the principal meats which the butcher handles. In cookery these meats are classified as: the dark or red meats, which include beef and mutton; and the white, embracing the remainder. When grilled, braised, or sautéed, the succulent qualities of the dark meats must be retained. This is accomplished only when the meat has not been too recently slaughtered and the cooking process not overdone. The white meats, be they broiled, braised, sautéed, grilled, or roasted should be sufficiently cooked so that when carved the juice is not of reddish or pinkish color, otherwise the meat will not be well digested by delicate stomachs.

This highly delectable dish derives its name from the fact that the chefs in Paris prepare their pork chops in this manner . . . *charcutier* being the French word for a pork butcher. It is an extremely popular luncheon dish, and very tasty.

LOUIS P. DE GOUY

Makes 6 servings

¼ cup chopped onions
4 or 5 tablespoons lard
1 teaspoon flour
1 cup meat stock
½ cup dry white wine
    salt and freshly crushed
      black pepper

6 pork chops (3 to a pound)
2 tablespoons thinly sliced
    small gherkins
1 teaspoon prepared mustard
    chopped chervil or parsley

1. Cook ¼ generous cup of chopped onions in a small saucepan with 2 tablespoons lard till tender, without browning; then sprinkle with flour, blending well with a wooden spoon over a gentle flame till mixture is of a golden color; gradually stir in meat stock mixed with dry white wine, stirring constantly, over a medium flame. When mixture begins to thicken, season to taste with salt and pepper; bring to a boil, then skim well. Lower the flame and let the sauce simmer very, very gently for 20 minutes.
2. Meantime, cook 6 nice, thick pork chops "Frenched" in 2 or 3 tablespoons of lard over a brisk flame at first so as

to sear on both sides; then over a gentle flame, until chops are tender, or about 20 minutes. Season to taste with salt and pepper.

3. Arrange on a hot dish. Skim the sauce, taste for seasoning, then add 2 tablespoons of thinly sliced small gherkins and 1 teaspoon of prepared mustard. Pour over the chops, dust with chopped chervil or parsley and serve at once.

The Gold Cook Book
LOUIS P. DE GOUY

SWEET AND SOUR PORK

Makes 3 or 4 servings

1 pound of pork (lean), cut into 1-inch cubes
½ cup flour
2 eggs, slightly beaten
½ teaspoon salt
oil for frying
1 cup pineapple chunks
6 small sweet pickles, sliced
1 green pepper, cut into 1-inch squares

3 small carrots, diced
1 clove garlic, chopped fine
1 cup water
2 tablespoons vinegar
1½ tablespoons sugar
1 tablespoon Chinese molasses
1 tablespoon cornstarch

1. Mix flour, eggs, and salt to make a batter.
2. Dip the cubed pork into batter. Fry in deep hot oil for 10 minutes. Remove and drain on absorbent paper.
3. Put pork cubes into frying pan, add pineapple, sweet pickles, green pepper, carrots, garlic, and ½ cup water. Cook covered for 10 minutes.
4. Combine the vinegar, sugar, molasses, cornstarch, and ½ cup of water and blend thoroughly.
5. Mix well with the meat and cook for another 5 minutes.

Oriental Cookbook
ALICE MILLER MITCHELL

SWEET DRY-COOKED SPARERIBS

Makes 3 or 4 servings

2½ pounds spareribs	3 tablespoons sugar
2 cups water	2 tablespoons sherry
4 tablespoons soy sauce	¼ can pineapple or some
1 teaspoon salt	fresh fruit

1. Wash ribs and cut into separate pieces with a bone and some meat on each.
2. Put ribs, water, sauce, and salt in a boiling pot. Use big fire till it boils, then turn down fire to simmer for 1 hour or 40 minutes if meat is tenderly bought.
3. Put ribs together with the juice in a frying pan. Now add the sugar, sherry, and fruit. Use big fire and stir constantly till all the water evaporates and all the sauce seems to have wrapped around the meat.

NOTE:
This can be kept in the oven for a while before eating.

How to Cook and Eat in Chinese
BUWEI YANG CHAO

SUCKLING PIG

1 suckling pig	fat for brushing
1 apple	salt and white pepper
1 potato	

1. Clean pig, wash well inside and out with clear water. Rub well with salt. Sprinkle with white pepper inside and out.
2. Stuff the cavity with dressing and sew up with linen thread or white cord. Cover ears and tail with pieces of well-greased paper.
3. Place in roaster, brush with a little fat and roast at 375° F. for 2½ hours, basting every 15 minutes. Pig's mouth should be opened and a potato inserted.

4. After roasting, remove the potato and place an apple in the mouth. If you want the skin of the pig to be soft, baste with hot stock; if you want it to be crusty, baste with oil or melted butter. Remove pig to hot platter and garnish with parsley or watercress.

DRESSING

1 loaf dry white bread	2 eggs
milk for soaking	1 teaspoon pepper
1 onion	2 tablespoons parsley, minced
pig's liver	1 teaspoon celery salt
4 tablespoons butter	1 teaspoon salt

1. Soak bread in milk. Press out surplus moisture and flake with fork. Chop onion and sauté in butter, add chopped liver.
2. Combine all ingredients and toss lightly.

Treasured Polish Recipes for Americans

FRIED RABBIT WITH CREAM GRAVY

Makes 6 to 8 servings

2 young rabbits	salt
¾ cup bacon fat	pepper
1 sliced onion	flour
¼ teaspoon allspice	1 cup sour cream
lemon	watercress
⅔ cup milk	

1. Beforehand preparation: Have your butcher hang the rabbits for several days. Order them cut into small pieces like a frying chicken.
2. Wipe them with a damp cloth. Rub all over with lemon juice, squeezing the lemon to get all the juice. Sprinkle with salt and pepper. Dip in milk. Roll in flour.
3. At the grill: Heat the fat in a skillet. Brown the rabbit. Add onion and allspice.

4. Cover skillet and simmer for an hour, turning every 15 minutes. Remove the rabbit pieces to brown paper to drain. Keep warm.
5. Thicken the juice in the pan with a tablespoon of flour. Add 1 cup of sour cream; simmer for a few minutes.
6. Serve over the rabbit. Garnish with watercress.

The Complete Barbecue Book
JOHN AND MARIE ROBERSON

BREAST OF CHICKEN WITH
SAUCE CHAMPIGNONS

This is a specialty of a delightful inn in Barbizon, France, called Les Pleiades. Its chef, M. Baratin, fortunately has a brother in New York, who serves breast of chicken in the Pleiades style at the always-busy Le Veau d'Or Restaurant.

Makes 6 servings

breasts of 3 (3-pound) chickens, fresh-killed
salt and pepper
8 ounces sweet cream butter
2 pounds button mushrooms

1 teaspoon shallots or onions, chopped very fine
1 pint extra-heavy sweet cream
2 ounces dry sherry

1. Skin the chicken breasts and sprinkle with salt and pepper. Place in frying pan with 4 ounces of the butter and cook slowly, until chicken is golden brown. (Ten minutes on each side should be enough.) Remove chicken from pan and keep warm.
2. Use the same pan without washing it and place in it the remaining 4 ounces of butter, the mushrooms and onions. Cook for 10 minutes over a very high flame.
3. Lower the flame, add sweet cream and sherry and let this sauce simmer till it thickens.
4. Place the breasts of chicken on a very hot platter, pour the mushroom sauce over them and serve with wild rice.

Le Veau d'Or Restaurant
New York City

POULTRY

CHICKEN SALTIMBOCCA

Since the veal available in America seldom has the delicacy
of French or Italian veal, Mrs. Peck has concocted this excellent saltimbocca with chicken, and it has a remarkable simi-
larity to the best veal saltimbocca you may have enjoyed in
Europe. First bone and skin the chicken breasts. Then, with a
mallet, pound each one thin between two sheets of wax paper.

Makes 6 servings

6 chicken breasts, boned, skinned, and cut in half	1 egg
	3 tablespoons milk
6 thin slices of Prosciutto, cut in half	2 cups fine bread or cracker crumbs
12 pieces of mozzarella cheese, about ¾-inch square	½ cup butter
	2 cloves garlic, finely minced
12 pitted black olives, cut in half	½ cup chopped parsley
	butter and olive oil, in equal
1 teaspoon monosodium glutamate	parts, to cover the bottom of a skillet to a depth of
1 teaspoon pepper	¼ inch
½ cup flour	

1. On ½ of each thin chicken breast, place half a piece of Prosciutto, a piece of mozzarella cheese, and 2 olive halves. Sprinkle with monosodium glutamate and freshly ground pepper. Fold unfilled side over to cover filling, and press edges firmly together to enclose filling.
2. Flour each little package, so it is well dusted on all sides. Beat egg slightly, adding milk. Dip chicken packages into egg mixture, on both sides. Then dip into bread crumbs. Chill for at least ½ hour.
3. Melt ½ cup butter in a small saucepan. Add chopped garlic and parsley, and keep warm until the chicken is cooked.
4. Heat butter and olive oil in a skillet until the fats are hot but not smoking. Place breaded chicken in skillet, and turn heat to medium high. Sauté chicken quickly, only till golden, turning once to cook the other side.
5. Remove to heated serving dish; pour warm garlic-parsley butter sauce on top and serve at once.

Paula Peck's Art of Good Cooking

LA TZE CHI

(CHINESE CHICKEN AND PEPPERS)

In the restrained and conservative areas of North China, highly seasoned food, garlic, and pepper are not considered the fare of a gentleman. This same conservatism is evident in the roof lines of Peking, which curve gently to the eaves as did the ancient tent ropes of nomadic princes, from which the curved roof design is derived. In the south where they are constructed by a people without the indigenous tradition of the north, the roof lines assume exaggerated curves and flaring upturned cornices. This lack of restraint is considered bad taste in staid Peking. The same is true of speech—even among the rickshaw coolies and workmen of Peking. Ordinarily they speak in the modulated cadences which are characteristic of the old court city, in contrast to the harsh tones and rough vulgarity of the more guttural south.

A similar comparison can be made of the art of cookery. In preparing a dish the northern *ta shih fu,* or chef, relies on a subtle blending of flavors, which to the newcomer may seem to be without designed taste until he learns to relish their delicacy on his palate. They are like the muted tones and the blend of soft colors under a bright blue sky, which are typical of northern landscapes. Not so in the south. There the native dishes run to *la,* or pepper. In rough and direct Hunan, the rice bowl of the middle Yangtze, the peppers are like fire and so are the tempers. And in the great red bowl of Szechuan (red for the color of its soil), the center of a 1500-year-old irrigation system which is still unrivaled today, the isolated inner citadel of China which has never been conquered by a foreign army, the independence and the tempers of the people are reflected in their love of pepper. The somewhat rebellious attitude of the great provincial cities and the enormous population are attested to by such dishes as La Tze Chi. It is of the common people. It was not meant to appeal to the refined esthetes of the northern court, but rather to deliver its peppery punch and to send the diner back to his rice field or his craft with renewed vigor to attack the soil or his lathe. It is a dish for the vigorous man who fights all comers for his living and who takes his pleasures in a hearty open fashion.

GENERAL FRANK DORN

Makes 4 servings

breasts of 2 chickens, uncooked
2 pounds green peppers (the hot peppery kind)
oil
1½ teaspoons salt
2 teaspoons sugar
1½ teaspoons finely chopped candied ginger
1 garlic clove, minced
pepper to taste, depending on type of green peppers used
2½ cups water
3 teaspoons cornstarch, mixed with water into smooth paste

1. Boil chicken breasts in water for 25 minutes. Remove from water, allow to cool, remove skin, and cut into small pieces.
2. Clean peppers and cut into small pieces (about the size of 25-cent piece). Boil for 4 minutes, rinse in cold water, and drain.
3. Place peppers in a hot skillet well greased with peanut oil (or salad oil). Cook for 2 minutes. Add chicken, salt, sugar, ginger, garlic, pepper, and water.
4. Cover and cook for about 6 minutes at a boil. Add cornstarch paste. Stir constantly and cook for 2 minutes more.

The Dorn Cookbook
GENERAL FRANK DORN

VOLAILLE ETUVÉE PAVILLON

This superb dish is one of the specialties of Chef Cristoff of the famous Le Pavillon restaurant in New York City. It calls for champagne and other good ingredients. Not an everyday dish, but certainly one for top occasions.

Makes 4 to 6 servings

5-pound young chicken (if 6 or more are to be served, two 3½-pound chickens will go further)	1 carrot, minced
	2 tablespoons butter
	2 mushrooms, minced
	1½ cups Champagne
salt and pepper	½ cup cream
1 onion, minced	

1. Clean, truss, and salt and pepper the chickens.
2. Put them in a casserole with the onion, carrot, 2 tablespoons butter, the mushrooms, and 1 cup of the Champagne.
3. Cook very slowly in the oven until the chicken is tender, basting frequently with the Champagne. Remove the chicken from the casserole and keep it warm.
4. Reduce the sauce to 1 cup over a low flame, then add the cream and the other ½ cup Champagne.
5. Put the sauce through a coarse sieve and see that it is seasoned right with salt and pepper.

6. Strain the sauce over the chicken and garnish with braised celery.

Menus and Recipes for All Occasions
STELLA STANDARD

CHICKEN LEGS FLAMED IN BRANDY

Reading a Sunday paper, after I had carefully studied the comics, I came to a column which described the delicious cuisine of several of the better New York restaurants. It told just enough about the various specialties to whet your curiosity but coyly ducked the issue as to just how you could turn out the dishes. With an abundance of adjectives and a plethora of social chit-chat, one description glossed over chicken legs stuffed with a "delicious concoction of chopped livers," which were served in flaming brandy. The pitch was there, but the ingredients were lacking. So William and I settled down to serious conference in the kitchen, and eventually came up with one of our favorite recipes.

GENERAL FRANK DORN

Makes 1 serving

2 chicken legs, including
  second joints, per person
chicken livers and giblets
  from one chicken, finely
  chopped
2 tablespoons finely chopped
  parsley
2 tablespoons finely chopped
  onion

1 clove garlic, finely chopped
1 tablespoon small seedless
  raisins
  salt and pepper to taste
1 cup dry white wine
2 tablespoons butter
6 tablespoons brandy, heated

1. Remove the bones and tendons from the chicken legs and second joints, keeping the meat in 1 piece slit down 1 side. Stuff with a mixture of chopped livers and giblets, parsley, onion, garlic, raisin, salt, and pepper. Sew up each leg.
2. Soak in wine for 8 to 12 hours.
3. Brown the legs in a skillet with butter until they are light gold in color. Place the chicken legs and the remaining

butter in a bake pan. Pour in the wine and cover tightly. Bake in a 375° F. oven for 45 minutes. Add wine if the juices begin to dry up.

TO SERVE:

4. Prepare a bed or ring of dry cooked rice on a serving platter. Surround the rice with fresh mushrooms cooked in butter, finely sliced string beans, and strips of buttered carrots.
5. Before serving chicken legs, remove all threads. Place chicken legs in the center of the rice, with the hot brandy in which they have been soaking briefly. Ignite the brandy in the kitchen just before serving. Quench the fire when ready to serve by pouring in the pan juice.

The Dorn Cookbook
GENERAL FRANK DORN

POLLO ALLA CACCIATORA

(CHICKEN HUNTER'S STYLE)

Makes 4 to 6 servings

1 frying chicken, 4 pounds	1 cup canned tomatoes
4 small onions	1 cup sliced mushrooms
5 tablespoons olive oil	1 large green pepper
½ cup flour	salt and pepper to taste
1 clove garlic, chopped	

1. Cut chicken into serving pieces. Season with salt and pepper; roll lightly in flour.
2. Heat oil in skillet and brown chicken on all sides about 10 minutes.
3. Stem, seed, and slice green pepper lengthwise. Mix with onions, garlic, and tomatoes; add mixture to chicken.
4. Cover; simmer slowly for 40 minutes. Add mushrooms; simmer 15 minutes or until mushrooms and chicken are tender. Serve very hot.

The Art of Italian Cooking
MARIA LO PINTO

CHICKEN PAPRIKA

The key to the success of this recipe is the paprika. There are three kinds: the sweet (or rose), the hot, and the mixed. Since paprika is called for in large quantities in making Chicken Paprika, the sweet type must be used. Sweet paprika is the product of Hungary and is available at many Hungarian or Czechoslovakian food stores. In New York City two suppliers are: Paprika Weiss, 1546 Second Avenue, and the Atlas Importing Co., 1577 First Avenue.

Makes 4 to 6 servings

1 broiler, 2½ pounds	1½ tablespoons paprika
4 tablespoons butter or chicken fat	½ teaspoon salt
	1 tablespoon flour
4 to 5 medium-sized onions, chopped rather fine	½ pint sour cream

1. Cut chicken into serving pieces, and put in a bowl with enough water to cover.
2. Melt butter or chicken fat in heavy-duty stew pot with tight-fitting cover. Add onions and cook slowly until they are yellow and glossy, not brown.
3. Add paprika and stir until mixed. Paprika is added at this point because browning produces bitterness.
4. Add the chicken with whatever water clings to it. Stir thoroughly, add salt and cover closely. Do not add any more water at this point since too much water produces a "boiled" taste. Cook over very low fire for ½ hour. The chicken will give considerable juice of its own—some give much more than others.
5. At the end of ½ hour, if not enough broth has been produced, a little water or chicken broth may be added. Cook chicken for 1 hour more, or until tender.
6. In another bowl stir flour into sour cream thoroughly.
7. Add hot gravy to cream by the tablespoon, one at a time, stirring after each addition to equalize the temperature until it is fairly runny.
8. Add cream mixture to chicken and mix lightly. At no time after this should the Chicken Paprika boil; the gravy still

might curdle. Continue cooking over very low flame until gravy is thick and rich.
9. Serve with broad noodles which have been sprinkled with bits of browned-in-butter noodles.

NOTE:
Veal, cut up as for stew, can be substituted for chicken, and served with dumplings. The title of this dish would be Veal *Pörkölt*.

An original recipe from
IRENE HARRIS

CHICKEN MARENGO

This historic recipe, supposedly invented by a desperate chef, in the field the night before the battle of Marengo, for his hungry boss Napoleon, has dozens of versions. This probably is not what he did but it is close enough to be plausible.

Makes 6 servings

2 broilers, about 2½ pounds each
4 tablespoons olive oil
2 shallots
a clove of garlic

1½ cups sliced mushrooms
6 medium-sized tomatoes
½ cup dry white wine
1 tablespoon brandy

1. Cut raw broilers in pieces—wings and legs off, white meat off each side of the breast bone, back in one hunk.
2. Fry the pieces till they are lightly colored in olive oil, turning so all sides are done evenly.
3. Lower the flame and cover for a scant 10 minutes; then remove the chicken from the oil.
4. Put in its place the shallots, garlic, sliced mushrooms, and tomatoes. Let them cook in the oil till the mushrooms are done. Add dry white wine and brandy; stir and blend till the liquid is reduced about a third.
5. Then return the chicken, cover, and let cook gently for perhaps 15 minutes, till you are sure the chicken is completely tender. Serve in the sauce.

André L. Simon's French Cook Book

MARYLAND FRIED CHICKEN

Makes 4 to 6 servings

2 broilers or 1 large fryer,
   or chicken parts
salt and pepper
flour

1 egg beaten slightly with
   2 tablespoons cold water
bread crumbs
1 pound salt pork
1 cup light cream

1. Cut chicken into serving pieces; season with salt and pepper, dredge with flour. Dip chicken into egg mixture and then cover well with bread crumbs.
2. Dice the salt pork and render it in heavy skillet to make fat 1 inch deep. When hot, add the chicken and brown quickly. Then cover and cook slowly until tender (35 to 50 minutes).
3. Make a sauce with cream .and some of the drippings. Pour over fried chicken.

BROWN CHICKEN FRICASSEE

Abraham Lincoln's favorite dish was said to be fricassee of chicken, and that is easily understood because he was a country boy who preferred good wholesome country cooking.

Makes 6 servings

1 fricassee chicken, 3½ to
   4 pounds, cut into pieces
½ cup rendered chicken fat
   or butter
1 cup mushrooms
1 carrot, chopped
1 onion, chopped
1 tablespoon chopped parsley
1 tablespoon chopped turnips

1½ cups tomato juice
   or tomato soup
¼ teaspoon powdered clove
2 tablespoons chives or
   chopped stuffed olives
flour
salt
pepper
paprika

1. Season the flour with salt and pepper, and dredge the chicken pieces with this. Then brown them in ¼ cup chicken fat.
2. While the chicken is browning, cook the carrot, onion, parsley, and turnip in the remaining ¼ cup fat until the vegetables are tender. Add tomato juice, 1 cup hot water, and season with salt, pepper, and paprika.
3. In this sauce, simmer chicken until tender. Sauté the mushrooms and add with chives or olives to the chicken and sauce 5 minutes before serving.
4. Place the chicken on toast triangles on hot plates or platter, pour on sauce and garnish with parsley sprigs or pimiento strips.

LE COQ AU VIN

"A chef has to be like a musician, like an artist," says Roger Fessaguet, possibly the greatest chef in America. "We have a recipe as an artist has a drawing, and you have to develop it, but none will be similar. Two pieces of music, two drawings, none will be similar, and it's the same with chefs. You never achieve perfection, it doesn't exist, but you have to come as close as you can."

This recipe for Coq au Vin comes from the kitchens of La Crémaillère, the country branch restaurant of New York City's La Caravelle.

Makes 4 servings

2 2-pound chickens	½ pint brown gravy
6 mushrooms	bouquet garni
8 small white onions	flour
1 slice salt pork, diced	butter
1 pint red wine	salt and pepper to taste

1. Separate the breasts and legs of the chickens. Season with salt and pepper and roll in flour.
2. Heat the butter in a saucepan and add the chicken.
3. Add the mushrooms, onions, and diced salt pork to the pan. Cover, and allow to cook slowly for 15 minutes.

4. Drain all the fat from the saucepan, then add the wine, brown gravy, and bouquet garni and cook for 15 minutes.
5. Season to taste and serve.

La Crémaillère
Banksville, New York

CHICKEN À LA KING

Chicken à la King is what you can call a serviceable dish, and that's probably why it's a main course at many hotel luncheons and dinners. Easy to prepare, easy to keep going, and stretchable. The Waldorf-Astoria probably serves as many portions of Chicken à la King as any establishment, and this is its recipe:

Makes 3 servings

1 boiled double breast of fowl, diced	1 cup heavy cream
4 sliced mushroom heads	2 egg yolks
1 ounce julienne of green pepper	1 glass excellent sherry
4 ounces sweet butter	1 ounce julienne cooked red pimiento
a little bit of flour	6 slices of truffle
	seasoning to taste

1. Warm the butter. Cook in it for 2 minutes the julienne of pepper. Add the mushrooms and cook for another 2 minutes.
2. Add the chicken and mix very well, then season and let simmer a moment.
3. Then add just a little bit of flour and pour in the cream. Let boil for 2 minutes, stirring all the while.
4. Remove from the fire. Add the egg yolks and mix thoroughly. Rectify the seasoning; then add the sherry and the red pimiento.
5. Serve very hot from a chafing dish. Pour over toast and top with slices of truffle.

Waldorf-Astoria Hotel
New York City

CHICKEN PIE WITH RELISH CRUST

Makes 6 servings

2 cups diced cooked chicken
1 cup cooked peas
½ cup cooked, diced celery
2 cups hot chicken gravy or medium cream sauce (see page 254) or 2 cups
diluted canned cream of chicken soup
1 teaspoon salt
1 tablespoon chopped parsley, if desired
Relish Crust Biscuits

1. Combine chicken, vegetables, and gravy.
2. Add seasonings and put into individual buttered baking dishes or 1½-quart casserole.
3. Top with relish crust biscuits.
4. Bake in a hot oven (425° F.) 20 to 25 minutes.

RELISH CRUST BISCUITS

2 cups biscuit mix
⅛ teaspoon paprika
1 tablespoon chopped parsley
2 tablespoons shredded raw carrot
1 tablespoon chopped green pepper
⅔ cup milk (about)

1. Combine the biscuit mix, paprika, parsley, carrot, and green pepper in a bowl.
2. Make a well in the biscuit mix. Add the milk and stir.
3. Turn onto floured board or pastry cloth and knead 6 times. Roll to ½-inch thickness.
4. Cut with round or diamond cutter and place over the hot chicken mixture.

Martha Logan's Meat Cook Book
BETH BAILEY MC LEAN AND
THORA HEGSTAD CAMPBELL

CHICKEN CHOP SUEY

Makes 2 or 3 servings

2 cups raw chicken, cut into
    1-inch pieces
1 cup celery, cut into
    1-inch pieces
12 water chestnuts, sliced
    (These may be bought in
    cans or fresh at Chinese
    and Japanese food stores)
½ pound fresh mushrooms,
    sliced

1 cup sliced bamboo shoots
    (or substitute celery
    cabbage)
1 cup Chinese greens, cut into
    1-inch pieces
2 tablespoons peanut oil
1 teaspoon salt
1 cup water

1. Heat peanut oil in a frying pan until very hot. Add salt and the chicken.
2. Cook until brown, then add water and all other ingredients.
3. Cover and cook for 15 minutes.
4. Add sauce.

SAUCE

1 tablespoon soy sauce
1½ teaspoons cornstarch
½ teaspoon sugar

½ jigger whisky or brandy
½ cup water

1. Stir all together until thickened.
2. Serve with rice or fried noodles.

Oriental Cookbook
ALICE MILLER MITCHELL

DUCKLING À LA BELASCO

David Belasco was one of the fabulous figures of the theatrical world in the heyday of the Barrymores, Sarah Bernhardt, Eleonora Duse, Nazimova, and others of their stature. Presumably this favorite dish of the patrons of the Café de Paris in Chicago was named in honor of the great David.

1 good-size duckling
  (or pheasant)
currant jelly
juice of 6 oranges
juice of 2 lemons

fine julienne strips of both
  the orange and lemon
  rinds (make these before
  squeezing the juices)
3 ounce of Curaçao liqueur
  arrowroot starch

1. Roast the duckling (or pheasant) very slowly until well done and skin is crisp.
2. After having strained the braising sauce or juice from the duck, completely remove the grease and reduce the juice with a large tablespoon of currant jelly for 10 minutes.
3. Strain through muslin and add the juice of the oranges and lemons. Cook this sauce slowly; add the julienne strips of the orange and lemon rinds and scald for 5 minutes. Finish by adding the Curaçao liqueur. If sauce is too thin add a little arrowroot starch.

Café de Paris
Chicago, Ill.

ROAST DUCK WITH ORANGE SAUCE

Unless Roast Duck with Orange Sauce is made just right— that is, with a delicate and knowing hand—it had better be left off the menu. One of the greatest meals I ever had was at Le Closerie des Lilas in Paris, a small bistro near the Luxembourg Gardens, which used to be frequented by Ernest Hemingway and other writers. The roast duck with orange sauce was simply superb, and I recommended it loudly to some of my friends visiting Paris; they went there, ordered it, and it wasn't so hot.

Gordon's, a small restaurant in Amagansett, in the heart of the Long Island duckling district, makes a good crisp duckling and a quite uniformly good orange sauce, but each time I order it, it is with fear and trepidation that it may not be up to standard.

The recipe here is Danny Kaye's favorite Chinese-style roast duck, and when properly made is undoubtedly one of the most delectable of dishes.

Makes 4 to 6 servings

4- 5 pound duckling
3 cups white rice
   small can crushed pine-
    apple
1 small onion, chopped

1 branch of celery, finely
   chopped
½ pound bulk sausage
   anise oil
   seasoning to taste
   sliced almonds

1. Wash duck and wipe dry. Rub inside and outside with anise oil, then let stand for 1 hour while preparing dressing, (Cook giblets separately and save stock.)
2. Cook and steam the rice until tender.
3. Fry sausage meat with celery and onion until golden brown. Add hot rice to sausage mixture. Add pineapple, Add 3 or 4 drops of anise oil, depending on taste, or 1 teaspoon of anise seed.
4. Fill duck with the above dressing.
5. Roast in open roasting pan for about 2½ hours, or until tender, at 350° F.
6. Before serving, garnish with sliced almonds, and serve with Orange Sauce.

ORANGE SAUCE

2 cups orange juice
1 cup broth from giblets
½ teaspoon grated orange rind

2 tablespoons white vinegar
½ cup sugar
   cornstarch

1. Cook all ingredients in double boiler and thicken with cornstarch until the consistency of heavy cream.
2. Serve separately to use over duck.

Stars in Your Kitchen
MARTA MICHEL

DUCKLING WITH GREEN GRAPES

Mabel Stegner, who created this recipe, is a well-known home economist working with various organizations to create new and better ways to cook their foods. Two of her clients— the Long Island Duckling Association and the Kitchen Bouquet people—are represented in this recipe. You can be sure that you will be proud when you serve any dish with the Stegner stamp upon it.

Makes 4 servings

1 Long Island duckling	¾ cup Muscatel wine
1 teaspoon Kitchen Bouquet	2 tablespoons currant jelly
1 teaspoon salt	1½ tablespoons cornstarch
⅛ teaspoon nutmeg	2 tablespoons cold water
2 tablespoons fat	1 cup halved seedless grapes

1. Skin duckling and cut in pieces. Place in bowl with Kitchen Bouquet, salt, and nutmeg. Stir to coat evenly.
2. Brown duckling in fat over moderate heat.
3. Add wine and jelly. Cover and bring to boil. Cook until duck is tender, about 45 minutes.
4. Blend together and stir in cornstarch and water to thicken sauce. Add grapes and heat thoroughly.

MABEL STEGNER

BREAST OF GUINEA HEN AU SHERRY

Makes 2 servings

2 breasts of guinea hen	1 cup heavy cream
4 sliced mushrooms	1 beaten egg yolk
steamed wild rice	grated cheese, if desired
small glass of sherry wine	

1. Brown the guinea hen all around in a saucepan, then add mushrooms and cook covered for 10 minutes in a 400° F. oven.
2. Place a layer of the steamed wild rice on an ovenproof platter and put the hen on top.
3. Pour the wine and the cream into a saucepan and cook slowly for 2 minutes. Add the egg yolk to the wine and cream and let cook, without boiling until the sauce thickens.
4. Pour the sauce over the guinea hen and brown under

broiler. Season to taste, and if desired sprinkle the grated cheese over the sauce before placing the platter under the broiler.

La Crémaillère
Banksville, New York

FILETTI DI TACCHINO ALLA BOLOGNESE

This is Vernon Jarratt's recipe for breast of turkey and you can be sure it is a treat. He is the chef-owner of the famous George's restaurant in Rome and author of *Spaghetti in My Hair* and *Eat Italian Once a Week*.

Makes 6 servings

5 fillets of turkey breast	consommé
flour	white truffles
butter	freshly grated Parmesan
salt	cheese
sherry	tomato purée

1. Flour the fillets of turkey breast and fry them quickly in butter.
2. Season them and add sherry, letting the fillets absorb the sherry.
3. Move them to the side of the pan and add a little good consommé to the pan, using a wooden spoon to mix it with the deposit left by the cooking of the fillets. Put the fillets back in the center of the pan and let them soak up the sauce.
4. On each fillet put a couple of slices of white truffle, using the tinned ones if you can't get them fresh, and cover generously with the grated Parmesan.
5. Put a few drops of consommé on each fillet and a small spoon of tomato purée, add a little more to the bottom of the pan, cover and leave it over the low flame for a few minutes until the Parmesan is melted.
6. Place the fillets on a service dish, surround with mashed potatoes.

VERNON JARRATT

ELEANOR ROOSEVELT'S TURKEY WITH CHESTNUT DRESSING

Visitors to the Roosevelt estate, which sits high above the Hudson River at Hyde Park, New York, almost always are struck by the simplicity of the home in which this noted family lived. "You mean to say," people exclaim, "that the Queen of England stayed in that little bedroom?" Such is the dignified simplicity that surrounded Eleanor Roosevelt's life. We are very happy to have Mrs. Roosevelt's recipe for this turkey and dressing.

turkey
6 cups chestnuts
boiling salted water
1 cup melted butter
2 teaspoons salt
¼ teaspoon pepper
½ cup cream
⅔ cup dry bread or cracker crumbs
3 tablespoons chopped parsley
1 cup chopped celery
2 tablespoons grated onion
broiled sausages (for garnish)

1. Shell and skin the chestnuts and drop them into boiling salted water. Cook them until they are soft.
2. Put them through a potato ricer and combine them with the remaining ingredients.
3. Fill cleaned turkey with the dressing.
4. Roast the turkey uncovered in a slow oven (300° F.) until tender.
5. Season with salt and pepper when it is half cooked.
6. Serve on hot platter and garnish with broiled sausages.

Stars in Your Kitchen
MARTA MICHEL

WILD RICE STUFFING FOR TURKEY OR CHICKEN

3 cups uncooked wild rice for a large bird (use 2 cups of rice for a 12-pound bird, and about 1½ cups of rice for a roasting chicken, in each case reducing the other ingredients in proportion)

6 or 7 pork sausages (1-inch lengths), sautéed

1½ cups sliced onions, sautéed

1 pound chicken livers, sautéed; or ½ pound mushrooms (halved), sautéed; or 1½ cups sliced pecans, browned in oil; or 2 cups boiled chestnuts

1 cup celery and leaves, chopped

3 tablespoons parsley, chopped

3 tablespoons simple syrup

2 teaspoons turmeric

1 teaspoon each: rosemary, basil, and thyme

salt and pepper

⅓ cup Madeira or sherry

1. Cook the rice, after washing it in many waters, in consommé or broth. Broth made of the giblets may be used. Some mushrooms may be used with the chicken livers if desired.
2. Sauté the sausages, remove them from the pan, then sauté the onions in the drippings.
3. Sauté the livers a little in oil or butter, the same with the mushrooms if used.
4. Toss all the ingredients lightly together and taste for seasoning. Do not add any other moisture to the dressing, as it must be light and fluffy. The steam from the bird while roasting is sufficient.
5. Never fill a bird too full. Sew it up and roast it slowly.

Whole Grain Cookery
STELLA STANDARD

VEGETABLES

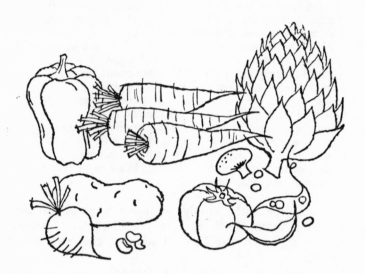

FRENCH FRIED POTATOES

There is a right and a wrong way for making French Fried Potatoes. Here is the right way:

1. Peel potatoes and cut all into the same size and length . . . ⅜ inch wide, ⅜ inch deep, by a uniform length of about 2 inches or the length of the potato.
2. Place in moderately hot oil or lard. Use enough oil so the potatoes are not crowded.
3. When potatoes come to the surface, remove from the fat immediately.

4. Reheat the fat quickly, on the highest flame.
5. The potatoes should now be plunged into the fat for a second time. This must be done within 2 minutes from the first cooking. Remove at once.
6. Sprinkle with salt and serve immediately.

HASHED BROWN POTATOES

1. Wash, peel, and slice spuds and let stand in cold salted water for ½ hour. Bring a pot of water to boil, toss in the slices. Boil for 5 minutes, pour off the water and allow steam to escape.
2. Chop the slices into pieces about the size of a pea. Mix in some chopped onion and mold into a cake.
3. Place it in a hot greased frying pan and brown evenly on both sides. Be careful not to break the cake when you flop it over.

The Outdoor Picture Cookbook
BOB JONES

HOLLYWOOD POTATOES

In California, an "Iowan" is any one of the innumerable visitors who come from "The East"—and decides to stay. Genevieve Callahan, whose *California Cook Book* supplied this recipe, actually was born in Iowa and became an active working-at-it Californian through sheer love of the place. She is widely known for her articles on foods, which have appeared in *Good Housekeeping, Better Homes and Gardens,* and other magazines.

medium-sized potatoes   grated cheese
melted butter

1. Boil medium-sized potatoes in their jackets.
2. While still hot, peel and roll each in melted butter, then in grated cheese.
3. Place in well-buttered shallow baking dish or pan and heat

under the broiler until lightly browned. They make a good surprise dish for a barbecue supper. No spuds are in evidence at the grill. Then, presto, as the chops are distributed, the big dish of potatoes arrives from the kitchen.

The California Cook Book
GENEVIEVE CALLAHAN

POTATOES ANNA

There are so many interesting ways to prepare potatoes, it is particularly difficult to select the World's Best potato recipes. Pommes Soufflés—those glamorous puffed-up potatoes—require two saucepans of fat, one at 400° F., the other at 350° F.—a tricky recipe. There are other styles of potatoes— Duchess Potatoes, Potatoes Lorette, Potatoes Brioche, Lyonnaise Potatoes—we should have liked to include. But in the interest of compactness, selectivity—and waistlines—the few favorites on these pages won out. Potatoes Anna is deservedly among them—simple yet gastronomically satisfying.

Makes 6 servings

6 to 8 good-sized potatoes
½ teaspoon salt
pepper

about ¼ pound softened butter

1. Peel the potatoes and slice very thin. Soak in cold water, then drain and dry well. Season with salt and a little pepper.
2. Butter a small round baking dish and line the bottom with potato slices. Spread 1 tablespoon of butter over the potatoes.
3. Repeat until the potatoes are all used, spreading butter over each layer and on top.
4. Bake in a hot oven (425° to 450° F.) for about 45 minutes, or until potato slices are soft. Test by inserting a small sharp knife.
5. To serve, turn the baking dish over onto a heated serving platter. The potatoes will be in a golden-brown molded form. Decorate with a few sprigs of parsley.

POPPY CANNON'S EASY
POTATO PANCAKES

Poppy Cannon, food editor of the *Ladies' Home Journal*, has had a tremendous impact upon the American way of eating. In her articles, books, TV appearances, and lectures she has proved to delighted millions her philosophy that truly fine cooking can be achieved with speed and ease through the use of modern "convenience" foods and modern kitchen appliances. This recipe calls for the use of a blender and comes from Miss Cannon's *The Electric Epicure's Cookbook*.

Makes 8 small pancakes

2 eggs	¼ cup parsley clusters
1 sliced onion	2 cups diced raw potatoes
1 teaspoon salt	¼ cup flour

1. Place eggs, onion, salt, parsley clusters, and 1 of the cups of diced raw potatoes into the blender. Turn on high.
2. Remove cover, add the flour and second cup of potatoes. Do not overblend.
3. Pour mixture in eighths onto hot greased griddle and cook until brown on both sides.
4. Serve hot with bacon or ham and warm applesauce, or as an accompaniment to pot roast or sauerbraten.

The Electric Epicure's Cookbook
POPPY CANNON

CANDIED SWEET POTATOES

Makes 4 servings

4 large sweet potatoes	1 tablespoon lemon juice
salt and paprika (optional)	little grated lemon rind
½ cup brown sugar	1½ tablespoons butter

1. Cook the potatoes in their jackets in a covered pot until they are almost tender.
2. Peel and cut them into slices. Put them in a shallow oven-proof pan and season.
3. Sprinkle over them evenly the brown sugar, lemon juice, and lemon rind. Dot with butter.
4. Bake in a moderate oven for 15 to 20 minutes.

VARIATION:

orange marmalade, thinned with a little water to make ¼ cup	2 tablespoons butter

1. After the potatoes have been peeled and sliced and arranged in baking pan, dot them with butter, and pour over them the thinned orange marmalade. Shake the pan to make sure potatoes are evenly coated with mixture.
2. Bake in a moderate oven for 15 to 20 minutes.

ITALIAN SPINACH TART

This is another interesting Robert Carrier recipe (see also Brandade Pâté of Smoked Trout and Onion Soufflé Soup). *Newsweek* Magazine asks this question: "What do Zero Mostel and Princess Margaret have in common? Answer: They're both mad for Robert Carrier's gourmet restaurant in London. . . . It sounds like a phony but it's the real thing— an *haute cuisine* restaurant run by an American in England that serves impeccable guinea fowl with sauce riche and ballotine of duck."

Carrier learned the art of fine French cooking from a clever woman named Fifine, who runs a successful restaurant in St. Tropez on the French Riviera. In 1952 he went to London for the Coronation of Elizabeth II and ended up as food columnist for *Harper's Bazaar, Vogue,* and the London *Sunday Times.* "Carrier's cheerful, expert, and gorgeously illustrated articles, along with his recipe cards," says *Newsweek,* "launched him as a glamorous evangelist crying out in a wilderness of boiled vegetables. Carrier became literally a household word."

Makes 4 to 6 servings

1 pastry shell	½ pound ricotta or cottage
dried beans for use in	cheese
setting crust	3 eggs, lightly beaten
1½ cups fresh spinach	½ cup freshly grated
4 tablespoons butter	Parmesan cheese
salt	½ cup heavy cream
freshly ground black pepper	grated nutmeg

1. Line a pie tin with pastry, fluting the edges. Chill. Prick bottom of pastry shell with a fork; cover bottom with a piece of wax paper.
2. Fill the pastry shell with dried beans and bake in a hot oven (450° F.) for about 15 minutes, just long enough to set the crust without browning it. Allow to cool.
3. Cook spinach with butter, and salt and pepper to taste. Drain thoroughly and add ricotta or cottage cheese with beaten eggs, grated Parmesan, cream. Add nutmeg to taste.
4. Spread mixture in pastry shell and bake the tart in a moderate oven (375° F.) for 30 minutes, or until the crust is brown and the cheese custard mixture has set.

ROBERT CARRIER

SOUFFLÉ AUX ÉPINARDS

(SPINACH SOUFFLÉ)

Makes 4 servings

1 cup finely chopped cooked	1 teaspoon salt
spinach	dash of cayenne
1 tablespoon butter	dash of Worcestershire
1 teaspoon salt	sauce
dash of nutmeg	5 eggs, separated
3 tablespoons butter	3 tablespoons finely
3 tablespoons flour	shredded Swiss cheese
1¼ cups milk	

1. Casserole in the making: Season spinach with 1 tablespoon butter, salt, and nutmeg. Cook over heat to remove any excess moisture.
2. Melt 3 tablespoons butter in a small pan. Blend in flour and cook until it bubbles and is lightly browned. Gradually stir in milk and seasonings. Cook over low heat, stirring constantly, for 10 minutes, or until thickened. Gradually beat in the well-beaten egg yolks a little at a time, until well blended. Add spinach purée. Cool.
3. Fold in egg whites beaten until stiff but not dry. Pour into a greased 2-quart soufflé dish. Sprinkle the top with grated cheese and bake in a moderate oven (375° F.) 35 to 40 minutes, or until the top is browned and the soufflé is nicely puffed.
4. Serve immediately.

The Casserole Cookbook
JOHN AND MARIE ROBERSON

ZUCCHINI ROMANO

Makes 4 to 6 servings

⅓ cup olive or salad oil
1 cup diced celery
1 sweet red pepper, diced
1 medium onion, diced
1 clove garlic, minced

2 pounds zucchini, washed and sliced
1 teaspoon salt
¼ teaspoon pepper
1 cup buttered bread cubes
½ cup grated Romano cheese

1. Casserole in the making: Heat oil in a Swiss-style casserole on an asbestos pad over low heat. Sauté celery, red pepper, onion and garlic. Cook until onion is tender.
2. Add zucchini, salt and pepper. Cover and simmer 10 minutes. Remove the cover and sprinkle the top with bread cubes and cheese.
3. Bake in a moderate oven (375° F.) 20 minutes, or until the cheese is melted and the bread is browned and crisp.

The Casserole Cookbook
JOHN AND MARIE ROBERSON

BRUSSELS SPROUTS, BON VIVANT

Makes 4 servings

1½ pounds Brussels sprouts	½ cup prepared poultry
2 teaspoons grated onion	dressing
1 cup chestnuts	butter
2 cups medium white sauce*	additional grated Swiss
⅓ cup grated Swiss cheese	cheese
⅛ teaspoon nutmeg	additional nutmeg

1. Cook the sprouts in salted water with the grated onion added.
2. Boil the chestnuts, shells slashed, about 15 minutes. Peel —outer and inner covering both—and slice.
3. *Make white sauce (2 tablespoons butter, 2 tablespoons flour, 2 cups milk), and beat the cheese into it. Add the nutmeg.
4. Sauté the poultry dressing and sliced chestnuts in plenty of butter to coat well.
5. In a buttered baking dish, put half of the sprouts, then half the poultry dressing, then half the sauce—and repeat. Grate additional cheese over the top. Sprinkle with additional nutmeg.
6. Bake at 400° F. until the cheese has melted, and the Brussels sprouts are bubbly hot.

NOTE:

Speaking of NUTMEG: A pretty way to hold your true love is as follows (according to an ancient adage): Cut a nutmeg into quarters. Toss one piece into the fire, bury another in the ground, chuck a third into the brook, and boil the fourth. Drink the water it has boiled up; put the boiled segment under your pillow. Ancients said you will dream of your real love.

Martha Deane's Cooking for Compliments
MARION YOUNG TAYLOR

ASPARAGUS ALMONDINE

A very little girl, the daughter of a lady connected with the court, once had the honor of being invited to have luncheon with Queen Victoria. The child had always been strictly disciplined never to apply her fingers to anything she was eating, excepting bread. Whenever she broke the rule, her governess would say in a shocked tone: "Oh, piggie, piggie." All went well and the child behaved admirably until she saw the Queen take up some asparagus with her fingers. Then, with a pained expression on her face she solemnly raised one of her fingers, pointed it at Victoria, saying: "Oh, piggie, piggie." The Queen, reports say, immensely enjoyed the incident and laughed heartily.

P.S. If Queen Victoria could do it, so can you. Of course, when the asparagus is served with dressing, like this Asparagus Almondine, the fork's the thing.

MILDRED O. KNOPF

Makes 6 servings

¼ pound butter
¼ cup slivered almonds
juice of ½ lemon

2 pounds asparagus
salt

1. Render butter in a skillet and brown until dark but not black. Fry finely slivered almonds in the butter. Add the juice of ½ lemon to the butter.
2. Boil asparagus in slightly salted water until soft, but not too soft (about 20 minutes, depending on the thickness of the asparagus).
3. Drain the asparagus, lay the spears evenly on a flat, hot platter, pour the brown butter over them, and sprinkle with the almonds. Salt very lightly.

NOTE:

This almond butter also lends itself excellently to string beans and to cauliflower.

I have found from experience that the most effective way to cook asparagus is to lay them flat covered with slightly salted water in a roasting pan. Set the roasting pan if necessary over two burners and cover until the water comes to a boil. Once the water is boiling, the cover may be removed. This method cooks the asparagus evenly and makes it simple to remove without breaking any heads. Do not pour the asparagus out of the water, but, with a spoon or spatula, lift onto a flat platter to drain. Drain them thoroughly of all water; otherwise need I warn you your sauce will be ruined! Asparagus is equally delicious served with Hollandaise Sauce, Sauce Mousseline, or with drawn butter and a thick covering of grated Parmesan cheese.

The Perfect Hostess Cook Book
MILDRED O. KNOPF

AMELIO'S ASPARAGUS DELLA CASA

On Powell Street, in San Francisco, near the turntable where you may have helped to swing around the famous cable cars to send them on their return journey, is Amelio's, the "casa" whose rich but delicious specialty this is. In selecting the asparagus, my own experience has been that unless you can personally harvest the asparagus as the shoots come up in your own garden, it is better to buy the finest deluxe brands of white asparagus in jars or cans. Pay the price or don't eat asparagus at all. In France, where food is still shopped-for daily, you can, in season, buy succulent asparagus at any market, but here tasty fresh asparagus is becoming a rarity.

Makes 2 servings

12 canned or fresh jumbo   paprika
     white asparagus   Parmesan cheese
½ pound butter

1. Cook and drain the asparagus; heat and drain if canned. Keep warm.
2. Brown the butter in a skillet. Keep shaking to prevent it from burning. Sprinkle paprika into the butter.
3. Arrange the asparagus in hot dishes, add a generous sprinkling of cheese and pour over the browned butter.

Amelio's Restaurant
San Francisco, Calif.

BEAN-POT BEANS

My grandmother's beans were prepared like this:

Makes 6 to 8 servings

4 cups small white beans ½ cup molasses
1- pound piece of salt pork 1 tablespoon salt
1 large onion, peeled 1 teaspoon pepper
1 heaping teaspoon mustard

1. Four cupfuls of small white beans were picked over to eliminate the worm-holed specimens and the small stones that so mysteriously intrude among all beans, then covered with water and left to soak overnight.
2. Early the next morning, usually around five o'clock, they were put in a saucepan, covered with cold water and heated until a white scum appeared on the water. They were then taken off the stove, the water thrown away, and the bean-pot produced.
3. In the bottom of the bean-pot was placed a 1-pound piece of salt pork, slashed through the rind at ½-inch intervals, together with a large peeled onion; then the beans were poured into the pot on top of the pork and onion. On the beans were put a heaping teaspoon of mustard, ½ cup of molasses, and a teaspoon of pepper; the bean-pot was filled with boiling water, and the pot put in a slow oven.
4. At the end of 2 hours, a tablespoon of salt was dissolved in a cup of boiling water and added to the beans. Every hour or so thereafter the cover was removed, and enough boiling water poured in to replace that which had boiled away.
5. An hour before suppertime, the cover was taken off for good, the salt pork pulled to the top, and no more water added. Thus the pork, in the last hour, was crisped and browned, and the top layer of beans crusted and slightly scorched.
6. When the beans were served, the pork was saved and the scorched beans skimmed off and thrown away. The two

great tricks of bean-making seemed to be the frequent adding of water up to the final hour of baking, so that no part of the beans had an opportunity to become dry, and the removal of the cover during the last hour.

Trending Into Maine
KENNETH ROBERTS

DELICATE CORN FRITTERS

Makes 6 to 8 servings

12 ears tender sweet corn
4 eggs, separated
2 teaspoons all-purpose flour
2 teaspoons granulated sugar
½ teaspoon salt
black pepper, coarsely
ground
4 tablespoons melted butter

1. Husk the corn, and remove all the silk. Run a sharp knife down the center of each row of kernels and scrape out the milky part or use a corn scraper, sold for that purpose.
2. Beat 4 egg yolks well, and beat into them flour, sugar, salt, and a very little black pepper. Add the scraped corn and mix well, and stir in the melted butter.
3. Beat the whites of the eggs stiff, and fold them carefully into the corn mixture.
4. Drop by tablespoonfuls onto a hot, lightly buttered griddle or iron frying pan and bake until brown on one side; then turn them over with a spatula or pancake turner and bake until brown on the other side.
5. Serve a few at a time on a hot platter. These are very delicate and should be eaten immediately and it is almost essential to have someone stay in the kitchen to bake them, if they are to come to the table in a state of perfection.

The Best I Ever Ate
SOPHIE KERR AND JUNE PLATT

BAKED CORN CUSTARD

Makes 4 servings

2 No. 1 cans niblet corn
3 tablespoons butter
3 tablespoons flour
2 cups milk
1 cup grated rattrap cheese
2 eggs
1 teaspoon sugar

2 leeks, chopped
1 canned pimiento, cut into
    small pieces
½ teaspoon marjoram
1 teaspoon minced onion
    breadcrumbs
    salt and pepper

1. Beat the eggs slightly. Sauté the onion in butter, blend
   flour, add milk and cheese slowly. Add seasonings, pimiento, sugar.
2. Stir in the corn and eggs. Put in low buttered casserole,
   sprinkle top with breadcrumbs, and dot with butter. Bake
   in medium oven (350°) for 35 minutes.

Casserole Cookery
MARIAN AND NINO TRACY

CARROTS-IN-HONEY, AU GRATIN

This dish is called Zanahorias al Miel de Abejas, au Gratin,
at Hotel Villarica, in the Chilean town of Abejas.

Here in the heart of Chile's incredible Lake Region you get
one of the world's truly exciting views of clear, chill trout-
filled lake water, encircling peaks that make the Alps look
like foothills with a snow-capped active volcano puffing smoke
into the wine-clear air, just for good measure. You not only
get some of the finest trout fishing on earth, but meet good
food and smart traveled people. To duplicate this easy yet
delicious dish . . .

carrots
strained honey
grated Swiss cheese

fine-chopped fresh
    marjoram or orégano
    (or chopped mint)

1. Scrub and trim plenty of really young fresh carrots. Cook in lightly salted water until crisply tender, not too soft.
2. Split from end to end, toss in plenty of strained honey mixed with a little fine-chopped fresh marjoram or orégano (we find chopped mint is better still).
3. Arrange neatly in oven dish, cover with grated Swiss cheese.
4. Brown under broiler or in very hot oven at 450° F. or so.

The South American Gentleman's Companion
CHARLES H. BAKER, JR.

EGGPLANT PROVENÇALE

1 firm eggplant	bread crumbs
salt, pepper and paprika	oil
parsley, chopped	1 medium-size tomato
garlic, chopped	

1. Choose firm eggplant, wash and peel, cut into ½-inch slices, season with salt, pepper, and paprika.
2. Sprinkle over a mixture of fine chopped parsley, garlic, and bread crumbs, then shake a few drops of oil over slices.
3. Place on a lightly greased pie plate or baking pan and grill in oven until lightly brown and tender.
4. Cut medium-size tomato in half, season with salt and pepper, sprinkle with mixture of fine-chopped parsley, garlic, and bread crumbs, then shake a few drops of oil over halves.
5. Place on a lightly greased pie plate or baking pan and grill in oven until lightly brown and tender.
6. When serving, place grilled tomato on top of eggplant.

Stars in Your Kitchen
MARTA MICHEL

PETITS POIS

Makes 4 servings

1 cup small pearl onions
2 cups shelled peas
½ pound small white
mushrooms

lemon juice
4 tablespoons olive oil
salt, pepper

1. Bring the onions to a boil in cold water and drain.
2. Bring the peas to a boil in cold water and drain.
3. Wash the mushrooms in lemon juice and water and cut in thick slices. Sauté in the hot oil.
4. Add the peas, onions, salt and pepper. Cover with the lid and shake over a slow fire for 10 to 15 minutes, or until the peas are just soft but not mushy.
5. Serve in a casserole.

The Cordon Bleu Cook Book
DIONE LUCAS

GREEN BEANS, VIENNESE STYLE

Makes 10 servings

3 pounds green beans
3 tablespoons fat
3 tablespoons flour
1 onion, chopped
1 tablespoon dill, chopped
½ teaspoon parsley, chopped

½ cup soup stock or
vegetable stock
1 tablespoon vinegar
dash salt, pepper
1 cup sour cream

1. Clean beans, cut off ends, wash. Cut into small pieces.
2. Cook in salted water about 20 minutes. Drain.
3. Melt fat, blend in flour, add onion and brown. Add dill, parsley, and soup or vegetable stock; bring to a boil.
4. Add beans, vinegar, salt, pepper, and sour cream. Bring to a boil again, stirring constantly.

Viennese Cooking
O. AND A. HESS

STRING BEANS VINAIGRETTE

Makes 6 servings

1½ pounds string beans whole canned pimientos	2 tablespoons red wine vinegar
¼ teaspoon salt	4 tablespoons olive oil
¼ teaspoon French mustard pepper	½ teaspoon chopped chervil or parsley
¼ teaspoon paprika	½ teaspoon chopped chives

1. Buy 1½ pounds of the youngest beans you can come by; cut off the tips and string them.
2. Then boil them rapidly in salted water till they are just barely tender. The excellence of this dish depends largely on the texture of the beans, so for goodness' sake do not let them cook till they are sage green, limp, and dejected. They should still be a pretty color and just exactly cooked through. Drain and cool.
3. Slice enough whole canned pimientos to give you 6 big red rings and slip a fagot of beans through each one.
4. Mix in a bowl, salt, French mustard, a generous sprinkle of pepper, and paprika. Dissolve it in red wine vinegar. Then add olive oil; beat briskly; add chervil or parsley and chopped chives. Beat some more and pour over the beans a good hour before you expect to serve them.

André L. Simon's French Cook Book

PEPPERS AU GRATIN

That Italy is a land of vegetables is evidenced by the fact that we in America use so many Italian vegetable names (broccoli, zucchini, finocchi); Jerusalem artichoke is a corruption of Italian *girasole,* and kohlrabi of *cavoli-rape* (cabbage-turnips). The names endive, celery, chicory, radish are barely disguised from the original Italian *indivia, sedano, cicoria,* and *radice.* Italians like their vegetables raw, in salad form (in which case they are usually accompanied by a dressing of olive oil, wine vinegar, salt, and pepper), or boiled and left to cool (whereupon olive oil, lemon juice and garlic predominate).

Many vegetables are fried (the Italian *fritto misto* includes celery, eggplant, mushrooms, artichokes, and other vegetable varieties); others are skilfully blended with fresh cheeses and tomato sauce, like the Eggplant Parmigiana. The ubiquitous tomato, which figures as an ingredient in so many sauces and dishes, appears in its own right in Rome, where it is hollowed out, stuffed with boiled rice which is mixed with the tomato's own juices plus olive oil, garlic, and chopped mint, then baked in the oven.

PROFESSOR MARIO A. PEI

Here is another fine Italian vegetable dish which is baked in the oven.

Makes 4 servings

4 large green peppers	4 tablespoons olive oil
1 tablespoon capers	2 tablespoons fine bread
4 anchovy fillets, cut into	crumbs
pieces	½ teaspoon salt
8 black olives, pitted and cut	½ teaspoon pepper
into pieces	

1. Roast peppers in very hot oven (450° F.) 10 minutes, or until skin is easily removed. Peel, remove seeds, and cut into wide slices.
2. Place in oiled baking dish, dot with capers, anchovies, olives and sprinkle with oil, bread crumbs, salt, and pepper.
3. Bake in moderate oven (375° F.) 20 minutes and add more olive oil. This dish can be served either hot or cold.

The Talisman Italian Cook Book
ADA BONI

PARSNIPS

Many people shun parsnips—but why? Parsnips have a sweet and delicate flavor, and when mashed like mashed potatoes, oŕ fried, boiled, baked, or steamed, they make an interesting addition to all sorts of meat dishes. Ancient Greeks and Romans thought well of parsnips according to historical notes, and they have been grown in this country since 1609.

CANDY-BAKED PARSNIPS

Makes 6 servings (1 pound serves 3 or 4)

1½ pounds parsnips	5 tablespoons brown sugar
salt	grated rind of 1 orange
⅓ cup orange juice	butter

1. Boil the parsnips until tender. Drain and peel.
2. Cut into lengthwise slices and arrange in a shallow, greased baking dish. Salt them.
3. Combine the orange juice, brown sugar, and grated rind, and pour over the parsnips.
4. Dot with butter, and bake at 375° F. until syrup has been pretty well absorbed.

PARTY PARSNIPS

1. Scrape them. Discard about ½ inch of the stem end if the parsnips are not young and tender. Slice diagonally into very thin chips.
2. Deep fry at 390° F. until they're a crisp brown. Put them in a few at a time—for best results. And "best results" are certainly very good!

SWISS CHEESE PARSNIPS

parsnips	salt and pepper
grated Swiss cheese	light cream
buttered bread crumbs	

1. Arrange cooked, sliced parsnips in a greased casserole, alternating with layers of grated Swiss cheese and buttered bread crumbs. Season with salt and pepper as you go. Add about 1 cup of light cream (more if the family casserole is large).
2. Bake at 350° F. until the mixture is bubbly hot—about 20 minutes.

Martha Deane's Cooking for Compliments
MARION YOUNG TAYLOR

BAKED GREEN SQUASH

Nicholas Tselementes, author of this recipe, established his reputation as a premier chef in Greece and on the continent of Europe. Then he heard the call to come to America and supervise the kitchens of the swank St. Moritz Hotel in New York City. Few assignments offer such a challenge, for probably no other hotel in America, with the possible exception of its neighbor The Plaza, caters to so varied a clientele and so wide a divergence of culinary backgrounds.

large squashes, cut lengthwise in thick slices	1 cup tomato sauce or sliced tomatoes
sliced onions (¼ of the weight of the squashes)	1 cup oil
1 cup chopped parsley and dill (or mint leaves)	salt and pepper to taste some dry bread crumbs

1. In a baking pan, make a layer with half the sliced onions and sprinkle with salt; then another layer of sliced squash and half of the parsley; then a layer with the rest of the onions, more salt and pepper, etc.
2. Pour over the tomato sauce diluted with a little water, or the fresh tomatoes, and sprinkle with salt. Top with bread crumbs, add the oil, and bake in a moderate oven for about 1 hour.
3. Serve lukewarm or cold.

Greek Cookery
NICHOLAS TSELEMENTES

SWEET AND SOUR CABBAGE

In *As You Like It* Shakespeare refers to chewing the food of sweet and bitter fancy. The idea of contrasting flavors exists in many recipes, and the sweet and sour motif is an outstanding example. Sweet and sour fish, sweet and sour sauce for beets, sweet and sour sauce for sauerbraten. Sweet and sour cabbage, while not a delicate dish to be sure, is an interesting one.

Makes 6 servings

4 cups shredded cabbage	⅓ cup vinegar
4 slices bacon, diced	salt
2 tablespoons brown sugar	pepper
1 tablespoon flour	1 small onion, sliced
½ cup water	2 cloves

1. Cook cabbage in boiling, salted water 7 minutes.
2. Fry bacon. Add sugar and flour to bacon fat; blend. Add water, vinegar, and seasonings; cook until thick.
3. Add onion, diced bacon, and cabbage; heat through.

Recipes Mother Used to Make
EDNA BEILENSON

STUFFED ARTICHOKES DELUXE

It took me a long time to acquire a taste for artichokes. It seemed so silly to have to pull big, buttered leaves through one's teeth just to get a little vegetable matter. What decided me to try artichoke in earnest was the following story by Andre Kostelanetz about Henri Matisse.

On Easter Sunday, 1945, the last year of the war, Kostelantz and his wife Lily Pons were in Marseilles, France. "We had just arrived for four days' rest, after a tour of entertaining the troops in Burma," says Kostelanetz. "It was a wonderful morning, sparkling but not too warm, there were no tourists of course, and we decided to drive along the Riviera to Venice and call on Matisse. We had never met the painter, but we knew well his son Pierre in New York.

"We found Matisse living in a small house, with a magnificent, sweeping view beyond his vegetable garden. In one room there was a cage with a lot of fluttering birds. The place was covered with paintings, most of them obviously new ones. I marveled at his production and I asked him, 'What is your inspiration?'

" 'I grow artichokes,' he said. His eyes smiled at my surprise and he went on to explain: 'Every morning I go into the garden and watch these plants. I see the play of light and shade on the leaves and I discover new combinations of colors and fantastic patterns. I study them. They inspire me. Then I go back into the studio and paint.'

"This struck me forcefully. Here was perhaps the world's most celebrated living painter. He was approaching eighty and I would have thought that he had seen every combination of light and shade imaginable. Yet every day he got fresh inspiration from the sunlight on an artichoke; it seemed to charge the delicate dynamo of his genius with an effervescent energy almost inexhaustible."

Artichokes make a colorful compliment to straight manly meat dishes like steak and chops. Serve plain cooked artichokes with ordinary melted butter or lemon butter. Or go a step further for these Stuffed Artichokes Deluxe.

Makes 4 servings

4 artichokes	1 teaspoon salt
1 large clove garlic, minced, or 1 small onion, minced	¼ teaspoon black pepper
	2 tablespoons grated Parmesan cheese
¼ cup butter, margarine, or oil	1 cup hot artichoke liquid, or meat stock, or water
1 cup dry bread crumbs	melted butter
¼ cup parsley, finely minced	

1. Wash artichokes several times in lukewarm water and drain, bottoms up. Remove loose discolored leaves around base and clip tip of each leaf. Drop into enough boiling unsalted water to cover (to retain color). Cover and let boil until outer leaves may easily be pulled from stem— about 20 to 30 minutes. Turn artichokes several times during cooking period. When almost done, add 1 teaspoon salt and continue to cook for several minutes longer. Remove from liquid and drain well with bottoms up on rack. Remove choke.
2. Sauté garlic or onion in shortening until delicately brown. Pour over dry bread crumbs and mix well.
3. To the crumb mixture add parsley, pepper, and cheese and mix thoroughly. Last, drizzle over ingredients the artichoke liquid or meat stock or water, mixing all gently with a fork, keeping ingredients moist without allowing them to become compact.
4. Pour a little melted shortening into each artichoke and sprinkle lightly with salt. Fill center and in between leaves with the dressing.

5. Place close enough together to prevent spreading, and bake in a covered pan at 350° F. for about 30 minutes.
6. Pour hot melted butter over dressing just before serving.

Antoinette Pope School Cookbook
ANTOINETTE AND FRANÇOIS POPE

PURÉE DE CHAMPIGNONS "PAVILLON"

Makes 8 servings

1½ to 2 pounds fresh white mushrooms
¾ cup rich Cream Sauce
salt and pepper

¼ teaspoon nutmeg
4 tablespoons fresh butter
¼ cup heavy cream

1. Wash the mushrooms, removing but 1/16 inch from the stems. Dry them well. Chop them fine in a wooden bowl —do not grind them. Put them in a well-greased casserole and let them dry out some more in the oven—about 7 minutes at 325° F., uncovered.
2. Then add the Cream Sauce, well seasoned with salt, pepper, and nutmeg.
3. Mix well and put back in the oven for 4 minutes at 350° F.
4. Boil up the butter with the cream, and add to the purée.

CREAM SAUCE

2 tablespoons butter
1½ tablespoons flour
½ cup cream

¼ cup milk
seasonings

1. Make the Cream Sauce with 2 tablespoons butter mixed with 1½ tablespoons flour in a saucepan over a gentle flame.
2. When it is smooth slowly add ½ cup cream and ¼ cup milk.
3. Cook 2 minutes and add the seasonings.

Le Pavillon
New York City

CELERY AND BONE MARROW

In or near the Western Hills outside Peking are some of the loveliest old temples in China—the Temple of the Azure Clouds with its 500-year-old white pines whose silvery trunks rise out of beds of wild violets in the spring—the Temple of the Sleeping Buddha—the shrines around the Jade Fountain —and many others. The most charming group is Pa Ta Ch'u (the Eight Great Temples); the most beautiful of all is Pao Chu Tung (the Temple of the Precious Pearl Cavern). Behind the temple buildings, the shrine was a cave in which a lacquered mummy of an old abbot looked out through clouds of incense as temple bells tolled out the prayers of pilgrims. Tillie Hoffman had leased the rather simple temple buildings and courtyard, and had fixed them up as a weekend and summer place. This is quite a common practice in China, and always has been, where temples are looked upon as places where both the gods and the people may live in tranquillity. On the edge of the almost precipitous mountainside stood a T'ing-erh, or open pavilion, which offered a breathtaking view over the roofs and trees of lower shrines, and across the Peking Plain to the hazy walls and golden roofs of the ancient capital.

On cold fall days Tillie served her guests Mongolian mutton cooked in the open on huge charcoal braziers. During the golden warmth of summer weekends, we loafed in the paved courtyard, walked to visit other temples, and stowed away huge meals under the upcurved roof lines of the T'ing-erh. Tillie's cook, Chiang, had a simple specialty that always raised cheers and called for more—Celery and Bone Marrow.

GENERAL FRANK DORN

Makes 8 servings

1 head of celery	1 ounce sherry, heated
salt and pepper to taste	4 or 5 large beef bones,
2 tablespoons soy sauce,	broken to convenient
heated	lengths for cooking

1. Cover broken beef bones with water in a pot, bring to a boil, and then lower heat to a simmer for about 2 hours, adding salt to taste.

2. Clean the celery and cut the stalks into pieces about 1-inch long. Either steam in a strainer over boiling water or cook in a tightly covered pot with a minimum of water, salt and pepper. Do not allow the celery to become waterlogged. It should be removed from the pot and drained while still fairly firm.

3. Place the celery on a serving platter. Force or dig out the marrow from the bones, collecting all loose pieces. As far as possible, slice the marrow into pieces about ¼-inch thick, and scatter over the top of the celery. Sprinkle with soy sauce and sherry, and serve.

The Dorn Cookbook
GENERAL FRANK DORN

RED-FLANNEL HASH

There is no record that the red men taught the early colonists to make red-flannel hash. The origin of the bulgy beet is shrouded in mystery—a fitting subject for a doctor's thesis in horticulture. One can only hope that the Indians, who knew corn, beans, and squashes, also knew the beet.

It is unfortunate that the word hash has become associated with this combination. The word has fallen into some disrepute. Mother's mystery is not enigmatic; it is good, solid, everyday grub.

Red-flannel hash, however, is on a different plane. It is an Oriental-looking, taste-tantalizing dish. Its color is exciting. It has allure and snap. A frying pan full of it on the kitchen stove sends a nostril-tickling aroma through the room. As a man comes through the woodshed with the milk pails on his arm, he inhales the smell and a smile lights his face. What better reward for a long day's work digging potatoes or picking apples?

How to make it? Heat an old iron spider on a wood-burning stove. Fry a few slices of bacon until they are crisp and break into small bits. Chop a dozen cooked beets into small pieces; mix in two or three boiled potatoes and two chopped onions. The countryman, who is meticulous regarding certain culinary points, says that correct red-flannel hash is 85 percent beet, 10 percent potato, 3 percent onion, and 2 percent bacon; and that never under any circumstances should it include meat (other than bacon), gravy, or extraneous vegetables. Serve it piping hot with yellow cornmeal muffins and green-tomato pickles. For dessert, a wedge of deep-dish apple pie, a piece of old sharp cheese, and a glass of cold, creamy milk are acceptable.

Country Flavor
HAYDN S. PEARSON

Mr. Pearson knows whereof he speaks. He was born in the New Hampshire hills fifty-three years ago, where his father, a country minister, owned and ran a 120-acre general farm with a dozen milk cows and an 800-tree orchard. He gained his early education in a one-room school and in the pursuit of the usual chores that are the lot of every farm boy. After he graduated from the University of New Hampshire, and since that time, he has been writing, lecturing, and teaching school, all the while, however, staying close to the soil on his own small farm in eastern Massachusetts. He therefore properly qualifies as a country-man.

The Rural New Yorker Magazine
WILLIAM F. BERGHOLD, Editor

SAUCES

SAUCE BÉARNAISE

Even experienced cooks get into a panic when Béarnaise
Sauce is mentioned. It is not really so fearsome to make, but
it does require great patience.

Any sauce with eggs in it must be made in a double saucepan, but I have found that Béarnaise and Hollandaise take
better to china and glass than aluminum or enamel; so into
the bottom half of a small double saucepan half-filled with
water put a Pyrex or china bowl, and cook the sauce in this;
it has a further advantage in that the sauce can be served in
the bowl in which it was cooked.

All the classic recipes for Béarnaise instruct you to use about 6 yolks of eggs and at least ½ pound of butter. To make enough for 4 people these quantities are unnecessary. Using the whites is supposed to harden the sauce and encourage curdling, but I have found that with extra care the whites can perfectly well be used, so fewer eggs are required.

ELIZABETH DAVID

Makes 4 to 5 servings

2 chopped shallots	½ glass red wine, or half red
parsley	wine and half tarragon
tarragon	vinegars
thyme	3 ounces butter
bay leaf	(6 tablespoons)
ground black pepper	2 whole beaten eggs

1. Into a small saucepan put shallots, a little piece of parsley, tarragon, thyme, a bay leaf, and ground black pepper. Add red wine, or wine and tarragon vinegars. Let this boil rapidly until it has reduced to 1 tablespoon of liquid. It is this preliminary reduction which gives a Béarnaise sauce its inimitable flavor.
2. Strain what is left of the vinegar into a Pyrex bowl, add a dessert spoon of cold water, and over the saucepan containing hot water, and an exceedingly gentle fire, proceed to add little by little, butter and whole beaten eggs, stirring with great patience until the sauce thickens, and becomes shiny like a mayonnaise.
3. If the fire becomes too hot, if the water in the double saucepan boils, or if you stop stirring for one instant the sauce will curdle; when it has thickened take it off the fire and keep on stirring; the sauce is served tepid, and is at its best with grilled tournedos, but can be used with many other dishes. A very finely chopped tarragon is stirred in before serving.

NOTE:

If all precautions fail and the sauce curdles, it can sometimes be brought back again by the addition of a few drops of cold water, and vigorous stirring; if this fails put the sauce through a fine sieve, add another yolk of egg and stir again.

The addition of a quarter of its volume of concentrated tomato purée to the Béarnaise makes Sauce Choron; 2 tablespoons of meat glaze added (to the initial Béarnaise) makes Sauce Foyot. Whatever variations are to be made are made at the end when the sauce has already thickened.

The Book of Mediterranean Food
ELIZABETH DAVID

SAUCE JOLIE FILLE

La Cuisine de France is a book of excellent modern French recipes by Mapie, the Countess de Toulouse-Lautrec. The name Mapie is known to most every French household because for some fifteen years her recipes have appeared weekly in the popular French women's magazine, *Elle,* and she is a regular contributor to *Realités* as well as being director of the cooking school of Maxim's Academy in Paris.

Mapie's recipes in *La Cuisine de France* have been translated and edited by Charlotte Turgeon, who is also well known on the American cookery scene.

Sauce Jolie Fille (Pretty Girl Sauce) is superb for boiled fish and boiled meats of every variety.

4 teaspoons butter	4 teaspoons chopped parsley
1½ tablespoons flour	½ teaspoon onion juice
⅓ cup soft breadcrumbs	2 hard-boiled egg yolks
⅓ cup consommé	4 teaspoons lemon juice
⅓ cup heavy cream	salt and pepper

1. Heat the butter in a small saucepan and add the flour, mixing well. As soon as it is pale golden in color, add the breadcrumbs and stir for a minute before adding the consommé.
2. Stir well, add the cream, and season with salt and pepper. Add the chopped parsley and the onion juice.
3. Mix well, and as soon as it reaches the boiling point, remove from the fire and add the egg yolks and the lemon juice.

La Cuisine de France

SAUCE PARISIENNE

3 egg yolks	juice of ½ lemon
¼ cup cream	¼ teaspoon dry mustard
2 tablespoons tomato purée	salt
3 tablespoons butter	

1. Blend, in upper part of double boiler, egg yolks, cream, and tomato purée. Stir constantly over hot water with a wire whisk until mixture thickens.
2. Add butter, 1 tablespoon at a time, stirring well each time. Add salt to taste, lemon juice, and mustard.

The Fireside Cook Book
JAMES A. BEARD

BASIC STANDARD RECIPES FOR CREAM SAUCES

Each makes 1 cup of cream sauce

THIN	MEDIUM	THICK
1 tablespoon butter	2 tablespoons butter	3 tablespoons butter
1 tablespoon flour	2 tablespoons flour	3 tablespoons flour
1 cup milk, or thin or heavy cream	1 cup milk, or thin or heavy cream	1 cup milk, or thin or heavy cream
½ scant teaspoon salt	½ scant teaspoon salt	½ scant teaspoon salt
⅛ teaspoon white pepper	⅛ teaspoon white pepper	⅛ teaspoon white pepper
1 beaten egg yolk	1 beaten egg yolk	1 beaten egg yolk

1. For any one of the 3 basic sauces, melt the butter; stir in the flour and blend thoroughly, but do not let brown, over a gentle flame.
2. Add seasonings, then gradually, while stirring constantly, stir in the milk, or thin or heavy cream, previously scalded with 2 thin slices of onion, a bit of bay leaf, 2 sprigs of parsley, and 1 whole clove.
3. Keep stirring, still over a low flame, until mixture thickens and bubbles. Let bubble for 3 or 4 minutes.
4. Remove from the fire and briskly stir in the egg yolk. Do not boil any more, unless you stir briskly and from the bottom of the pan, lest mixture curdle.

The Gold Cook Book
LOUIS P. DE GOUY

BÉCHAMEL SAUCE

Béchamel Sauce, a simple combination of butter, flour, and milk, is a foundation sauce which everyone should know how to make. An onion cooked in it gives added flavor, and other seasonings such as mustard are often added. For a richer sauce it can be combined with eggs, cream, cheese, and so on. Béchamel Sauce, or any of its variations, is served on vegetables, fish, hard-cooked eggs, poultry, and other cooked foods.

⅓ cup butter
½ medium onion, minced
⅓ cup flour
3 cups hot milk

1 teaspoon salt
few grains white pepper
2 sprigs parsley
a little nutmeg

1. Melt butter in a saucepan, add onion and cook until onion becomes very light brown.
2. Add flour, cook a few minutes longer, add milk and seasoning, stirring vigorously.
3. Cook gently 25 to 30 minutes, stirring constantly until sauce is thick and smooth and then occasionally for the remaining time. Strain.
4. If sauce is not to be used immediately, stir occasionally as it cools to prevent a crust forming on top.

French Cooking for Americans
LOUIS DIAT

MORNAY SAUCE

Makes about 1½ cups of sauce

1 cup Cream Sauce (sec page 254) or hot Béchamel Sauce (see page 255)
¾ scant cup of dry white wine

2 tablespoons of grated cheese
1 tablespoon sweet butter seasoning to taste

1. To each cup of Cream Sauce or hot Béchamel Sauce add ¾ scant cup of dry white wine and let this reduce to ⅓ its volume over a bright flame, stirring frequently.
2. Then stir in 2 tablespoons of your favorite grated cheese or equal parts of 2 different kinds.
3. When ready to use, blend in 1 tablespoon of sweet butter and taste for seasoning.

NOTE:

When using Mornay Sauce to top a dish to be made au gratin, it is usually, in the French cuisine, considered improved if a tablespoon or two of whipped cream is folded into each half cup of Mornay Sauce before spreading over top of fish or other main ingredient. The top then takes on an even golden brown glaze.

Home Style Mornay Sauce: Simply add ⅓ cup of grated cheese to each cup of cream sauce and stir until the cheese is melted. It is merely a cheese sauce.

Mornay Sauce cannot be boiled when it is made, lest it curdle, so, if for any reason it has to stand, keep it over hot, never boiling water. This applies to any sauce containing eggs.

The Gold Cook Book
LOUIS P. DE GOUY

VELOUTÉ SAUCE

Velouté is another foundation sauce which acts as the base of many other sauces. It can also be used in making croquettes.

It can be kept covered in the refrigerator for a week and then boiled up and put in a clean jar to keep it longer.

Makes about 2 cups of sauce

⅓ cup butter
⅓ cup flour
 3 cups white stock (part of
    this may be liquid in
    which mushrooms were
    cooked)

½ teaspoon salt
 2 or 3 peppercorns
 1 sprig parsley
    few gratings nutmeg

1. Prepare stock by cooking veal or chicken bones (and meat if available) in water, or use chicken bouillon cubes and water.
2. Melt butter (or substitute), add flour and cook, but do not let brown.
3. Add stock and cook, stirring all the time until flour and fat are combined with the liquid.
4. Add remaining ingredients and cook gently about 1 hour when there should be 2 cups of sauce.
5. Strain, cool, and use as needed.

French Cooking for Americans
LOUIS DIAT

TOMATO SAUCE, ITALIAN STYLE

Makes about 3 pints

2 cups chopped onion
3 cloves garlic, chopped
3 tablespoons olive oil
1 No. 2½ can (1 pound 13
   ounces or 3½ cups)
   Italian-style plum
   tomatoes
2 cans tomato paste

2 cups water or meat broth,
   approximately
1 bay leaf
½ teaspoon salt
¼ teaspoon pepper
½ teaspoon orégano or ¼
   teaspoon each orégano
   and basil

1. Sauté onion and garlic in olive oil until brown, stirring often.

2. Add tomatoes, tomato paste, water or broth, bay leaf, salt, and pepper. Simmer uncovered, stirring occasionally, about 2 hours. Add additional water as needed.
3. Add orégano and basil and continue cooking about 15 minutes. The sauce should be thick.

The New York Times

SWEET MUSTARD SAUCE

This sauce is excellent for baked ham. The Colony and the Baroque restaurants in New York, and probably other good restaurants, too, make a rather thick mustard-and-mayonnaise sauce to accompany broiled fillet of sole and other broiled fish. No sugar in it, of course.

Makes about 10 servings

5 tablespoons dry English mustard

10 tablespoons confectioner's sugar
cider vinegar

1. Mix enough vinegar with the mustard and sugar to make a smooth paste.
2. Stir until sugar is completely dissolved.

SAUCE HOLLANDAISE

Makes 6 to 8 servings

½ lemon
4 tablespoons vinegar
big pinch of salt
⅛ teaspoon white pepper (coarsely ground black pepper may be substituted, but it will show)

2 tablespoons cold water
4 egg yolks
butter
cayenne

1. Squeeze and strain the juice of ½ lemon.
2. Put vinegar in top part of enamel double boiler with a big pinch of salt and white pepper. Reduce the vinegar by simmering until only 2 teaspoons are left. Add cold water and the yolks of 4 eggs, making sure not to include any of the whites. Beat well with wire whisk or rotary beater, and add ⅛ pound butter cut in little pieces.
3. Place the pan directly on a very, very low heat (or to be safer still, place over boiling water in bottom part of double boiler, on low flame, being sure that the bottom part of the top pan does not actually touch the boiling water) and beat constantly with wire whisk until the mixture has thickened.
4. At this point, remove the pan from the fire entirely, and add little by little (beating constantly with wire whisk) ½ pound butter. When all the butter has been added, stir in the lemon juice and season to taste with salt, pepper, and cayenne. Serve in warm, not hot, bowl.

The Best I Ever Ate
SOPHIE KERR AND JUNE PLATT

SAUCE MOUSSELINE

See recipe under Alice B. Toklas' Cauliflower Salad with Shrimps, page 274.

This sauce is suitable with cold fish, asparagus, and shellfish salads.

TEXAS BARBECUE SAUCE

There is no greater authority than Helen Corbitt to give you the correct recipe for the hot, smoky sauce used by Texans for outdoor picnics. It is great as a steak sauce or for oven barbecuing—great, that is, if you can take it.

Makes 3 cups

1 tablespoon salt	1 teaspoon Liquid Smoke
½ teaspoon pepper	sauce
3 tablespoons brown sugar	1 cup water
¼ cup catsup	2 tablespoons chili sauce
3 tablespoons prepared	½ cup vinegar
(brown) mustard	1 cup melted butter or
2 tablespoons Worcestershire	cooking oil
sauce	

1. Mix ingredients in order given, using rotary egg beater as oil is added. Simmer slowly until slightly thickened. This makes enough sauce for 6 pounds of meat. Keep hot.
2. Brown meat over coals of charcoal broiler, add sauce, and bake at 350° until tender. This is for such cuts of meat as shoulder chops, short ribs, lamb shoulder, and breast: the cheaper cuts of meat.
3. If barbecuing a steak of the cheaper variety, soaking it in beer for a few hours will help tenderize it; then swish it around in the barbecue sauce before broiling over the grill. Brush frequently with the sauce while broiling.

Helen Corbitt's Cookbook

CHINESE BARBECUE SAUCE

The way of the English is much meat and little sauce. The art of the Chinese—along with the French—is little meat and generous servings of sauce. Certainly the savoriness of Chinese barbecued spareribs depends upon the generous use of this sauce.

¼ cup soy sauce	1 piece fresh or dried ginger
2 tablespoons honey	root, 1½ inches long,
1 tablespoon brown sugar	grated
1 teaspoon salt	1 garlic clove, minced
½ teaspoon pepper	½ jigger brandy

Combine all ingredients and mix well.

Oriental Cookbook
ALICE MILLER MITCHELL

CHILI SAUCE

½ peck tomatoes	1 cup vinegar
2 cups chopped celery	1 tablespoon mustard seed
2 cups chopped onions	3 tablespoons salt
2 cups chopped green	2 tablespoons cinnamon
peppers	1 teaspoon cloves
2 cups sugar	

1. Cook the vegetables for 20 minutes.
2. Add sugar, spices and vinegar.
3. Cook until thick.

Massachusetts Cooking Rules Old and New
MRS. GEORGE J. BATES

CHASEN'S CRACKED-CRAB SAUCE

Enough for 4 servings of Dungeness crab—a Pacific Coast delicacy—or for other types of cold boiled crab meat.

1 medium-sized Bermuda onion	2 teaspoons Worcestershire sauce
½ teaspoon dry mustard (English type)	¼ teaspoon freshly ground black pepper
1 tablespoon prepared mustard (French type)	4 tablespoons mayonnaise

1. Grate onion. Place in center of linen napkin; squeeze out juice.
2. Combine onion juice and dry mustard; blend into a paste.
3. Add prepared mustard and Worcestershire sauce. Sprinkle pepper over mayonnaise; add to first mixture. Blend all ingredients thoroughly.

Holiday Book of Food and Drink

CHART FOR

Here's a chart for barbecue sauces to serve as a guide in mixing something special of your own. They all began with "dipney"—a blend of sweet country lard, salt, and the strongest vinegar, thick and hot with red and black pepper—which was used to baste the roasting meat at the all-American barbecues of the last century. Later on, other ingredients were

	"Dipney" Basting sauce for all meats	Basic all-round sauce, beef, lamb, veal
Fat	sweet lard	2 tablespoons butter or margarine
Salt	to taste	to taste
"Pepper uppers" black, white, red pepper, paprika, Tabasco	black and cayenne	black pepper and paprika to taste
Vinegar and/or lemon juice	strong cider vinegar	¼ cup vinegar (malt or cider)
Onion and garlic		⅓ cup chopped onion
Tomato sauce, catsup		1 cup catsup
Sugar white, brown		1 tablespoon white
Mustard powdered, prepared		2 tablespoons prepared
Other spices and herbs		

Prepared sauces ⟶

BARBECUE SAUCES

added to improve the texture of the meat or brighten the flavor of the sauce. Now the sky's the limit. You can perform magic with the addition of herbs and spices—not to mention the handy flavored additions available at epicurean food stores.

Mexican	For Pork	For chicken
½ cup oil or butter	fat from pork is sufficient	2 tablespoons butter or chicken fat
to taste	scant	to taste
Mexican red pepper, very sparingly used	freshly ground black or white	freshly ground black or white pepper to taste
½ cup red wine vinegar (half water if desired)	3 tablespoons	½ cup to 1 cup white wine vinegar
1 small onion; 1 clove chopped garlic	1 small chopped onion; garlic juice	onion juice
1 cup canned tomato sauce	3 tablespoons catsup	½ cup catsup
	2 tablespoons brown	1 teaspoon white
	1½ teaspoons dry	¼ teaspoon dry
1 teaspoon chili powder	to taste	to taste

Use as directed to taste ←⎯⎯⎯⎯⎯⎯⎯⎯⎯⎯⎯⎯

The Complete Barbecue Book
JOHN AND MARIE ROBERSON

MUSHROOM SAUCE

Makes 2½ to 3 cups sauce

½ pound mushrooms,
    washed and sliced thin
1 teaspoon chopped onion
½ teaspoon chopped parsley
6 tablespoons butter
4 to 5 tablespoons flour

1 cup stock (or use bouillon
    cube)
¼ cup sour cream
salt to taste
½ tablespoon lemon juice

1. Melt the butter (about 2 tablespoons of it) and sauté the onion and parsley.
2. Add the mushrooms and allow to cook for about 5 minutes.
3. In another pan melt the remaining butter. Blend the flour in well. Gradually add the stock and mix thoroughly. Blend in the sour cream, then add the salt.
4. Pour the sour cream-stock mixture into the pan with the mushrooms, stirring constantly and allow to cook gently for 15 minutes.
5. Remove from flame and add the lemon juice.

HOT HORSERADISH SAUCE

Makes about 1½ cups sauce

1 cup medium white sauce
½ cup white bread crumbs
¼ cup horseradish (freshly
    grated if possible)

2 tablespoons lemon juice or
    mild white vinegar
½ teaspoon salt

1. Freshly grated horseradish is preferred. If you grate your own you will shed tears during the process, but it is worth it, and is perhaps good for your sinus. Freshly grated horseradish needs either lemon juice or a mild white vinegar. If you use the prepared horseradish, omit the lemon juice or vinegar.
2. Add the bread crumbs and horseradish to the white sauce.

Mix well and add the lemon juice or vinegar and salt gradually.

3. Serve hot with ham, roast beef, and fried or broiled fish.

You Can Cook If You Can Read
MURIEL AND CORTLAND FITZSIMMONS

HOMEMADE KETCHUP

"Such was the passion for my grandmother's ketchup in my own family that we could never get enough of it," says Kenneth Roberts. "We were allowed to have it on beans, fish cakes and hash, since those dishes were acknowledged to be incomplete without them; but when we went so far as to demand it on bread, as we often did, we were peremptorily refused, and had to go down in the cellar and steal it—which we also often did. It had a savory, appetizing tang to it that seemed—and still seems—to me to be inimitable. I became almost a ketchup drunkard; for when I couldn't get it, I yearned for it. Because of that yearning, I begged the recipe from my grandmother when I went away from home; and since that day I have made many and many a batch of her ketchup with excellent results.

"The recipe has never been published, and I put it down here for the benefit of those who aren't satisfied with the commercial makeshifts that masquerade under the name of ketchup."

Makes about 1 gallon

1 peck of ripe tomatoes, cooked and strained or 1 dozen cans of concentrated tomato juice
1 pint sharp vinegar
6 tablespoons salt
4 tablespoons allspice
2 tablespoons mustard
1 tablespoon powdered cloves
1 teaspoon black pepper
¼ teaspoon red pepper
olive oil

1. With a large spoon rub cooked tomatoes through a sieve into a kettle, to remove seeds and heavy pulp, until you have 1 gallon of liquid. One peck of ripe tomatoes, cooked and strained, makes 1 gallon. (This operation is

greatly simplified by using one dozen cans of concentrated tomato juice.)
2. Put the kettle on the stove and bring the tomato juice almost to a boil.
3. Into a bowl put a pint of sharp vinegar, and in the vinegar dissolve 6 tablespoons of salt, 4 tablespoons of allspice, 2 tablespoons of mustard, 1 tablespoon of powdered cloves, 1 teaspoon of black pepper and ¼ teaspoon of red pepper.
4. Stir the vinegar and spices into the tomato juice, set the kettle over a slow fire and let it simmer until it thickens. The mixture must be constantly stirred, or the spices settle on the bottom and burn. If made from concentrated tomato juice, 1½ hours of simmering is sufficient; but if made from canned tomatoes, the mixture should be allowed to cook slowly for 3 or 4 hours.
5. When the kettle is removed from the fire, let the mixture stand until cold.
6. Then stir and pour into small-necked bottles. If ½ inch of olive oil is poured into each bottle, and the bottle then corked, the ketchup will keep indefinitely in a cool place. It's better if chilled before serving.

Trending Into Maine
KENNETH ROBERTS

SKORDALIA

(GARLIC SAUCE)

From its earliest recording up until the glorious Golden Age, Greek history makes frequent mention of those culinary techniques which developed from a primitive to a refined art. History records many illustrious cooks who lived in that period and who elevated cooking to new deserving heights. Such men were Thimbron the Athenian; Archistratus, who had also written a cookbook; Soteriades the Sage, who claimed that he prepared different dishes for different moods and ages—the young, the lovers, the older men, and the philosophers.

The Romans adopted this cooking years later by acquiring the services of Athenian cooks as they later procured the services of Greek tutors for the education of their children. Thus, Greece conquered Rome firstly with her excelling culinary artfulnss, and secondly with her superior education. It is no coincidence that famed Roman gluttons like Apicius and Lucullus make their appearance at about this time.

Makes about 3½ cups of sauce

2 cups oil, select quality
3 or 4 cloves garlic
1 or 2 medium-size boiled and mashed potatoes, or 1 cup moist bread crumbs

¼ cup vinegar
salt and pepper to taste
if desired, add about ¼ cup blanched and crushed almonds to the sauce

1. Crush the garlic in a mortar. Add either the mashed potatoes or the bread crumbs. Then add blanched almonds.
2. Pound well until blended to a paste. Add olive oil and vinegar alternately in very small quantities, stirring the sauce briskly with the pestle. Add salt and pepper.
3. Continue to stir in a rotary motion until the sauce is stiff enough to hold its shape.

Greek Cookery
NICHOLAS TSELEMENTES

BILLY MILLS'S CORN RELISH

If, when fresh corn is in season, you are fortunate enough to have the urge to do some pickling, try this prize recipe. It comes (via Leonard Levinson's book on pickles and relishes) from a man who made a hobby of pickling despite his quite different profession of musical director on the famous radio show "Fibber McGee and Molly."

Billy Mills says, "I discovered the recipe written in pencil on the margin of an old cookbook, yellowed with age. It was almost unintelligible. The book belonged to my mother, and the recipe was probably given to her by her mother, as it had been passed down through generations. We came from Michigan and my mother put up this relish every fall during harvest time when the ingredients were plentiful. It keeps indefinitely and does not require refrigeration, although its flavor is enhanced if it is served chilled.

"I found this recipe in 1941 and made a batch of it to see if it was as good as I had remembered it as a boy back in

Michigan. It was so good that a friend persuaded me to allow it to be taken and entered in the Los Angeles County Fair at Pomona. I thought so little of the idea that I didn't want to be bothered, so my friend entered it for me.

"I was away on a cruise at the time the judging was done and on my return found that the news services, Fair officials, and publicity offices were frantically trying to locate me because my Corn Relish had won first prize. Because of my connection with the Fibber and Molly show, the winner of a blue ribbon had great publicity potential.

"The success of the Relish gave me an idea—why not bottle it and send it out for Christmas? It seemed an ideal way to take care of those who 'had everything' and could be given nothing they didn't already have. Don Quinn drew me a label and I bought suitable containers and went ahead with the idea.

"This went on for several years, until the list got so large that I had to discontinue making it. At regular periods up until the present, I have made new batches and entered it in the Los Angeles County Fair. It always repeats and never has failed to win."

Makes about 6 pints

5 or 6 ears fresh green corn (about 1 quart when cut from cobs)
3 cups chopped ripe tomatoes, without seeds
1½ cups chopped green peppers (3 peppers)
¾ cup chopped sweet red pepper (1 small)

1 cup chopped, unpeeled green cucumber
1 cup chopped onion
PICKLING SOLUTION:
1 cup sugar
1 pint vinegar
1 tablespoon salt
1 teaspoon celery seed
1 teaspoon mustard seed

1. Wash and drain vegetables. Cut corn from cob. Scrape cobs to get all of the milk from the kernels.
2. Combine with all of the other prepared vegetables in a large pot or preserving kettle.
3. Mix the pickling solution separately; pour over the vegetables; simmer for 1 hour and place in jars. Seal while hot to preserve flavor.

The Complete Book of Pickles and Relishes
LEONARD LEVINSON

SALADS

GREEN SALAD

I go mad, the way green salads are served in most restaurants —chewed-up lettuce in little bowls, with a dash of bottled dressing dribbled on top. In France and Italy, green salads are treated with respect, and salad-making is an art. In preparing the simple Italian Insalata Verde (for two servings), a tablespoon is filled about one third full of salt, and the rest of the spoon is filled with white wine vinegar. With a fork, the salt and vinegar are mixed in the spoon and sprinkled over the greens from a height of about a foot. The salad is given a few gentle turns with fork and spoon, and then, from about two feet above it, a very thin stream of oil is poured from a bottle or tin held in one hand, while the other hand starts turning the salad. When your judgment tells you there is enough oil to coat the leaves, both hands are used to turn the greens over and over, gently, with fork and spoon. I must confess that I have never been able to duplicate the precise flavor of salad dressings made by even the most *paisan* waiter in Italy—perhaps the oil is different, or the lettuce—but even a near miss is good. In Stockholm—I am thinking of the Grand Hotel in particular—mustard is used successfully in the dressing. A little restaurant in New York called La Piazetta makes a great salad with a finely diced beet dressing, and another small but fashionable place named The Running Footman serves a good salad of raw spinach with a crisp bacon dressing. The following is the best classical French salad, the typical green salad served with every French meal in every province. It is never eaten with the main dish—it is almost always a course in itself, though sometimes an accompaniment to cheese.

Makes 4 servings

1 head lettuce: Boston, iceberg, or chicory (or 8 heads of endive)	½ teaspoon salt freshly ground pepper
3 tablespoons fine salad oil: peanut or olive oil preferred	OPTIONAL: garlic for the bowl ½ teaspoon dry mustard ¼ teaspoon sugar
1 tablespoon tarragon vinegar, light wine vinegar, or lemon juice	2 tablespoons finely chopped dill, scallions, or parsley

1. You can wash the salad greens or just remove the outer leaves and use the rest without washing. If you wash it, remember you will never get a good salad if water remains on the leaves. After washing, use a salad basket or a clean cloth and shake and shake, then let the greens dry in the air for 10 minutes and shake again in a dry cloth. They should be crisp yet dry.
2. In a medium-size bowl, prepare the dressing in the amounts given above. We suggest peanut oil because it is so light and does not have the strong taste of many olive

oils—but the oil used is a matter of preference; so is the type of vinegar. Use the pepper mill fairly generously. If you like mustard and sugar in your dressing, this is the place to add them.

3. For the salad mixing, you need a very large bowl—big enough to turn the greens readily without their falling all over the place. If you like the flavor of garlic (and it likes you), rub the bowl gently with a garlic clove. Don't add the greens yet.

4. Pour the dressing into this extra-large bowl and put in *half* the greens. Turn them over and over until all the leaves are well coated with the dressing. Now add the other half and continue turning lightly but thoroughly. Don't mash or the leaves will become soggy.

5. If you desire, you can sprinkle the finely chopped dill, parsley, or scallions over the top of each serving. And/ or, if you are particularly fond of tomatoes, add quarters or slices, but most salad sybarites will say, "Let it be all green."

SALAD BOWL À LA LAWRY'S

This is the famous salad served at Lawry's The Prime Rib Restaurant, in Beverly Hills, California.

Makes 6 servings

1 small head romaine
1 small head lettuce
1 cup endive, torn in pieces
½ cup watercress, torn in sprigs
1 cup shoestring beets, well drained

1 hard-boiled egg, sieved
Lawry's Seasoned Salt
Lawry's Seasoned Pepper
¾ cup Lawry's Sherry French Dressing

1. Tear the romaine and lettuce in 2-inch pieces into a salad bowl. Add the endive, watercress, beets, and egg.

2. Sprinkle with the seasoned salt and seasoned pepper. Toss with the Sherry French Dressing.

CAESAR SALAD À LA CHASEN

Dave Chasen may not have created the Caesar Salad, but his Hollywood restaurant is famous for it . . . as well as for spareribs, soups, chili, and other specialties.

Those of us with long memories recall Dave as the sort of witless assistant to a comedian named Joe Cook. As writer Budd Schulberg puts it, Dave Chasen was "the stubby red-thatched clown with the droopy lids and the blacked-out teeth who climaxed one of the most elaborate gags ever to clutter up a stage. The orchestra in the pit would engage itself in a pseudo-classical rendition, gathering steam until it reached the point where the score called for the tingle of a triangle—at which point Joe Cook would press a button setting in motion his memorable Rube Goldberg contraption. Balls rolled down inclines, wheels revolved, weights were released onto levers thereby shifting gears—this entire mechanical phantasmagory culminating in the tap of a hammer upon the head of the droll figure who drowsed, to all appearances, unsuspectingly. Thus interrupted from his reveries, Dave would come to with a pixy smile, sound a single significantly insignificant note on his triangle and move his hand, palm outward, in a slow half-circle in front of his face. If it isn't quite so funny, here in words, as it was to see, that's because Dave was, like all good comedians, a visual artist, a clown of the old school who has made people laugh with a move of the eye, the droop of a lip, from caveman days to the reign of Fields, Chaplin, and Durante.

"But effective as he was on stage, Dave reached even greater heights of artistry after the curtain fell, when he could move onto the stage he loved best, with two-inch beefsteaks for props, and a charcoal fire with which to work his magic."

Makes 4 servings

6 cups mixed salad greens, washed, dried, and broken into fair-sized pieces

1 cup ½-inch croutons, preferably made from sourdough bread

2 tablespoons garlic oil (cut 1 clove garlic into oil; let stand several hours; remove garlic pieces)

6 tablespoons French dressing

4 tablespoons grated Parmesan cheese

juice of 1½ lemons

1½ teaspoons Worcestershire sauce

1 1-minute coddled egg

1 teaspoon freshly ground black pepper

1. Prepare in advance the salad greens, croutons, garlic oil, French dressing and grated Parmesan cheese.
2. At serving time beat together in a small bowl lemon juice, garlic oil, Worcestershire sauce, French dressing, and the coddled egg.
3. Next toss well in large wooden bowl the salad greens, croutons, mixture from the small bowl, black pepper, and Parmesan cheese. Serve immediately.

MIXED SALAD

For more than twenty years, Ann Batchelder was food editor of the *Ladies' Home Journal*. She was responsible for some of the most beautiful food pictures that have ever been published. She helped to create many fascinating dishes and presented innumerable recipes in a manner understandable alike to blushing bride and bouncing matron. Above all, Ann Batchelder speaks not alone with authority but with good humor. She was a native of Vermont and, like many other good Vermonters, she carried herself with an air of confidence, dignity, and human understanding that befits true Americanism.

This is one of Ann Batchelder's favorite recipes. Another is her Ham and Eggs Jersey in another section of this book (page 106).

Makes 8 servings

¼ pound sliced Swiss cheese	1 bunch radishes
¼ pound sliced boiled	½ cucumber
smoked tongue	2 tomatoes
¼ pound sliced boiled ham	assorted greens
4 hard-boiled eggs	

1. Cut Swiss cheese, tongue, and ham into thin strips. Slice the eggs and radishes. Slice cucumber and cut all the slices into quarters. Cut tomatoes into quarters or eighths, depending on the size.
2. Line a salad bowl with a good bed of crisp assorted greens. Arrange the above ingredients in groups on the greens. Have a big bowl to begin with, as you're going to toss it at the table.

DRESSING

1 clove garlic	4 finely chopped anchovies
1 teaspoon salt	2 tablespoons chopped water-
½ cup salad oil	cress
1 raw egg	¼ teaspoon paprika
3 tablespoons wine vinegar	⅛ teaspoon pepper

1. Mash garlic to a pulp with salt. The salt hurries things up. Add salad oil and raw egg. Now beat with a fork. Add wine vinegar, anchovies, watercress, paprika, and pepper.
2. Beat again to blend smooth. The egg gives this dressing body, but it shouldn't be thick.

Ann Batchelder's Cookbook
ANN BATCHELDER

ALICE B. TOKLAS' CAULIFLOWER SALAD WITH SHRIMPS AND SAUCE MOUSSELINE

During the forty years that she was the constant companion of Gertrude Stein, Alice B. Toklas expressed her creativity through the preparation of superb food for the author and her many distinguished guests. During all this time, Alice B. Toklas harbored the secret ambition to write a book of her own, which materialized upon Miss Stein's death as *The Alice*

B. Toklas Cook Book, a volume full of sensitive observations as well as fine foods.

We could have brought you many unique recipes from *The Alice B. Toklas Cook Book*—her Singapore Ice Cream, Scheherezade's Melon, Mirrored Eggs, or perhaps her recipe for Hashish Fudge, which has evoked almost as much comment as Gertrude Stein's famous "a rose is a rose is a rose." For those many exotic or erotic dishes we refer you to the book itself. For *The World's Best Recipes,* we have chosen a simple yet delectable salad with a sauce of many uses.

Makes 6 servings

1 large whole cauliflower	1 pound giant shrimps, cooked and shelled

1. Boil the whole cauliflower in salted water until the flowerets are tender but no more than that.
2. Drain and press head down in a bowl while still hot so that when cold and removed from the bowl it will keep its shape.
3. Place cauliflower flat side down on a flat round serving dish.
4. Place the giant shrimps between the flowerets, tails out.
5. Serve sauce separately.

SAUCE MOUSSELINE

3 egg yolks	¼ pound butter
¼ teaspoon salt	1 tablespoon lemon juice
pinch of pepper	½ cup whipped cream
pinch of nutmeg	

1. Place egg yolks in top of double boiler. Add salt, pepper, and nutmeg.
2. Put over very hot but not boiling water. Stir constantly with a wooden spoon, particularly around the sides and at the bottom.
3. Add the butter in very small pieces. Allow each piece to melt before adding the next one.
4. When all the butter has melted and the mixture has thickened, remove from the heat and very slowly add the lemon juice.

5. When the sauce is tepid, add the whipped cream. Stir gently and serve. This sauce is also good with cold fish, asparagus, and shellfish salads.

The Alice B. Toklas Cook Book

DRUNKARD'S DREAM

In Nashville there is a society of men, The Society of Amateur Chefs, who take pride in their cookery and have developed a number of original dishes. The following all-inclusive original recipe was given me by the Society with explicit strings attached: The cup of ham gravy served over the salad MUST be poured over the moment before serving; the gravy must be piping hot! This salad may be made for a large or a small group. This recipe is for a large platter of guests. Drunkard's Dream is basically composed of:

shredded leaf lettuce
chopped radishes
chopped spring onions
diced dill pickles

chopped tomatoes
several slices of crisp
   fried bacon
1 cup of red ham gravy, *hot*

1. Build up ingredients in alternate layers on a large meat platter.
2. Top with bacon slices.
3. Just before serving, pour 1 cup of red ham gravy, *hot,* over all.

The Southern Cook Book
MARION BROWN

BISMARCK SALAD

1 stalk of celery
1 small heart of lettuce
2 medium size carrots
1 Bismarck herring

⅓ cup homemade French
   dressing
2 tablespoons chili sauce

1. Finely shred the lettuce heart and the celery. (Have lettuce and celery crisp and cold before cutting.)

2. Grate raw carrot and thinly slice the herring.
3. Combine all together and moisten with French dressing and chili sauce.
4. Toss lightly with salad fork and spoon until salad is thoroughly mixed with dressing.

GERMAN POTATO SALAD

Salads are not listed among the recipes found in Grandmother's old-fashioned cookbook. This fact is not too surprising, since the idea of having a salad with every dinner is a twentieth-century innovation.

However, many of the foods we use in salads were a part of the diet of our great-grandparents. Those dishes of former days, although not called salads, consisted of lettuce, onions, and radishes in late spring; cole slaw during the summer; endive, turnip slaw, and celery during crisp autumn days; and dandelion and water cress in early spring. In the absence of beautiful salad plates, these were served in fancy glass dishes, and were just another of the tasty foods arranged on Grandmother's table.

Most interesting is this bit of helpful advice found written among a list of home remedies in a quaint old recipe book: "At this season of the year (spring) too much cannot be said in favor of onions. Whether raw or cooked they are especially good, both medicinally and as a skin beautifier."

MARY EMMA SHOWALTER

Makes 8 servings

6 frankfurters, cooked and chopped	1½ teaspoons salt
	1 tablespoon flour
4 cups hot, diced potatoes	2 tablespoons fat
½ cup chopped celery	⅓ cup sugar
1 medium-sized onion, chopped	⅓ cup vinegar
	¼ teaspoon pepper
1 tablespoon chopped parsley	⅔ cup water

1. Fry chopped onion in hot fat until light brown. Add flour and blend. Then add sugar, salt, vinegar, and water. Bring to a boil, stirring constantly. Mix in the celery and parsley.

2. Pour dressing over the diced potatoes and chopped frank-furters. Sprinkle with pepper and serve hot.

The Mennonite Community Cookbook
MARY EMMA SHOWALTER

BLISSFUL BEAN SALAD

Holt Delyner is the name of the colorful "Bachelor Gourmet" whose recipes appear on cards in New York City buses. When it comes to cooking, Holt, they say, has the inferiority complex of a taxi driver. . . . He claims the girls at the picnic would think they were in heaven eating his Blissful Bean Salad if there were just some trumpets in the background. In making his specialty, Holt says it isn't necessary to add thin slices of onion, but he always does. It may set the court-ship back temporarily, but, as George Meredith said, "Kissing don't last; cookery do."

Makes 8 servings

1 tall can wax beans	1 green pepper, thinly sliced
1 tall can green beans	½ cup salad oil
1 tall can kidney beans	¾ cup cider vinegar
½ cup diced celery	½ cup sugar

1. Drain all the beans well and place in large bowl.
2. Add the celery and green pepper, and mix carefully with a fork.
3. Make a smooth dressing of the oil, vinegar, and sugar. Pour this over the mixture, cover the bowl, and set it in the refrigerator for 8 hours or so. Every now and then, take it out and tenderly toss the beans around in the dressing.

CHEF'S SALAD

There are times when a Chef's Salad just touches the spot, and there are times when you make it to use up leftover ends of meat . . . and there are times when it serves as a satisfying, filling-but-not-fattening item on a weight-watching diet. Those who are not on a diet can enrich this salad with a Roquefort dressing or a hearty Russian dressing.

Makes 4 servings

1 head lettuce	6 ounces white meat of
1 head romaine	chicken
1 head chicory	6 ounces baked ham
1 head escarole	6 ounces Swiss cheese
8 sprigs watercress	6 ounces tongue
4 small tomatoes, quartered	French dressing

1. Chop coarsely lettuce, romaine, chicory, and escarole. Mix and divide equally, placing in 4 wooden bowls.
2. Place tomato quarters on top of greens.
3. Cut julienne-style, chicken, ham, tongue, and Swiss cheese. Place on top of salad.
4. Garnish with watercress. Serve with French dressing.

Longchamps Restaurants
New York City

NEW LEEK SALAD

Unless you know the robust yet gentle flavor of leeks, you are not fully flavor-wise. We are too ready to confine leeks to the soup pot, never knowing their uncooked fineness of flavor. But there was a time, while England was still peopled with Angles and Saxons, when leeks were important food. In fact, a garden was known then as a leac-ton, and a gardener was a leac-ward. The wise men of early times said:

Eat leeks in oile, and ramsines in May,
And all the year after physicians may play.

In case you were wondering, ramsines were old-fashioned broad-leafed leeks. So copy the Angles and Saxons—eat leeks in your salad.

IRMA GOODRICH MAZZA

3 leeks
1 large tomato
romaine
1 teaspoon sweet basil
1 teaspoon chervil

garlicked chapon of bread
olive oil
salt, pepper
vinega.

1. Cut up coarsely the white parts of leeks that are young and tender.
2. Cut a large tomato into sections and add these and the leeks to a bowl of romaine.
3. Sprinkle with a teaspoon sweet basil and the same amount of chervil. (Chervil is the salad herb *par excellence*.)
4. Add a garlicked chapon of bread, and dress with olive oil, salt, pepper, and vinegar.

NOTE:

To make a chapon of bread, take the heel of a loaf of French bread and rub over it a clove of garlic, first dipped in salt. A chapon is frequently used in vegetable salads to give an additional bit of flavor.

Herbs for the Kitchen
IRMA GOODRICH MAZZA

BOUQUET OF FLOWERS SALAD

Say it with flowers from love's sweetest bowers,
And you'll find her waiting, waiting for you.
     —Neville Fleeson, "Say It With Flowers"

This salad will give the effect of a bouquet of flowers.

Makes 4 to 6 servings

1 medium-size cauliflower
2 medium-size boiled
    potatoes
2 medium-size tomatoes
1 green pepper
4 hard-boiled eggs

2 tablespoons mayonnaise
2 tablespoons oil
2 tablespoons lemon juice
salt and pepper to taste
heart of lettuce or sprig of
    parsley

1. Cut off stem of cauliflower and wash. Cover and cook whole in a small amount of salted water until tender. Overcooking must be avoided because it makes cauliflower mushy. Drain well. Place in a salad bowl in the shape of a mound. Sprinkle with salt, pepper, oil, and lemon juice.
2. Mash the potatoes. Add salt, mayonnaise dressing, and a little milk. Mix and spread evenly with a spatula all over the cauliflower, applying most of this mixture around the base of the mound.
3. Dip a small pointed knife in cold water and make lengthwise slits in cauliflower.
4. Garnish the top of the salad with the hard-boiled eggs cut in quarters. Place pointed ends of eggs up with the yolks on the outside, to give the appearance of a flower. Place a small heart of lettuce or a sprig of parsley in the center.
5. Slice the tomatoes and cut with a round biscuit cutter. Garnish bottom part of the salad bowl. Cut green pepper in strips and place on the tomatoes. Cut a few green olives in half and place them around the eggs.

Greek Cookery
NICHOLAS TSELEMENTES

WALDORF SALAD

Makes 6 to 8 servings

4 cups of diced apples	lettuce leaves
2 cups of diced celery	chopped walnuts
1 cup of mayonnaise	

1. Mix the apples and celery, then add the mayonnaise and mix well again, so that the apples and celery are well coated.
2. Serve in a salad bowl topped with chopped walnuts with a border of lettuce leaves.

Waldorf-Astoria Hotel
New York City

BULGARIAN BRANDIED FRUIT SALAD

(FRUKTOVA SALATA)

Makes about 6 servings

3 apples, peeled and sliced thin
3 pears, peeled and sliced thin
2 oranges, peeled and sliced thin

1 cup pitted cherries, fresh or frozen
1 cup melon balls, fresh or frozen
½ cup sugar
2 cups white wine
½ cup brandy

1. Combine the apples, pears, oranges, cherries, and melon balls. Sprinkle with the sugar.
2. Mix the wine and brandy together. Pour over the fruit and mix gently but thoroughly.
3. Chill for at least 3 hours. Serve very cold.

The Complete Round-The-World Cookbook
MYRA WALDO

DELUXE CHICKEN SALAD

Makes 6 servings

2 cups chicken cubes
1 cup diced celery
1 cup green peas
½ cup French dressing

lettuce
1 cup mayonnaise
2 tablespoons capers
1 hard-boiled egg, sliced

1. Be sure the peas are not overcooked. Fresh garden peas or quick-frozen ones are usually a fresher green in color than the canned ones.
2. Marinate the first 3 ingredients in the French dressing for an hour.

3. Drain. Bind this salad mixture with mayonnaise. Serve on lettuce.
4. Garnish with capers and sliced hard-boiled eggs.

400 Salads
FLORENCE A. COWLES AND
FLORENCE LA GANKE HARRIS

CRAB LOUIS

California is more than a state—it's a way of life. That is what designers of sports clothes say. Architects and decorators recognize the fact. Visitors from other parts of the country feel it, comment upon it.

Just what is this California way of life? As I see it, it's a pleasant mixture of outdoor and indoor living, with emphasis on the out-of-doors. It's a blending of comfort and style, casualness and care, functionalism and fun.

That way of living explains why we demand clothes that are comfortable, casual, colorful, good-looking, suitable for indoors and out; why we make the garden or patio or terrace an integral part of the house we live in. It explains, too, why we Californians like to eat so many of our meals under the skies; why we are constantly figuring ways to cut down kitchen time indoors to give us more time outside; why we like to substitute informality for formality, imagination for elaboration, flavor for fussiness.

Crab Louis is a good luncheon salad—a favorite on the Pacific Coast.

GENEVIEVE CALLAHAN

½ crab per serving
shredded lettuce
finely chopped hard-boiled
eggs

sliced eggs
chopped chives

1. Allow half a good-sized cooked crab per serving. (West Coast crabs are big fellows.) Flake the meat in as big pieces as possible, removing all bits of shell and cartilage.
2. On each individual plate put a bed of shredded lettuce, and on it a mound of the crab, topped with big pieces from the legs. Around the crab arrange a ring of finely chopped

hard-boiled eggs. Top with a few slices of egg and a sprinkling of chopped chives.

3. Pass the following dressing separately:

DRESSING

1 cup mayonnaise	1 teaspoon horseradish
¼ cup French dressing (made with tarragon wine vinegar)	1 teaspoon Worcestershire sauce
¼ cup chili sauce or catsup	salt and coarse black pepper
2 tablespoons chopped chives	

1. Mix and chill well.
2. Some cooks add chopped pimiento or chopped pickle relish to the dressing; some, chopped rice or stuffed olives. Follow your own wishes. If served as a first-course salad at dinner, make the serving portions much smaller than for lunch.

The California Cook Book
GENEVIEVE CALLAHAN

LUNCHEON AND SUPPER DISHES

JAPANESE TEMPURA

In Japan you will find almost as many tempura eating places as there are hot dog or hamburger stands in the United States. This Japanese favorite is not too difficult to prepare, and many Americans are wild about it. I well remember visiting Rafael Steinberg, an American friend in Tokyo, whose lovely Japanese wife had prepared an enormous amount of tempura in honor of the occasion. "I'm so delighted that you came," he exclaimed. "Tamika seldom has tempura anymore, but for you she made it!" . . . and to this day I'm not sure whether he was as glad to see me for old time's sake as for the tempura.

To the Japanese, the appearance of food is as important as its taste, so the idea is to prepare it to perfection and serve it with some grace.

Makes 6 servings

½ pound large fresh shrimp, shelled and deveined
1 10-ounce package frozen lobster tails
2 10-ounce packages frozen scallops
6 large parsley sprigs
½ small eggplant, cut in strips 2 inches by ¼ inch
¾ pound sweet potatoes, pared and sliced ⅛ inch thick
1 large green pepper, sliced lengthwise in ¼-inch strips
salad oil
Batter (page 287)
Sauce (page 287)

1. Drop shrimp into boiling salted water to cover; bring back to the boil. Reduce heat; simmer, covered, 5 minutes. Then drain, and let cool.
2. Cook lobster tails as package label directs. Drain; cool. With scissors, cut shell away from meat; halve meat crosswise.
3. Drop unthawed scallops into boiling salted water to cover; bring back to the boil. Reduce heat; simmer, covered, 5 minutes. Then drain, and let cool.
4. On platter, arrange shrimp, lobster, and scallops in attractive pattern with parsley, eggplant, sweet potatoes, and green pepper.
5. Refrigerate, covered, until you are ready to cook tempura.
6. Tempura is best served immediately, cooked at the table. In electric skillet or deep-fryer, heat oil (at least 3 inches deep) to 350° F. on deep-frying thermometer.
7. With tongs, dip shrimp, lobster, scallops, and vegetables into batter to coat lightly.
8. Deep-fry, a few pieces at a time, until lightly browned— about 3 minutes.
9. Serve a combination of seafood and vegetables to each guest, along with a small bowl of sauce for dipping.

BATTER FOR TEMPURA:

3 eggs
2½ teaspoons shoyu or
    soy sauce
1¼ cups water

1⅔ cups sifted all-purpose flour
2 tablespoons sugar
1 teaspoon salt

1. Make batter just before it is to be used. Beat eggs in medium bowl with rotary beater.
2. Add shoyu and water. Gradually add flour, sugar, and salt, beating until smooth.

SAUCE FOR TEMPURA:

½ cup sherry
½ cup beef bouillon
1 cup shoyu or soy sauce
1 teaspoon monosodium
    glutamate

radishes, freshly grated
horseradish, freshly grated
ginger root, freshly grated

1. In small saucepan, combine sherry, bouillon, shoyu, and monosodium glutamate; bring to a boil.
2. Divide into 6 individual serving bowls. Place on tray, along with 3 small bowls filled with grated radishes, horseradish, and ginger root.
3. Each guest adds radish, horseradish, or ginger root to dipping sauce to suit his own taste.

McCall's Cookbook

STEAK AND KIDNEY PIE

Our meat packers must send kidneys to England by the shipload because so many Americans seem averse to any kind of kidneys, and the English are so fond of them. My wife and I had never tasted good steak and kidney pie until, one day in London, we happened to drop in to the Cock & Lion, a pub on Wigmore Street, and that's all they were serving for lunch (except "bubble and squeak," an everyday dish using leftover meats and vegetables, often cabbage). The steak and kidney pie was so good that we understood why this dish was a favorite of George and Martha Washington, who, they say, set a good and bountiful table.

Makes 6 servings

1½ pounds rump or round steak
4 small veal or beef kidneys
1 cup sliced mushrooms
1 cup dry red wine
2 onions (1 sliced, 1 diced)
2 bay leaves
½ cup chopped celery
½ cup chopped parsley
bacon drippings or suet
flour
1 teaspoon coarse black pepper
1 teaspoon marjoram
pastry or puff paste, pie crust, or biscuit dough to cover casserole

1. Separate the kidneys; clean out fat and gristle. Sprinkle with salt and marinate the kidneys for 2 hours in the wine, bay leaves, pepper, and sliced onion.
2. With side of cleaver or mallet, pound flour onto the steak and cut into 1-inch cubes. Heat bacon drippings or suet in iron skillet; cook diced onion until clear.
3. Remove onion and brown the steak cubes well over medium heat.
4. Drain the kidneys, saving the marinade. Dredge kidneys with flour; brown them, stirring carefully. Add a cup of hot water and the chopped celery, parsley, and marjoram. Stir well.
5. Mix together all the ingredients except the mushrooms, and transfer into a cooking-serving casserole with a tight lid. Strain in the marinade. Cover, and bake for 1 hour at 325° F.
6. Brown the mushrooms in additional bacon drippings or oil, and add them to the casserole. Cover with the topping dough, return to a 400° F. oven and bake 20 to 30 minutes, or until brown. Serve immediately.

STEAK, KIDNEY, AND OYSTER PUDDING

This is a variation on plain steak and kidney pie, and is an old, favorite specialty of Simpson's on the Strand. We thank

Bill Hinks, former head of London's J. Walter Thompson Advertising Agency, for suggesting and obtaining this recipe.

Makes 6 servings

2 pounds beef steak	salt
¾ pound ox kidney	fresh ground black pepper
½ pound mushrooms	1½ pounds suet paste
12 oysters	½ ounce flour

1. Cut meat and kidney into small pieces. Peel and wash mushrooms, cut, and add to meat.
2. Take salt, pepper, and flour and mix well with meat.
3. Wash oysters and add to meat.
4. Line basin with suet paste, place ingredients inside, and cover with water.
5. Put suet paste topping on pudding and cover with grease-proof paper, then with cloth. Steam for 4½ hours.

Simpson's Restaurant, London, England

THE WHITE TOWER'S MOUSSAKA

Everybody who is anybody eventually finds his way to John Stais's White Tower restaurant in the Soho section of London. There the Moussaka is prepared differently from that of the Taverna Ta Nissia, and because it is equally good, we urge you to try them both.

2 pounds of chopped beef	Béchamel Sauce
12 medium-size onions,	(see page 255)
chopped	Parmesan cheese
8 to 10 small to medium-size	olive oil
eggplants, sliced	

1. Sauté the onions in olive oil until brown.
2. Place the chopped beef and onions between layers of sliced eggplant and cover with the creamy Béchamel Sauce.
3. Sprinkle with mature Parmesan cheese and place in oven until cooking is complete and the top is golden-brown.

White Tower, London, England

TAVERNA TA NISSIA'S MOUSSAKA

Moussaka is a dish which probably originated in Syria, but the Turks, who for centuries were rulers of so much of the Near East, spread its fame throughout the area. It is in Greece that Moussaka has been made known to many travelers . . . and the Athens Hilton Hotel has done its share in that respect. The Taverna Ta Nissia in the Athens Hilton is a distinguished restaurant, reflecting the life and character of the Greek islands. *"Ta Nissia"* means "The Islands."

Makes 4 servings

12 ounces chopped meat (beef or veal)	½ cup grated cheese
¾ ounce butter	1 tablespoon chopped parsley
1½ ounces onion, chopped	½ cup white wine
½ cup tomato sauce	salt, pepper, nutmeg to taste
3 large eggplants	Béchamel Sauce
2 ounces bread crumbs	butter

1. Brown the onions in butter or lard. Add the chopped meat, mixing constantly until mixture becomes crumbly. Add tomato sauce, wine, water, salt, pepper, parsley, and nutmeg.
2. Cover pan and cook for 1 hour over low heat. In the meantime, cut the eggplants lengthwise in slices about ¼ inch thick. Salt, strain in colander, and fry in deep fat.
3. Arrange half the eggplant in shallow pan with a few bread crumbs in pan. Remove chopped meat from heat (by this time it should have only ½ the gravy it had when it started to cook), add ½ the grated cheese, and a little of the breadcrumbs. Spread evenly over the eggplant.
4. Add the rest of the eggplant. Pour Béchamel Sauce evenly over this and spread remaining cheese and bread crumbs over all. Do not pour sauce to more than ¼-inch thickness. Pour some melted butter over the top, and bake for 15 minutes until golden brown.
5. Cool slightly and cut in squares as you would macaroni au gratin. Serve with a little juice of veal.

BÉCHAMEL SAUCE FOR MOUSSAKA

1 quart milk	salt
½ cup flour	pepper
1 egg	nutmeg
2 tablespoons butter	

Melt butter; stir in flour, milk and seasonings. Add egg. Cook, stirring until thickened.

BROILED TRIPE À LA PARKER HOUSE

No matter what I say, there will, I know, always be skeptics to insist that my memories play me false: that these simple old Maine dishes couldn't actually have been as good as I think they were.

Fortunately the Parker House in Boston is able to broil scrod and tripe the way my grandmother did. . . .

KENNETH ROBERTS
(Author, *Northwest Passage, Arundel,* and other novels)

Makes 5 servings

fresh honeycomb tripe	olive oil
flour	sifted bread crumbs
salt and pepper	

1. Cut fresh (not pickled) tripe in pieces about 5 x 7 inches. A single strip serves 1 portion. Season with salt and pepper.
2. Sprinkle with flour, then dip in olive oil and sprinkle generously with sifted bread crumbs.
3. Broil slowly 2 or 3 minutes on each side or until the crumbs are brown (a charcoal fire is best). Serve with Mustard Sauce.

MUSTARD SAUCE

1 tablespoon minced onion	2 tablespoons dry mustard
3 tablespoons butter	1 tablespoon water
2 tablespoons cider vinegar	1 cup brown gravy

1. Sauté onion in butter. Add vinegar and simmer 5 minutes.
2. Moisten dry mustard with water and blend; then add brown gravy.
3. Let simmer a few minutes. Strain and serve very hot.

Parker House Hotel
Boston, Mass.

SUKIYAKI

Suki means plow and *yaki* means roasted. According to a story, probably apocryphal, this dish originated in Japan a century or more ago at a time when Buddhism forbade the eating of beef. A farmer slaughtered a steer in secret on a lonely mountain and then cooked it, using part of his plow as a grill over the fire. Hence, the term, "plow-roasted"—sukiyaki.

Sukiyaki calls for some slicing and cutting behind scenes, but very little toil at the dining-table, where the ingredients are cooked all together for less than ten minutes. One of the new electric skillets is highly recommended as a cook-serve piece. An electric hot plate and a heavy pan are also useful for the preparation.

The ingredients listed here may be cooked together at one time in a medium-sized frying pan (9 inches in diameter). For more servings, double the recipe and use either two skillets or one of giant size.

The hibachi, the Japanese brazier used for making sukiyaki, is now being sold by almost every house furnishings or hardware store, since it has become so popular for general outdoor cooking. Bamboo shoots and other Japanese foods can be obtained in numerous Japanese or Chinese grocery stores in New York, in West Coast cities, and elsewhere. *Sake* is available at most good liquor stores, or it can be ordered for you.

Makes 2 to 3 servings

1 small piece beef suet	¼ cup sliced mushrooms
8 to 10 paper-thin slices very tender beef of about 3 x 4 inches (have butcher slice meat)	1 sliced bamboo shoot
	3 1-inch cubes soybean curd
	2 tablespoons special vermicelli (*shirataki*)
1 cup sliced onions	1½ tablespoons sugar
2 cups sliced celery	¼ cup soy sauce
½ cup steamed spinach (thoroughly drained)	2 tablespoons *Sake* (sherry may be substituted)
6 scallops cut in 3-inch lengths	

1. Heat skillet very hot. Rub it thoroughly with the suet.
2. Add meat and sear on both sides.
3. Add the remaining ingredients and cook all together over high heat for about 3 minutes.
4. Reduce heat to low and simmer 5 to 7 minutes longer. Stir gently several times. Vegetables should be crisp when eaten.

In preparing sukiyaki, Japanese often use dried mushrooms (*shiitake*) of very intense flavor and fragrance. These are soaked a couple of hours before they are added to the dish.

Adapted from recipe of
Miyako, oldest Japanese
restaurant in New York

BITOK

Baron George Wrangell, the man with the eye-patch who used to pose for Hathaway shirts, cooks occasional suppers, starting them off with the Baron Special: five parts Smirnoff Vodka, one part Dubonnet blond; iced in cocktail shaker and served with twist of lemon peel. Then follows the *Bitok:*

1 loaf bread	½ teaspoon pepper
1 cup milk	1 teaspoon salt
1 pound ground beef	dash of onion powder
½ teaspoon orégano	butter

1. Cut bread in half crosswise and scoop out insides.
2. Soak crumbs in milk. Mix with beef and seasonings.
3. Fill hollowed loaf with mixture.
4. Cut in 1-inch slices and sauté in butter.
5. Serve with mushroom sauce and red wine.

Look Magazine

CHICKEN AND HAM CASSEROLE

Makes 6 servings

7 slices white meat of
   cooked chicken, cut in
   uniform size
3 slices boiled ham, cut
   same size
½ small Bermuda onion,
   finely minced
¼ cup butter

½ cup sliced mushrooms
1 teaspoon paprika
1 teaspoon salt
¼ teaspoon grated nutmeg
¾ cup cream
3 to 4 tablespoons Parmesan
   cheese, grated

1. Cook the minced onion in the butter for 5 minutes, stirring constantly, and do not let it brown. Add the sliced mushrooms and seasonings, and let simmer for 15 minutes.
2. Then turn the mixture into an oblong baking dish, and arrange chicken and ham on the top. Add enough hot cream to cover the meat; let simmer in a hot oven (400° F.) for 10 minutes. Cover with Parmesan cheese; let remain in the oven until the cheese is browned.

Cook It in a Casserole
FLORENCE BROBECK

CHICKEN PORTOLLA

Makes 1 serving

1 coconut	salt
4 tablespoons butter	Maggi seasoning
1 small green apple	½ cup cooked light meat of
1 small onion	chicken
1 small bay leaf	1 red pepper
3 tablespoons curry powder	1 large mushroom
1 cup chicken stock	½ cup cooked corn
½ cup cream	pie crust
1 tablespoon flour	

1. Cut off the top of the coconut and drain out the milk. Remove enough meat to make 2 tablespoons when shredded. Melt butter in a shallow pan. Chop apple and onion coarsely and add with bay leaf to butter. Cook until soft but not brown. Add flour and stir until blended; then add curry powder and blend. Add chicken stock and cook, stirring constantly, until thickened. Strain and add cream. Season to taste with salt and Maggi.
2. Cut chicken into bite-size pieces. Chop pepper and mushroom coarsely and add with shredded coconut meat and corn, to the sauce. Simmer 10 minutes.
3. Place mixture in the coconut and replace the top, sealing it with a narrow collar (1 inch wide) of pie crust. Bake for 20 to 25 minutes in a moderate oven (350° F.).
4. Remove coconut top and serve in shell.

Hotel Ambassador
Chicago, Ill.

POLENTA WITH CHICKEN LIVERS

It isn't always that a dish high in nutritional value is one you can relish. Beatrice Trum Hunter has written a cookbook with an accent on health, and it contains many delectable concoctions, one of which follows. The "nutritional yeast" of which she speaks is powdered brewer's yeast, which may be obtained at health food stores or by mail from the U.S. Health Club, 25 North Broadway, Yonkers, New York 10702.

Makes 6 servings

1 pound cornmeal
½ cup stock, cold
1¼ quarts stock, boiling
1 teaspoon salt
3 tablespoons oil
1 pound chicken livers, chopped

½ teaspoon sage
3 tablespoons nutritional yeast
¼ cup tomato juice
3 slices bacon, broiled and chopped

1. Mix cornmeal with cold stock. Gradually add to boiling stock. Add salt.
2. Cook, stirring frequently for 30 minutes, or until cornmeal leaves side of pot easily.
3. Heat oil and sauté chicken livers. Add sage, yeast, and tomato juice. Cover and simmer for 10 minutes.
4. Turn polenta onto large warm platter. Garnish with liver mixture and top with bacon bits.

The Natural Foods Cookbook
BEATRICE TRUM HUNTER

PUMP ROOM CHICKEN HASH

Makes 2 servings

½ cup chicken broth
¼ cup diced celery
1 cup diced cooked chicken
1 tablespoon cream
1 ounce Escoffier Sauce (or A1 Sauce)
salt, pepper
3 ounces Madeira wine

1 egg yolk
paprika
parsley
½ cup Béchamel Sauce (page 255) with addition of bay leaf
pastry shell

(For this dish you will need 2 skillets)

1. In skillet No. 1, place some chicken broth, diced celery, and chicken and simmer well.
2. Pour Supreme Sauce into skillet No. 2 and heat. Add cream to thin. Then add Escoffier Sauce, salt, and pepper. Allow to simmer well and then add Madeira wine.
3. Now strain off liquid from skillet No. 1 and pour chicken and celery into contents of skillet No. 2.
4. Take yolk of egg and whip, adding a dash of cream; mix all well and allow to cook until done.
5. Serve in pastry shell using paprika and a sprig of parsley as decor.

Pump Room, Hotel Ambassador
Chicago, Ill.

FETTUCINI ALFREDO

In Rome today there are several "original Alfredo" restaurants, but I remember the *real* original Alfredo, who was a character right out of an Italian opera. When he came from the kitchen with a heaping platter of fettucini, he carried it high, and the lights were dimmed for a brief moment as he crossed the room to your table. There, he personally added the cream, butter, and cheese. He had one further, typical Alfredo touch: If there were four guests at a table, three would be served the prepared fettucini on regular plates and the fourth, the customer of longest standing, would receive his or her portion on the big service platter. I also remember with fondness his enormous guest book, which included names and notes from worldwide travelers, many of them famous in politics, the theatre, and other walks of life.

Makes 4 servings

8 ounces broad egg noodles   ½ pound freshly grated
¾ cup heavy cream   Parmesan cheese
½ pound butter   freshly ground black pepper

1. Cook noodles until tender, about 10 minutes. Drain well.
2. Place noodles in warm bowl, add cream, and then add

chunks of butter. Mix well by constantly turning the noodles, rather than tossing them.

3. Add the grated cheese and continue turning, or folding it in, until all the noodles are thoroughly coated. Signor Alfredo took at least 10 minutes to do this. Season with freshly ground black pepper and serve from the bowl or transfer to a hot platter.

PIZZA SICILIANA

"It is to the highly developed civilization of the Chinese that we owe our greatest cookery debt," says James A. Beard. "The golden road to Samarkand was traveled by many hardy ancients of western Europe who returned . . . with tales of the wondrous foods they had eaten in far Cathay."

When Marco Polo introduced pasta to the Italians, little did he dream that one day there would be an America where every day Americans would consume tons of spaghetti-and-meat-balls and thousands of pizzas. The pizza, if not a noble dish, is at least a nourishing one, with plenty of appetite appeal and tang. Real Sicilian pizzas are simple and satisfying to make once you get the knack. Here is Maria Lo Pinto to tell you how to fill your kitchen with magnificent aromas, and your table with munificent pizzas.

1 cake yeast	2 tablespoons peanut or
1 cup lukewarm water	olive oil
1 pound flour	Anchovy Tomato Sauce
1 teaspoon salt	½ cup Italian cheese, grated

1. Dissolve yeast in lukewarm water. Place flour and salt on board. Add dissolved yeast. Knead thoroughly for 10 minutes. Add oil and continue kneading until smooth.
2. Cover well. Set aside in warm place about 2 hours or until dough has risen to double its size. Pound dough, cover, and set aside for ½ hour.
3. Spread in large well-greased baking pan about ½ inch thick. Dent here and there with fingertips. Cover and set aside ½ hour.
4. Pour generous layer of Anchovy Tomato Sauce over dough and sprinkle liberally with grated cheese.

5. Bake in hot oven (425° F.) for ½ hour. Lower heat to 375° F. and continue baking 15 minutes or until pizza is golden brown.
6 Remove from oven and cut into pieces about 4 to 5 inches square. Serve very hot.

ANCHOVY TOMATO SAUCE

1 large onion, sliced	3 anchovy fillets
3 tablespoons olive oil	2½ cups water
1 can tomato paste	salt and pepper to taste
½ teaspoon orégano	

1. Fry onion in oil about 5 minutes or until medium brown.
2. Add paste and fry 3 minutes, stirring constantly. Add orégano, anchovies, salt and pepper, 2½ cups water, and cover.
3. Simmer over low flame for 25 minutes.

The New York Cookbook
MARIA LO PINTO

CANNELLONI

Whether Sardi's originated the cannelloni, or simply helped to make it popular, I do not know. The recipe that follows outlines the manner in which it is prepared at the Villa Camillo restaurant in New York.

Makes 4 to 8 servings

TO MAKE CANNELLONI

1. Make the filling and the sauce. While the sauce cooks, make the crêpes. (If you are using very wide noodles in place of the crêpes, parboil them and let cool slightly.)
2. Put about 3 tablespoons of the filling on a crêpe, or spread it along 1 edge of a noodle.
3. Roll and place in a flat greased baking dish.

4. When the crêpes and the filling have been used up, either refrigerate for heating later, or cover with the sauce and heat through in a 350° oven for 15 minutes.
5. Finally, run the dish under the broiler to brown the top.

FILLING:

1 pound boneless chicken	½ pound Parmesan cheese
½ pound lean pork	4 eggs, beaten
¼ pound Prosciutto ham	1 teaspoon salt
½ pound veal	pepper to taste
1 bay leaf	small pinch thyme
½ pound ricotta	small pinch nutmeg
½ pound spinach, chopped	1 clove garlic, minced

1. Cut the meats into small pieces; add the bay leaf, onion, and garlic, and brown in a 350° oven for 45 minutes.
2. Cool and put through a very fine meat chopper (removing the bay leaf first).
3. Add the ricotta, Parmesan cheese, spinach, and eggs, along with the spices. Mix into a smooth paste and chill.

SAUCE:

2 cups consommé	1 cup ricotta
1 cup flour	chopped parsley
½ pound Mozzarella cheese, cut into very small cubes	salt and pepper

1. Mix the consommé with the flour and the Mozzarella. Cook over hot water in a double boiler until you have a smooth paste.
2. Remove from the heat and add the ricotta, chopped parsley, and salt and pepper to taste. Pour over the cannelloni.

CRÊPES:

1½ cups water	¾ teaspoon salt
1½ cups milk	3 cups sifted flour
6 eggs	6 tablespoons melted butter

1. Mix ingredients in a blender at high speed for 1 minute. Refrigerate for a few hours or overnight.
2. Cook the crêpes in a 6-inch skillet that has been brushed lightly with oil. Pour ¼ cup of batter in the pan, tilt it so it covers the bottom, and cook until it's delicately browned.
3. Turn the crêpe with a spatula and brown on the other side. Spread out on waxed paper until ready to use.

Esquire Party Book

RAVIOLI

Makes 12 ravioli

FILLING:

1¼ cups ricotta, or dry
    cottage cheese
¼ cup Parmesan cheese,
    grated
2 eggs, beaten

½ cup cooked beets, grated
1 tablespoon raisins,
    chopped
½ teaspoon salt

DOUGH:

1 cup flour
2 eggs

Parmesan cheese

1. Combine all the ingredients for filling.
2. Mix flour and eggs together to form paste for the dough. After kneading this thoroughly, roll it out thin and cut into 2-inch sections, using a square or round cutter.
3. Spread filling mixture on ½ of each section of dough. Moisten edges and fold the other half over the filling, pressing the edges together firmly.
4. Cook in rapidly boiling water. When done, drain and serve with Parmesan cheese.

LASAGNE

"What do you suppose she means by this headline?" I asked my wife as I handed over Isabel McGovern's cooking page in *This Week Magazine*. "Pastas put heart in your meals," it read.

"I suppose it means that pastas make hearty dishes, or that they can be the heart of the meal," replied my wife, but then her eyes became sort of dreamy, and I waited for more. "The way I see it, though, is that when you eat a good *paisano* Italian dish like a lasagne with a glass of *vino*, you find in it the heart of Italy. To me it brings back that lovely sweet smell of the lemon groves near Amalfi, the wonderful band in the square in Capri, the jolly time we had singing with the natives in the little restaurant near San Geminano, and . . ."

That's what Italy does: it gets in your heart and becomes part of you.

Makes 10 servings

SAUCE:

½ can tomato paste
½ cup hot water
2 cloves garlic
    salt and pepper to taste

4 tablespoons olive oil
1 stalk celery, diced
1 large can plum tomatoes, strained

Blend tomato paste with hot water. Brown garlic in hot olive oil about 3 minutes. Add celery, blended tomato paste, and plum tomatoes. Boil over high flame for 3 minutes, then lower flame. Cover and simmer for 1 hour. Add pepper and salt.

STUFFING:

1 pound sausage
1 pound lasagne (*very* broad noodles or dough strips)
1 cup Parmesan cheese, grated

1 pound Mozzarella, sliced (or Swiss cheese if Mozzarella is not available)
1½ pounds ricotta (or uncreamed cottage cheese if ricotta is not available)
salt and pepper to taste

1. Broil sausage under high flame about 15 minutes or until brown on both sides. Cut into small pieces.
2. Cook lasagne in rapidly boiling salted water with 1 tablespoon oil about 15 minutes or until tender, but not too soft. Drain.
3. Pour ½ cup sauce into bottom of baking pan and over this place layer of noodles, then layer of grated Parmesan cheese, a layer of sauce, a layer of Mozzarella, sausage, and a tablespoon of ricotta here and there. Repeat this process in layers until all ingredients are used. Top layer should be sauce and grated cheese.
4. Bake in moderate oven (350° F.) for 20 minutes or until firm.
5. When done, the lasagne is cut into serving portions. Place on individual plates and top with more sauce and grated cheese. Serve hot.

NOTE:

One pound of ground beef or pork may be substituted for sausage. In that event just add meat to sauce when sauce starts cooking.

The New York Cookbook
MARIA LO PINTO

KREPLACH

Kreplach are very much like Italian ravioli or Chinese Won Ton, except that the fillings are different. Kreplach is pronounced with a soft *e* as in *crept;* the *a* is said "ah," and the *ch* has a sort of gargling sound. But never mind trying to say it—make kreplach, eat 'em, and you'll pronounce them good.

The Jewish people, like all other peoples, have food customs traditionally associated with their daily lives, their holidays and festivals, celebrations in the home and out of it. In addition to these, regulations are prescribed in a code of dietary laws, from the slaughter of animals used for food, and rules for other food combinations, to the kinds of dishes prepared for special holidays and festivals as well as the Sabbath. These food traditions have accumulated through the long, historic experience of the Jewish people. Some food customs and traditions cluster about historic events that have become the basis for annual observance. All of this has contributed to the national continuity of an ancient people.

While kreplach are a year-round dessert delicacy, this kreplach recipe is designed especially for the springtime holiday called Purim (poor-rim), the Feast of Esther. The holiday commemorates the downfall of a wicked councillor of an ancient king. The triangular shape of these kreplach is like the three-cornered hat worn by that enemy of the people. There is evidently great satisfaction in eating up a symbol of this tyrant.

LEAH W. LEONARD

Makes 24 to 36

2 cups sifted flour (approximately)

2 eggs
2 or 3 teaspoons cold water

1. Sift flour into mixing bowl or on kneading board. Make a well in the center. Add eggs and combine with a fork adding spoonfuls of water as necessary to form a ball of dough that is compact but not hard. Knead dough until as smooth and elastic as possible.
2. Roll out on a lightly floured board. Use the rolling pin from the outer edges toward the center, turning the board as necessary in order to achieve easier rolling. When dough is rolled evenly thin through the whole round, cut into 1½-inch squares.
3. Place ½ teaspoon filling in center of squares and pinch together securely into triangular puffs. Pinch together points. Drop into boiling salted water. Cook 10 to 15 minutes. When done, kreplach rise to the top. Skim out. Serve with clear soup or gravy.

CHICKEN FILLING

1½ cups finely cut leftover chicken
1 egg

1 tablespoon minced parsley
1 teaspoon onion juice

Blend together in the order given.

CHICKEN LIVER AND EGG FILLING

1. Chop together broiled chicken livers and as many hard-cooked eggs as desired to make a smooth mixture.
2. Season with minced parsley, poultry seasoning, salt and pepper.

NOTE:
Variation: Greben (cracklings from rendered chicken or goose fat) and broiled liver, chopped fine and seasoned to taste.

CHEESE FILLING

1 cup dry cottage cheese	dash of pepper
1 egg	2 tablespoons fine crumbs
¼ teaspoon salt	

Blend together with a fork.

Jewish Cookery
LEAH W. LEONARD

RISOTTO ALLA MILANESE

Risotto is a specialty of Milan, probably because it lies in the heart of the rice-growing district of Italy. *Risotto* is usually eaten alone, as the first dish of a typical Italian meal, but sometimes it is served together with certain dishes, such as *osso-buco* or *spezzatino* which is actually the Italian version of our veal stew.

There are many variations on the *risotto* theme; it is sometimes cooked with mushrooms, or tomato sauce, or shrimps or served with white truffles, an exquisite and very expensive delicacy which can be found in this country only in tins. The quality of rice to be used for *risotto* should be of the tough, long-cooking kind. Preferably use imported Italian rice. Rice should retain a certain consistency—what the Italians call *al dente,* so that your teeth (*dente*) can still "feel" it. *Risotto* should have the consistency of our rice pudding.

Makes 10 to 12 servings

20 ounces rice
6 ounces butter
1 onion about the size of a golf ball
1 quart good homemade stock, either chicken or beef; or use canned consommé or bouillon cubes. (More or less stock is needed according to quality of rice— some absorbs more liquid than others.)

1 pinch saffron (can be omitted if flavor is not agreeable)
1 cup white wine (also can be omitted if more stock is substituted)
4 heaping tablespoons fine imported Parmesan cheese, grated
salt should be added if stock is not sufficiently seasoned

1. Melt 4 ounces of the butter in saucepan; brown onion which has been chopped very fine. When onion is well browned throw in the rice. Stir continuously. When rice has absorbed all the butter, add wine.
2. When wine has been absorbed, add saffron, which has been diluted in a bit of stock or water.
3. Add stock, a cup at a time. Stir continuously. Never put in more than one cup of stock at a time so that when cooked, the risotto will not be too liquid.
4. When rice is cooked, remove from fire and add rest of butter and cheese and stir well until both are absorbed into the risotto.
5. Serve piping hot. More grated cheese can be added at the table.

Giannino's Restaurant
Milan, Italy

FRIED RICE

Makes 2 to 4 servings

2 cups rice (long grain,
1 egg
2 chicken legs, cooked and diced (or other cooked meat or shrimps)

2 teaspoons peanut oil
½ teaspoon salt
1 teaspoon soy sauce
scallions, if desired

1. Wash the rice in 4 washings until water is clear. Place in saucepan and cover with water (about 3½ cups). Cover pan and bring to slow boil.
2. When very little steam seeps from under cover, turn flame very low. Let heat for about 10 minutes more. Allow rice to get cold.
3. Put the peanut oil in a pan, add the egg and swirl it around. Add the diced chicken, then the rice, salt and soy sauce (and scallions, if desired).
4. Stir vigorously and cook for about 3 minutes.

PAELLA A LA VALENCIANA

It has been said, and rightly, that paella is one of the glories of Spain. Paella is a dish that is beautiful to look at and even better to eat. It can be part of a formal dinner or an informal buffet. It tastes good on the first serving and improves on reheating. You will be following the Spanish tradition when you make your own mixture of seafood and meat, depending upon your preferences, the season, and local supplies. I've eaten paella laden with mussels, squid, octopus, slices of hot Spanish, Italian, or Polish sausages, pieces of pork, and so on. Lorenzo de Granados, whose recipe follows, has his own ideas about paella—he doesn't use black olives, as they usually do in Spain, and he is dead against tomatoes, because he feels they are too acid-y for paella. Whatever you put into your paella, make sure you serve it with some dash—if you do not have a Spanish paellera (as who does?), use a large earthenware baking dish or casserole. Recently we served paella to twelve people out of a round hammered copper tray twenty-one inches in diameter, that bellied out to about three inches deep. It made such a wonderful impression, with the clam and mussel shells and the shrimp sticking out from the saffroned rice, that the guests flatteringly called it a work of art instead of just a dish of food.

Makes 4 servings

1 (3-pound) chicken (broiler)	2 teaspoons paprika
	½ teaspoon orégano
1 coffee cup of olive oil	2 teaspoons salt
2 cloves garlic	chopped parsley
2 medium-sized onions, chopped	leek
	2 cups of raw rice
1 green pepper, diced	8 clams
½ teaspoon saffron (whole, dried)	16 shrimps
	2 lobsters

1. Make a stock of the neck, feet, and gizzard of the chicken using 6 cups of water.
2. Cut the chicken into quarters or eighths and sauté in the oil until brown. Then add the garlic, cut lengthwise; the onions, and the green pepper.
3. When the onions are crisp (but not burned), add the saffron, paprika, orégano, salt, chopped parsley, and an equal amount of leek.
4. Pour into a heavy casserole. Strain the stock into the chicken mixture.
5. Add the raw rice and stir well. On top of the mixture put the clams, shrimps, and lobsters, which have been cut up.
6. Cover and cook over slow fire for 30 minutes.

Granados Restaurant in Greenwich Village
New York City

PINK POODLE

As I made my way about the city [of San Francisco], I found that the cooking had taken on a curious melting-pot quality, in which the Spanish influence of its origin, the pioneer West, the Orient, and Mexico were all blended into a cuisine as varied as it is good.

In a small jolly unpretentious place, I savored for the first time highly seasoned and romantic tamale, enchilada, chile con carne, and Spanish rice, all delicious and all very hot.

In a restaurant known as the Poodle Dog, I was introduced to a combination of cheese and tomatoes, named for the place of its inception, Pink Poodle. It was a kind of glorified pink Welsh Rabbit, and a mighty welcome snack when San Francisco was wrapped in as thick a fog as any London might boast of.

HERMAN SMITH

Makes 6 servings

3 tablespoons butter	½ teaspoon salt
1 tablespoon minced onion	¼ teaspoon pepper
1 tablespoon flour	dash of powdered clove
2 tablespoons claret, or other dry wine	¾ pound sharp cheese, cut in small pieces
1 can cream of tomato soup	1 egg, slightly beaten
½ teaspoon dry mustard	1 pinch soda

1. Cook the onion in the butter till soft and yellow. Add the flour and, when well blended, the claret and tomato soup.
2. Stir in the seasonings, then the cheese, stirring till the cheese is melted. Add the soda, then the egg slightly beaten. Stir till very smooth.
3. Serve on thin hot toast with more of the claret on the side.

Kitchens Near and Far
HERMAN SMITH

ENCHILADAS

(MEXICAN STYLE)

Makes 4 to 6 servings

12 corn tortillas (Editor's Note: Excellent ready-made tortillas are available in cans—made by Ashley's, Inc., El Paso, Texas.)	1 cup pitted and chopped black olives
	2 cups yellow cheese, grated
	½ teaspoon crushed orégano
1 large onion, chopped	pork lard
1 large clove garlic, minced	1 tablespoon flour
	2 teaspoons salt
	2 dozen dried red chilis

1. Rinse chilis, slit and wash out seeds. Cover with boiling water. Cover and let soak until pulp is soft. Drain (save liquid for further use), grind through chopper with medium knife. Press through sieve using a small amount of the chili liquid to make a medium chili sauce.
2. In 1 tablespoon of lard on a slow fire, fry garlic, do not brown. Add flour, stir until it browns slightly. Add chili sauce, salt, and orégano and stir well. Let simmer 10 minutes, then set aside and keep warm.
3. Now heat good and hot ⅔ cup lard. Fry tortillas one at a time for just a second.
4. On half of each tortilla, put 1 teaspoon each of onion, olives, cheese, and 1 tablespoon chili sauce. When all tortillas are used up, pour rest of chili sauce over all. Sprinkle with rest of onion, olives and cheese.
5. Set in oven for 15 minutes at 350° F. and serve.

NOTE:
Chicken or turkey enchiladas may be made by including a few small pieces of cooked chicken or turkey meat in each enchilada.

The Spanish-Mexican Cook Book
DON CARLOS

PEG BRACKEN'S TAMALE BEAN POT

Her deliciously gay books, which present with honesty and good humor her rejection of woman's historical functions in the home, have made Peg Bracken one of the most popular authors and speakers in America. She hates to cook, and not only states it, but has written a book to prove it—and added an appendix to that book to prove it even more so. As she says, "You don't recover from hating to cook, any more than you get over having big feet."

Makes 6 to 8 servings

1 pound ground beef
1 minced garlic clove
1½ teaspoons chili powder
1 can garbanzo beans, drained
2 cans red kidney beans,
   drained

1 can Mexicorn, drained
1 can tomato sauce
a spatter of Tabasco sauce
2 cans of tamales, papers
   peeled off, and cut in
   1-inch chunks

1. Brown the ground beef with the minced garlic and chili powder. If you like a more distinctly south-of-the-border taste, add another teaspoon of chili powder.
2. Then mix with all the other ingredients and bake, covered, for 4 hours at 200° or 2 hours at 350°.

The I Hate to Cook Book
PEG BRACKEN

MAMA'S RED BEANS AND CHILI CON CARNE

At first thought, most people suppose that chili con carne is a Mexican dish. The truth is, of course, that it is a North American development, being either purely Texan or anyway Southwestern in origin. One thing is sure: chili con carne, made right, is uniquely satisfying and tantalizing at one and the same time.

Naturally, there are about as many ways to make chili con carne as there are makers.* Nobody has ever undertaken to

---

* Editor's Note: The chili made at the Texas ranch of former President Lyndon B. Johnson—Pedernales River Chili—calls for the following ingredients:

4 pounds ground chili meat
   (coarsely ground round)
8 tablespoons bacon drippings
1 large onion, chopped
2 cloves garlic
1 teaspoon ground orégano
1 teaspoon cumin seed
1 string dried mushrooms

6 teaspoons chili powder
1½ cups canned whole tomatoes
2 No. 2½ cans kidney beans
2 to 6 generous dashes hot
   pepper sauce
salt to taste
2 cups hot water

count them, but there may be almost as many recipes for "chili" as for barbecue. We have tried our share; but we have found none that can match Mama's. We can still call to mind winter days in the Panhandle, at Clarendon, just below the Caprock, when we would come straggling in after a long hunt under dark gray skies, maybe with snow in the air, in the clean cold wind, and be met at the door with the coursing fragrance of cooking chili. And it tastes just as good today as it did then, which is eloquent testimony to its qualities.

ARTHUR AND BOBBIE COLEMAN

Makes 6 servings

red beans	2 small onions or 1 large
3 tablespoons shortening	onion
4 tablespoons chili powder	shortening for frying
salt to taste	1½ pounds ground round
	steak (top grade)

1. Soak red beans overnight. Cook them in unsalted water. When they are soft, add 3 tablespoons of shortening, 2 tablespoons of chili powder, and salt to taste.
2. Chop onions. Fry the onions in a skillet in shortening until they are soft. Add ground round steak, 2 tablespoons of chili powder, and salt to taste. Stir until the meat is seared.
3. Cover with water and cook slowly until done. Then add the meat mixture to the red beans and simmer for a few minutes longer, to blend well. If the chili seems too thick, add water.

Incidentally, chili con carne is especially good when served with pickles and crackers. Sour pickles are much better with chili than are dill.

The Texas Cookbook

BAKED GUVETSI WITH MEAT

It is a known fact that most of our Greek culinary preparations have Turkish names. I could explain how this has come to pass by comparing the case with the prevalence of French terminology in the cuisine of English-speaking countries. It is common knowledge that French cooks—who held key positions in hotels and mansions—spread the use of this cuisine outside the narrow limits of private homes. But as time went on there arose a justified demand to have menus written in the English language. And so the French cuisine has finally established itself in the English language. Similarly after the fall of Constantinople, Greek cooks were forced to refer to their dishes in the Turkish language; that is why many are parading today under assumed Turkish names and are thought of as preparations of Turkish culinary art.

NICHOLAS TSELEMENTES

Makes 4 to 6 servings

2 pounds lamb (cut in pieces)
1 pound macaroni or
    spaghettini (or any other
    type of pasta)
1 cup butter

3 tablespoons tomato paste
    diluted in 1 glass water
3 tablespoons minced onion
    salt and pepper

1. Brown meat in butter along with the onion. Add enough water to cover the meat. Add the tomato, salt and pepper and cook for 30 minutes.
2. Add macaroni and stir 2 or 3 times until the macaroni starts to boil slowly. Cover and cook until the macaroni is ready and the meat is tender. If the liquid is absorbed before the macaroni is cooked, add a little hot water.
3. When serving, grated cheese may be sprinkled on top, if desired.

Greek Cookery
NICHOLAS TSELEMENTES

HAMBURGER AND POTATO ROLL

Makes 5 to 6 servings

1 medium onion, chopped
1 small clove garlic, minced
1 tablespoon drippings
1 pound hamburger
1 egg
2 slices bread, top crust removed
1 teaspoon salt
¼ teaspoon orégano, rosemary or basil
pepper to taste
2 tablespoons dry bread crumbs
2 cups seasoned mashed potatoes
1 tablespoon minced parsley or green pepper, optional
3 strips bacon, optional

1. Sauté onion and garlic in drippings till yellow. Add to hamburger. Add egg.
2. Soften bread in water, press out excess water and add to hamburger. Add salt, herb, and pepper. Mix thoroughly.
3. Sprinkle a piece of waxed paper with crumbs. Press meat out on crumbs to make a rectangle about ½ inch thick.
4. Beat mashed potatoes with parsley or pepper and spread on top of meat. (If leftover potato is used, reheat it in a double boiler before spreading.)
5. Using waxed paper to help, roll meat and potatoes, jelly-roll fashion, and place in a loaf pan or on a shallow pan. Grease pan if meat is very lean. Place bacon on top or brush with additional drippings and baste at least once during baking.
6. Bake in a moderate oven (350° F.) about 1 hour. Serve with a brown sauce made from pan drippings or with mushroom, tomato, or other sauce.

The New York Times

CLUB SANDWICH
À LA WALDORF-ASTORIA

The club sandwich has become an American institution of the higher brackets, somewhat above the hamburger and the hot dog on the social scale. The club sandwich is an elegant emergency item, quickly made with foods on hand; if you don't happen to have slices of chicken or turkey around, the canned variety will do. The main quality of a club sandwich is inherent in the manner of serving—the freshness of the toast, the crispness and greaselessness of the bacon, the excellence of the tomato—and the garnishing with which it is served.

3 freshly toasted slices of white bread
4 to 6 slices of white meat of boiled fowl or roasted chicken
2 strips of bacon
4 thin slices of tomato
1 lettuce leaf
mayonnaise

1. Butter the toast.
2. Between the first 2 slices, put the chicken and the bacon.
3. Between the top 2 slices, put the thinly sliced tomato, the lettuce, and the mayonnaise.
4. Make sure the toast is still hot when served.

Waldorf-Astoria Hotel
New York City

SWISS CHEESE PIE

(QUICHE LORRAINE)

Quiche Lorraine is a marvelous main dish for lunch or supper . . . or, when cut in smaller wedges, as a first course for dinner. It's as delicious as it is nutritious—as rich in flavor as it is in protein.

Some recipes call for twelve strips of bacon, but June Platt's recipe calls for more. In New York, the most famous producer of Quiche Lorraine is probably Colette, whose bake-shop supplies it to numerous fine French restaurants as well as to many private patrons. Colette uses diced ham in her Quiche.

Makes 6 to 8 servings

1½ cups pastry flour
½ teaspoon salt
¼ pound salt butter
4 tablespoons ice water
    (about)
1 cup grated Swiss cheese
1½ dozen strips bacon
    (about)

4 eggs
2 cups thick or thin cream
1 pinch nutmeg
1 pinch sugar
¾ teaspoon salt
1 big pinch cayenne
   black pepper

1. First make a paste in the following manner: Sift pastry flour with salt. Work into it with fingertips the bar of salt butter. Moisten with just enough ice water to make it hold together.
2. Make a smooth ball of it, wrap in waxed paper, and place in refrigerator for ½ hour or so, before rolling it out thin on a lightly floured board. Line a large 10-inch Pyrex pie pan with it, trim the edges, roll them under and crimp prettily. Prick the surface with a fork and place in refrigerator, while you prepare the following ingredients. (But first set your oven at 450° F. and light it.)
3. Fry or grill about 1½ dozen bacon strips until crisp, but don't overcook. Break or cut into small pieces.
4. Break eggs into a bowl and add to them thick or thin cream, nutmeg, sugar, salt, cayenne, and plenty of freshly ground black pepper. Beat with rotary beater just long enough to mix thoroughly. Now rub a little soft butter over the surface of the pastry and sprinkle the bacon over the bottom, sprinkle the cheese over the bacon, and pour the egg mixture over all.
5. Place in preheated hot oven and bake 10 to 15 minutes, then reduce the temperature to 325° F. and continue cooking until an inserted knife comes out clean, showing the custard has set (about 25 to 30 minutes). If not a light golden brown on top, place under a hot grill for a second before serving piping hot. Cut in wedge-shaped pieces.

The Best I Ever Ate
SOPHIE KERR AND JUNE PLATT

DELICATE MUSHROOM SOUFFLÉ

Frederica L. Beinert tells the story of a bride who wanted her first "real" dinner party to be a gourmet's dream. She planned a fairly elaborate menu, with soufflé for dessert, and engaged a part-time helper to cook and serve the meal. All went smoothly until midway through dinner, when the cook slipped a note onto the hostess's lap. She unfolded it as unobtrusively as possible and read, with horror, "Heavenly days ma'am, what do I do now—the wind's gone out of the puddin'?"

Frederica L. Beinert is a nationally known food consultant and the author of several good cookbooks. She says, "A soufflé is a dramatic production, to be sure, but its basic ingredients are quite ordinary." So buy your pound and a half of mushrooms, add them to the "ordinary ingredients" as listed, and serve a beautiful, delicate mushroom soufflé.

Makes 6 to 8 servings

1½ pounds fresh mushrooms
¼ cup butter or margarine
¼ cup flour
1½ cups cold medium cream
    or undiluted evaporated
    milk
    fine dry bread crumbs

1½ teaspoons salt
¼ teaspoon pepper
    few grains cayenne pepper
6 egg yolks, well beaten
6 egg whites, beaten stiff but
    not dry

1. Have ready: 2-quart soufflé dish, buttered and dusted with bread crumbs.
2. Wash and trim mushrooms. Chop fine. Melt butter or margarine in saucepan or skillet over low heat. Add mushrooms and sauté, stirring occasionally, for about 10 minutes, but do not let them brown.
3. Blend flour and cream or undiluted evaporated milk to a smooth mixture in top of double boiler. Cook and stir over boiling water until thick and very smooth. Add seasonings and sautéed mushrooms, and remove from heat to cool for 5 minutes.
4. Gradually add about 1 cup of warm sauce to beaten egg yolks, stirring briskly. Return mixture to rest of sauce in

double boiler. Cook and stir over hot water until sauce thickens.

5. Remove from heat and let cool for 15 to 20 minutes. Fold in beaten egg whites gently but thoroughly. Pour into prepared 2-quart soufflé dish set in a pan containing 1 or 2 inches of hot water.

6. Bake in moderate (375° F.) oven for 50 to 60 minutes.

The Art of Making Soufflés
FREDERICA L. BEINERT

STUFFED TOMATOES

(TOMATES FARCIES)

Tomatoes, like onions and potatoes, are used so much in our cooking today it almost seems impossible that there was a time when people did not eat them. We look to their flavor and acidity to enhance dishes of all kinds and depend upon their bright red color to put a spot of interest in many an otherwise colorless plate.

One of the problems, however, in using fresh tomatoes in salads and in cooked dishes is that they are full of seeds and extremely watery. There is a trick that careful cooks use to take care of this. To remove seeds—and surplus liquid at the same time—cut in half crosswise and then, grasping the half in the palm of the hand, squeeze very gently so that seeds and juice run out. If handled gently the pulpy dividing parts and shell will remain intact. This juice need not be wasted but can be used in soups or sauces that will be strained anyway. In using canned tomatoes in sauces that are to be cooked quickly, the canned purée is usually preferable to canned whole tomatoes because quick cooking will not reduce the volume of liquid.

Tomatoes in season are always so plentiful that using them up is a problem. In France we not only ate them raw but we cooked the nice firm ones in many ways—sautéed, creamed, stuffed and so on. Stuffed Tomatoes, we call them *Tomates Farcies,* are a favorite of mine. I think you could hardly find a more delicious way of using those bits of leftover meats that at first glance seem almost useless.

LOUIS DIAT

finely chopped meat (leftover cooked lamb, veal,
beef, or poultry) sea-
soned with finely
chopped onion

tomatoes
salt and pepper
fine bread crumbs
melted butter

1. Select firm tomatoes, not overripe. Cut a hole in the top about 1½ inches in diameter. Turn upside down and press very gently to remove seeds and water.
2. Stuff with finely chopped meat which has been seasoned with finely chopped onion or stuff with cooked rice pressing the stuffing down into the tomatoes and rounding it over the tops. Sprinkle with fine bread crumbs and a little melted butter.
3. Arrange on a heatproof dish and pour a little stock or water around them.
4. Bake in a moderately hot oven of 400° to 425° F. about 15 to 20 minutes or until the tomatoes are soft and the crumbs on top are brown.

French Cooking for Americans
LOUIS DIAT

VEGETABLE CASSEROLE PROVENCALE

(RATATOUILLE)

The author of this recipe is Paul Vasseur, an extraordinary Parisian personality. Monsieur Vasseur is called a genius in the field of the rhythmic dance . . . and in the art of cooking as well.

In many vegetable casserole recipes, the vegetables lose their identity, but that is not so here. *Ratatouille* excites the appetite and is very satisfying as a supper or luncheon dish, or even as the vegetable course for a dinner.

Makes 6 servings

6 medium-sized tomatoes, sliced thin	1 stalk celery
	scant ¼ cup olive oil
1 medium-sized eggplant, sliced thin	2 cloves of garlic
	2 laurel leaves (if available)
4 to 5 green peppers, sliced thin	1 sprig of thyme
	4 to 5 sage leaves
1 pound of onions, sliced thin	2 whole cloves
	salt and pepper to taste
1 pound of pumpkin (approximately), sliced	

1. Heat the olive oil in a casserole with a cover. Sauté the onions.
2. Remove onions and sauté the tomatoes for about 10 minutes in the same oil.
3. Put the remaining vegetables in the casserole in alternate layers; salt and pepper each layer.
4. Add the spices and 1 glass of water and allow to cook, covered, for ½ hour.

NOTE:
If you prefer a thicker sauce, remove the cover for the last 5 to 10 minutes of cooking.

PAUL VASSEUR

CLEMENTINE'S APPLE FRITTERS

Clementine is the lovable cook made popular by Phineas Beck, who says, "It has been said many times that it is less difficult to discover a new star than to create an entirely new dish. Neither Clementine nor the Becks make the slightest claim to the latter distinction. We have merely sought out and adapted dishes to American measures and conditions. Our sources frequently go so far back into the folklore of French cooking that the recipes are anonymous."

The secret of this Apple Fritter dish is the batter. It is beautiful batter for any sort of fritters.

6 tablespoons flour	5 tablespoons (more or less) tepid water
1 generous tablespoon oil	
1 egg, separated	sugared slices of apple
pinch of salt	

1. Mix the flour gradually with the water; add the yolk of the egg and oil beaten up together and a pinch of salt. Put aside to "rest" for 2 hours at room temperature.
2. Just before using, add the white of egg, well beaten. This should have the consistency of heavy cream.
3. Dip sugared slices of apple in this batter for fritters and fry in hot oil. When golden, drain on paper, sprinkle with sugar, and serve.

NOTE:
Clementine, generous soul that she is, adds this simple supper suggestion: Place in the bottom of a dessert dish some mashed and strained stewed apricots. Cover with a layer of whipped cream flavored with powdered sugar and a few drops of vanilla. Serve cold. Delicious!

Clementine in the Kitchen
PHINEAS BECK

BRENNAN'S CRÊPES FITZGERALD

The name Fitzgerald usually makes one think of John Fitzgerald Kennedy and his grandfather, Boston's famous "Honey Fitz." But here it is associated with that French-Irish restaurant in the French Quarter of New Orleans. To make sure you prepare the dish in the Brennan fashion, we give you their recipe for the crêpes as well.

Makes 1 serving

2 crêpes	sugar
2 heaping teaspoons Philadel-	butter
phia Cream Cheese	strawberry liqueur
2 tablespoons sour cream	Kirsch
½ cup strawberries	

1. Roll cream cheese and sour cream in crêpes and put on plate. In a chafing dish, cook strawberries in sugar and butter.
2. Flame them in strawberry liqueur and Kirsch and pour over crêpes.

CRÊPES:

2 eggs
¾ cup sifted flour
pinch of salt

1 teaspoon sugar
milk

1. Mix eggs with flour, salt, and sugar. Add milk until batter is the consistency of condensed milk. Beat until smooth.
2. Heat a 6-inch skillet oiled with a pastry brush dipped in vegetable oil. Pour 2 tablespoons of batter into pan, tilting quickly to distribute batter evenly.
3. Cook 1 minute or so, until brown, then turn and brown other side. Oil pan with brush and repeat with rest of batter. Keep cooked cakes warm in a towel.

BLINTZES

The author of this recipe is Kathryn Murray, the petite wife of Arthur Murray, the man who taught America to dance.

Blintzes are more substantial than crêpes suzette, yet they must not be made with a heavy hand. Follow Mrs. Murray's clear-cut directions and you will enjoy good blintzes. Serve them as a main dish for luncheon or supper, with a generous blob of sour cream or blueberry sauce. We have an artist friend who gives Sunday afternoon blintz parties. With his blintzes he offers a selection of sauces, which includes raspberry and chocolate.

Makes about 14 thin pancakes
(average servings—3 to 4 per person)

PANCAKES

6 eggs, beaten
1 teaspoon salt

4 tablespoons flour
2 tablespoons water

1. Beat eggs and salt. Mix flour and water in small bowl and gradually add to it about a cupful of the beaten egg. Then add this mixture to the rest of the beaten egg. (This is to prevent lumping.)

2. Cover work surface near your stove with wax paper on which pancakes can be tossed as cooked.
3. The secret of making thin, tender blintzes is to watch the heat of the pan carefully. Use a 6-inch iron skillet. Heat this gradually until a bit of butter dropped in it will sizzle but not spatter or smoke. Try to keep pan at this same heat.
4. Grease pan lightly but completely with butter. Hold handle of pan with your left hand as you pour enough batter to make a thin layer that will just cover the pan. Turn your left hand back and forth as you are pouring so that the pan will be covered quickly and evenly.
5. If your pan is correctly heated, the thin pancake should start bubbling almost immediately. Give the pancake just a few seconds until "set" and then invert pan over wax paper so that pancake will drop out. *Note:* Pancake is now lying raw side down, cooked side up.
6. Continue making rest of pancakes, greasing pan with butter as needed.

FILLING

1 pound cottage cheese	½ teaspoon salt
1 egg, beaten	dash of pepper

1. Blend filling.
2. Then place heaping tablespoon full in center of cooked side of each pancake. Roll pancakes and place, side by side, in greased, open baking pan.
3. Twenty to 30 minutes before serving, place baking pan in preheated 350° F. oven. Bake until pancakes are golden brown.
4. Serve on very hot plates and pass garnishings. These can include sour cream, cinnamon, apple sauce or apricot, blueberry or strawberry jam.

KATHRYN MURRAY

POPPY CANNON'S SOURDOUGH HOT CAKES

Poppy Cannon's entertaining and original articles on food and travel have appeared in many publications, including *Town and Country, House Beautiful,* and *Ladies' Home Journal* (of which she is Food Editor). Internationally known as an authority on wines as well as foods, Poppy Cannon is one of the few American women to be honored in France with the decoration of the Chevaliers des Tastevins, the renowned and ancient society of Burgundy wine tasters. Her sourdough hot cakes are the king of Sunday breakfast treats, especially when served with lots of sweet whipped butter and real first-run maple syrup or wild blackberry jam. Note that you must begin this recipe the night before, by setting up a sourdough starter.

Makes about 18 hot cakes

3 eggs, well beaten	1 tablespoon baking soda
1 cup milk	1 teaspoon baking powder
2 cups sourdough starter	1 teaspoon salt
1¾ cups all-purpose flour, sifted	¼ cup sugar

1. Combine eggs with milk and sourdough starter.
2. Separately, add the flour, soda, baking powder, salt, and sugar.
3. Combine these mixtures and bake on a greased electric griddle. These can be made on an ungreased griddle, but in that case ¼ cup melted fat must be added to the batter. To make thinner cakes, add more milk. The old recipe says, "Test griddle as usual by flipping a drop of water in center, and if it bounds off slowly it is the right temperature." Set your thermostat between 380° and 390° F.
4. At serving time, keep cakes on an electric hot tray. Do not stack.

SOURDOUGH STARTER:

½ yeast cake	1½ cups light rye flour, sifted
1 cup lukewarm water	

1. Dissolve yeast in water. Gradually add the sifted rye flour. Stir into paste.
2. Cover and store overnight in a warm place 80° to 85° F.

The Electric Epicure's Cookbook
POPPY CANNON

MOSAIC OR CHECKERBOARD SANDWICHES

3 slices white bread   creamed butter
3 slices graham bread

1. Cut 3 slices each of white and graham bread ½ inch thick. Spread a slice of white bread with creamed butter and place a slice of graham on it; spread this with creamed butter and place on it a slice of white bread; repeat this process, beginning with a slice of graham.
2. Put both piles in a cool place under a light weight. When butter has become firm, trim each pile evenly, and cut each pile in 3 half-inch slices.
3. Spread these with butter and put together in such a way that a white block will alternate with a graham one. Chill under light weight.
4. When butter is perfectly hard, cut in thin slices.

The New Fannie Farmer
Boston Cooking School Cook Book

SUGGESTIONS FOR DANISH OPEN-FACED SANDWICHES

On toasted French bread:
   Warm scrambled eggs sprinkled with chopped chives
   Shrimp topped with scrambled eggs
   Roquefort cheese
   Russian caviar and two raw oysters
   Two oysters, raw or toasted
   Sardines with sliced tomatoes or sliced stuffed olives
   Anchovies with scrambled eggs

On rye and pumpernickel bread:

Raw scraped T-bone steak and Russian caviar

Shrimp, heavily covered with mayonnaise or other thick dressing

Flaked crab boiled with dill

Fresh smoked salmon

Scrambled eggs with a strip of smoked salmon in center

Fried fish with tartar sauce (usually sole)

Marinated mussel, or toasted mussel with curry mayonnaise

Smoked eel, halved and boned, with scrambled eggs

Fresh jellied herring fillet with dill

Sardines with sliced hard-boiled eggs

Liverpaste with strips of sliced pickled beets

Pressed lamb

Pressed meats or head cheese

Lamb roast or veal roast with sliced cucumber

Roast beef with sliced tomatoes

Pork roast with sliced pickled beets

Ham with scrambled eggs

Roast lamb with parsley center

Roast beef with two slices of jellied meat juice and grated horseradish

Cheeses of different kinds

Slice bread very thin. Use plenty of butter.

From Danish Kitchens

CAKES AND COOKIES

POUND CAKE

This recipe comes from Mrs. Harry S. Truman, one of our friendliest First Ladies. "I hope you include this recipe in your book," Mrs. Truman wrote me, "because it has been in our family for generations. The recipe is 200 years old." Pound cake was popular with another First Lady, Dolly Madison, wife of the fourth President. Her favorite was called Williamsburg pound cake, and it used 12 eggs, ½ pound of pitted dates, 8 almonds instead of the walnuts called for in Bess Truman's recipe, and honey for glazing instead of the white icing. The Williamsburg pound cake is decorated with the dates and almonds and glazed with the honey when it has cooled. The secret of making a pound cake is in its slow, careful baking.

1 pound (2 cups) sugar
1 pound butter (scant)
9 large eggs, separated
1 pound (4½ cups) cake flour

1 teaspoon lemon extract
white icing
12 walnut halves

1. Mix sugar and butter; add well-beaten egg yolks.
2. Add flour gradually. Then fold in the egg whites, which have been beaten stiffly. Add lemon extract.
3. Pour into tube cake pan and bake for 1 hour in 300° to 325° F. oven.
4. Ice with white icing and decorate with walnut halves.

MRS. HARRY S. TRUMAN

BUTTERCREAM POUND CAKE

Each year the Pillsbury flour people run a Busy Lady Bake-Off contest, with a $25,000 first prize. In their nineteenth such contest, Mrs. Phyllis Lidert of Oak Lawn, Illinois, was the big winner with this buttercream pound cake. Set the oven at 325° and use a 10-inch tube pan.

2 cups butter, softened
1 package Pillsbury Regular Size Buttercream Lemon or Vanilla Frosting Mix
6 eggs

4 cups Pillsbury's Best All Purpose Flour (Self-Rising Flour not recommended for this recipe)
2 teaspoons baking powder
1 12-ounce can poppy seed cake and pastry filling
confectioners' sugar or glaze

1. In large mixer bowl, cream sugar and dry frosting mix at medium speed, until light and fluffy, at least 5 minutes. Add eggs, 1 at a time, beating 1 minute after adding each.
2. Gradually beat in flour and baking powder. In small mixer

bowl, combine 3 cups batter with poppy seed filling; blend well.

3. Spread half of plain batter over bottom of greased 10-inch pan. Then alternately add spoonfuls of poppy seed batter and remaining plain batter.

4. Bake at 325° for 1 hour and 30 minutes. Let cake cool in pan for 15 minutes before removing. Let cool completely.

5. Sprinkle with confectioners' sugar or drizzle with glaze. For glaze: Combine 1 cup confectioners' sugar and 2 tablespoons lemon juice or milk.

BASIC CAKE VARIATIONS

1. Add 3 tablespoons lemon juice along with Vanilla Frosting Mix.

2. Substitute 1 package Pillsbury Buttercream Brown Sugar Frosting Mix for Lemon Frosting Mix. After removing the 3 cups batter, add to the remaining plain batter either ½ teaspoon cinnamon and ⅛ teaspoon ground cloves, OR ¼ teaspoon maple flavoring.

TO SUBSTITUTE FOR POPPY SEED FILLING

1. Combine 1 cup poppy seeds, 1 cup milk, 2 tablespoons butter, 2 tablespoons honey, and ½ cup ground nuts in saucepan. Cook and stir until thick. Cool completely.

2. Combine 1½ cups (2 packages, 3¾ ounces each) ground hazelnuts or almonds, 1 cup milk, 2 tablespoons butter, 2 tablespoons light corn syrup, and 2 tablespoons almond extract in saucepan. Cook and stir until thick, about 10 minutes. Cool completely.

3. Combine 1½ cups (12 ounces) pitted dates, ⅓ cup light corn syrup, ⅓ cup water, ¼ cup sugar, ½ teaspoon lemon juice, ¼ teaspoon salt, and ⅛ teaspoon ground cloves in saucepan. Cook and stir until mixture is thick and no liquid remains. Cool completely; beat well.

4. Combine 1 12-ounce can date cake and pastry filling with ½ cup ground or finely chopped nuts; mix well.

5. In small mixer bowl, combine 1 8-ounce can almond paste and 2 tablespoons light corn syrup and beat until smooth.

OLD-FASHIONED MAPLE SUGAR CREAM CAKE

1 cup maple sugar	¼ teaspoon cinnamon
1 egg	pinch of salt
1 teaspoon soda	2 cups flour
1 cup sour cream	granulated maple sugar

1. Mix the maple sugar with the egg and beat thoroughly. Dissolve the soda in a little cold water and stir into the sour cream. Combine the mixtures.
2. Sift the cinnamon and salt with the flour and fold in. Sprinkle the top with granulated maple sugar.
3. Bake in a 7 x 10-inch pan for ½ hour in a moderate oven (350° F.).
4. Serve hot or cold, plain or with whipped cream.

MAPLE WHIPPED CREAM

1 cup cream	⅓ cup maple spread

Whip the cream until stiff. Add the maple spread and beat slowly until well mixed. Then beat rapidly until firm.

Secrets of New England Cooking
ELLA SHANNON BOWLES AND
DOROTHY S. TOWLE

ROBERT E. LEE CAKE

This is one of the most famous Southern historical cakes. No two authorities seem to agree on the egg content (ranging from eight to ten eggs). The icing varies with each recipe. Some variants use grated orange rind or lemon in icing; others use a pure lemon filling and white icing.

10 eggs, beaten separately
2 cups flour
½ teaspoon salt
2 cups sugar

1 teaspoon lemon juice
1 teaspoon orange juice
grated rind of 1 lemon
boiled icing

1. Beat the egg yolks until lemon-colored; add the sugar and fruit juices.
2. Fold in the stiffly beaten egg whites; lastly add the flour sifted with salt, by sprinkling in the flour gently by the handfuls.
3. Bake in round ungreased pans, making 3 medium layers or 4 thin layers.
4. Ice with a boiled icing. (Or a lemon icing with coconut and orange and lemon rind to flavor. An old Williamsburg recipe calls for an uncooked lemon and orange juice filling made by combining fruit juices with sugar and grated rinds. Grated coconut is added and sprinkled over cake.)

BOILED ICING

3 cups sugar
1 cup water
1 tablespoon lemon juice
3 egg whites beaten until stiff

grated rind of 1 orange
grated rind of 1 lemon
1 cup grated coconut

1. Boil sugar and water until syrup spins a thread. Pour into whites of eggs, stirring constantly.
2. Add lemon juice and grated orange and lemon rind to icing.
3. Spread between layers and on top and sides of cake. Sprinkle the grated coconut all over top and sides of cake.

The Southern Cook Book
MARION BROWN

FRENCH CHERRY LAYER CAKE

This recipe comes from the Château de Mimont, via William I. Kaufman's *Cooking in a Castle*. This château-hotel, located some fifty miles from Paris, en route to the Mediterranean, is one at which you can stay, living *en famille,* among exquisite antiques, a pink marble staircase, floors of Louis XIV parquet, and Regency chandeliers with Baccarat pendants. The great woods that surround the castle will beckon to you before or after the enjoyable meals. Hopefully, you will visit on a day when the dessert is Gâteau aux Cérises à la Française.

Makes 1 9-inch cake

2 cups cake flour, sifted	4 egg whites
2 teaspoons baking powder	½ cup butter
½ teaspoon salt	1¼ cups sugar
⅔ cup milk	1 tablespoon Kirsch

1. Sift together the flour, baking powder, and salt.
2. Pour these sifted dry ingredients into a bowl alternately with the milk, beginning and ending with the dry mixture.
3. Beat egg whites until stiff but not dry. Fold into the batter.
4. Turn into 2 greased and floured 9-inch layer-cake pans. Bake in 375° oven for 25 to 30 minutes.
5. Cool and frost with the cherry icing, made by creaming the butter, gradually adding the sugar, then whisking until light and fluffy and blending in the Kirsch.

Cooking in a Castle
WILLIAM I. KAUFMAN

LADY BALTIMORE CAKE

Makes 2 cakes

(Preheat oven to 350° F.)

½ pound butter	10 egg whites
2 cups sugar	4 teaspoons baking powder
1 cup milk	1 tablespoon almond extract
4 cups flour	

1. Cream butter with sugar until very light and smooth. Add milk, a little at a time, and beat well.
2. Sift flour. Measure and resift. Beat egg whites until stiff. Add flour and egg whites alternately to the batter, *reserving the last cup of flour.*

3. Add 4 level teaspoons baking powder to the reserved cup of flour. Then add to batter, blending well with a gentle, folding motion. Fold in almond extract.
4. Bake in a 350° F. oven until done (approximately 25 minutes). This makes 6 layers, enough for 2 cakes.

THE FILLING

4 cups sugar	1 cup chopped nuts
1 cup water	nuts
4 egg whites	maraschino cherries
1 cup chopped raisins	raisins

1. Cook sugar with water until it threads.
2. Beat egg whites until stiff. Pour the syrup into the egg whites very slowly in a long, thin stream, beating all the while.
3. Place half of this mixture into another bowl. Add chopped raisins and chopped nuts. Put this mixture between the layers. Use the second half of the icing for the top and sides of the cake. Decorate with nuts, maraschino cherries, and raisins.

The Perfect Hostess Cook Book
MILDRED O. KNOPF

CRAIG CLAIBORNE'S
ELEGANT GENOISE CAKE

The *genoise* is one of the most elegant of cakes, and Craig Claiborne, one of America's most notable cookery experts, tells you how to make the *genoise* with an electric mixer . . . and also how to use a sheet of *genoise* cake to make *petits fours*.

Mr. Claiborne says "The *genoise* is a superb French pastry. It does not contain a leavening agent other than the air that is beaten into the eggs. Originally it was necessary to beat the eggs by hand over low heat in order to give the eggs volume. With today's electric mixers the method is greatly simplified. It is important, however, that the eggs be at room temperature or warmer and that the mixing bowl of the electric mixer be warmed before the beating begins.

"The power of electric mixers varies. Care should be taken that the mixer does not become overheated.

"Finally, the utmost care must be taken when folding the flour and butter into the *genoise* batter."

Makes 2 9-inch or 3 8-inch layers

6 eggs, at room temperature or warmer
1 cup extrafine granulated sugar
1 teaspoon vanilla extract
1 cup cake flour, sifted
¼ cup butter
Quick Butter Frosting
Rich Butter Cream

1. Warm the bowl of an electric mixer. Beat the eggs with the sugar and vanilla at the highest speed until the mixture stands in stiff peaks when the beater is withdrawn. Depending on the power of the mixer, this should take from 5 to 30 minutes. It is important not to underbeat the mixture. Scrape the sides of the bowl with a rubber spatula from time to time so that the ingredients will be well blended.
2. Meanwhile, grease 2 9-inch or 3 8-inch cake pans that are 1½ inches deep. Line the pans with waxed paper and grease the paper. Melt the butter and cool to lukewarm. Set heat control at moderate (350° F.) and place rack in the lower third of the oven.
3. Divide the flour into 6 to 8 portions and sift it over the egg mixture a portion at a time. Use a rubber spatula to fold the flour in gently after each addition.
4. Add the butter, about a teaspoon at a time, and fold it in gently but completely.
5. Turn the batter into the prepared pans and bake 35 to 40 minutes. When done, the cake will rebound to the touch when pressed gently in the center.
6. Turn the cakes out onto a cooling rack, remove the paper, and let cool. Frost with desired frosting and *genoise* praline powder.

GENOISE PRALINE POWDER

1 cup granulated sugar
⅛ teaspoon cream of tartar
⅓ cup water
1 cup blanched almonds

1. Boil the sugar, cream of tartar, and water, stirring until the sugar dissolves. Add the almonds and cook without stirring until the almonds have browned and the syrup is a golden brown color. Turn into a buttered pan and cool until brittle.
2. Turn the brittle out of the pan, break into pieces and, working with about a quarter at a time, cover with a towel and crush to a powder with a mallet or rolling pin. (Yields enough for use with either butter cream or butter frosting over a 3-layer, 8-inch *genoise*.)

To Frost the Genoise:

Reserve half the praline powder and add the remainder to the selected frosting. Spread frosting between the layers and over the top and sides of the cake. Stand the cake on waxed paper and toss the remaining powder over the sides, pressing it in gently. Any powder on the paper may be used for a border around the top of the cake.

If the Rich Butter Cream is used, chill the cake after frosting until ready to serve.

Quick Butter Frosting

¼ cup butter, at room temperature
1 pound (3½ cups) sifted confectioners' sugar
¼ teaspoon salt
4 to 5 tablespoons heavy cream
1 teaspoon vanilla extract

Cream the butter, add about 1 cup of the sugar and the salt, and cream well. Add the remaining sugar alternately with the cream, using enough cream to give a slight gloss and a good spreading consistency. Add the vanilla.

Rich Butter Cream

1 cup granulated sugar
⅛ teaspoon cream of tartar
⅓ cup water
6 egg yolks
1 cup butter, at room temperature
1 teaspoon vanilla extract

1. Mix the sugar and cream of tartar. Add the water and bring to a boil, stirring until the sugar dissolves. Continue boiling to 246° F. (a drop of the mixture forms a firm ball in cold water). Set aside to cool to lukewarm.
2. Beat the egg yolks in an electric mixer or with a rotary hand beater until very thick and fluffy. Add the syrup slowly while beating. Beat until cool.
3. Add the butter, a tablespoon at a time, beating well after each addition. Beat until very smooth and creamy. Chill until firm enough to spread. After frosting, chill the cake until ready to serve.

PETITS FOURS

Frost a sheet of *genoise* cake smoothly with Quick Butter Frosting or Rich Butter Cream. Cut the sheet with cookie cutters or a knife into desired shapes. Garnish with candied cherries cut in half or into sixths for petals of flowers, angelica cut into diamonds or leaves, whole or chopped nuts, candy sprinkles, melted chocolate, coconut, etc.

The New York Times Cook Book
CRAIG CLAIBORNE

HOT MILK SPONGE CAKE

Makes 1 7-inch square cake

2 egg whites	salt
2 egg yolks	½ cup hot milk
1 cup sugar	1 tablespoon butter
1 cup flour	½ teaspoon lemon extract
1 teaspoon baking powder	½ teaspoon vanilla

1. Beat egg whites stiff. Beat yolks until light and add to whites and beat together. Slowly add sugar. Beat with a spoon for 5 minutes.
2. Sift together flour, baking powder, and salt. Add to egg mixture. Beat in milk in which butter has been melted. Add dry ingredients and hot milk as soon as possible.

3. Turn into 7-inch square pan lined with wax paper. Bake in a 360° F. oven for 25 to 30 minutes.

NOTE:

Usually no flavoring is used in sponge cake, but we add lemon extract and vanilla to this recipe.

The Toll House Cook Book
RUTH WAKEFIELD

MARIE'S CHOCOLATE ICING

4 squares sweet chocolate	3 tablespoons water
¼ cup water	1 heaping teaspoon butter
½ cup sugar (scant)	2 tablespoons heavy cream

1. Place squares of sweet chocolate in a pan with water. Melt slowly over a low flame.
2. Make a syrup of sugar and water. Add the chocolate and stir until it boils. Add butter and heavy cream. Cook a little longer. Stir when it begins to thicken, then remove from fire. As soon as it cools, use as icing.

NOTE:

Once your cake or pastry is iced, never place it in the refrigerator as this icing has an unusually high glaze, which it loses when chilled.

The Perfect Hostess Cook Book
MILDRED O. KNOPF

PETITS FOURS GLACÉS

(LITTLE PARTY CAKES)

Petits fours are those insidious little items which by their colorful frosting attract as flowers do the bee. Then—*petit a petit on va bien loing*—little by little one goes very far.

Bake sponge cake, angel cake, or pound cake in shallow pan. Cool and cut in strips 1¼ inches thick. Cut in rectangles or triangles. Arrange cakes in rows on a cake cooler with a fine mesh, allowing plenty of space between the pieces of cake. Have spotlessly clean marble or enamel table or pan beneath cake cooler.

FROSTING

2 cups sugar	confectioners' sugar, sifted
⅛ teaspoon cream of tartar	(1 cup or more)
1 cup hot water	

1. Cook sugar, cream of tartar, and water in enamel saucepan without a lid, to 226° F. or to a thin syrup. Cool to slightly above lukewarm (100° F.) and add enough confectioners' sugar to make mixture the right consistency to pour over cake. Always add the sugar to the syrup, not the syrup to the sugar. Avoid adding too much sugar. Test by pouring a little over one cake.
2. For a series of colors, tint frosting delicately with vegetable coloring and frost one row of cakes, scrape up frosting, reheat, and add more coloring for next row, and so on. The following series may be used: (1) yellow, green, brown (with melted chocolate); (2) white, pink, rose, red; or (3) white, yellow, pale orange, deep orange.
3. Heat frosting over hot water until thin enough to pour. Start pouring over a row of cakes onto the table or pan, moving steadily to end of row and then back over them. Lift cake cooler gently, then move it back and forth to loosen the dripping frosting.
4. Make borders, flowers, or other designs with colored frosting put on with pastry bag and tube, or use tiny colored candies, chocolate shot or chocolate bits, confectioners' decorations, sliced gumdrops arranged like flowers, nut meats, coconut, or candied fruits, etc.

The New Fannie Farmer
Boston Cooking School Cook Book

PLUM CAKE

This is another of Paula Peck's fine baking recipes—a French cake with an English name, and a very special fruitcake in anybody's country.

¾ cup mixed candied fruits, diced
½ cup candied orange peel, diced
½ cup dark sultana raisins
1 teaspoon grated lemon rind
½ cup blanched almonds, sliced
¼ cup cognac
1 teaspoon vanilla
5 eggs
¼ cup sugar
¾ cup butter
½ cup almond paste
1 cup flour, sifted
½ cup cornstarch, sifted

1. Set oven at 350° F. Grease and dust with flour a deep 9-inch tube pan.
2. Combine all fruit, grated lemon rind, and nuts in a bowl. Add cognac and vanilla. Let stand at least 20 minutes, then drain excess liquid from fruit.
3. In a large bowl, combine 4 of the eggs with the sugar. Beat for a minute, then set bowl over a saucepan of hot water. Place saucepan over low heat for about 10 minutes, or until eggs are slightly warmer than lukewarm. Do not let water boil. Stir eggs occasionally while they are being heated to prevent them from cooking on bottom of bowl.
4. While eggs are warming, cream butter and almond paste together. Add remaining egg to this mixture, beating it in well.
5. When eggs are warm, beat until they are cool and thick and have tripled in bulk. Fold ¼ of beaten eggs into creamed butter-almond paste mixture. Pour mixture and drained fruit on top of remaining lightly beaten eggs. Fold all together, sprinkling in flour and cornstarch at the same time. Fold only till ingredients are combined. Be careful not to overmix.
6. Pour into prepared pan. Bake about 55 minutes, or until cake is golden brown and pulls away from sides of pan.

The Art of Fine Baking
PAULA PECK

SCRIPTURE CAKE

A recipe to be read rather than followed. And remember the words of St. Luke (12:19): "And I will say to my soul, Soul, thou hast much goods laid up for many years; take thine ease, eat, drink and be merry."

1 cup butter, JUDGES 5:25[1]
3½ cups flour, I KINGS 4:22[2]
2 cups sugar, JEREMIAH 6:20[3]
2 cups raisins ⎫
2 cups figs ⎭ I SAMUEL 30:12[4]
1 cup water, GENESIS 24:17[5]
1 cup almonds, GENESIS 43:11[6]
a little salt, LEVITICUS 2:13[7]

6 eggs, ISAIAH 10:14[8]
sweet spices to taste,
I KINGS 10:2[9]
1 tablespoon honey,
EXODUS 16:31[10]

Sift 2 teaspoonfuls of baking powder with flour, blanch almonds, chop figs. Follow Solomon's advice for making good boys and you will have a good cake, PROVERBS 23:14.[11]

A Cookbook for Poor Poets

---

[1] He asked water, and she gave him milk; she brought forth butter in a lordly dish.

[2] And Solomon's provision for one day was thirty measures of fine flour, and threescore measures of meal.

[3] To what purpose cometh there to me incense from Sheba, and the sweet cane from a far country? Your burnt offerings are not acceptable, nor your sacrifices sweet unto me.

[4] And they gave him [David] a piece of cake of figs, and two clusters of raisins: and when he had eaten, his spirit came again to him: for he had eaten no bread, nor drunk any water, three days and three nights.

[5] And the servant ran to meet her, and said, Let me, I pray thee, drink a little water of thy pitcher.

[6] And their father Israel said unto them, If it must be so now, do this, take of the best fruits in the land in your vessels, and carry down the man a present, a little balm, and a little honey, spices, and myrrh, nuts, and almonds.

[7] And every oblation of thy meat offering shalt thou season with salt; neither shalt thou suffer the salt of the covenant of thy God to be lacking from thy meat offering: with all thine offerings thou shalt offer salt.

[8] And my hand hath found as a nest the riches of the people: and as one gathereth eggs that are left, have I gathered all the earth; and there was none that moved the wing, or opened the mouth, or peeped.

[9] And she [Sheba] came to Jerusalem with a very great train, with camels that bare spices, and very much gold, and precious stones: and when she was come to Solomon, she communed with him of all that was in her heart.

[10] And the house of Israel called the name thereof manna: and it was like coriander seed, white; and the taste of it was like wafers made with honey.

[11] Thou shalt beat him with the rod, and shalt deliver his soul from hell.

MÜRBETEIG

(SHORT DOUGH)

1 cup butter
2½ cups flour
2 egg yolks
   pinch of salt

3 to 4 tablespoons sour cream,
   or light cream and a
   few drops of lemon juice
sugar, if desired

1. Put flour on board and, with a pastry cutter, cut butter into the flour. Add egg yolks, salt, and finally enough sour cream to make a soft dough that barely holds together.
2. Wrap in a cloth and chill in refrigerator.
3. Roll and pat out about ¼ inch thick for tart crust or piecrust.

STRAWBERRY SHORT CAKE

Makes 1 9-inch cake

6 eggs
1 cup sugar
¾ cup sifted flour
1 teaspoon lemon juice
1 teaspoon vanilla
2 tablespoons cold water

⅓ teaspoon salt
1 pinch baking powder
3 packages frozen sliced
   strawberries (or fresh if
   in season)
1½ pints heavy sweet cream

1. Separate eggs. Beat yolks well, add sugar, then lemon juice and vanilla. Beat until creamy.
2. Sift flour 3 or 4 times, add salt, and then add to egg yolk mixture.
3. Add baking powder to egg whites and beat well. Then fold into first mixture.
4. Flour 9-inch spring form and pour in the mixture.
5. Bake in 400° F. oven for 20 minutes, then lower to 350° F. for another 20 minutes, or until cake leaves the sides of the pan.
6. Strain berries and add pulp to whipped cream. Spread on

middle, top, and sides of the cake. Put in the refrigerator for a few hours before serving.

An original recipe from
STELLA GELLER

CHOCOLATE ICEBOX CAKE

Makes 6 servings

2 squares chocolate	4 egg whites, beaten stiff
½ cup sugar	lady fingers
¼ cup water	whipped cream, or
4 egg yolks	pistachio nuts and
1 cup confectioners' sugar	candied cherries
1 cup butter	

1. Melt chocolate in top of double boiler. Add sugar, water and egg yolks. Cook until thick and smooth. Cool.
2. Cream together confectioners' sugar and butter. Add chocolate mixture and fold in stiffly beaten egg whites.
3. Line mold with lady fingers and turn mixture into mold. Chill thoroughly.
4. Unmold. Decorate with whipped cream or with pistachio nuts and candied cherries, cut fine.

The Toll House Cook Book
RUTH WAKEFIELD

CHOCOLATE ROLL

8 eggs, separated	8 teaspoons cocoa
8 tablespoons sugar	whipped cream

1. Beat the egg yolks, sugar and cocoa together.
2. Fold in the stiffly beaten egg whites.
3. Line long baking dish with waxed paper and pour in the dough.

4. Bake at 450° F. for 15 to 20 minutes.
5. Turn quickly onto towel, roll up, and cool.
6. Unwrap and spread with whipped cream and roll up again. Cover the outside with whipped cream.

An original recipe from
MRS. FRED STORKS

LINDY'S CHEESE CAKE

Makes 1 9-inch cake

2½ pounds cream cheese
1¾ cups sugar
3 tablespoons flour
1½ teaspoons grated orange rind
1½ teaspoons grated lemon. rind

pinch of vanilla bean (inside pulp) OR ¼ teaspoon vanilla extract
5 eggs
2 egg yolks
¼ cup heavy cream

1. Combine cheese, sugar, flour, grated orange and lemon rind, and vanilla. Beat in electric mixer at second speed.
2. Add sugar gradually, then remainder of ingredients in order given. Add eggs and egg yolks, one at a time, stirring lightly after each addition.
3. Stir in cream.

COOKIE DOUGH

1 cup all-purpose flour, sifted
¼ cup sugar
1 teaspoon grated lemon rind
¼ teaspoon vanilla
1 egg yolk
¼ cup butter, melted

1. Combine flour, sugar, lemon rind, and vanilla. Make a well in center and add egg yolk and butter. Work together quickly with hands until well blended.
2. Wrap in waxed paper and chill thoroughly in refrigerator for about 1 hour.
3. Roll out ⅛ inch thick and place over oiled bottom of a 9-inch spring form cake pan. Trim off the dough by running a rolling pin over sharp edge.

4. Bake in hot oven (400° F.) 20 minutes or until a light gold. Cool.
5. Butter sides of cake form and place over base. Roll remaining dough ⅛ inch thick and cut to fit the sides of the oiled band.
6. Fill form with cheese mixture.
7. Bake in very hot oven (550° F.) 12 to 15 minutes. Reduce temperature to slow (200° F.) and continue baking 1 hour. Cool before cutting.

Lindy's Restaurant, Broadway
New York City

NO-COOKING LEMON CHEESECAKE

This tasty, no-fuss cheesecake by Robert Carrier calls for a crust of ground-up chocolate-covered wholemeal biscuits and Nabisco sells a good chocolate-covered graham cracker (perhaps other bakers do, too).

Makes 6 to 8 servings

½ package chocolate-covered wholemeal biscuits (graham crackers), finely ground
3 to 4 tablespoons butter, softened
3 packages Philadelphia Cream Cheese
3 tablespoons sugar
1 teaspoon vanilla extract
juice and grated rind of ½ lemon
2 egg yolks, beaten
½ ounce powdered gelatin
3 egg whites
½ pint heavy cream, whipped plain chocolate (for decorating cake)

1. Prepare crust by combining the finely ground chocolate-covered graham crackers with the softened butter.
2. Press into a loose-bottomed cake pan. Bake 10 to 15 minutes in a slow oven (325° F.). Allow to cool.
3. Prepare the filling by combining the cream cheese and vanilla extract. Add the lemon juice, rind and beaten egg yolks and whisk the mixture. Add the gelatin which you have dissolved in 2 tablespoons warm water.

4. Beat egg whites until stiff and fold gently into the cheese mixture. Then fold in the whipped cream.
5. Spoon the filling into the crumb crust and chill in refrigerator until ready to serve. Then grate the chocolate coarsely into curls and decorate the cake with them.

ROBERT CARRIER

BABA AU RHUM

1 package active dry, or cake, yeast	⅓ cup citron or currants, or a combination of both, cut up
1¼ cups warm water	
2 cups all-purpose flour, sifted	¾ cup granulated sugar
3 large eggs, beaten	2 thin orange slices
⅓ cup butter or margarine, melted	2 thin lemon slices
	¼ to ½ cup white rum
2 tablespoons granulated sugar	½ cup apricot jam
	1 tablespoon lemon juice
½ teaspoon salt	

1. Sprinkle or crumble yeast into ¼ cup warm water in measuring cup; stir until dissolved. Meanwhile, measure flour into large bowl. Stir up yeast; stir into flour; let stand 5 minutes.
2. Now stir in eggs; with spoon, beat dough 5 minutes. (If you sit down, 5 minutes won't seem so long.) Let dough rest for 30 minutes.
3. Next, gradually stir in melted butter. (Dough will ooze butter, but don't worry.) Then stir in 2 tablespoons sugar, salt, and citron. Now, with spoon, "knead" dough in bowl 5 minutes; although it is soft and sticky, don't add more flour. Pat dough into greased 9-inch tube pan. Let rise in warm place (80° F. to 85° F.) until triple in bulk and ½ inch from top of pan. Then bake baba at 375° F. for 35 to 40 minutes or till a rich brown.
4. Meanwhile, in small saucepan, covered, simmer ¾ cup sugar and 1 cup water, with orange and lemon slices, 5 minutes. Cool sauce; add rum to taste.
5. Remove baba from pan and place on cake rack. When slightly cooled, set on plate with bottom side up and

spoon rum sauce over it. Let stand 2 hours. Just before serving, if desired, press apricot jam through strainer, combine with lemon juice, and spread over top of Baba au Rhum. Cut into 1-inch wedges and serve as a dessert.

VARIATIONS

PETITE BABAS: Make dough as for Baba au Rhum; use to fill 18 greased 2½-inch muffin cups ⅓ full. Let rise till doubled in bulk; then bake at 375° F. 15 to 18 minutes. Arrange babas in deep serving dish or on individual dessert plates. Spoon rum sauce (step 4) over each baba. Serve warm or cold as dessert.

PETITE BABAS WITH FRUIT: Make Petite Babas, omitting rum sauce. Serve, topped with thawed frozen strawberries and whipped cream cheese or sour cream, as dessert.

PETITE BABAS WITH ICE CREAM: Arrange one Petite Baba on each dessert plate; pour rum sauce (step 4) over each; then place small scoop of strawberry ice cream beside baba.

BREAKFAST BABAS: If desired, serve half of babas with rum sauce for dessert. At breakfast the next morning, reheat remaining babas in 375° F. oven 3 minutes; serve with jam or split and butter, then toast in broiler.

LARGE BABA AU RHUM: Double all ingredients. Place in greased 10-inch tube pan (4 inches deep) or a 4-quart mold. Bake at 375° F. 40 to 45 minutes.

The Good Housekeeping Cookbook

PUFF PASTE DESSERTS

Puff Paste, or *Pâté Feuilletée*, is the basis for some of the elite in desserts—Napoleons and Palm Leaves being among the most popular.

Few cooks are better able to talk about puff paste desserts than Ann Seranne, to whom Craig Claiborne gives three cheers in the opening pages of this book. Her directions for making Puff Paste follow, as well as her recipes for Napoleons and Palm Leaves.

PUFF PASTE
(Pâté Feuilletée)

1 pound sweet butter or
    margarine
  ice water
4 cups (1 pound) enriched

flour, unsifted
½ teaspoon salt
1½ cups ice water

1. Put butter into a bowl containing ice water and knead until it is the consistency of putty and is free of lumps. Form it into a ball and squeeze firmly to extract any pockets of water that may have been trapped in it.
2. Roll the washed butter in a little of the flour, wrap in waxed paper, and chill. It must be firm when it is used, but not hard. In warm weather the butter should be kneaded well in advance of making the paste. Chill the rolling pin as well, as the paste must be kept cold at all times.
3. Wash a table top with ice water, dry it thoroughly, and sift flour and salt on it in a mound.
4. Work the 1½ cups ice water gradually into the flour, adding a little more, if needed, to make a very firm dough, never soft or sticky. Work quickly and lightly, for the dough must not be handled or kneaded too much. Kneading gives the dough an elasticity that must be avoided in this particular paste.
5. The dough thus formed is called the *détrempe,* and in France, where the ingredients are weighed rather than measured, the rule is that the weight of the kneaded butter should be equal to half the weight of the *détrempe,* or about 1 pound. It is most important that both butter and *détrempe* be of the same firmness. Form the dough into a rough ball and chill for 30 minutes.
6. Put dough on a floured board and roll it out away from you in a long rectangle ½ inch thick. Turn dough so that it is horizontally in front of you. Press the butter into a flat cake about ½ inch thick and put it in the center of the dough. Fold the flap of dough on the left to cover the butter, then fold the flap of dough on the right over the left flap. The butter is now completely covered with two layers of dough. Press edges of dough firmly together to entrap as much air as possible and chill for 20 minutes.

7. The dough with butter must be cold, but never so cold that it is difficult to manipulate.
8. Put dough on the floured board in the same position as it was before it was chilled and again roll it out into a rectangle about ½ inch thick and 20 inches long. Roll it within ½ inch of either end, and be careful not to let the enclosed butter break through the layers of dough. If the butter breaks through, it means the air trapped between the layers of dough will be lost, and it is this enclosed air that is going to puff the pastry. If the *détrempe* is firm enough, and both *détrempe* and butter are of the same firmness, the butter will not break through.
9. MAKING TURNS: When dough is rolled out into a rectangle, turn it so it is horizontal and fold as before. Fold left-hand third of dough over the center, then fold right-hand third of dough over the two layers, making three layers of dough. This rolling, turning, and folding is called a "turn." Make another turn and chill dough for 20 minutes. Make another turn and chill dough for 20 minutes. Make 2 more turns, always making sure to place dough on table in same position as before the chilling. Two more turns are needed to complete the paste. If it is going to be used immediately, make these turns, chill again, then roll, cut, and bake. The first 4 turns, however, may be made a day or two before the paste is actually required. Store dough in a bowl in the refrigerator, covered with a cloth wrung in cold water, and save the last 2 turns until the paste is to be used. Chill dough for 20 minutes before rolling and cutting. Chill dough again before baking.

This amount of paste will make 12 Puff Paste Patty Shells, 1 large *gâteau,* or 24 small cakes.

NAPOLEONS
(Petits Mille-jeuilles)

1. Roll out Puff Paste on lightly floured board into a rectangle ⅛ inch thick and cut it into strips 2½ inches wide. Put strips on a baking sheet lined with several layers of heavy brown paper, prick surfaces with a fork, and chill. Bake in a hot oven (450° F.) for 10 minutes.
2. Reduce temperature to 350° F. and bake for another 10

minutes. Place another cold baking sheet under the pastry, reduce oven temperature to 300° F., and bake for another 20 minutes, or until the strips are dry and golden brown.

3. Cool and put 3 strips together, one on top of the other, with cream between. The cream may be Pastry Cream (page 387), almond cream, or sweetened whipped cream flavored with strawberries. Dust top with confectioners' sugar and cut crosswise with a serrated knife into slices 2 inches wide.

PALM LEAVES
(Palmiers Glacés)

1. Press scraps of Puff Paste gently into a ball and roll out on a lightly floured board into a long band. Give the paste 2 turns (see Puff Paste recipe), sprinkling the rolled-out paste heavily with sugar between each turn.
2. Roll out the paste into a square ⅛ inch thick. Fold 2 sides of the square over to the middle, making a rectangle. Then fold the rectangle in half lengthwise, making 4 layers of paste.
3. Slice across the layers at 1-inch intervals, put the slices on a moistened baking sheet 1 inch apart, and bake in a hot oven (450° F.) for 8 minutes.
4. Turn with a spatula so that they do not burn on the bottom, reduce oven temperature to 350° F., and continue to bake for another 8 minutes.

The Complete Book of Desserts
ANN SERANNE

BANBURY TARTS

Makes 6 to 8 servings

PASTRY

2½ cups all-purpose flour
1 teaspoon salt
6 tablespoons vegetable shortening

¾ bar (6 tablespoons) sweet butter
ice water

1. Sift flour with salt. Add it to vegetable shortening and sweet butter. Work the shortening into the flour lightly, using your fingertips.
2. When mealy in consistency, moisten with not more than 6 tablespoons ice water. Wrap it in waxed paper and chill in refrigerator while you make the filling for the tarts.

FILLING

1 cup shelled English walnuts	1 tablespoon boiling water
1 cup white seedless raisins	1 tablespoon butter
grated rind and strained	1 egg
juice of 1 large lemon	1 teaspoon vanilla
1 cup granulated sugar	2 tablespoons cracker crumbs

1. Chop walnuts fine in a wooden chopping bowl and add raisins, likewise chopped fairly fine. Place the 2 together in a bowl and add the grated lemon rind and juice. Stir in sugar and moisten with the boiling water in which you have melted the butter. Beat egg lightly and stir it into the rest and flavor with vanilla. Sprinkle the whole with cracker crumbs and mix once more.
2. Now butter 2 large cookie sheets lightly. Roll out the pastry until ⅛ inch thick, then cut it carefully into 4-inch squares. Separate one from the other slightly and place a scant tablespoon of the filling on each. Dip your fingers in cold water and moisten the edges of each square. Then fold them over to form triangles and press the edges firmly together. Last of all, dip a fork in flour and crimp the cut edges of each. Lay them on the cookie sheets and prick each one 3 times with a fork. Place in refrigerator for 15 minutes to chill.
3. Light your oven and set it at 450° to 475° F. Gather up all the leftover scraps of pastry and use them to make more tarts until all has been used. In all, this quantity should make 12 full-sized tarts and a few baby ones for private sampling when done.
4. When chilled, paint each one with a little milk and place in preheated hot oven and bake for 20 to 25 minutes until lightly browned. Remove from oven and serve while still warm if possible. If not, reheat them slightly.

5. Just before serving, sprinkle lightly with confectioners' sugar in which you have kept a vanilla bean.

The Best I Ever Ate
SOPHIE KERR AND JUNE PLATT

CHOCOLATE-CINNAMON TORTE

Makes 12 servings

2¾ cups all-purpose flour, sifted
2 tablespoons cinnamon
1½ cups butter
2 cups granulated sugar
2 eggs, unbeaten

1 square unsweetened chocolate
2 squares semisweet chocolate
4 cups heavy cream
2 tablespoons cocoa
12 candied cherries
12 walnut halves

Several days ahead, make these "cookies":

1. Start heating oven to 375° F. Grease, line bottom with wax paper, then grease again, 2 or 3 9-inch layer-cake pans. Sift the flour with cinnamon.
2. In large bowl, with mixer at medium speed, mix butter with sugar, then with eggs, until very light and fluffy. Then, at low speed, mix in flour mixture, a little at a time, until smooth.
3. With spatula, spread ⅓ cup "cookie" dough in a very thin layer in each layer-cake pan. Bake, at one time (place on 2 racks, making sure pans are not directly over one another), about 8 to 12 minutes, or until golden.
4. Then immediately and carefully remove each "cookie" from pan to wire rack, and cool. Continue baking "cookies" until all dough is used, making at least 12. Store, carefully stacked, in tight container.

About 1 hour before serving:

1. Grate unsweetened chocolate medium fine; with vegetable parer, shred semisweet chocolate into curls; whip cream.
2. Place 1 "cookie" on flat cake plate; then spread with ¼

to ⅓ cup whipped cream. Continue building the layers in same way until you have a 12-layer torte.

3. Now fold cocoa and unsweetened chocolate into leftover whipped cream; heap over top of torte.
4. As a finishing touch, decorate top edge of torte with cherries and walnuts; then heap chocolate curls in center.
5. Refrigerate torte for about ½ hour before serving, so it will be easy to cut into 12 wedges.

The Good Housekeeping Cookbook

SAND TORTE

Makes 1 9- or 10-inch torte

1¾ cups butter	1½ teaspoons double-action
1¾ cups sugar	baking powder
9 medium-sized eggs,	juice and grated rind of
separated	½ lemon
1¾ cups flour	2 tablespoons rum or brandy
1¾ cups cornstarch	

1. Cream butter until very light. Add sugar and egg yolks alternately, mixing well after each addition.
2. Sift together flour, cornstarch and baking powder, and add to the butter-sugar-egg mixture alternately with lemon juice and rum or brandy. Stir in lemon rind and finally fold in the egg whites beaten stiff, but not dry.
3. Pour into a greased 9- or 10-inch tube pan and bake in a moderate oven (350° F.) for 45 minutes to 1 hour.
4. Dust with confectioners' sugar and serve with whipped cream on the side.

NOTE:

This cake may also be baked in 2 small loaf pans or 1 large one (4 x 8 inches), but the time should be increased to 1 hour and 15 minutes.

The Viennese Cookbook
IRMA RHODE

OLD-FASHIONED GINGERBREAD

According to Carl Sandburg, the poet and great Lincoln biographer, young Abraham Lincoln once said, "I don't suppose anybody likes gingerbread better'n I do—and gets less'n I do." Abraham Lincoln also said, "My father taught me to work; he didn't teach me to love it." Now, if *you* and your family like good homemade gingerbread, but don't love to work at it, here is an easy recipe. Gingerbread cut in squares makes a good coffee-cake or serve it as a dessert, topped with sweetened and vanilla-flavored whipped cream.

2 teaspoons powdered ginger	1 cup molasses
1 teaspoon cinnamon	2 cups flour, sifted
½ cup sugar	1½ teaspoons baking soda
¼ pound butter	¼ teaspoon salt
2 eggs, well beaten	powdered sugar

1. Preheat oven to 350° F. Cream the butter with the granulated sugar. When light and fluffy, add the well-beaten eggs.
2. Add the molasses. Combine the buttermilk and baking soda and add to the mixture, beating thoroughly.
3. Combine the sifted flour with the ginger, cinnamon, and salt; resift and add gradually to the batter.
4. Into a well-buttered and floured glass baking dish, pour the batter and bake 40 minutes in the 350° oven. While still hot, sprinkle with fine powdered sugar.

DUTCH APPLE CAKE

Makes 4 to 6 servings

1½ cups all-purpose flour, sifted before measuring	1 egg, well beaten
½ teaspoon salt	4 large sour apples, peeled and cut into eighths
2 teaspoons baking powder	2 tablespoons brown or granulated sugar
1 tablespoon sugar	1 teaspoon cinnamon
4 tablespoons shortening	
½ cup milk	

1. Seven x 11-inch shallow pan . . . Preheated oven—
   400° F. . . . Baking time—30-35 minutes.
2. Sift flour with salt, baking powder, and sugar.
3. Cut in the shortening. Add milk to beaten egg. Stir into
   flour mixture. This will make a soft dough.
4. Spread dough in greased pan. Arrange apples, pointed
   sides down, in parallel rows on dough. Mix sugar and
   cinnamon together and sprinkle over top. Bake.
5. Serve hot with lemon sauce or top milk.

The Betty Furness Westinghouse Cook Book
BETTY FURNESS AND JULIA KIENE

PAULA PECK'S APPLE STRUDEL

There are some people who have a "green thumb" in the
garden, and others who have a magic touch in the kitchen.
Paula Peck is such a person, as her cookbooks reveal.

This apple strudel has the virtue of being a perfect offering not only for dinner or lunch, but even for breakfast, and
it certainly stands up well doing a solo at an afternoon kaffee-
klatsch. Before attempting the apple strudel itself, you'll need
Mrs. Peck's general advice on making strudel—which follows
—as well as her basic strudel recipe.

STRUDEL-MAKING:

Why is strudel in the same category with puff paste? Both
pastries are crisp, light, and flaky after they are baked. Both
are created from alternate layers of dough and fat, and in
both pastries it is the fat that keeps the layers of dough from
sticking together. In making puff paste, however, the dough
and butter, after they are combined, are treated as one, while
in strudel, the dough is first stretched paper-thin, then brushed
all over with melted butter before being filled and folded.

Bread flour makes the best strudel because of its high
gluten content. The dough itself is much softer than puff-
paste dough. It must be worked, beaten, and slapped against
the table until it no longer sticks to hand or table. This will
give it enough elasticity that it can be stretched and pulled to
tissue-paper thinness.

Homemade strudel will remain crisp for several days after it has been baked. It is at its best when served slightly warm. Baked strudel can be frozen for a few weeks but should be reheated before serving. Unbaked dessert strudels should not be frozen, because many uncooked fillings do not freeze well.

BASIC STRUDEL RECIPE

1½ cups flour (preferably bread flour)
¼ teaspoon salt
1 tablespoon lemon juice
2 egg whites
4 tablespoons peanut oil

¼ to ½ cup warm water
2 cups fine white bread crumbs sautéed in ⅔ cup butter
4 cups filling (approximately)

1. Place flour in a bowl. Make a well in the center. Add salt, lemon juice, egg whites, and peanut oil. With your hand, work ingredients together, adding enough water to make a very soft, sticky dough. Knead and beat well, slapping dough against table top or pulling it against bowl, whichever you find easier. If kneading on table, keep a spatula handy to push dough together when it spreads too far.
2. When dough has been beaten at least 15 minutes and is very elastic and smooth, place it in an oiled bowl. Brush top with oil. Cover bowl with a plate, place in a pan of medium-hot water, and let dough become lukewarm. Turn dough in bowl once or twice. Warming will take 10 to 15 minutes.
3. Cover table top with a pastry cloth, particularly in the center. Place dough on cloth. Sprinkle heavily with flour. Roll out thin to the size of a large handkerchief. Brush all over with oil.
4. Dip your fists into flour. Then, by working fists under the dough (palms down), stretch dough, working from center out, until it is as thin as tissue paper. If it should begin to dry in spots before it is thin enough, brush with oil. If holes appear, ignore them. When dough is evenly stretched it may hang over edges of table. Let it dry about 10 minutes. Do not allow it to become brittle.
5. After it has dried slightly, pull or cut off thick edges. Brush remaining dough all over with melted butter. Sprinkle sautéed bread crumbs over dough. Arrange a 2-inch

strip of filling across one end. Fold over flaps of dough to right and left of filling. Brush them with butter. Lift up end of cloth nearest filling and make the dough fold over on filling. By raising the cloth, continue this procedure until dough is completely rolled around the filling. Flip onto greased pan. Bake it in a 350° oven for 1 hour, basting occasionally with melted butter, until strudel is golden brown.

APPLE STRUDEL

stretched strudel dough
1 cup butter, melted
2 cups fresh bread crumbs, sautéed lightly in butter
½ cup walnuts, ground
4 cups apples, peeled and sliced
1 cup raisins
1 teaspoon grated lemon rind

⅔ cup cinnamon sugar (2 tablespoons cinnamon to 2 cups granulated sugar)
vanilla sugar (bury 3 or 4 vanilla beans in a canister containing a pound of confectioners' sugar)

1. Brush strudel dough generously with melted butter. Sprinkle all over with sautéed bread crumbs and ground walnuts. Place a 2-inch strip of sliced apples along one end of dough.
2. Brush apples with butter and sprinkle with raisins, grated lemon rind, and cinnamon sugar. Fold in flaps of dough at sides of filling. Brush them with butter.
3. Lift up end of cloth nearest filling and make the dough fold over apples. By raising the cloth, continue to roll up apple filling until it is completely enclosed in the sheet of dough. Roll loosely.
4. Transfer strudel to lightly greased baking sheet, making a horseshoe shape if it is too long for the pan. Bake in a 350° oven for about 1 hour, basting occasionally with melted butter, until strudel is golden brown. Dust with vanilla sugar. Serve slightly warm.

The Art of Fine Baking
PAULA PECK

STOLLEN

5 cups sifted flour
5 ounces butter or part lard
½ cup granulated sugar
¾ cup milk, slightly warmed
1 teaspoon salt
3 yeast cakes
⅜ pound seedless raisins
⅛ pound almonds, blanched
and sliced

⅛ pound chopped citron
2 tablespoons orange juice
1 tablespoon orange rind,
finely grated
1 teaspoon vanilla extract
¼ teaspoon bitter almond
extract

1. Dissolve yeast in the slightly warmed milk. Add salt, sugar, half of the butter, and 4 cups of the flour. Mix thoroughly. Cover and let rise in a warm place until double in bulk.
2. Add the remaining ingredients, 1 at a time, mixing well with a wooden spoon throughout. Allow to rise again to double in bulk in the mixing bowl.
3. Turn out on a floured pastry board, dust with flour, and pat out with your hands to 1 inch thickness.
4. Cut the dough into 2 rectangles, 3 inches shorter than the length of your baking tins. Fold the dough lengthwise applying considerable pressure to the edges so that they do not disengage in rising or baking. Set to rise to a little less than double in bulk on greased tins.
5. Bake at 350° F. for 30 to 35 minutes.
6. Brush generously with melted butter immediately after removing from oven. Allow to cool. Then cover with confectioners' sugar.

A Treasury of Fine Desserts
MARGARET AND JOHN STORM

STREUSELKUCHEN

1 cake yeast (1 ounce), or
equivalent in fast-granu-
lated yeast
½ cup milk, scalded and
cooled to lukewarm
2 tablespoons sugar

1 teaspoon salt
2 eggs, well beaten
grated rind of 1 lemon
2 to 2½ cups flour
6 tablespoons melted butter
or shortening

1. Dissolve yeast in milk, add sugar and salt, and stir. Let stand for 5 minutes. Add eggs, lemon rind, and gradually the flour, alternating with the butter. Beat well while mixing.
2. Turn out on a floured board. Let stand for 10 minutes, then knead until elastic and very smooth. Put dough, covered lightly with cheesecloth in a greased bowl and let rise over hot water.
3. When doubled in bulk, punch together and roll out on a baking sheet with a rim, dusted with flour to a thickness of ¼ inch. Let rise again for about 45 minutes, until not quite doubled in bulk.

STREUSEL
(Crumbs)

¾ cup butter	1 tablespoon cinnamon
⅓ cup flour	⅓ cup melted butter for
1 cup sugar	brushing

1. While dough is rising on the baking sheet, cut together all ingredients for Streusel, with either a knife or a pastry cutter, until crumbly.
2. Brush top of dough with melted butter, then sprinkle heavily with Streusel. Bake for 35 to 45 minutes in a moderate oven (350° F.).

The Viennese Cookbook
IRMA RHODE

SCHNECKEN

(VIENNESE SNAILS)

Coffee cake and coffee!

Need anything more be said to conjure up a vision of warm hospitality, crisp conversation, and the tranquillity of a fall or winter late afternoon?

The occasion, which can only be described as coffee and coffee cake, has an informal charm such as no other meal we eat has. It bespeaks only of conviviality and ease. You are invited to tea, but you "drop in" for coffee and coffee cake. You fuss over setting up a tea table, but you "sit down" to your coffee and coffee cake.

You can serve your coffee cake hot and fresh, cold, or reheated, with or without sweet or salted butter. To reheat it, sprinkle it lightly with cold water and put it in a brown paper bag in an oven at 400° F. and bake it 10 to 15 minutes, depending upon the size of the cake.

1 yeast cake	½ cup assorted glazed fruits,
2 cups warmed milk	chopped
5 cups sifted flour	½ cup dried seedless raisins
½ pound sweet butter	½ cup dried currants
1½ cups granulated sugar	1 teaspoon cinnamon, ground
3 eggs	1 egg yolk and 2 tablespoons
½ cup toasted almonds,	milk, beaten slightly
coarsely chopped	

1. Dissolve the yeast in ¼ cup warmed milk.
2. Combine 2¼ cups sifted flour with the remainder of the milk and stir to a smooth paste in a large mixing bowl. Mix the dissolved yeast with the paste. Set in a warm place and allow to rise until double in bulk.
3. Add ¼ pound melted butter, ½ cup sugar, eggs, and the balance of the flour and mix until it forms a smooth dough.
4. Roll out on a lightly floured board to a thickness of ¾ inch. Combine the almonds, glazed fruits, raisins, currants, and ground cinnamon with the remaining melted butter and sugar. Mix well.
5. Spread the mixed fruits over the dough, then roll the dough carefully into a long cylinder. Cut off slices ½ inch thick and set them on a greased cookie sheet. Let them rise for 30 minutes. Brush the "snails" with the egg yolk and milk mixture.
6. Bake at 250° F. until golden brown.

A Treasury of Fine Desserts
MARGARET AND JOHN STORM

KOLACHKY

2 cups potato water	6 cups flour
2 cups hot milk	1 cup sugar
2 yeast cakes	2 tablespoons salt
1 cup flour	½ cup melted butter
2 eggs or 4 yolks	fruit filling or cottage cheese

1. Heat milk to boiling point, add to cold potato water. Crush 2 yeast cakes into this liquid, add flour, beat until smooth and let rise ½ hour.
2. Add remaining flour, sugar, salt, eggs, and butter and knead very thoroughly until dough forms soft ball. Cover and let rise until double its bulk, about 2 hours.
3. Roll out on floured board until dough is 1 inch thick. Cut into 2-inch squares.
4. Fill squares with fruit filling (prunes, dates, apricots) or cottage cheese. Pinch corners of squares together, being certain fruit is completely enclosed in square.
5. Place in buttered pans and let rise 1 hour. Brush tops with melted butter and bake in moderate oven, 350° F., for 45 minutes or until nice and brown.

VARIATION:
One cup of raisins may be added to dough while kneading and dough may be spread out on pan into coffee cake. Sprinkle top with brown sugar, butter and cinnamon.

Treasured Polish Recipes for Americans

HELEN CORBITT'S COFFEE CAKE

Helen Corbitt is Director of Restaurants at Dallas' Neiman-Marcus, the great fashion center of the Southwest. She lectures on fashions and foods to women's groups throughout the country and once a year conducts an enormously popular three-day cooking school at Neiman-Marcus. In 1961 she became the first—and so far the only—woman to receive the

Golden Plate Award of the Food Service Industry. In addition to her *Cookbook,* she has written *Helen Corbitt Cooks for Looks* and *Helen Corbitt's Potluck.*

This coffee cake is expensive, but worth it.

1¾ cups sugar
¾ cup butter
1⅛ cups milk
3 cups flour, sifted
4 teaspoons baking powder
1 teaspoon salt

4 egg whites
2 cups pecans, chopped
1⅛ cups brown sugar
2 tablespoons cinnamon
¾ cup flour
¾ cup butter

1. Cream the sugar and butter till soft and smooth. Add the milk alternately with the flour, baking powder, and salt sifted together.
2. Fold in the egg whites, beaten stiff.
3. Pour into a buttered baking pan.
4. For topping, combine pecans, brown sugar, cinnamon, flour, and butter, till mixture looks like cake crumbs. Spread topping over cake and bake at 350° for 40 to 50 minutes. Cut in squares.
5. If any crumbs are left over, roll balls of vanilla ice cream into them and serve with butterscotch sauce.

Helen Corbitt's Cookbook

DUTCH TEA CAKES

KLETSKOPPEN

This recipe is more than four hundred years old and originated in the Dutch city of Leyden.

1½ cups brown sugar
2 tablespoons water
¼ cup butter

1 teaspoon cinnamon
1 cup almonds, ground
1 cup flour

1. Mix sugar and water to make a thick paste. Add butter, cinnamon, almonds, and flour.

2. Shape in small rounds, about 1 inch in diameter, on a baking sheet, greased with unsalted fat. Place at least 2 inches apart.
3. Bake about 15 minutes in moderate oven (325° F.).
4. Remove from oven, let stand ½ minute, and lift from baking sheet with a spatula. If wafers become too hard to take off easily, return to oven for a minute and then remove.

BUTTERCAKE
(Boterkoek)

1 cup white sugar	4½ cups flour
½ pound (1 cup) brown sugar	2 whole eggs
1 pound butter	grated rind of 2 lemons

1. Blend together the butter, brown sugar, and white sugar. Then add the eggs and the lemon rind.
2. Mix in the flour thoroughly.
3. Pour dough into a pie pan and bake in a slow oven for about ½ hour.
4. Remove from oven and cut into very narrow wedges.

JANHAGEL

3 ounces (6 tablespoons) brown sugar	5 ounces (½ cup and 2 tablespoons) flour
5 tablespoons butter	1 whole egg
	1 teaspoon baking powder

1. Mix butter, sugar, and egg with about 2 soup spoons of water. Blend thoroughly.
2. Add flour and baking powder.
3. Spread in pan or on cookie sheet and bake in moderate oven until crisp. This should take about 15 minutes.
4. Remove from oven, cut in squares, and serve.

Served on ships of the Holland-America Line

HARTSHORNS

4 eggs
1 generous cup sugar
1 teaspoon ground cardamom

1 tablespoon brandy
4½ cups flour
2 teaspoons baking powder

1. Beat eggs and sugar well. Add ground cardamom and brandy. Sift flour with baking powder; add to ingredients.
2. Take small lumps of dough and roll into strips between hands, joining ends to form small rings.
3. Make 4 slits through outer edge of rings and cook in boiling lard or oil.

Cook Book of Norwegian Recipes
MRS. ESTHER KLAUSEN

CAT'S TONGUES

¼ cup butter
4 tablespoons flour, sifted
4 tablespoons rice flour

¼ cup sugar
1 egg white

1. Soften the butter. Stir the flour and rice flour in smoothly. Add the sugar. Stir 5 minutes. Add the stiffly whipped egg white.
2. Pour into greased baking tray or spread in a baking pan and divide into long narrow strips (4 x 1 inch).
3. Bake in a moderate oven (350° F.) until browned, about 15 minutes.

The Home Book of French Cookery
GERMAINE CARTER

CHINESE ALMOND CAKES

¼ pound sweet butter
1 cup flour, sifted
4 tablespoons granulated sugar
¼ teaspoon baking powder

2 tablespoons toasted almonds, finely chopped
1 teaspoon dry gin
¼ teaspoon almond extract split blanched almonds

1. Combine the flour and baking powder.
2. Cream butter, sugar, flour, and baking powder to a smooth paste. Work in the chopped almonds.
3. Add the gin and almond extract and mix thoroughly.
4. Roll in small balls and set on lightly floured cookie sheet.
5. Flatten the balls to ¼-inch thickness and poke half a split blanched almond into each.
6. Bake at 350° F. for approximately 20 minutes, or until faintly brown.

A Treasury of Fine Desserts
MARGARET AND JOHN STORM

TOLL HOUSE CHOCOLATE COOKIES

Makes 100 cookies

1 cup butter	2¼ cups flour
¾ cup brown sugar	1 teaspoon salt
¾ cup white sugar	1 cup chopped nuts
2 eggs, beaten	2 packages semisweet
1 teaspoon soda	chocolate morsels
1 teaspoon hot water	1 teaspoon vanilla

1. Cream butter. Add brown sugar and white sugar and the beaten eggs.
2. Dissolve soda in hot water. Add alternately with flour sifted with salt. Then add chopped nuts, chocolate morsels, and vanilla.
3. Drop by half-teaspoonfuls onto greased cookie sheet. Bake at 375° F. for 10 to 12 minutes.

NOTE:

At Toll House, we chill this dough overnight. When ready for baking, we roll a teaspoon of dough between palms of hands and place balls 2 inches apart on greased baking sheet. Then we press balls with fingertips to form flat rounds. This way cookies do not spread as much in the baking and they keep uniformly round. They should be brown through, and crispy, not white and hard as I have sometimes seen them.

The Toll House Cook Book
RUTH WAKEFIELD

GERMAN COOKIES

Makes about 6 dozen cookies

1 cup shortening	1 teaspoon soda
1¼ cups molasses	2 teaspoons ginger
¾ cup brown sugar	1 teaspoon cinnamon
4 cups flour, sifted	1 teaspoon cloves
1 teaspoon salt	

1. Melt shortening. Add the molasses and sugar and heat, stirring, until sugar dissolves. Pour into a bowl and cool.
2. Sift together flour, salt, soda, ginger, cinnamon, and cloves. Add to molasses mix, stir, and then knead until no flour shows. Add more flour if necessary to make a firm, nonsticky dough. Wrap well in waxed paper, aluminum foil or a vapor-moisture-proof freezer wrap, and chill. Well wrapped, the dough ripens without drying and may be kept several days.
3. Heat oven to moderately hot, 375° F.
4. On a well floured board, or preferably a floured canvas, pat and then roll cookie dough to about ⅛ inch thickness with a rolling pin covered with a sleeve. Use ¼ of the dough at a time. Cut into fancy shapes, using floured cutters.
5. Place cookies on greased baking sheet and bake in preheated oven about 10 minutes. Gather up scraps of dough, add some fresh dough, and repeat process.
6. Remove cookies to cooling rack with spatula and let stand until crisp. Packed in a tightly sealed container, they will keep well for many weeks.

The New York Times Magazine
RUTH P. CASA-EMELLOS

ALMOND COOKIES

This is a special recipe from Evelyn Kaufman, wife of the well-known New York illustrator Joe Kaufman. These almond cookies are terrific, and I urge you to try them. The crucial part of the recipe comes when you remove the cookie sheet from the oven. If the cookies get too cool, they won't roll, and when they are too hot, you can't loosen them from the cookie sheet with a spatula. However, after doing a couple, you will know exactly the right moment to take action.

Makes about 18 cookies

⅔ cup canned slivered blanched almonds
½ cup butter

½ cup granulated sugar
1 tablespoon flour
2 tablespoons milk

1. Grind almonds in blender, ⅓ cup at a time. Heat ground almonds in skillet with butter, sugar, flour, and milk.
2. Cook over medium heat; stir with a rubber spatula until completely blended.
3. Butter cookie sheet and sprinkle with flour. Drop by teaspoonfuls, far apart, on cookie sheet.
4. Bake 4 to 6 minutes in 350° oven until edges are golden. Remove cookie sheet from oven and let stand a second or two. Loosen cookies, then roll them over the wooden handle of a spoon, and slip off the handle. Put on a rack to cool.

EVELYN KAUFMAN

PETTICOAT TAILS

When one of the French princesses married an English king, she took over to England with her the chef she had employed in her castle kitchen. He made these interesting little cookies which he and his mistress, then Queen of England, referred to by the French name *petits gâteaux tailes.* The English people heard this name spoken in what seemed to them rapid French gibberish and out of what they heard concocted the name petticoat tails, which is what these cookies are called to this day in England.

FLORENCE LA GANKE HARRIS

1 cup butter
¾ cup sugar
1 egg

1 tablespoon cream
4 cups flour
¼ teaspoon salt

1. Cream the butter and sugar together thoroughly in a basin. Add well-beaten egg, cream, and flour sifted with salt.
2. Turn out on a floured baking board; knead until smooth. Roll out into a large round.
3. Cut out a small round from the center, then divide the remaining portion into 8 pieces. Pinch the edges, mark all over with a fork, and lay on a greased baking tin.
4. Bake in a preheated (350° F.) oven for 15 minutes.

Cooking with a Foreign Flavor
FLORENCE LA GANKE HARRIS

HERMITS

Why these tasty cookies should be called Hermits, we cannot say, except that there's a bit of hermit in every man—and Hermits belong in every man. As Campbell wrote in his *Pleasures of Hope,*

Man, the hermit, sighed—till woman smiled.

One thing you can be sure of, if there are boys in your household, five dozen Hermits won't last long. I know!

Makes about 5 dozen

1 cup shortening (half
  butter)
2 cups brown sugar
2 eggs
2⅔ cups flour
½ teaspoon salt
2 teaspoons baking powder

½ teaspoon soda
1½ teaspoons cinnamon
½ teaspoon each cloves and
  nutmeg
⅓ cup milk
⅔ cup chopped raisins
⅔ cup chopped nuts

1. Cream shortening and sugar together. Add eggs and beat until fluffy.
2. Sift flour. Measure and add salt, soda, baking powder, and spices. Sift again.

3. Add sifted dry ingredients alternately with milk. Beat after each addition. Add chopped nuts and raisins and blend into mixture.
4. Drop by teaspoonfuls onto greased baking sheet about 2 inches apart. Bake at 350° F. for 12 to 15 minutes.

The Mennonite Community Cookbook
MARY EMMA SHOWALTER

EISENHOWER'S SWEDISH "SPRITZBAAKEN" COOKIES

Makes 100 cookies

1 pound butter	2 extra yolks
1 cup sugar	4½ cups sifted flour
2 whole eggs	vanilla

1. Cream sugar and butter.
2. Add beaten eggs, then flour gradually, then vanilla to taste.
3. Use cookie press and form your own design.
4. Bake in a moderate oven (350° or 375° F.) 20 minutes or until done. Should be light in color.

NOTE:
These bake very quickly and need to be watched constantly.

Stars in Your Kitchen
MARTA MICHEL

FASTNACHTS
(RAISED DOUGHNUTS)

This famous Pennsylvania Dutch recipe comes from Mary Emma Showalter's *Mennonite Community Cookbook*. Good cooks from all over the United States and Canada contributed 1,400 recipes to the *Mennonite Cookbook*. Mennonite women come by their skill through a knowledge of kitchen art that goes back centuries . . . to forebears who came here in search of religious freedom.

In addition to the Fastnachts recipe below, you'll find easy directions for making Shoofly Pie (page 380), German Potato Salad (page 277) and Snitz and Knepp (page 200) in this book. Other Mennonite favorites include Cinnamon Pie, Old-fashioned Ginger Cookies (Leb Kuchen), Apple Grunt, Huckleberry Roly-Poly, Cherry Cobbler, Watermelon Cake, Peppernuts (Pfeffernusse), and Sour Cream Raisin Pie.

Makes 3 dozen

1¼ cups milk	3 eggs, beaten
¼ cup shortening	¾ cup sugar
1 teaspoon salt	¼ teaspoon nutmeg
1 small yeast cake	4½ to 5 cups flour, sifted

1. Scald the milk; add shortening and salt. Cool until luke-warm; then add crumbled yeast cake and stir. Gradually add 2⅔ cups sifted flour, beating batter thoroughly.
2. Put in a warm place and allow to stand until full of bubbles.
3. Mix the sugar with nutmeg and combine with beaten eggs. Stir into yeast mixture and add remaining flour. Knead well, cover, and let rise in a warm place for about 1 hour.
4. Turn out lightly on floured board and roll ¾ inch thick. Cut with doughnut cutter or biscuit cutter, shaping into a ball, or make into twists. Cover with a thin cloth and let rise on board until top is springy to touch of finger.
5. Drop into hot fat (365° F.) with the raised side down, so the top side will rise while under side cooks. Drain on absorbent paper.

The Mennonite Community Cookbook
MARY EMMA SHOWALTER

BERLIN JELLY DOUGHNUTS

("Shrove Tuesday Cakes")

Doughnuts and crullers are the special cakes of the Mardi Gras, or "Fat Tuesday." Most of Germany celebrates Fasching, a pre-Lenten carnival that reaches its peak on Fastnacht, or what we know as Shrove Tuesday. On this day the costumed and masked carnival is at its wildest in Cologne and Munich, where "anything goes."

In the United States the jelly doughnut used to be the single most popular piece of pastry, but with the passing of the small German bakeries, many young people have yet to enjoy its delightful squooshiness as you try to squeeze it into your mouth. You think you've bitten at the spot where the jelly won't spurt out, but, sure enough, you haven't, and out it comes.

"To fry in deep fat correctly," says Mimi Sheraton, "you need a deep saucepan, a slotted spoon for removing the cakes as they brown and, the most important piece of equipment of all, a fat thermometer. Without the latter, your cakes will be underdone or burned. If you have an electric deep fryer that is controlled by a thermostat you need no thermometer. Corn or peanut oil, lard or any of the canned white solid vegetable shortenings are best for deep frying."

Makes about 30 to 34 doughnuts

1 envelope dry powdered yeast	3 egg yolks
1 teaspoon sugar	3 to 4 cups flour
1 cup milk	oil or melted butter
⅓ cup butter	1½ cups apricot jam or
¼ cup sugar	marmalade
1 teaspoon salt	fat for deep frying
grated rind of 1 lemon	vanilla sugar

1. Soften yeast in a little water according to instructions on package, adding a little sugar to speed the process, if you like. Let stand in a warm place until bubbly.
2. Scald milk. Cream butter with sugar, salt, and lemon rind. When blended, add scalded milk and stir until butter melts. When cooled to lukewarm, mix in egg yolks and 1 cup flour and dissolved yeast. Add remaining flour gradually until dough is soft and light, but smooth and not sticky.
3. Knead on floured board until elastic and smooth. Shape into ball and place in floured bowl. Brush top of dough

with oil or melted butter, cover with thin kitchen towel, and set to rise in a warm, draft-free corner of kitchen.

4. Let rise 1 hour, or until double in bulk. Punch down and roll on floured board to ¼-inch thickness and cut rounds with a 3-inch cookie cutter.

5. Put a generous dab of marmalade or jam in center of half the circles, then top each with a plain circle of dough. Pinch edges together with a little water or egg white.

6. Cover with towel and let rise about 45 minutes, or until again double in bulk. Heat fat to 365° and deep-fry doughnuts a few at a time, keeping fat temperature constant. Fry about 3 minutes on first side, then turn so second side can brown. Remove with slotted spoon and drain on absorbent paper. When cool, dredge with sugar.

VARIATIONS:

1. These are sometimes made without any filling. In that case, it is not necessary to roll dough. After it has risen, punch down and pinch off pieces about the size of limes. Let rise again until double in bulk and fry.

2. Fill doughnuts with jelly after they have been fried. Either roll out dough to ½-inch thickness or pinch off pieces, let rise, and fry. When cool, fill by splitting and spooning jam into them, or squirt jam in through a long-necked pastry tube.

3. Bohemian Crullers *(Böhmische Krapfen)* are made just like unfilled doughnuts but in long narrow rolls instead of rounds. Shape by pinching off dough, then rolling between hands.

The German Cookbook
MIMI SHERATON

PIES AND PASTRIES

LEMON MERINGUE PIE

Probably the most talked-of food at [the famous] Toll House [Restaurant] is the tall meringues on our pies. But we have no secrets. It is all accomplished by using plenty of egg whites. For the filling of our Lemon Meringue Pie, we use one and one-half times the recipe—instead of the 3 egg yolks specified below we allow 5 egg yolks for the filling of a 9-inch pie . . . and 5 egg whites for the meringue with 10 tablespoons granulated sugar. Guests vie with each other in guessing its height and rulers are brought out to settle wagers. Children call it sailboat pie!

RUTH WAKEFIELD

Makes 1 9-inch pie

1 9-inch baked pie shell of plain pastry	2 tablespoons flour
1 tablespoon butter	3 egg yolks, beaten
1 cup hot water	grated rind and juice of
1 cup sugar	1 lemon

1. Melt in top of double boiler butter in hot water. Mix in a bowl sugar, flour. Add beaten egg yolks and lemon rind and juice. Add all to melted butter.
2. Cook until thick, stirring constantly. Cool thoroughly. Turn into baked pastry shell and cover with Meringue Topping.
3. Place in 400° F. oven for 12 to 15 minutes to brown.

MERINGUE TOPPING

5 egg whites	pinch of salt
10 tablespoons granulated sugar	

1. When you make meringue for pie, beat the egg whites with a pinch of salt until they hold a firm peak. Then add the granulated sugar, 1 tablespoon at a time, allowing 2 tablespoons for each egg white. Beat thoroughly to dissolve the sugar. Keep adding sugar until all 10 tablespoons are absorbed by the egg whites and a marshmallowlike, shiny, silky consistency results. Some cooks add ¼ teaspoon cream of tartar or baking powder at the very end of the beating to insure stiffness.
2. Our meringue is so stiff we have to "pack" it down on the pie fillings. We spread the top smoothly as a too rough top results in uneven browning. The meringue should remain in the 400° F. oven (preheated) for 12 to 15 minutes. Then it will be thoroughly cooked and will stay high and fluffy. Do not expect a good meringue to result from quick broiler browning.

NOTE:
Much also depends upon the eggs. They should be over 1 day old, but preferably not more than 1 week old. Old eggs may have "watery" whites which are not likely to give good results.

The size of eggs varies. If eggs are small or of pullet size, measure ½ cup of egg whites for a high meringue on a 9-inch pie and allow the same 10 tablespoons sugar.

If meringue is cooked too long, the top is apt to be leathery and it "weeps." After spreading and cooking meringue topping, place pie in refrigerator or other cold place.

The Toll House Cook Book
RUTH WAKEFIELD

LEMON CHIFFON PIE IN
GRAHAM CRACKER CRUST

CRUST

16 graham crackers	½ cup butter or pie shortening, or half and half
1 tablespoon flour	1 teaspoon cinnamon
¼ cup sugar	⅓ teaspoon salt

1. Roll graham crackers until they are in very fine crumbs.
2. Add other ingredients for crust. Mix well.
3. Press into pie tin to form lining.
4. Bake 10 minutes at 375° F.

FILLING

1 tablespoon plain gelatin	1 cup sugar
¼ cup cold water	1 large lemon
4 eggs, separated	pinch of salt

1. Soak the gelatin in the cold water.
2. Squeeze juice from lemon, grate the yellow rind into the juice.
3. Make custard with the egg yolks, ½ cup of sugar, lemon juice and salt, cooking it over hot water and stirring constantly.
4. Beat up whites with ½ cup sugar and have these ready.
5. When egg yolk mixture is of custard consistency, add softened gelatin and mix thoroughly. Then fold in the beaten egg whites and sugar.

6. Pour the completed mixture into the pie shell. Let pie set in cool place. Spread each piece as served with a thin layer of whipped cream.

NOTES:

As much as ½ cup lemon juice can be used in making Lemon Chiffon Pie. Should you wish to make *Orange Chiffon Pie,* use ½ cup of orange juice and 1 tablespoon of lemon juice, and use 1 teaspoon grated orange rind instead of grated lemon rind.

For *Lime Chiffon Pie,* use ½ cup lime juice and a little grated rind, instead of lemon juice and grated lemon rind.

For *Strawberry Chiffon Pie,* use ½ cup of strawberry juice instead of lemon juice and rind.

FRESH STRAWBERRY PIE

Take away those strawberry pies loaded with gelatin and stiff as a board. Here is the ooziest, drooliest, most delicate and dreamiest strawberry pie that ever was made. It is the pie heaven where all good strawberries should go. It is a recipe as rare as a day in June and as full of flavor as the air is full of sweet scent when the strawberry is first in bloom. For it we are indebted to Blanche D. Small, who warns that the directions must be followed carefully for perfect results.

Makes 1 9-inch pie

¼ cup Crisco	1 tablespoon sugar
2 tablespoons butter	3 pints of strawberries
½ teaspoon salt	juice of ½ lemon
1 cup flour	⅔ cup sugar
¼ cup beef drippings or chicken fat, unseasoned	2 tablespoons flour

1. Blend shortenings, salt, flour, and 1 tablespoon sugar together with fingertips, handling as lightly and briefly as possible. Add more flour as needed, so that mixture re-

sembles coarse grain. With mixing spoon blend in just enough ice water, added slowly, to hold together, but not so much that it becomes sticky.

2. Remove dough from bowl with hands and place on floured board. Dough should not stick to hands—if it does, use a little more flour. Divide into 2 uneven units, and roll the larger one out with a floured rolling pin. Fit this into the bottom and sides of a 9-inch pie plate. Then flour slightly. If it breaks it can be patched, then pressed to match the thickness of the rest of the dough.

3. Pile in the strawberries which have been washed and well drained. Sprinkle with the juice of ½ lemon and then with a mixture of the sugar and 2 tablespoons of flour.

4. Roll out the smaller piece of dough to about 12 inches in diameter and cut into ½-inch strips with knife or pastry wheel. Lay strips diagonally both ways across the top of the pie, and pinch the surplus ends into a standing edge all the way around.

5. Sprinkle top with sugar and place in refrigerator to get ice-cold before baking. Pie can remain there for several days if desired, and can be baked just before using.

6. To bake, preheat oven for 15 minutes to about 400° F. Pie should bake in 30 minutes. Crust should gradually become a very pale tan color. If it becomes brown, oven is too hot. Berries should soften, but retain their shape.

BLANCHE D. SMALL

TOM BENSON'S AVOCADO PIE

Tom Benson is the chef-director of one of the superlative restaurants of the Western world—Parke's, located in the basement of a small house near Harrods department store in London.

Avocado Pie is not Parke's highest achievement, but it is one of their best. Breast of turkey with a thick cherry sauce is another one that we recall with pleasure. The menu changes constantly, each more dazzling than the one before. Your first course will probably be decorated with a gardenia, a touch which my good wife has unashamedly copied for dinner parties.

Makes 4 to 6 servings

2 ripe avocado pears
½ pint whipped cream
Demerara rum ⎱ both to
sugar ⎰ taste

1 sponge flan case, approximately 8 inches in diameter*
chopped toasted almonds

1. Sprinkle a little rum in the flan case. Sprinkle sugar over that.
2. Put into a low oven until the outside of the case is crisp. Allow to cool.
3. Peel and stone the avocados. Liquidize with a little rum; add sugar to taste (lots of sugar).
4. Blend the avocado mixture with half the lightly beaten whipped cream and set into the flan case level with the top.
5. Smooth over the rest of the whipped cream and sprinkle with chopped toasted almonds.

Parke's Restaurant
London, England

MAMA'S APPLE PIE

"I give you here," says Marye Dahnke, "the recipe for the very best apple pie I know. This is the one my mother wouldn't even lend for the missionary-circle cookbook! The pastry recipe is a sure-fire method for making flaky pastry."

Eugene Field, who wrote "Little Boy Blue" and so many other beautiful poems for children, was a strong advocate of serving a slice of cheese with apple pie. He wrote:

---

* Tom Benson adds: "A sponge flan case is a tart case made from sponge cake mixture. The outside rim is approximately 1 inch high and ¼ inch thick. In London we usually buy an 8-inch sponge flan case ready-made for about one shilling." Myra Waldo defins flan as an open tart usually filled with fruits or custard. It is baked in a flan ring, a ring of metal about an inch high. The pastry is rolled out into a circle, then carefully pressed into the buttered flan ring, which is placed on a buttered baking sheet. It may be baked before or after the filling is added, depending on the recipe.

> But I, when I undress me
> Each night upon my knees
> Will ask the Lord to bless me
> With apple pie and cheese.

Makes 1 9-inch pie

pastry
1 tablespoon flour
1 tablespoon sugar
3½ cups diced apples
½ cup sugar

¼ teaspoon nutmeg
5 tablespoons thin cream
1 cup shredded aged
   Cheddar cheese

1. Line a 9-inch pie pan with pastry and sprinkle the bottom with the flour and sugar mixed together.
2. Toss together the diced apples, sugar, and nutmeg, and place in the pastry-lined pan.
3. Pour the cream over them, cover with a lattice pastry top, and bake in a hot oven, 425° F., 30 to 35 minutes, or until well done and lightly browned.
4. Remove from the oven and sprinkle with the shredded cheese.

PASTRY
(*Single 9-inch Crust*)

1½ cups sifted flour
½ teaspoon salt

3 tablespoons water
½ cup shortening

1. Sift the flour and salt together. Add the water to ¼ cup of the flour mixture to make a smooth paste. Cut the shortening into the remaining flour mixture, using a pastry blender or 2 knives.
2. Add the paste to this mixture and blend lightly with a fork until the dough holds together.
3. Roll the dough on a lightly floured board and fit into a 9-inch pie pan. Flute the edge.

The Cheese Cook Book
MARYE DAHNKE

WASHINGTON APPLE PIE

4 or 5 Washington State
apples
1 cup sugar
¼ teaspoon cinnamon
2 tablespoons flour

⅛ teaspoon salt
1 tablespoon lemon juice
1 tablespoon melted butter
finely grated peel of apples

1. Peel apples and grate peeling.
2. Cut each apple into 16 pieces and place in heavy skillet or baking dish. Combine sugar, cinnamon, flour, salt, and grated apple peel and sprinkle over apples. Dribble lemon juice and butter over all.
3. Steam in oven or over direct heat on an asbestos pad, until apples are soft but not done.
4. Spoon apples into unbaked crust, cover with top crust and press edges together. Bake at 450° F. 15 minutes.

Columbia Hotel Apple Pie

Apple pie is a specialty at the Columbia Hotel in Wenatchee, and they believe that the following special handling of the filling accounts for its excellent texture and flavor:

1. To the apple slices, add the sugar and desired spices and let stand for 2 hours. Drain off the resulting juice into a small pan.
2. Put apple slices into unbaked pie shell, dot with butter and cover with top crust.
3. Bake 15 minutes at 475° F.; reduce to 350° F. and continue baking 45 minutes.
4. Just before pie is through cooking, simmer juice until it becomes syrupy. When pie is removed from oven, pour juice into pie through steam escape hole in top. Serve warm.

SHOOFLY PIE

The Pennsylvania Dutch *hausfrau* would set out her molasses pies, and all the while they were cooling, the flies would gather, so that she was continually saying, "Shoo flies!" Thus, the pie became known as Shoofly Pie.

You may recall the fly problem of A. A. Milne's famous imaginary bear, Winnie the Pooh:

> ... His arms were so stiff from holding on to the string of the balloon all that time that they stayed up straight in the air for more than a week, and whenever a fly came and settled on his nose he had to blow it off. And I think—but I am not sure—that *that* is why he was always called Pooh.

A. A. MILNE

Makes 1 9-inch pie

BOTTOM PART:

¾ cup dark molasses (sorghum or dark Karo)   ¾ cup boiling water
½ teaspoon soda

TOP PART:

1½ cups flour   ½ cup brown sugar
¼ cup shortening   pastry for 1 9-inch crust

1. Dissolve soda in hot water and add molasses.
2. Combine sugar and flour and rub in shortening to make crumbs.
3. Pour ⅓ of the liquid mixture into unbaked pie crust.
4. Add ⅓ of the crumb mixture. Continue alternate layers, putting crumbs on top.
5. Bake at 375° F. for approximately 35 minutes.

The Mennonite Community Cookbook
MARY EMMA SHOWALTER

PECAN PIE*

1 cup corn syrup	3 eggs
1 cup pecans, chopped coarse	1 teaspoon vanilla
½ cup granulated sugar	½ teaspoon salt

1. Beat eggs slightly, add sugar, syrup, nuts, salt, and vanilla.
2. Put in unbaked shell and bake 30 minutes in a slow oven 350° F. The pecans will float to the top forming a crust that will brown nicely if baked slowly.

The New Orleans Cook Book
LENA RICHARD

BROWN DERBY BLACK BOTTOM PIE

Makes 1 10-inch pie; serves 8

2 teaspoons unflavored gelatin	1 teaspoon vanilla
½ cup milk	1 egg yolk
1 ounce sugar	3 ounces sweet chocolate
1 pinch salt	1 pint cream, whipped
	1 pie shell, prebaked

1. Soak gelatin in small amount of cold water for 15 minutes. Bring milk to boiling point.
2. Beat together sugar, salt, half of vanilla, and egg yolk until light, thick and creamy. Add ½ of the boiling milk over egg mixture. Blend well, then add to remaining hot milk.
3. Return to heat, stirring constantly for a few seconds. Remove from fire before boiling point is reached. Press

---

* Ruth Wakefield's recipe at Toll House calls for a richer pie. She combines 4 eggs, 1 cup sugar, 1 cup dark corn syrup, 1 tablespoon flour, ½ teaspoon salt, 3 tablespoons melted butter, 1 cup pecan meats, and 2 teaspoons vanilla. Plain pastry shell. 9-inch pie plate. Bake at 350° for 40 minutes. Chill and top with whipped cream.

soaked gelatin free of any excess water and dissolve in hot mixture. Strain through a very fine sieve.

4. Add 2 ounces of the chocolate, which has been shaved; beat until smooth. Cool until it reaches creamlike consistency. Fold in ½ of the whipped cream and remaining half of vanilla.

5. Fill prebaked pie shell and place in refrigerator for 30 minutes.

6. Top with remaining whipped cream 1 inch thick. Remaining chocolate is now shaved into curled spears and stuck in top. Dust with grated chocolate.

The Brown Derby Restaurant
Hollywood, Calif.

PUMPKIN PIE

Makes 1 9-inch pie

1½ cups cooked or canned pumpkin, mashed
1 cup brown sugar
½ teaspoon salt
1½ cups rich milk (or light cream)
4 eggs
1 teaspoon cinnamon

½ teaspoon ginger
½ teaspoon nutmeg
¼ teaspoon cloves
¼ teaspoon mace
1 9-inch pie shell (unbaked)
2 tablespoons rum or brandy (optional)

1. Combine the pumpkin, sugar, salt and spices in a large mixing bowl.

2. Beat the eggs and milk or cream (and rum or brandy, if desired) together and add to the pumpkin mixture. Blend thoroughly.

3. Pour into unbaked pie shell.

4. Bake in a hot oven (450° F.) for 5 minutes, then lower the heat to 350° F. for an hour or until a knife, inserted in center, comes out clean.

LINZER TORTE

This is one of the many specialties of Demel's great pastry shop in Vienna. What one visitor—Art Buchwald—has to say about Demel's follows this recipe.

Makes 1 9-inch torte

1½ cups blanched almonds, coarsely chopped
1 cup butter, very cold
2 cups flour sifted with
1½ teaspoons powdered cinnamon

1 cup sugar
2 eggs
⅛ teaspoon powdered cloves
2 teaspoons cocoa
½ teaspoon baking powder
2 to 4 cups any red jam

1. Put almonds through a food chopper, using the coarse blade.
2. Put almonds and very hard butter together in a wooden bowl and chop until butter is cut into pieces the size of peas. Add sugar and eggs and mix well.
3. Sift flour with spices, cocoa, and baking powder and work it in to make an elastic dough. Remove the dough from the bowl, wrap it in a towel, and put it into the refrigerator for at least an hour.
4. When it is well chilled, divide into 2 parts, one a little larger than the other. Roll out the larger portion and fit it into a well greased 9-inch pie pan or spring mold.
5. Fill the shell with red jam (raspberry, currant, strawberry, cherry, or a mixture). Roll out the other portion of the dough, cut it in strips, and arrange a lattice-like top over the jam.
6. Bake in a moderate oven (350° F.) for 30 to 40 minutes. Cool and fill the lattice openings with more jam.

NOTE:
Variation: Two tablespoons of chopped citron and the same amount of chopped candied orange peel may be added to the dough during mixing.

The Viennese Cookbook
IRMA RHODE

LICKING HISTORY'S FINGERS IN SWEET VIENNA
By Art Buchwald

VIENNA, AUSTRIA—There are many people in Vienna who consider the State Opera House the most important building in the city. But there are others of us, mostly on the highest cultural levels, who would trade three performances of "Fidelio" and two performances of "Lohengrin" for one plate of *schlag* at Demel's, the grandmother of all Viennese pastry shops.

Demel's is to Austria what the Tower of London is to England. Inside the hallowed mirrored walls are displayed the treasures of the country—foaming mountains of custard, strata upon strata of chocolate cakes, bottomless lakes of fruit-flavored mousse, tunnel after tunnel of apple strudel, and glaciers of ice cream and frozen tarts.

It has been said that if Austria had an Aga Khan, he would be weighed each year at Demel's and given the equivalent in whipped cream and strawberry icing.

The first thing I saw on entering Demel's was a large marble stand filled with homemade candies. On top of the stand was a handwritten sign advertising the specialty of the day.

It was a strawberry mousse with vanilla cream, grilled almonds and hazelnuts, sherbet, and assorted candied fruits.

"A strong man," Si Bourgin, an international food patrolman, told us, "would quail at such a dish, but the average Austrian woman can eat ten of them."

As my eyes became used to the light, I saw a room to the right with about twenty tables. The decor was late nineteenth century, and very little has been changed since Emperor Franz Josef used to pop in for an apple turnover. In the center of the shop was the high altar, filled with pastries and *gugelhupf*.

I started to shake uncontrollably, and Bourgin had to slap me in the face to bring me back to my senses.

The women who wait on people are known as the Sisters of Demel's. They are dressed in shapeless black smocks and have all taken vows never to serve any pastry unless it has been made with butter. Tattooed on their arms are the words: "Death before shortening."

Reprinted by permission of the author.

As I sat at a table and prepared to eat six pastries, I heard a low rumbling, groaning, and moaning.

"What's that?" I asked Mr. Bourgin.

"That's what is known as the Demel Lament. Each afternoon the women come here and start moaning, 'Oh, I can't eat this—it's so fattening. Oh, I can't take another bite, I shouldn't! Tomorrow I will eat nothing all day. I swear this is the last Sacher Torte I will touch for a month.' They never stop eating while they're talking. You could compare the Demel Lament to a Gregorian Chant."

"What kind of people come here?"

"The Viennese aristocracy, tourists, beautiful women, and people who are trying to forget their unhappy childhoods. You must never talk to a beautiful woman at Demel's. The way to strike her fancy is to send over a pound of butter with your compliments. If she accepts it you can then formally introduce yourself."

SACHER TORTE

The Sacher Hotel in Vienna has long been an assembling place for those who appreciate the truly good things of life—music, talk, friendliness, leisure, food. Though its red-velveted walls have become a little worn with age, much of the old atmosphere still exists. As Oliver Wendell Holmes said, "Age, like distance, adds a double charm."

The fame of the Sacher Torte, or rich chocolate cake, is universal . . . so much so that a special shop exists largely to take mail orders. One year we sent various sized Sacher Tortes to a list of friends and family—to arrive just before Thanksgiving . . . and the Sacher Tortes made a great hit. The recipe given here came to us through the courtesy of Mrs. Anna Sacher.

Makes 1 8 x 9-inch cake

¾ cup butter	8 egg yolks
6½ ounces semisweet chocolate	1 cup flour
	10 egg whites, stiffly beaten
¾ cup sugar	2 tablespoons apricot jam

1. Beat butter until creamy. Melt chocolate. Add sugar and chocolate to butter; stir.
2. Add egg yolks 1 at a time. Add flour. Fold in egg whites.
3. Grease and butter 9-inch cake tin. Pour mixture in.
4. Bake in 275° F. oven about 1 hour. Test with toothpick or straw. Remove to board; cool. Cut top off and turn bottom up.
5. Heat apricot jam slightly and spread over top.
6. Cover with chocolate icing, prepared as follows:

CHOCOLATE ICING

1 cup sugar	7 ounces semisweet
⅓ cup water	chocolate

1. Cook sugar and water to thin thread.
2. Melt chocolate in top of double boiler. Add sugar gradually to chocolate. Stir constantly until icing coats the spoon. Pour on top of cake.

NOTE:
If desired, split cake into 2 or 3 layers. Fill with apricot jam or whipped cream.

Viennese Cooking
O. AND A. HESS

CHOCOLATE ECLAIRS

Makes 12 large eclairs

1 cup hot water	1 cup plus 2 tablespoons
¼ pound butter	sifted all-purpose flour
1 teaspoon sugar	4 or 5 eggs
⅛ teaspoon salt	

1. Combine the water, butter, sugar, and salt in a saucepan and bring them to a rapid boil. Remove the pan from the heat and dump in all the flour at once, stirring rapidly.

2. Reduce the heat to simmer, and stir the mixture on the stove until the dough forms a ball that sticks neither to the sides nor to the bottom. This drying process is important. Remove the pan from the stove.
3. Break the eggs one by one into the dough, beating hard after each addition. If you have an electric beater you can facilitate the process by putting the hot dough into the mixing bowl quickly and adding the eggs as directed.
4. Break the final egg, if it is needed, into a bowl, blend with a fork, and add only as much as is necessary. The dough should be golden, smooth, and glossy, and the addition of the fifth egg is necessary only if the dough is too stiff. It should be just stiff enough to hold its shape. The dough is now ready to be shaped and baked.

PASTRY CREAM

2 cups milk
6 egg yolks
1 cup sugar
9 tablespoons sifted
   all-purpose flour

1 teaspoon vanilla or
2 tablespoons Kirsch, rum
   or brandy

1. Scald the milk.
2. Beat the egg yolks and sugar until lemon colored.
3. Sift the flour into the egg mixture. Stir until mixed and gradually add the hot milk, stirring constantly.
4. Pour the mixture back into the saucepan in which the milk was heated and bring to a boil, still stirring.
5. Remove from the stove, add the flavoring, beat until smooth, and strain. Cool before using.

CHOCOLATE BUTTER FROSTING

2 squares unsweetened
   chocolate
½ cup sugar

⅓ cup water
2 tablespoons butter

This is a rich bittersweet frosting.

1. Melt the chocolate over hot water. At the same time boil the sugar and water until it threads from a spoon.

2. Add the syrup gradually to the chocolate, stirring constantly. Add butter in small pieces stirring until blended.
3. Spread the frosting over the cake and smooth it into place with a knife dipped in hot water. Let the frosting dry near an open window if you want it to be shiny.

ECLAIRS

cream-puff pastry
1 egg yolk
1 teaspoon water

pastry cream
chocolate butter frosting

1. Preheat the oven to 375° F.
2. Make the pastry. Let it cool and place it in a pastry bag fitted with a large plain tube.
3. Butter a baking sheet and dust it with flour. Force the paste onto the baking sheet in strips 4 inches long and ¾ inch thick. The strips should be about 2 inches apart from one another. Hold the pastry bag at an oblique angle and retrace your direction at the end of each strip with a quick jerk in order to cut off the pastry neatly.
4. Blend the egg yolk and water and paint each strip twice.
5. Bake the eclairs for 30 minutes. Reduce the oven temperature to 300° F. and bake 10 minutes longer, or until all beads of moisture have disappeared. Cool the eclairs on a wire rack.
6. Meanwhile make the Pastry Cream and flavor with vanilla. Cool thoroughly, stirring occasionally.
7. Slit the eclairs down the center top with scissors or knife and fill them with pastry cream.
8. Re-form the tops and cover with frosting.

NOTE:
While you are preparing one recipe of French pastry dough or fillings you might as well do two or three. In a very little while your freezer will have the makings of a variety of cakes and pastries.

Tante Marie's French Pastry
CHARLOTTE TURGEON

CREAM PUFFS WITH CREAM CUSTARD FILLING

Makes 8 cream puffs

½ cup butter or margarine   1 cup water
1 cup flour   salt
4 eggs

1. Put butter and water in a pan and bring to boil.
2. Add flour and a pinch of salt. Lower heat to medium, and beat hard until mixture forms a ball and comes away from sides of pan. Remove from heat.
3. Add 4 eggs, unbeaten, 1 at a time. Beat hard after each egg is added until mixture is smooth.
4. Drop from spoon onto greased baking sheet. Spoonfuls of mixture should be several inches apart.
5. Bake 20 minutes in hot oven (400° F.); reduce heat to 350° F. and bake for 25 minutes longer.
6. When the cream puffs have cooled, either make a slit in one side or cut off the top, and fill with cream custard filling.

FILLING

¾ cup cream   ½ cup flour
2¼ cups milk   ⅓ teaspoon salt
¾ cup heavy cream   3 eggs
¾ cup sugar   flavoring

1. Combine milk and cream in double boiler and heat.
2. Sift dry ingredients together, and add hot milk and cream gradually.
3. Return mixture to double boiler, stirring constantly to keep it smooth until it thickens.
4. Beat eggs until they are light and frothy; add the hot mixture gradually.
5. Return to double boiler again, and cook a few minutes longer, constantly stirring.

6. Cool. Fold in stiffly whipped heavy cream, and flavor with vanilla, almond or lemon extract as desired.

NAPOLEONS

Makes 4 servings

1 cup flour	½ to ¾ cup ice water
level teaspoon salt	1 cup butter

1. Put 1 cup flour on a slab or pastry board and make a well in the center; add salt; then work quickly to a paste with ice water. Roll out to the size of a man's handkerchief. In the middle place the butter. Fold up like a package and put in the refrigerator for 15 minutes.
2. Remove and roll out into a long strip. Fold in thirds with open edges out; roll again; fold and wrap in a napkin and put in the refrigerator for ½ hour. Repeat this 3 times. It is well to leave the paste in the refrigerator several hours before using.
3. On the last time, roll very thin and cut in 3 long strips, the length of a cookie sheet by 3 inches wide. Place on cookie pans, which have been moistened with water and set in the refrigerator for ¼ hour; then bake until golden brown in a 400° F. oven for about 15 minutes. Remove from the oven, let cool and sandwich with Cream Filling.

CREAM FILLING

1 egg	1 teaspoon vanilla
1 egg yolk	¾ cup hot milk
3 heaping tablespoons flour	2 tablespoons rum
3 tablespoons sugar	2 stiffly beaten egg whites
1 tablespoon dry gelatin	¾ cup whipped cream

1. Put egg and egg yolk, flour and sugar in a bowl. Beat well; then mix in gelatin and vanilla.
2. Pour on hot milk and stir over the fire until the mixture just comes to a boil; remove and stir over ice until it

begins to thicken. Add rum, stiffly beaten egg whites and whipped cream.

3. After sandwiching layers, spread a thin coating of the cream on top layer, sprinkle with crumbled bits of baked scraps of pastry and dust generously with confectioners' sugar. Serve in a long strip or cut into individual portions.

The Cordon Bleu Cook Book
DIONE LUCAS

DESSERTS

MICHAEL FIELD'S CHOCOLATE TORRONE LOAF

Michael Field is one of today's cooking masters. After his many years of experience at his celebrated cooking school in New York, he is able to present complete and readily understandable directions for many of the most challenging dishes. A dessert you and your guests will long remember is Michael Field's Chocolate Torrone Loaf

Makes 8 servings

½ pound semisweet chocolate
4 tablespoons dark rum
½ pound unsalted butter, softened
2 tablespoons sugar, "instant" or "verifine"
2 egg yolks
1½ cups almonds (about 5 ounces), grated
2 egg whites
pinch of salt
10 to 12 Petit Beurre Biscuits, or Social Tea Biscuits, cut into 1-inch-by-½-inch pieces
1 teaspoon vegetable oil
powdered sugar
½ cup heavy cream (optional)

1. Break the chocolate into small pieces and combine it with the dark rum in a small heavy saucepan. Stir over moderate heat until the chocolate melts. To avoid having the rum boil, remove the pan from the heat before the chocolate is fully dissolved and continue to stir; the heat remaining in the pan will be sufficient to melt the chocolate completely. Let it cool to room temperature.
2. Cream the softened butter with the sugar in an electric mixer, beating at medium speed until the butter is smooth and satiny. (To do this by hand, use a mixing bowl and wooden spoon, and mash the butter against the sides of the bowl until it is pliable enough to beat easily; still beating, slowly add the sugar.) Then incorporate the egg yolks, adding them 1 at a time and mixing until not a trace of them shows. Follow this with the grated almonds (pulverized dry in the electric blender, or grated by hand with a Mouli grater) and the cooled chocolate—and the chocolate must be cool, or the butter will melt and become oily.
3. Now, with a rotary beater or a wire whisk, beat together the egg whites and salt until the whites are thick enough to cling solidly to the beater without drooping. With a rubber spatula, fold them into the chocolate mixture until streaks of white no longer show.
4. Scatter the cut-up biscuits over the top of the torrone mixture (it doesn't matter if the biscuits are ragged and uneven, but don't use the crumbs) and, with a large spoon and gentle hand, mix them in, distributing the pieces evenly. Be careful not to break them.
5. With a pastry brush or a crumpled paper towel, lightly coat the inside of a 1½-quart loaf pan with vegetable oil,

and turn it upside down on a paper towel to allow any excess oil to run off. Spoon the torrone into the pan, and rap the pan sharply once or twice on the table to make sure the mixture settles evenly without air bubbles. Cover it tightly with Saran wrap or waxed paper, and refrigerate for at least 4 hours, or preferably overnight, until it is firm.

6. To unmold the torrone, carefully run a small sharp knife around the sides of the pan, cutting all the way down to the bottom. Then, for about 15 seconds, dip the bottom of the pan in a shallow pan filled with hot water. Unmold the torrone by placing a chilled platter upside down over it and, gripping the pan and platter together, quickly reversing them. Still holding them together tightly, rap the platter sharply on the table and the torrone should emerge without any difficulty. If it doesn't (this has been known to happen), repeat the dipping process.

7. Smooth the top and sides of the unmolded loaf with a spatula and return it to the refrigerator until ready to serve; because of its high butter content, the torrone tends to soften rapidly. Just before serving, sieve a little powdered sugar over the top; do not do this in advance or the sugar will dissolve. Serve the torrone cut in the thinnest of slices, accompanied, if you wish, by a bowl of whipped cream.

NOTE:
Afterthought: Don't attempt to chill the torrone in an ornamental mold. Dipping it in hot water to unmold it inevitably softens the surface and the torrone won't retain any of the designs.

Michael Field's Cooking School

AMY VANDERBILT'S BAKED ALASKA

I have at least a few things in common with Amy Vanderbilt —we both love New York, we both love good food, and we both take dancing lessons at Tom Tobin's school. The difference is that Amy's feet do the right things and mine don't.

As to Baked Alaska, it certainly is a party dish, makes a

great impression—and is not so difficult to prepare if you follow Amy Vanderbilt's directions.

Makes 6 servings

5 egg whites
⅛ teaspoon cream of tartar
⅛ teaspoon salt
1 cup sifted confectioners' sugar

1 round 6-inch angelfood cake
1 round pint strawberry ice cream, frozen hard
fresh whole strawberries

1. Start oven at hot (450° F.). Use board about 9 inches square. Lay strip of brown paper on board.
2. Make meringue. Whip egg whites until frothy. Add cream of tartar and salt and continue whipping until stiff but not dry. Add sugar, 2 tablespoons at a time, whipping after each addition. Continue to whip until meringue stands in stiff peaks when beater is withdrawn.
3. With sharp knife, enlarge center hole in cake enough to hold roll of ice cream. Use any other favorite ice cream, such as peach, pistachio, mocha, chocolate, or maple.
4. Place cake on prepared board. Run spatula inside ice cream carton. Slide ice cream into hole in cake. Quickly cover cake and ice cream with meringue, swirling thickly on top and sides. Cake and ice cream must be completely and thickly covered all over.
5. Set board in oven 5 minutes or until meringue is golden brown. Remove immediately to serving platter. Pull Alaska on strip of brown paper onto serving platter. Pull paper off platter and discard. Garnish Alaska quickly with berries. Serve at once.

Amy Vanderbilt's Complete Cookbook

CRÊPES SUZETTE

You may not believe it, but the best Crêpes Suzette we have ever eaten, and God knows we have eaten plenty, were made at a small hotel restaurant in England! It was the Mitre Hotel in Hampton Court, a short boat ride on the Thames from London. This is the Mitre recipe.

Makes 2 servings

SAUCE:

2 ounces granulated sugar	3 ounces Orange Curaçao
2 ounces butter	liqueur
6½ ounces fresh orange juice	6 crêpes (3 to each)
few drops lemon juice	cognac to flame
	powdered sugar

1. Put the sugar into the crêpe pan to "dissolve" it. Add the butter and let it melt with the dissolved sugar to a *light* brown color.
2. Add the orange juice and start reducing the liquid. Add the few drops of lemon juice and the Curaçao liqueur and reduce to a medium-thick liquid.
3. When the right consistency of the sauce is obtained, place the crêpes one by one into the sauce and carefully fold each one of them into quarters. Then flame with the cognac and, while the flame is still on, sprinkle a little powdered sugar over the crêpes and serve on a hot plate. And that's it!

CRÊPES:

Makes about 20 crêpes. Unused crêpes should be separated with wax paper, wrapped tightly in foil or freezer paper, and frozen for future use.

1 cup flour	¼ teaspoon vanilla extract
2 eggs	¼ teaspoon salt
1½ tablespoons granulated	1¼ cups milk
sugar	3 tablespoons melted butter

1. Mix the flour and sugar in a mixing bowl. Add the eggs, vanilla, and salt.
2. Add milk gradually and wire-whisk it constantly as you do so. Use only enough milk, a cup or less, to make a very thin batter.
3. Strain the batter into a fresh mixing bowl and add the melted butter. Stir in well.
4. Heat a size 18 crêpe pan (7 inches) over moderate heat.

Spoon a little batter into the pan, then tilt the pan quickly to coat the bottom evenly. If the batter is too thick for a delicate crêpe, stir in a little more milk.

5. Cook the crêpes until golden on one side, then turn with spatula and cook the other side until light brown. Transfer each crêpe, as it is done, onto a clean dish towel.

Mitre Hotel
Hampton Court,
England

CRÊPES MA POMME

This is one of the memorable *spécialités* of New York's La Caravelle restaurant, where the renowned Roger Fessaguet is king of the kitchen. It is a dessert which, since it calls for that potent apple brandy Calvados, must have roots in Normandy. Its preparation calls for an experienced hand, with the ingredient quantities left pretty much to "feel."

Makes 1 serving

1 apple, preferably of the
    Golden Delicious type
    brown sugar
    butter
    Calvados brandy

Cognac brandy
1 crêpe (see page 396)
Crème Chantilly (whipped
    cream with vanilla sugar)

1. Slice the apple into bite-size pieces. Sauté these in brown sugar for a few minutes.
2. Add fresh butter and toss the apple pieces until they are brown and moist. *Do not overcook.*
3. Flambé with Calvados.
4. In a crêpe pan prepare a crêpe, using Cognac and Calvados. Fold the apple into the crêpe and let it reduce. Flambé with Calvados.
5. Serve with Crème Chantilly. Do not use aerosol "whipped cream"; use real Crème Chantilly.

La Caravelle,
New York City

CRÊPES "SIR HOLDEN"

This is a dessert fit for the gods. It comes from the Restaurante Horcher, the top restaurant in Madrid and probably the best in all Spain. Horcher's is run by Otto Horcher and his sons, who are members of a notable family of restaurateurs: the famous Three Hussars Restaurant in Vienna, as well as restaurants in Berlin and Brussels, were under the Horcher regime.

This is one of those recipes in which experience and taste are the deciding factors when it comes to quantities. However, you can't go far wrong. The crêpes, by the way, are not folded, but laid open across the ice cream.

Makes 2 servings

berries—raspberries, strawberries, or wild strawberries
butter
cream
powdered sugar
mixture of liqueurs—Grand Marnier, Himbeergeist,
Cognac, and Kirschwasser
2 thin crêpes
2 large balls of vanilla ice cream
whipped cream
almonds, crushed

1. Heat the berries in a frying pan with butter, cream, and powdered sugar.
2. Flame this with a mixture of liqueurs.
3. Moisten the thin crêpes in the pan and then place one on top of each ball of vanilla ice cream.
4. Add the syrup and fruit from the frying pan.
5. Top this with a little whipped cream and a sprinkling of crushed almonds.

Restaurante Horcher
Madrid, Spain

PALATSCHINKEN

Vienna at the turn of the century was a paradise for epicures. In the restaurants and cafés people gathered at any and all hours. This was a happy and wholesome time in Vienna's history. Laughter and song went hand-in-hand with fine food. Crusty bread was delivered by the baker at dawn and eaten, while still warm, with good sweet butter. Rich soups, noodle dishes, boiled beef, wiener schnitzel, fancy cakes called torten, coffee with mounds of whipped cream, and wondrous pancakes called *Palatschinken*. These are but a few of Old Vienna's contributions to noble cooking. *Palatschinken* are similar to crêpes suzette or blintzes—but different. Make them thin or thick, depending on the way they are to be used. Serve plain with cinnamon and sugar, or filled.

IRMA RHODE

Makes 8 servings

2 cups cake flour, sifted	1 cup milk
6 tablespoons sugar	3 tablespoons sweet butter
pinch of salt	½ cup sweet cream
5 eggs	

1. Sift flour into a good-sized bowl. Add sugar and salt. Make a well in the center and break the eggs into it. Stir with a wooden spoon until the mixture is smooth and sticky.
2. In a saucepan, warm the milk, the sweet butter, and the cream. Stir together well. Add to the flour-egg batter and beat for several minutes until the batter is very smooth and flows freely.
3. Allow batter to stand for about an hour before frying the pancakes very carefully.
4. Into a hot frying pan, about 6 inches in diameter, put a small piece of butter, rotating the pan to distribute the fat evenly. Then pour in 2 to 3 tablespoonfuls of the batter. Tilt the pan with a rotary motion to spread the batter as much as possible. Lower the heat and let the pancake cook a few seconds.

5. Check the color by lifting part of the edge and when it is yellow, but not brown, turn the cake with a pancake turner or a spatula and cook until the other side is also done. It is often advisable, especially when making the first few pancakes of a batch, to add a little more fat to the pan when the cakes are turned.

6. Remove them from the pan, if desired, sprinkle with sugar or fill with Cottage Cheese Filling (see below) or with chicken hash.

The Viennese Cookbook
IRMA RHODE

TOPFENFÜLLE

(COTTAGE CHEESE FILLING)

Makes 8 servings

¾ pound cottage cheese
2½ tablespoons butter
3 eggs, separated
½ cup sugar

½ cup raisins, measured, then plumped in water
3 to 4 tablespoons milk or cream

1. Press cottage cheese through a fine sieve. Cream butter. Add egg yolks and sugar. Beat well. Add cottage cheese and plumped and dried raisins. Fold in the egg whites, beaten stiff but not dry.

2. Cook pancakes, following recipe for *Palatschinken.*

3. Spread mixture over pancakes, roll, and place on a shallow, well-greased ovenproof baking dish or in a frying pan. Add enough milk or cream to cover the bottom of the dish and bake in a moderate oven (350° F.) for 20 minutes. If desired, the tops may be sprinkled with sugar.

The Viennese Cookbook
IRMA RHODE

CRÊPES MONTE CARLO

Makes 8 servings

1½ cups flour, sifted
¼ cup granulated sugar
¼ cup blanched almonds,
  finely grated
¼ cup sweet butter, melted
5 whole eggs, beaten well

1 cup milk
  Grand Marnier liqueur
  Cherry Heering or Kirsch
  Crème de Menthe
  yellow Chartreuse
  Maraschino liqueur

1. Combine, in order, the sifted flour, sugar, and almonds with the beaten eggs. Add the melted butter, stirring briskly to form a smooth paste.
2. Now thin the paste with the milk to form a batter the consistency of rather thin cream.
3. Heat a small cast-iron skillet. Grease it well, then remove the excess grease with wax paper.
4. Pour a thin layer of batter into the pan. Bake until the pancake draws away from the sides of the skillet. Turn it and allow it to bake for another ½ minute. Remove to a sheet of brown paper in a warm place.
5. Stack the pancakes 5 to a serving, brushing each pancake generously with a different liqueur.
6. Shower with confectioners' sugar and serve hot.

A Treasury of Fine Desserts
MARGARET AND JOHN STORM

STRAWBERRY BAVARIAN CREAM

Makes 6 servings

4 cups strawberries, washed
  and hulled
1 tablespoon lemon juice
¾ cup sugar

2 tablespoons gelatin
¼ cup cold water
2 cups heavy cream, whipped

1. Mash the berries and press them through a fine sieve.
2. To this strawberry purée add the lemon juice and sugar and stir until the sugar is completely dissolved.
3. Soften the gelatin in the cold water, stir over hot water until dissolved, and fold into the strawberries.
4. Stir this mixture over cracked ice until it begins to thicken, then fold in the whipped cream, and pour into a serving dish.

Delectable Desserts
ANN SERANNE

STRAWBERRIES À LA CRÈME CHANTILLY*

strawberries
whipped cream

few drops of vanilla
powdered sugar

1. Stir handsome strawberries cut in halves into a fluffy mass of whipped cream flavored with powdered sugar and a few drops of vanilla.
2. Let stand in the refrigerator 2 hours before serving. The berries will be nicely chilled and the cream streaked with the pink of the strawberry juice.

Clementine in the Kitchen
PHINEAS BECK

VANILLA MOUSSE

¾ cup sugar
½ cup water
4 egg yolks

1-inch stick of vanilla bean
2 cups heavy cream

---

*An all-season variation is Banana Chantilly. A good ripe banana is sliced in half lengthwise and laid on a plate so that the ends touch, with a bow-legged effect. The Chantilly or sweetened-and-flavored whipped cream is then squeezed on the banana slices out of a pastry tube, forming wiggles. —M.S.

1. Combíne the sugar and water, bring to a boil, and cook for 5 minutes. Cool.
2. Beat 4 egg yolks in the top of a double boiler. Stir in the syrup gradually, add the pulp from the vanilla bean, and cook over hot, but not boiling, water, stirring constantly, until the mixture is thick and creamy.
3. Rub the cream through a fine sieve and cool.
4. Whip the heavy cream until it is stiff and fold it into the cream.
5. Freeze in a refrigerator tray or in a mold buried in equal parts of rock salt and ice.

Delectable Desserts
ANN SERANNE

PEG BRACKEN'S POT-DE-CHOCOLAT

One of the reasons Peg Bracken has written an appendix to her original *I Hate to Cook Book* is that she had noticed some misconceptions being disseminated by new or newish cookbooks. "To take only one," she says, "consider those odd little books that keep comparing cooking with sex. For instance, how to cook him a Sunday morning breakfast that will make him propose. . . . Now we who hate to cook wouldn't dream of cooking Sunday morning breakfast for a man until he *has* proposed. Preferably in writing. Even then, it will be good old-fashioned bacon and eggs.

"Most people like chocolate," says Peg Bracken, "and this pot-de-chocolat recipe—from a blender booklet I'd gladly credit if I knew which one it was—is a good velvety affair."

Makes 6 servings

1 cup semisweet chocolate chips
1¼ cups scalded light cream (coffee cream)

2 egg yolks
3 tablespoons brandy (or rum)

1. Place these ingredients into the blender bowl. The cream should be heated till just below boiling.
2. Turn the switch to high speed and blend till the racket stops.
3. Pour into any small pretty cups—Japanese teacups or demitasse cups—something small, because it's rich.
4. Chill about 3 hours.

The I Hate to Cook Book
PEG BRACKEN

MOHR IM HEMD

(MOOR IN GOWN)

The trick is to blend the bittersweetness of a hot chocolate pudding with the cold bland sweetness of stiffly whipped cream. Good at the end of a light meal.

Makes 4 to 6 servings

4 tablespoons (2 ounces) butter	2 ounces unblanched almonds, grated
2 ounces sugar	2 ounces bittersweet chocolate
3 eggs, separated	½ pint heavy sweet cream, whipped

1. Cream butter and fold in sugar, egg yolks, almonds, grated chocolate, and stiffly beaten egg whites.
2. Grease inside of pudding mold with butter. Sprinkle and spread with powdered sugar.
3. Fill mold with creamy batter and cover tightly.
4. Put mold in water bath and boil for 1 hour.
5. Turn hot pudding carefully onto a serving dish and garnish with wreath of chilled sweet whipped cream. Whipped cream may be flavored with strong black coffee.

An original recipe by STEFAN SALTER

CHOCOLATE CUSTARDS

Makes 6 servings

3 heaping tablespoons corn-
    starch dissolved in
    ½ cup milk
2½ cups milk
5 heaping tablespoons sugar

2 tablespoons water
1 square cooking chocolate
½ teaspoon vanilla extract
cream

1. The first step in making chocolate custards is to buy 2 or 3 dozen glass goblets—the sort shaped like large egg cups.
2. The cornstarch is dissolved in ½ cup milk.
3. Two-and-one-half cups of milk are heated in a double boiler. Into a saucepan are put the sugar, water, and cooking chocolate.
4. This is dissolved over boiling water, then placed on the fire, boiled for 2 minutes, and added to the hot milk.
5. When the mixture has the appearance of chocolate milk instead of plain milk, the ½ cup of milk and cornstarch is poured in. It is stirred until slightly thickened, when the vanilla extract is added.
6. It is then poured into the goblets, and the latter, when cool, are placed in the icebox. Before serving, cream is added to the surface with a gentle hand, so as not to break the delicate scum.

Trending Into Maine
KENNETH ROBERTS

HOT CHOCOLATE SOUFFLÉ

Makes 4 servings

2 tablespoons butter	5 tablespoons sugar
3 level tablespoons flour	2 tablespoons rum
¾ cup milk	5 egg yolks
4 ounces dark sweet chocolate	5 stiffly beaten egg whites confectioners' sugar
½ ounce bitter chocolate	1 egg
3 tablespoons water	2 tablespoons Marsala wine

1. Melt the butter in a small thick pan, stir in the flour and pour on the milk. Stir over the fire until it thickens; it must not boil.
2. Add the chocolate, dissolved in 3 tablespoons cold water over a slow fire.
3. Add 3 tablespoons sugar and rum. Beat in 4 egg yolks and 5 stiffly beaten egg whites.
4. Grease a soufflé dish, tie a band of greased waxed paper around the outside and dust out with granulated sugar. Pour in the soufflé mixture, place in a pan of hot water and bake in a 375° F. oven for 45 minutes. Carefully remove the paper and dust with confectioners' sugar.
5. Put in a small bowl 1 egg, 1 egg yolk, 2 tablespoons sugar and the Marsala. Put the bowl in another pan of hot water and beat over a slow fire with a rotary beater until thick. Serve this sauce at once, separately, with the soufflé!

The Cordon Bleu Cook Book
DIONE LUCAS

PROFITEROLES AU CHOCOLAT
(CHOCOLATE CREAM PUFFS)

Makes 4 servings

1 cup water	1¼ cups flour
2 tablespoons butter	5 eggs

1. Put the water and butter in a thick pan and bring slowly to a boil. When bubbling add the sifted flour.
2. Remove from the fire and beat until smooth. Beat in, 1 at a time, 4 eggs. Cool in the refrigerator for 1 hour.
3. Butter a cookie sheet well and place the mixture on the cookie sheet in very small balls or with a pastry bag and small round tube. Brush tops with beaten egg.
4. Bake in a 375° F. oven for 20 minutes and then in a 300° F. oven for 5 minutes. They should be a good golden-brown color and firm to the touch.
5. Cool and make a small hole in the bottom with a small knife.

FILLING

1 cup whipped cream	little vanilla
little confectioners' sugar	

1. Fill with whipped cream, which has been flavored with a little sugar and vanilla.
2. Pile on a serving dish and sprinkle well with confectioners' sugar.

SAUCE

½ ounce bitter chocolate	6 ounces dark sweet chocolate
6 tablespoons water	1 tablespoon rum

1. Break up the chocolate and put in a thick pan with 6 tablespoons water.
2. Stir over a slow fire until it dissolves. Add the rum and cook a little longer.
3. Serve separately, piping hot.

The Cordon Bleu Cook Book
DIONE LUCAS

DAMPF KNEPP

(CARAMEL DUMPLINGS)

Makes 6 servings

1 cup warm water
1 egg
1 teaspoon salt
3 tablespoons sugar

1 tablespoon shortening, melted
1 yeast cake (small)
flour (approximately 2½ to 3 cups)

1. Dissolve yeast in warm water.
2. Beat egg and add sugar and salt.
3. Combine yeast and egg mixture. Add flour and melted fat and work to a smooth soft dough. Turn out on a floured board and knead for several minutes.
4. Place dough in a greased bowl and brush surface with melted shortening. Cover and let rise in a warm place until double in bulk.
5. Divide dough into 6 parts, work into smooth round balls, and let rise until light.
6. Place on top of boiling syrup. Cover and cook slowly for 25 to 30 minutes. Do not remove lid.

SYRUP

3 cups water
2 cups brown sugar

1 tablespoon butter

Combine water, brown sugar, and butter and cook together for 5 minutes.

NOTE:
Raisins may be added to syrup if desired.

The Mennonite Community Cookbook
MARY EMMA SHOWALTER

ENGLISH PLUM PUDDING

Special occasions call for special foods, and nothing is more special than the traditional ending to a good Christmas dinner —a flaming plum pudding. The joy and excitement of its arrival at the table was never told better than by Charles Dickens in *A Christmas Carol:*

> In half a minute Mrs. Cratchit entered—flushed, but smiling proudly—with the pudding like a speckled cannon-ball, so hard and firm, blazing in half a quartern of ignited brandy, and bedight with Christmas holly stuck into the top.
>
> Oh, a wonderful pudding! Bob Cratchit said, and calmly too, that he regarded it as the greatest success achieved by Mrs. Cratchit since their marriage. Mrs. Cratchit said that now the weight was off her mind, she would confess she had her doubts about the quantity of flour. Everybody had something to say about it, but nobody said or thought it was at all a small pudding for a large family.

Makes 10 to 12 servings

½ pound (1¼ cups) pitted dates, chopped
⅔ cup candied citron, cut fine
1 cup seedless raisins
1 cup dried currants
¼ pound candied lemon peel, cut fine
¼ pound candied orange peel, cut fine
½ cup blanched almonds, slivered
2 tablespoons apple, pared and chopped
1 teaspoon ground ginger
3 teaspoons cinnamon
½ teaspoon nutmeg
½ teaspoon allspice
¼ teaspoon ground cloves
¼ teaspoon salt
1 cup light brown sugar
1 6-ounce glass red currant jelly (or raspberry preserves)
4 eggs, well beaten
2 tablespoons milk
2 cups fine dry bread crumbs
¼ pound (⅔ cup) beef suet, ground
dry white wine
brandy
sprig of holly with a few berries on it

1. Combine all the fruits, spices, sugar, jelly, and salt with the suet and bread crumbs. Mix thoroughly in a large bowl.

2. Mix together the eggs, milk, and 6 tablespoons each of wine and brandy.
3. Fold the egg mixture into the fruit mixture until thoroughly blended. If not moist enough to cling together, add a little more milk. Turn this into a well-greased 2-quart pudding mold with a tight-fitting cover. Make certain it is on tight; wrap with metal foil if in doubt.
4. Place a trivet in a large kettle and set the mold on it. Pour in enough boiling water to reach halfway up the sides of the mold.
5. Cover the kettle and steam the pudding for 4 to 5 hours. Let water boil gently and add water as needed.
6. Before turning out the pudding, plunge the closed mold into cold water for a few minutes, or set on a wire rack 5 minutes to cool.
7. Just before bringing it to the table, warm ¼ cup brandy slightly in a small saucepan. Ignite with a match and pour blazing over the pudding. Quickly stick the sprig of holly into the top of the pudding. Serve with Hard Sauce separately.

HARD SAUCE

1 cup confectioners' sugar
⅓ cup butter

1 teaspoon flavoring—vanilla, rum, or almond

Cream the butter in electric mixer. When soft and light, stir in the sugar and flavoring until smooth and fluffy. Set in cool place until ready to serve.

LEMON POSSET

We have two interesting recipes in this book by the famous "Mapie," Countess de Toulouse-Lautrec, and several by Robert Carrier. Now here is a dessert that Bob Carrier served to Mapie on her visit to his home in North London. She calls his Lemon Posset "an ingenious, delicate adaptation of an old English cold cure." The dictionary definition of a posset is "a hot drink of sweetened and spiced milk curdled with ale or wine."

Makes 4 servings

1 pint heavy cream
½ cup dry white wine
3 egg whites

grated rind and juice of
  2 lemons
freshly grated orange peel
powdered sugar

1. Add the grated lemon rind to the heavy cream and whisk until stiff.
2. Stir in the lemon juice and white wine. Add sugar to taste.
3. Whisk egg whites until they form peaks and fold into whipped cream mixture.
4. Serve in individual glasses or glass serving dish. Garnish with a little freshly grated orange peel.

ROBERT CARRIER

SYLLABUB

The following rule was taken from the first cookbook published in the United States—*American Cooking,* by Amelia Simmons, "an American orphan," in 1796—and is very kindly contributed by Mrs. Arthur L. LeBaron of Duxbury, who is in possession of a copy of the original book:

To make a fine syllabub from the Cow—Sweeten a quart of cyder with double refined sugar, grate nutmeg into it, then milk your Cow into your liquor, when you have thus added what quantity of milk you think proper, pour half a pint or more in proportion to the quantity of syllabub you make, of the sweetest cream you can get all over it.

Here is a syllabub recipe in the modern manner:

1 pint heavy cream
¼ cup sugar
2 egg whites

¼ cup sugar
4 tablespoons Sauterne wine

1. Beat cream until stiff and fold in ¼ cup sugar.
2. Beat egg whites until stiff and add ¼ cup sugar.

3. Add to cream and mix well; then add Sauterne, slowly.
4. Serve over Trifle (page 418), sponge cake, or sliced bananas.

Massachusetts Cooking Rules Old and New
MRS. J. VERITY SMITH

ZABAGLIONE

Makes 6 servings

6 egg yolks
½ cup sugar

⅔ cup Marsala wine

1. In top of large double boiler, place egg yolks in sugar. Beat until thick and pale in color.
2. Gradually beat the wine into the mixture.
3. Place the pot over boiling water, and continue beating mixture until it foams up and starts to thicken. Be sure to beat constantly while cooking—and be careful not to overcook. Remove from the fire immediately upon sign of first boiling bubbles.
4. Strain into sherbet glasses and serve hot. If desired, the sherbet glasses may be lined with lady fingers. Or, place in parfait glasses, chill in refrigerator, and serve cold.

CRÈME BRULÉE

Makes 6 servings

3 cups heavy cream
6 tablespoons sugar
6 egg yolks

2 teaspoons vanilla
½ cup light brown sugar

1. Heat the cream over boiling water and stir in the sugar. Beat the egg yolks until they are light in color and pour the hot cream gradually over them, stirring rapidly.
2. Stir in the vanilla and strain the mixture into a baking dish.

3. Put the dish in a pan containing 1 inch of hot water and bake in a slow oven (300° F.) for 35 minutes, or until a silver knifeblade inserted in the center comes out clean. Be careful not to overbake—and remember, custard continues to bake from its own heat when it is removed from the oven. Cool and chill thoroughly.
4. Just before serving, cover the surface of the cream with the light brown sugar. Set the dish on a bed of cracked ice and put the cream under the broiler flame until the sugar is brown and melted. Watch very carefully, for sugar burns easily.
5. Serve immediately, or chill again and serve very cold.

Delectable Desserts
ANN SERANNE

CHARLOTTE RUSSE

Makes 6 servings

¾ tablespoon gelatin
¼ cup cold water
⅓ cup milk, scalded
⅓ cup powdered sugar
½ teaspoon maple flavoring

2 tablespoons strong coffee
1 cup heavy cream
lady fingers
flavored custard

1. Soak gelatin in cold water. Dissolve it in scalded milk. Beat in powdered sugar. Cool these ingredients. Flavor them with maple flavoring and coffee.
2. Whip heavy cream until stiff. Fold it lightly into the chilled ingredients.
3. Line a mold with lady fingers. Pour the pudding into it. Chill it thoroughly. Unmold it and serve it with Boiled Custard flavored with rum.

BOILED CUSTARD:

1. To make about 2½ cups custard, beat slightly 3 or 4 egg yolks; add ¼ cup sugar and ⅛ teaspoon salt. Scald 2 cups milk and stir in slowly.

2. Place custard over very slow fire. Stir constantly . . . take care that it does not boil.
3. Strain, cool, and add rum, sherry, vanilla, or a little grated lemon rind.

The New Joy of Cooking
IRMA S. ROMBAUER AND
MARION ROMBAUER BECKER

SOUFFLÉ AUX FRAISES
OU FRAMBOISES

There is a small Parisian restaurant in the neighborhood of the Cathedral of Notre Dame called Le Bossu (The Hunchback), where one of the excellent *spécialités de la maison* is a raspberry soufflé (another delicious specialty is a lobster quiche). It was interesting, therefore, to learn that a respected American cookbook author, Stella Standard, also found and enjoyed the same great dessert at a restaurant of the same name, Le Bossu, in Lyons—the restaurant of Mme Blanc, on the Quai Bourbon. Stella Standard, incidentally, was born in Nebraska, has lived most of her life in New York, and has won three gold medals for her cookbooks.

Makes 4 servings

3 cups fresh berries and
   ¼ cup light brown sugar
   (or 1 10-ounce package
   frozen berries and 2
   tablespoons lemon juice)
3 tablespoons flour

½ cup heavy cream
4 egg yolks
5 egg whites
   pinch of salt
1 teaspoon almond extract
   powdered sugar

1. Sieve enough fresh strawberries or raspberries to make 1 full cup purée, add the light brown sugar, and let stand for an hour. (If they are frozen berries, purée them in the blender; if you are using raspberries, put the purée through a fine sieve to extract the seeds. The frozen berries are usually too sweet, so add the lemon juice and omit the sugar.)

2. Put the flour in the top of the double boiler and blend in the cream slowly so that there are no lumps. Stir continually with a rubber spatula over boiling water until it begins to thicken, then stir in 1 egg yolk at a time.
3. Add the purée, cook for a minute or 2, then set aside. (This may be made ahead of time.)
4. When ready to make the soufflé, have ready a greased 7½-inch soufflé dish, sprinkled, sides and bottom, with granulated sugar. Add a pinch of salt to the egg whites and beat them stiff. To the purée, add the almond extract and ¼ of the egg whites, so that the purée is very light.
5. Fold purée into the rest of the whites, stirring no more than necessary. Empty into the soufflé dish and put in a preheated 400° oven, then turn heat quite low (325°). The soufflé will begin to rise immediately. Don't open the oven for 25 minutes. It will be creamy inside, and another 3 minutes will make it firmer. Sift powdered sugar over the top and serve immediately.

The Art of Fruit Cookery
STELLA STANDARD

POIRES VÉFOUR

Le Grand Véfour is one of the few restaurants in Paris given top rating by the Guide Michelin. From its famous host, M. Olivier, Stella Standard has extracted this elegant fruit dessert recipe, which is served at Le Grand Véfour in lovely individual covered compotes on pedestals.

Makes 8 servings

4 Anjou or Comice pears
simple vanilla syrup
macaroons

Grand Marnier liqueur
6 egg yolks, beaten
1 teaspoon vanilla

CRÈME NO. 1:

2 tablespoons cornstarch
1 cup milk
1 cup light cream
½ cup powdered sugar

CRÈME NO. 2:

3 egg yolks, beaten
⅓ cup powdered sugar
Grand Marnier liqueur
1 cup cream, whipped

1. Select fine juicy pears. Peel, halve, and core them. Make vanilla syrup by boiling 1 cup sugar and ½ cup water for 5 minutes; add vanilla. Poach the pears until they are tender but still quite firm. Let them cool in the syrup, chill, and, when ready to use, drain them.
2. Make Crème No. 1: blend the cornstarch with a little of the cold milk, then add the rest; add the cream and powdered sugar and cook until mixture thickens.
3. Add the 6 beaten egg yolks and cook a little more, stirring continually over hot water, until it coats the spoon. Remove and chill. Add the vanilla and enough Grand Marnier to thin it a very little.
4. Make Crème No. 2: beat the egg yolks, add the powdered sugar gradually, and beat mixture until thick. "Perfume" the egg mixture with 2 or 3 tablespoons Grand Marnier and combine with the whipped cream. *Dressage:* sprinkle each macaroon with a teaspoon of Grand Marnier.
5. In a good-sized individual compote dish, put a layer of Crème No. 1, then a macaroon, then another spoonful of Crème No. 1, then a half pear; then cover with Crème No. 2.

The Art of Fruit Cookery
STELLA STANDARD

COEUR À LA CRÈME

Ferdinand: Here's my hand.
Miranda: And mine, with my heart in it.
—*The Tempest,* SHAKESPEARE

Makes 6 servings

2 pounds cottage cheese
2 cups heavy cream
salt
Maraschino cherries
strawberries

fresh mint
powdered sugar
heart-shaped ceramic molds

1. Add salt to cottage cheese and beat to smooth consistency while stirring in heavy cream.

2. When ingredients are thoroughly blended, place in colander and set in refrigerator to drain overnight.
3. Line a heart-shaped dessert mold with cheesecloth and pack the cheese tightly into the mold.
4. At serving time, unmold on a large platter and strip off the cheesecloth. Garnish with Maraschino cherries, fresh mint, and strawberries which have been sprinkled with powdered sugar. Fresh raspberries sprinkled with sugar may also be used.

MACEDOINE OF FRUITS

What lifts this from an ordinary fruit cup or fruit cocktail is, of course, the liquor or liqueur and the strawberries in sugar syrup.

orange sections	rum, brandy, Kirsch, or
strawberries	port wine
pineapple	strawberries in sugar syrup
peaches	or strawberry purée

1. Peel and slice the fruits.
2. Place in alternate layers in a crystal or glass dish. Pour over all rum, brandy, Kirsch, or port to suit your taste.
3. Chill well in the refrigerator and add the strawberry purée or strawberries in syrup.

NOTE:
Other fruits such as Bartlett pears, bananas, apricots, and raspberries may be used for this dish.

BANANAS AL CORDIAL

The *Esquire Party Book* calls this delicious dessert "a Spanish taste flame-enco" because it is a flamed dessert served at one of the world's best eating places, the Restaurante Horcher in Madrid.

You can, if you wish, have everything set up beforehand, reheat it while you eat, and flame it at serving time.

Makes 6 servings

9 bananas	1 small flat can crushed
1 cup brown sugar	pineapple
¼ teaspoon powdered cloves	3 tablespoons butter, melted
¼ teaspoon powdered ginger	¼ cup rum
1 teaspoon powdered	
cinnamon	

1. Allowing 1½ bananas per person, split the fruit length-wise, then cut it across. Pour the melted butter into a baking dish, dip the bananas in brown sugar, and put a layer in the bottom of the dish.
2. Add a heavy dusting of the brown sugar mixed with the spices. Repeat with as many layers as you need to use up your bananas.
3. Top with a ¼-inch layer of crushed pineapple, plus juice, then a final sugar-spice dosage.
4. Heat in a 350° oven for 15 minutes, basting it occasionally. Pour the hot rum over it and serve flaming.

Esquire Party Book

ENGLISH TRIFLE

English Trifle was a favorite dessert of George Washington and his family. This recipe comes from our favorite Scotsman, Thomas Clarkson. Tom admits that it is a wee bit Scotch in that it uses (or rather, "uses up") stale cake. There's no law against fresh cake, although Tom says it isn't quite cricket.

stale pound or sponge	strawberry jam
cake	bananas
sherry wine	vanilla pudding

1. Line a loaf pan with the stale cake. You can slice it either vertically or horizontally.
2. Soak with sherry wine.
3. Cover with a layer of strawberry jam.

4. Over this put a layer of sliced bananas—either lengthwise or cut in rounds will do.
5. Pour a layer of cooled vanilla pudding over all. Then repeat for a second layer.
6. Chill thoroughly and serve with whipped cream.

THOMAS CLARKSON

DIMPAS DAMPAS GRAND'MÈRE

As the wife of movie producer Edwin O. Knopf, Mildred O. Knopf was for years a famous hostess of the motion picture colony. She has traveled widely, and one of the chief joys in her travels has been the discovery of interesting foods. Through the years she has concerned herself with testing and improving her collection of recipes.

"Dimpas Dampas Grand'mère," says Mrs. Knopf, "was my grandmother's idea of an ideal children's dessert. The fact that it was perfect for adults, with a steaming cup of coffee, never seemed to have occurred to anyone in the family until later."

3 eggs	4 green apples
1 tablespoon sugar	2 tablespoons butter
2 heaping tablespoons flour	sugar
¼ teaspoon salt	cinnamon
¼ cup milk	1 tablespoon lemon juice

1. Preheat oven to 375° F.
2. Beat eggs until light. Then sprinkle in sugar and continue to beat well. Add flour and salt alternately with milk. Beat thoroughly until smooth.
3. Peel, core and slice 4 green apples into thin slices. Fold into batter until well covered. Melt 1 tablespoon butter in preheated glass pie plate. Pour in the batter and bake for 35 minutes in 375° F. oven. After the first 20 minutes cover with an inverted pie plate and continue to bake for 15 minutes more, at which time the apples should be soft.
4. Remove from the oven and dot immediately with 1 tablespoon butter broken into bits. As soon as the butter has melted, sprinkle generously with a mixture of sugar and

cinnamon to taste and lemon juice. Allow to cool slightly, but be sure to serve while still warm.

The Perfect Hostess Cook Book
MILDRED O. KNOPF

PENNSYLVANIA APPLE PANDOWDY

"This makes a superb dessert," says Emily Post. "It is a favorite in any household. It is my own favorite."

fingers of bread, dipped in melted butter	4 tablespoons dark brown sugar
4 large green cooking apples	½ teaspoon cinnamon
	½ cup water

1. Line a Pyrex baking dish, bottom as well as sides, with fingers of bread which have been dipped in melted butter.
2. Fill in the center with apples—peeled, cored, and sliced.
3. Sprinkle apples with dark brown sugar (if lumpy, pulverize with rolling pin) and cinnamon. Add water and cover top with a layer of well-buttered fingers of bread. Sprinkle top with additional sugar.
4. Cover and bake 1 hour in a moderate (350° F.) oven.
5. Serve with whipped cream.

The Emily Post Cookbook

MONT BLANC

Makes 6 to 8 servings

MERINGUE

4 egg whites	2 drops vanilla
8 ounces granulated sugar	

1. Beat the egg whites until stiff. Add the granulated sugar and the vanilla.

2. Put into a piping bag with a star tube, and pipe a base in a circle about 3 inches in diameter and ½ inch high—1 for each serving.
3. Allow to dry in a warm oven and then let get cold.

CRÈME CHANTILLY

| 1 pint heavy cream | 4 drops vanilla |
| 2 ounces fine sugar | |

1. Whip cream and sugar and vanilla.
2. Put into a piping bag and pipe onto each meringue base, making a mound, on each, about 3 inches high.

CHESTNUT PURÉE

1½ pounds chestnuts   sweetened milk

1. Cook the chestnuts in the sweetened milk. Allow to cool and then mash dry.
2. Press this chestnut purée through a coarse sieve over the mounds of whipped cream, covering the top and sides entirely.
3. Press down with a spatula so that the Chestnut Purée will adhere to the whipped cream.

Restaurant Voisin
New York City

NUTS IN WINE

No one has done more to improve the national standard of cooking in England than has Ambrose Heath. He has encouraged good cooking and discouraged bad. He has helped to sharpen the standards of restaurateurs by inspiring their customers to be more discriminating. Among his many interesting stories, Ambrose Heath tells this one about himself and the custom of eating nuts in wine.

When we were children, my father used to have a habit of allowing us to have a taste of wine, not by tint-ing our glasses of water an insipid pink with red wine, but by a much more subtle and delicious method. At dessert-time, when we were old enough, we used to find waiting for us a spare glass of sherry heaped full to the brim with a mixture of nuts and sherry which had been left just long enough for the nuts to be very finely flavoured but not impregnated with the golden wine. These, picked out from their vinous bath, were always savoured with the utmost delight and remain one of my earliest memories of this lovely wine. Fresh cobnuts (hazelnuts) and filberts were commonplace, but fresh walnuts were—and still are—ineffable. But whatever the nut, it must be completely and cleanly skinned or the fullest joy will not be fulfilled.

AMBROSE HEATH

LEMON RICE PUDDING

4½ cups milk	juice of 2 large lemons
½ cup brown rice	3 egg yolks, beaten
4 tablespoons brown sugar	MERINGUE:
1 tablespoon butter	3 egg whites, beaten
few grains salt	4 tablespoons sugar
grated rind of 1 lemon	2 tablespoons lemon juice

1. Wash the rice and cook it in the top of the double boiler with the milk, sugar, butter, and salt until it is tender, about 50 minutes to an hour.
2. Add the rind, juice, and beaten yolks and put into a baking dish.
3. For the meringue, beat the whites until stiff, add the sugar and lemon juice, and pile on top of the rice.
4. Brown in a hot oven about 8 minutes. The rice should be quite moist. It thickens as it cools.

Whole Grain Cookery
STELLA STANDARD

RICOTTA WITH CRUSHED STRAWBERRIES

Mapie, Countess de Toulouse-Lautrec, asked Robert Carrier, the American who helped to gourmetize England, what he himself most enjoyed eating, and Carrier replied, "The simple things. I'm often never happier than with a perfectly poached egg and an absolutely fresh salad—with a little wine, of course. Whenever I get off a plane in America I get frantic for New England boiled dinners, homemade pea soups, clams and pumpkin pies." I agree with Carrier—there are times when your palate shouts for simplicity.

Another cookbook author recently asked me to name my one most favorite dessert, and I spontaneously answered, "Ricotta cheese with a generous topping of crushed strawberries." And it's so simple to prepare! There used to be a time when you could get ricotta cheese only in Italian food stores, but today many supermarkets carry it or can get it for you. Cheese shops, which seem to be springing up all over the place, can, of course, supply ricotta. If you still have trouble finding it, ask an Italian restaurant or pizzeria where they get theirs.

You merely defrost a package of frozen crushed strawberries and pour as much as you like over as much of the ricotta as you like. That's it. To me, this dessert is a lot better than strawberries over ice cream, because ricotta isn't sweet and complements the strawberries perfectly. We have successfully served ricotta and strawberries at the most elegant dinner party and for the simplest Sunday night supper.

STUTTGART APPLE RICE

I feel that one of the most important parts of living is to collect good memories. Sometimes these are memories of little unexpected occurrences, moments that stay with you forever after, like something that happened to me in the old town of Freiberg in Germany, at the edge of the famous Black Forest. We had hired a car in Stuttgart to drive to Baden-Baden, that dowager of German health spas, and then on to Colmar in

Alsace-Lorraine, to see the fabulous altarpiece of Mathias Grünewald. So there we were in Freiberg, relaxing at a café across from the beautiful cathedral. Finally, time told us we must leave this friendly, *gemütlich* atmosphere, and we got into our hired Mercedes—but no sooner had we started to drive away than, from across the square, the happiest, lustiest near-inebriate came trotting in front of us, waving his arms high over his head and shouting at the top of his lungs, "Hi, Stuttgarter! Hi, Stuttgarter!" We were completely at a loss as to the cause of this joyous outburst, until it suddenly dawned on me that, since we had hired the car in Stuttgart, it bore Stuttgart-identified license plates. For this brief moment, the license plates had made us that warmest of warm friends, brother townsmen away from home. Now when I write of Stuttgart Apple Rice, there flashes merrily across the screen of my memory the picture of that ruddy, red-faced man and how he spontaneously drew my wife and me into his radiant aura of happy brotherliness.

Makes 10 servings

10 medium cooking apples (firm red ones, not sour greenings)	1 envelope Knox gelatin (or ½ cup red currant jelly)
1 pound washed rice	1 teaspoon vanilla extract
1 pound and ⅔ cup sugar	juice and rind of 1 lemon
4 cups milk	½ cup rum
5 tablespoons raisins	

1. Cook rice in almost all the milk, with ⅔ cup sugar. By the time rice is done, all milk should be absorbed. Do not stir rice while cooking. If mixture becomes too thick, add the rest of the milk. Rice should be tender but not mushy.
2. Add vanilla. While rice is cooling, mix the pound of sugar with 1 quart cold water in a pot large enough to set the 10 apples later. Cook slowly 5 to 10 minutes to make a syrup. Add lemon juice and rind.
3. Peel and core the apples and fill each core with raisins (or chopped brandied fruits, if you have them). Place the apples in the pot of syrup, cover, and cook slowly (below simmering) about 10 minutes, or until just tender. Do not let apples overcook.

4. Remove apples carefully and let cool. Remove lemon rind. Mix the rum into the syrup and mix a cup of this into the rice. Then pour the rice into a wide glass serving bowl and chill.
5. Soften the gelatin in 4 tablespoons of cold water and stir this (or the ½ cup red currant jelly) into the remaining hot syrup until the gelatin or jelly is completely mixed in. Let this cool until the syrup just starts to thicken. Should the mixture set, heat it slightly.
6. Cover the cooled apples with this thickened syrup, re-applying the syrup with a spoon or brush until they are thickly glazed. Place the glazed apples into the chilled bowl of rice. After setting the entire dish on the table, serve each apple with a scoop of rice.

RIZ AUX FRAISES

Earle R. MacAusland, as some of you may know, is the dedicated publisher of *Gourmet* Magazine. We should like to quote the closing paragraph of his Introduction to Volume II of the attractive *Gourmet Cookbook:*

> And now, as always, I wish you bon appetit! This classical salutation, in its various national forms—buon appetito!, guten Appetit!, priyatnyi appetit!, or simply good appetite!—is a hearty wish that all of you will enjoy your food and drink. It is a toast to your health, but also a hope that you will experience all the pleasures—gustatory, esthetic, emotional, and imaginative—that fine food and drink can afford. It is the summation of what *Gourmet* has always stood for.

Makes 4 servings

¼ cup rice	1 cup whipped cream
2 cups milk	1 teaspoon eau-de-vie de
2 teaspoons gelatin	framboise (or use
juice of 1 lemon	raspberry syrup)
2 egg yolks, lightly beaten	2 cups sliced strawberries
1 egg white, stiffly beaten	

1. In a heavy saucepan cook the rice and milk over low heat, stirring constantly, until the mixture comes to a boil.
2. Soften the gelatin in the juice of 1 lemon, dissolve it over hot water, and stir it into the hot rice.
3. Remove the pan from the heat, pour a little of the hot mixture into the lightly beaten yolks of 2 eggs, and add the eggs to the rice.
4. Put the pan in a bowl of crushed ice and stir the cream until it is cold. Carefully fold in the stiffly beaten egg white, whipped cream flavored with eau-de-vie de framboise, and sliced strawberries.
5. Turn the cream into a serving bowl and chill.

The Gourmet Cookbook

MACAROON PUDDING

In Hamburg, Germany, there is the original Hagenbeck Tierpark, which is the model for the modern zoos without bars now in Chicago, New York, San Diego, Cincinnati, and other American cities.

Perhaps it is the animal in us that associates this unrelated fact with so ecstatic a dessert. Hamburg, it just so happens, is the origin of this remarkable recipe, because Mrs. Hennie Hirsch brought it from there. She passed it on to Blanche Small, who added her own touches and then gave it to us. It undoubtedly is one of *The World's Best Recipes*—gorgeous to look at on the platter, beautifully shimmering on one's plate, and a touch of paradise to the palate.

2 dozen plain almond macaroons	5 eggs, separated
3 heaping teaspoons gelatin	½ teaspoon vanilla extract
1 pint milk	½ teaspoon almond extract
1 cup sugar	¼ cup liquor (optional)
salt	2 dozen Maraschino cherries

1. Mix sugar, salt, and gelatin into milk and allow to stand over hot (not boiling) water about 15 minutes. Then stir thoroughly and blend in the beaten egg yolks.
2. Cook over gently boiling water till slightly thickened,

mixing every few minutes. Remove from lower part of double boiler to cool. Add vanilla and almond extract and whatever liquor desired.

3. Then strain into the beaten egg whites and blend.
4. Pour very carefully into a quart pudding mold, which has been lined with the cherries and macaroons. Cherries may be halved before arranging, and macaroons, if double, should be split.
5. Set in refrigerator to chill. The gelatin should form a translucent layer at the bottom, and the custard portion should rise to the top, while the cherries and macaroons remain where they were placed. When unmolded and reversed (and this process does not require hot water, but just a little pressure of the fingers around the edges), the gelatin portion will be on top.
6. After being turned out on serving plate, the pudding can be enhanced with a decoration of whipped cream sprinkled with macaroon crumbs.

BLANCHE D. SMALL

NOODLE PUDDING

½ pound fine noodles
4 eggs, separated
1 cup powdered sugar

2 tablespoons grated
almonds

1. Boil noodles.
2. Beat yolks light with the sugar, add almonds and drained noodles and, lastly, stiffly beaten whites.
3. Pour into a well-greased pudding dish, set in a pan half filled with boiling water, and bake ½ hour.

The Settlement Cook Book
MRS. SIMON KANDER

BAKED INDIAN PUDDING

Makes ½ gallon

1 cup yellow granulated cornmeal	¼ teaspoon salt
½ cup black molasses	¼ teaspoon baking soda
¼ cup granulated sugar	2 eggs
¼ cup lard or butter	1½ quarts hot milk

1. Mix all the ingredients thoroughly with ½ of the hot milk (¾ quart) and bake in very hot oven until it boils.
2. Stir in remaining (¾ quart) hot milk, and bake in slow oven heat for 5 to 7 hours.
3. Bake in stone crock, well greased inside.

The Durgin-Park Restaurant
Boston, Mass.

TIPSY PUDDING

Makes 4 servings

2 eggs	½ cup rum
4 tablespoons sugar	shredded coconut
½ cup flour	

1. Beat the eggs and sugar until creamy. Then lightly stir in the flour.
2. Butter 4 ovenproof custard cups, sprinkle the insides with sugar, and pour in the mixture till each cup is about ¾ full.
3. Bake for 20 minutes in a moderate (325° to 350° F.) oven.
4. Pour an equal amount (about 2 tablespoons) of rum over each serving and garnish with shredded coconut.
5. Cool, then chill in refrigerator.

SWEET POTATO PONE

This is a dessert peculiar to the Deep South, and the ingredients vary according to what the household possesses. I remember the time my friend Moe accepted, somewhat to my distress, an invitation to a family Christmas dinner my first year in Florida. He made no comment as he made his way through the meal that had taken me days to prepare. I said to him, "This is a typical Yankee Christmas dinner. Now tell me, what is a typical Cracker Christmas dinner?" "Whatever we can git, Ma'am," said Moe. "Whatever we can git." Sweet potato pone is made according to whatever we can git.

The must rudimentary sweet potato pone is a thick gelatinous pudding. Small fry among poor blacks and whites consider it a treat of treats. Old colored Martha makes this type by peeling and grating raw sweet potatoes. To two cups of the grated potato she adds two tablespoons of flour, three tablespoons of grease from fried white bacon, one-half teaspoon soda, one cup of Florida cane syrup, and enough water to make a rather thin mixture. This is baked in a shallow pan in a slow oven until set and slightly browned. When Martha has eggs, she adds an egg or two. When she has milk, she uses milk instead of water. When "the chillen" are coming to visit, she uses butter instead of the bacon grease. On these occasions she may have cream to churn, and she chants:

Come, butter, come.
Grandma waitin' for the chillen to come.

From this simple basic recipe, sweet potato pone graduates to an elegant recipe like this.

MARJORIE KINNAN RAWLINGS

2½ cups raw sweet potatoes
   (yams), grated
1 cup molasses
2 eggs
2 cups rich milk
1 tablespoon butter, melted

1 teaspoon ground ginger or
   grated orange rind
1 tablespoon brown sugar
½ teaspoon powdered
   cinnamon

1. Add the molasses, well-beaten eggs, milk, melted butter, and ginger or orange rind, in order, to the grated potatoes.
2. Turn into a well-greased baking pan and bake about 45 minutes in a moderate oven, sprinkling the brown sugar and cinnamon over the top at the end of the first 25 minutes.

Cross Creek Cookery
MARJORIE KINNAN RAWLINGS

FLEMISH WAFFLES

The waffle is generally regarded as a Southern invention, because it is most often served in tearooms as an accompaniment to fried chicken. Actually, the first waffle dates from the time of the Crusades. One October day in the year 1204, Sir Giles Wimple returned from Jerusalem to his country place in Cornwall. It was a Friday, and his good Lady Ermintrude was in the midst of baking cakes when he arrived; but she dropped everything to greet him.

"And now sitte downe and tell me all about ye pilgrimage," said Lady Ermintrude after she had bussed him on both cheeks. "Didst bagge any Saracens, pardee?"

Sir Giles, who was attired in full suit of chain armor, sat down heavily on the settle by the stove. "Ye feete are damme near kyllynge me!" he sighed. "Well, to beginne with . . ." And for the next half-hour he regaled his good lady with an account of his journey to Jerusalem.

"I hadde a hunche thou wolde be back today," said Lady Ermintrude when he had finished, ". . . and did thy favorite oaten cake-y bake."

"Hot dogge!" exclaimed Sir Giles, slapping his mailed thigh. "Fain wolde I eat it now."

Lady Ermintrude glanced into the oven. "I wist not," she began, puzzled. Then she uttered a cry of dismay. "Giles! Methinks 'tis on ye settle."

LOUIS P. DE GOUY

4 cups of flour	½ ounce yeast, dissolved in a little warm water
8 eggs, lightly beaten	
1 cup of cream	½ glass of brandy or cognac
¼ cup of butter	dash of salt
	pinch of sugar

1. In a mixing bowl put 1 cup of the flour and work into it the yeast which has been dissolved in warm water. Blend thoroughly and set aside to rise.
2. Let the cream come to a boil and add the butter, allowing it to melt.
3. To the first mixture add the rest of the flour, the salt and sugar, the beaten eggs, the brandy and the cream and butter. Blend all ingredients well and put in a cool place for about 2½ hours.
4. Pour the batter into a well-greased waffle iron until the iron is ⅔ full.
5. When waffle is brown and crisp, remove from iron, sprinkle with sugar, and serve immediately.

The Gold Cook Book
LOUIS P. DE GOUY

CHERRIES JUBILEE

Makes 6 servings

2 cups of Bing cherries	¼ cup Kirsch
½ teaspoon arrowroot	vanilla ice cream

1. Drain the juice from the cherries into the blazer of a chafing dish and bring to a boil directly over the flame.
2. Dissolve the arrowroot in cold water and stir into the juice to thicken.
3. Heat the cherries through in the sauce.
4. Pour the Kirsch over the cherries and set it ablaze.
5. The flaming cherries can be served alone or over vanilla ice cream.

MYRA WALDO'S CHAMPAGNE MOUSSE

One of the most prolific of cookbook writers is Myra Waldo. From all the vast number of recipes she has created and collected, we have chosen this favorite for our own collection.

Makes 8 to 10 servings

2 envelopes (tablespoons) gelatin	1 cup sugar
¼ cup water	2 cups champagne
8 eggs	1½ cups heavy cream, whipped

1. Soften the gelatin in the water. Separate 5 of the eggs. Put 5 egg yolks and the 3 whole eggs in the top of a double boiler, stir in the sugar, and beat until light and fluffy. Beat in the champagne.
2. Place over hot water and cook, stirring constantly until thickened. Stir in the gelatin until dissolved. Cool.
3. Beat the 5 egg whites until stiff but not dry; fold them into the champagne mixture.
4. Fold in the whipped cream; pour into a 2½-quart soufflé dish or mold and chill until set.

The International Encyclopedia of Cooking
MYRA WALDO

SPUMONI

Makes 10 to 12 servings

OUTSIDE CUSTARD

4 tablespoons cornstarch	1½ cups sugar
4 cups milk	3 tablespoons chopped nutmeats
¼ teaspoon salt	
5 egg yolks	

1. Blend cornstarch in ½ cup cold milk. Combine with balance of milk, salt, egg yolks, and sugar. Beat briskly in deep saucepan. Cook over very low flame, stirring constantly, 10 minutes, or until mixture thickens and comes to a boil. *Do not boil.*
2. Remove from fire immediately; cool. Fold in chopped nuts. Pour into freezing trays of refrigerator. When firm but not hard, transfer to chilled bowl; whip vigorously and place bowl in refrigerator.

CREAM FILLING

1 cup heavy cream
½ cup powdered sugar

3 tablespoons chopped
    candied fruit, mixed
1 ounce bitter chocolate,
    grated

1. Pour cream into chilled deep mixing bowl; whip until frothy. Gradually add powdered sugar; whip until stiff. Combine candied fruit and grated chocolate; fold into whipped cream. Place in refrigerator until ready to use.
2. Prepare molds. If large ice cream or melon-shaped molds are not available, use 10 to 12 individual aluminum covered molds. Chill before using.
3. Remove first mixture (outside custard) from refrigerator. Line individual chilled molds with ¾-inch thickness of this partially frozen custard, packing it in with teaspoon. Leave center of mold hollow. Fill hollow quickly with second mixture (cream filling). Cover with outside custard. Cover molds. If molds have no covers, protect Spumoni by covering with 2 thicknesses of heavy wax paper held in place with elastic or string.
4. Place molds in freezing compartment of refrigerator set at freezing temperature, or pack in ice, for several hours.

NOTE:
As a delightful variation, serve each portion with a dash of apricot brandy or Cointreau.

The Art of Making Italian Desserts
MARIA LO PINTO

BISCUIT TORTONI, DOM PEDRO II

Serves 6

¼ pound sugar
1 teaspoon vanilla
4 egg yolks
1 tablespoon Maraschino
liqueur (or cherry
brandy)
3 tablespoons macaroon
crumbs
1 tablespoon citron, finely
chopped

3 tablespoons pistachio nuts
(or chopped blanched
almonds)
1 pint thick cream
red Maraschino cherries
(or finely chopped
candied orange or
lemon peel)

1. In top of double boiler mix a trifle over ¼ pound sugar with vanilla, and lightly beaten fresh yolks. Stir constantly and, when thick, take off heat and whisk until nice and light.
2. When cool, mix in Maraschino liqueur or cherry brandy and macaroon crumbs—crushed and put through coarse sieve—finally pointing up with fine-chopped citron and the pistachio nuts or chopped blanched almonds.
3. Now mix with a trifle over 1 pint nice thick cream; whisk all gently.
4. Load into paper cases, filling a trifle above edge; or in sherbet glasses of Tortoni size.
5. Put in freezer; when frozen take out; moisten tops with Maraschino or cherry brandy; dip first in a small mound of macaroon crumbs, then crown with a few chopped red Maraschino cherries, or a little fine-chopped candied orange or lemon peel.

The South American Gentleman's Companion
CHARLES H. BAKER, JR.

PHILADELPHIA WONDER ICE CREAM

We have one ice cream recipe which we prefer above all others. According to the definitions of various kinds of ice creams found in various cookbooks, this one should be classified as French. But it came to us in Philadelphia, and Philadelphian we will always consider it. The people of Philadelphia are specialists in the evaluation of ice creams. There are very few Philadelphians who are not connoisseurs of ice cream. The fact of the matter is that Philadelphia could justifiably be considered "The Ice Cream Capital of the World." Only such a capital could have produced our Philadelphia Wonder Ice Cream.

We made it first in vanilla—as you will find it here. But it has stood up masterfully to any other flavoring we've ever tried. We include some of the most successful variations.

It is important to remember two things about this recipe: (1) It is made in a freezer only, and (2) except for vanilla and chocolate, all the other flavorings are added just as the cream begins to stiffen.

MARGARET AND JOHN STORM

3 cups milk, scalded	¼ teaspoon salt
4 egg yolks, slightly beaten	1½ cups heavy cream
¾ cup granulated sugar	1 tablespoon vanilla extract

1. Beat sugar, salt, and egg yolks. Slowly stir in the scalded milk.
2. Pour the entire mixture into the top of a double boiler and cook over water until the mixture coats a wooden spoon.
3. Cool. Strain if necessary. *Do not chill.*
4. Warm cream to the same temperature as the custard. Add vanilla.
5. Freeze in an ice cream freezer, using 3-to-1 mix of ice to rock salt, not table salt. Ice cream should be frozen *slowly* to insure a fine grain.

BUTTER RUM ICE CREAM:

1. Melt 2 tablespoons sweet butter and combine it with 2 tablespoons dark rum.
2. Add to the cream just as it begins to stiffen.

BANANA ICE CREAM:

1. Mash 5 ripe bananas well.
2. Add them to the cream when it begins to stiffen.

BURNT ALMOND ICE CREAM:

1. Use ½ teaspoon almond extract instead of vanilla.
2. Add 1 cup almonds, blanched, toasted, and chopped, to the cream as it begins to stiffen.

CHOCOLATE ICE CREAM:

Melt 5 squares of bitter chocolate with the ¾ cup of granulated sugar and proceed as for the vanilla ice cream.

MARRON ICE CREAM:

Add 1 cup of chopped marrons (chestnuts) with their syrup to the cream as it begins to stiffen.

CRÈME DE MENTHE ICE CREAM:

1. Add 4 drops of green vegetable coloring to the cooled custard.
2. Add ½ cup crushed peppermint candy and 2 ounces of Crème de Menthe to the cream as it begins to stiffen.

PEACH ICE CREAM:

1. Combine 2 cups of crushed peaches and ¾ cup granulated sugar and allow to stand overnight.
2. Add to the cream as it begins to stiffen.
3. Also add 1 tablespoon peach brandy.

PISTACHIO ICE CREAM:

1. Scald ¾ cup of pistachio nuts in the milk. Drain the nuts and set them aside.
2. Add 4 drops of green food coloring to the custard before adding the cream. Omit the vanilla extract.
3. Toss the nuts into the freezing cream when it begins to stiffen.

STRAWBERRY ICE CREAM:

1. Combine 1 cup of crushed strawberries and ½ cup granulated sugar and allow to stand overnight.
2. Add to the cream as it begins to stiffen.

TUTTI FRUTTI ICE CREAM:

1. Marinate ½ cup crushed pineapple (drained), ½ cup crushed peaches, ½ cup crushed raspberries or strawberries, and ½ cup assorted glazed fruits in ½ cup Maraschino liqueur overnight.
2. Add to the cream as it begins to stiffen.

A Treasury of Fine Desserts
MARGARET AND JOHN STORM

TANGERINE SHERBET

Marjorie Kinnan Rawlings writes, in her *Cross Creek Cookery*, "This is a Cross Creek *spécialité de la maison*. Friends cry for it. It is to my winter what mango ice cream is to the summer. It has an extremely exotic flavor and is a gorgeous color. Actually, it is very simple. . . . In the days when black 'Geechee lived with me, it was always her choice for desserts, knowing its popularity. We usually had a crowd and served buffet, and 'Geechee would race through the farmhouse, cap awry, bearing a loaded tray, and shouting at the top of her strong lungs, 'Tangerine sherbet comin' up! Sherbet comin' up.' "

Makes 4 to 6 servings

1 cup sugar	4 cups tangerine juice
1½ cups water	grated rind of 4 tangerines
juice of 1 or 2 lemons	

1. Boil sugar and water 10 minutes.
2. Add the grated tangerine rind to syrup while hot.

3. Let cool slightly and add tangerine juice and lemon juice. Taste for sweetness and acidity, as the tangerines vary.
4. Chill thoroughly, strain, and freeze.

Cross Creek Cookery
MARJORIE KINNAN RAWLINGS

CASSATA

In Sicily there are many tangible evidences of bygone civilizations—Phoenician pots, Greek temples, Roman statuary—but it is also the birthplace of a marvelous twentieth-century dessert—cassata. To sit in a plaza café in Taormina, people-watching, looking out at the sea below, and enjoying a dish of cassata, is indeed a combination worth traveling for. Myra Waldo gives us this home recipe for cassata, which you must begin with the best quality ice cream.

Makes 6 to 8 servings

½ cup candied fruits, chopped   1 pint chocolate ice cream
2 tablespoons Marsala or   ¾ cup heavy cream
   sweet sherry   ¼ cup very fine sugar
1 quart vanilla ice cream   1 egg white, stiffly beaten

1. Combine the fruits and wine; let stand 15 minutes, mixing frequently. Let the ice cream stand at room temperature until soft enough to spread.
2. Dip a large spoon in warm water and spread the vanilla ice cream on the bottom and sides of a 1½-quart round mold. Spread the chocolate ice cream over it, leaving a hollow center, and freeze 30 minutes.
3. Whip the cream; mix in the sugar, then fold in the fruits and the egg white. Fill the center of the mold with the mixture and level off the top with a knife.
4. Cover with a piece of buttered waxed paper and then the cover of the mold or a piece of aluminum foil. Freeze until very firm. Unmold and cut into wedges.

The International Encyclopedia of Cooking
MYRA WALDO

CAFFÈ GRANITA

When Grayce and Rosario Murabito ran the Peacock Cafés—one in Greenwich Village and the other behind old Carnegie Hall—they tried to transplant the casual air of an Italian coffee house to New York. They believed that the atmosphere of, let us say, the Greco Café in Rome—a meeting place for writers, artists, and other creative people—would be popular in America. Apparently, too many Americans are hasty not casual, even about consuming dessert and coffee, since the Peacocks have gone, and so have the Murabitos—back to their castle on the hill near the ancient town of Lucca, Italy. But they have left their recipe for Caffè Granita, which is one of the traditional specialties of Lucca and the neighboring cities of Florence and Pisa.

Caffè Granita is served in a parfait glass, with whipped cream in the bottom of the glass and more on top of the coffee ice, so that you get a little whipped cream with each spoonful of the Granita.

You use a strong demitasse coffee for Granita—one heaping teaspoonful to each demitasse cupful of water. They prepare the coffee in an Italian espresso machine; you can now get these for home use.

You'll make a hit with Caffè Granita at an afternoon or evening party—or if you serve it as an after-dinner dessert.

1. Prepare good strong coffee. Add about 1 teaspoonful of sugar for each cupful of coffee. Freezing heightens the sweetness, so do not be too generous with the sugar.
2. Let the coffee cool, then ice it in refrigerator before freezing in ice cream freezer . . . be sure not to whip it too hard. If you have no freezer, just use the freezing tray of the refrigerator.
3. Don't take the Granita out of your refrigerator until the moment you are ready to serve it. Use chilled glasses, as Granita melts quickly.

GRAYCE AND ROSARIO MURABITO

PRALINES

America is the land of the sweet tooth, with special confections to represent every section: New England wintergreen candies, Atlantic City salt water taffy, apple-flavored Turkish paste from the state of Washington—and many others. But none is more characteristic than the Louisiana praline—and none is so easy to make.

2 cups white sugar	1 teaspoon vanilla
1 cup old-fashioned brown sugar	2 tablespoons butter pecan halves
2 cups cold water	

1. Cook 2 minutes or until threads form. Add butter. Add pecans.
2. Then drop in spoonfuls on wet board or platter or buttered tray or waxed paper.

The New Orleans Cook Book
LENA RICHARD

WINE JELLY

Thomas Jefferson is said to have been the best connoisseur of wines ever to live in the White House. He considered fine wines a necessity of life, and it is therefore no wonder that one of his favorite desserts was wine jelly. At his famous Virginia home of Monticello (which my architect son Roger insists on pronouncing in the Italian manner—Monti-chello), the preparation of this jelly began with the cooking of calves' feet to make the gelatin; but, thanks to Mr. Knox and others, unflavored gelatin is now available in handy packets.

Makes 6 or 8 servings

2 envelopes unflavored gelatin	¾ cup sugar
2 cups strained fruit juice— grape, raspberry, or cranberry	1 pint red wine—Madeira, burgundy, or sherry juice of 3 lemons, strained salt

1. Dissolve gelatin in ½ cup cold water. Bring fruit juice to a boil and add gelatin mix.
2. Add a pinch of salt and the sugar. If your taste says it is tart, add another ¼ cup sugar. Let cool and add the wine and lemon juice.
3. Pour into chilled mold. Set in refrigerator until stiff, about 2 hours. Unmold and serve cold.

BEVERAGES

CAFFÈ CAPPUCCINO

Is there any better aroma in the world than that of hot coffee?
Maybe only that of coffee combined with another spicy aroma,
such as cinnamon.

Makes 2 cups or 5 servings
(3 ounces each plus cream)

3 or 4 tablespoons good
    instant coffee
2 cups boiling water

½ cup whipped cream
cinnamon

1. Dissolve coffee in boiling water. Whip the cream. Place spoonfuls of whipped cream in 5 demitasse cups.
2. Add a dash of cinnamon. Pour hot coffee over cream. Serve with sugar, if desired.

The Coffee Cookbook
WILLIAM I. KAUFMAN

CAFÉ LIÉGEOIS

From the birthplace of some of the world's most exciting pastries, Demel's of Vienna, comes this rich, royal coffee concoction.

Makes 6 servings

1 cup sugar	1 pint heavy cream
8 egg yolks	whipped cream
1 cup very strong black coffee	

1. Mix the sugar with the egg yolks and add the coffee and the cream. Cook over hot water in a double boiler, stirring, until the mixture coats a spoon.
2. Strain through a fine sieve or wet cheesecloth into a large porcelain container and keep stirring (with the container in a pan of ice water) until the mixture is cool.
3. Freeze in the deep freeze or in refrigerator trays. Serve with a spoon from flute-shaped glasses, topped with whipped cream.

Esquire Party Book

REAL IRISH COFFEE

Abraham Lincoln once said that he could tell when he was in New England by the shape of the noses of the sheep— they had to be long and pointed to get between the rocks. In Galway, Ireland, the rocky soil is enough to try the stamina of any man, but the people seem to do it, and they live a hearty, zestful life. The weather may be cold, windy, raw, rainy, but the folks who live there are warm, robust, friendly.

In Galway stands the Great Southern Hotel—one of a chain of Great Southern Hotels—where we once spent a most memorable Saturday night. On the roof is a surprisingly good gourmet restaurant, and in the main ballroom, on the Saturday night we were there, there was a fine program of fun—dancing to bagpipes, singing of old Irish tunes, and other entertainment, which you might call "corny," but which was so good for the soul in this earthy atmosphere.

In Ireland there are many sources of good Irish coffee, but nowhere will you find it better made than at this Great Southern Hotel, and so we present their recipe. The true flavor of this drink is obtained by imbibing the blend of hot coffee and Irish whisky through the cream.

1 ounce Irish whisky
5 ounces freshly made black
   coffee, not too strong
   (The coffee must be
   boiling.)

1 or 2 teaspoons granulated
   sugar
2 ounces fresh chilled
   pouring cream

1. Heat a stemmed Irish coffee glass or whisky goblet over a spirit lamp or with boiling water.
2. Pour in the Irish whisky and set alight.
3. Pour boiling black coffee over flaming whisky. Add granulated sugar and stir well, making sure that the sugar is dissolved and the ingredients well mixed.
4. Add the chilled pouring cream by pouring it into a teaspoon and letting it run down the sides of the glass so that it floats on the surface of the coffee. After adding the cream, serve at once.

Great Southern Hotel
Galway, Ireland

TURKISH COFFEE

Many of the Hilton hotels are too commercial for my taste, but the Hilton Istanbul is a rare exception. It sits high above the Bosphorus, and has a decor befitting its Turkish surroundings. There used to be a cute little girl in a flowing harem costume who served coffee in the lounge, whom I well remember because my young son John couldn't keep his eyes off her. The coffee she served was, in true Turkish style, thick and syrupy and strong, but you can prepare a good imitation with caffein-free Sanka that won't keep you up all night condemning the Turks.

Makes 4 servings

   3 tablespoons Sanka, finest   • 8 lumps sugar
      grind

1. Since you probably do not have a special Turkish coffeepot, an ordinary aluminum coffeepot or, better yet, a small aluminum mug, will do. You will also need very tiny cups, like eggcups. No saucers or spoons.
2. Place 5 eggcupfuls of cold water into the mug or coffeepot. Add the coffee and sugar. Heat slowly and stir well.
3. As this begins to boil and a thick foam appears, give it another couple of stirs and wait for the foam to rise.
4. When the foam sinks, in a moment or two, return the pot to the flame. The foam will soon rise again—watch that it does not boil over: Remove from the heat, let the foam drop, and return. Do this 3 times in all, so that the coffee is well cooked.
5. Pour through small strainer into the tiny cups. A dash of rose essence—available in some drug stores and in Middle Eastern grocery stores—can be added to the coffee, but some people do not care for it. Better serve Turkish paste candy ("Turkish Delight") to give your Turkish coffee an authentic air.

ESPRESSO-TYPE COFFEE

In Italy, and wherever else you find real espresso, a special roast of coffee is brewed in a special coffee maker. But you can easily prepare coffee with a very similar flavor by blending instant and brewed coffee. Use good-quality coffees.

Makes 2 cups, or 6 servings, about 3 ounces each

   2 tablespoons instant coffee   2 cups hot brewed coffee

Dissolve instant coffee in brewed coffee. Serve hot in demitasse cups.

COFFEE NEAPOLITAN:

Prepare Espresso-Type Coffee, then pour 1½ teaspoons cognac in each whisky-sour glass and fill with the hot coffee. Top with sweetened whipped cream and a sprinkle of cinnamon. Serve at once. Makes 4 servings, about 4 ounces each, plus cream.

COFFEE CHOCOLACCINO:

Prepare Espresso-Type Coffee, adding 4½ teaspoons sugar and 4½ teaspoons chocolate syrup. Blend. Serve in demitasse cups topped with sweetened whipped cream and shaved sweet chocolate.

The Coffee Cookbook
WILLIAM I. KAUFMAN

MILK-FRUIT SHRUB

This is a really wholesome, nonalcoholic drink. Good if you are looking for vitamins (vitamin C and A in particular). Good if your throat is a bit scratchy. Good for sipping before bedtime.

Makes 4 to 6 servings

1 cup fresh berries	2 cups milk
1 tablespoon lemon juice	pinch of salt
1 tablespoon honey	sprig of mint

Blend all ingredients. If thinner drink is preferred, add more milk.

The Natural Foods Cookbook

CHURCHILL DOWNS MINT JULEP

Derby Day in Kentucky! To the uninitiated this phrase has little meaning, but lovers of horse racing all over the country thrill at the mention of the words. For the Derby is the most important race of the year. Thousands of visitors pour into Louisville just for this event on the first Saturday of May, the date when the Derby is usually held. Excitement is in the air, a spirit of carnival prevails, all roads into the city are crowded as the vast mob slowly wends its way in the direction of Churchill Downs.

This is the julep you would be served at the famous Louisville race track. A silver julep cup is preferable for making this famous old drink, although it is by no means essential. If you are lucky enough to own such heirlooms, chill the cups thoroughly before mixing the juleps. Glass tumblers may be substituted for silver cups if necessary—they will not frost, however!

MARION W. FLEXNER

Makes 1 serving

1 or 2 ounces Kentucky
  bourbon whiskey
1 tablespoon chopped mint
  leaves
1 tablespoon water

1 teaspoon sugar, or more
  to taste
shaved or crushed ice to
  fill cup
1 small bunch fresh mint
2 straws, cut short

1. Place sugar and chopped mint in a small crockery bowl. Bruise the leaves well with a muddler, or the back of a wooden spoon, until mixture forms a paste. Add water and continue stirring. There should be a thick green syrup by this time.
2. Now you are ready for the whiskey. Fill a julep cup ½ full of crushed or shaved ice. Add the mint syrup and the whiskey. Fill the cup or glass with crushed ice. Slip the bunch of mint into the ice and, beside it, the straws. They should be no taller than the mint.
3. Lift the cups onto a tray, being careful not to touch the sides with the fingers, and put them into the icebox to frost. This will take from ½ to 1 hour.

4. Serve at once. This appears to be a most innocuous concoction, but it has a potent kick, as anyone who has tasted
it for the first time can testify. It should be sipped slowly,
not tossed off at a gulp!

Out of Kentucky Kitchens
MARION W. FLEXNER

CAFÉ BRÛLOT

Makes 6 to 8 servings

1 cup brandy
8 lumps sugar
  peel of 1 orange

4 sticks cinnamon
10 whole cloves
3 cups strong, fresh coffee

1. Behind the scenes: Peel the orange into 1 long thin ribbon.
2. Make the coffee by your favorite method. Heat the bowl
   of the chafing dish with hot water just before serving.
3. Before the guests: Place the peel, cinnamon, cloves, and
   6 lumps of sugar in the bowl and pour in the brandy. Dip
   up some brandy in the ladle. Drop in the 2 remaining
   lumps of sugar and ignite.
4. Ladle and pour back the flaming liquid, scooping up the
   peel and sugar so that they also burn.
5. Slowly and carefully add coffee and, as the flame flickers
   out, ladle the café into demitasse cups.

NOTE:

Variation: For Café Diablo, use even amounts of coffee and
brandy, omit the cinnamon, and add the thinly sliced peel of
lemon. Proceed as above.

The Chafing Dish Cookbook
JOHN AND MARIE ROBERSON

ORANGE BRÛLOT

Café Brûlot may be familiar to you, but have you tasted Orange Brûlot, served in the Napoleon Patio of Broussard's notable restaurant in New Orleans?*

Makes 1 serving

1 orange, thin-skinned brandy	1 lump sugar

Cut through the skin all around the circumference of the orange, taking care not to cut into the pulp. With the handle of a teaspoon, turn the skin back until it forms a cup. Do this at both ends and you'll have a peeled orange, with a cup of skin at each end, like an hourglass. Place 1 cup on a plate, pour some brandy in the upper cup, put a lump of sugar in the brandy, light it, and as it burns, stir gently. When the flame dies, drink it. The flavor of the burned brandy, sugar, and orange peel is great.

Esquire Party Book

BLOODY MARY

The name "Bloody Mary" is enough to make one cringe, but, as it's served by such experts as the bartenders of Brennan's in New Orleans or the Delegates' Lounge of the United Nations in New York, this drink can be a potent pick-me-up. To make it, first assemble all the ingredients so that you can work quickly. The drink must be peppery, pungent, and thick. And it must never be served on the rocks.

---

* Other specialties created by Joseph Broussard are Chicken en Papilotte, Shrimp Remoulade, and Crêpes Suzette Soufflé.

Makes 1 serving

½ jigger fresh lemon juice
2 jiggers vodka
½ teaspoon salt
    several grinds of pepper
      from the peppermill
2 dashes Tabasco sauce
4 dashes Lea & Perrins
    Worcestershire Sauce

1 teaspoon onion juice
1 heaping teaspoon horse-
    radish, grated
4 ounces thick tomato juice
    (Lucky Boy or Sacra-
    mento), well chilled

1. Pre-chill the shaker. Measure out ½ jigger of fresh lemon juice.
2. Put this, the vodka, and ice into the shaker.
3. Add salt and pepper, Tabasco and Worcestershire sauces, and onion juice.
4. Squeeze the liquid from the grated horseradish and add.
5. Finally, add the tomato juice.
6. Shake hard.

PLANTER'S PUNCH

There used to be a place on St. Thomas in the Virgin Islands called the Pirate's Den, or some such name, and they served a version of a Planter's Punch guaranteed to make you want to walk the plank to perdition. But that was overdoing it. . . . A good Planter's Punch is a "gentleman's drink," aimed to cool and refresh—effective but not after-effective.

Makes 1 serving

2 to 3 ounces light cream
1 ounce lime juice
1 to 2 ounces grenadine syrup
2 or 3 dashes Angostura
    Bitters

crushed ice
club soda
1 sprig fresh mint
1 slice lime
1 stick fresh pineapple

1. Combine rum, lime juice, grenadine, and bitters.
2. Pour over crushed ice in tall glass. Fill with club soda. Stir briskly to give the glass a frosting.

3. Garnish the top of the glass with the slice of lime; set in the sprig of mint and the stick of pineapple.

TONGA

From the Pacific to the Atlantic, and overseas too, wherever there is a Trader Vic's (or one of his imitations), you can enjoy the giant cocktails and over-oversize drinks made with that rarest of ingredients, Imagination. The Tonga is one of Trader Vic's more popular numbers.

Makes 1 serving

1½ ounces fresh orange juice	dash of grenadine
¾ ounce fresh lemon juice	dash of Jamaica rum
juice of 1 lime	½ cup shaved ice
2½ ounces light rum	fruits for decoration
¼ ounce Curaçao	

1. Mix all ingredients in a blender.
2. Serve in 14-ounce glass, decorated with fruits.

COLD DUCK

Look out for this one! The first time I drank it, I was with a party of four, and not one of us could remember afterward where we had parked our cars. It is a concoction originated in Germany, and there it is called *Kalte Ente,* which translates as "Cold Duck." I don't know why they call it that—perhaps because it was first served with cold duck— more likely because it can lay you out like a cold duck. It's a good drink, worth trying. When you pour the wines, the Moselle and the champagne, do it dramatically, holding a bottle in each hand and pouring them simultaneously.

2 bottles Moselle wine, well chilled	ice to fill a glass punch bowl
1 bottle dry champagne, well chilled	2 tablespoons lemon juice
	3 tablespoons powdered sugar
	2 long lengths lemon peel

1. Chill the punch bowl and set a small chunk of ice in it, if you have one, building up a mound of ice cubes to surround it. Dissolve the sugar in the lemon juice and pour it over the ice. Rub the spirals of lemon peel over the inside of the bowl and then leave them in the bowl.
2. Pour the wines over this mound of ice, pouring the Moselle more slowly than the champagne to make the 2 bottles of Moselle come out even with the 1 bottle of champagne.
3. Let stand for a few minutes and serve straight or with an ice cube in each punch cup.

MULLED WINE

Traditionally, in the days of fireplaces and heavy pokers, mulled wine was mixed in a jug and heated by plunging a red-hot poker into it. A modern method is to make it at the table in a chafing dish or a suitable electric appliance. For the teenage crowd, substitute cider for wine and sweeten to taste.

Makes about 12 servings

1 quart Burgundy or claret yellow peels of 1 orange and 1 lemon	1 whole nutmeg, crushed
	6 whole cloves
2 to 3 inches of stick cinnamon	1 tablespoon sugar

1. Mix all ingredients in a saucepan and simmer gently 5 to 10 minutes.
2. Strain to remove spices and serve hot.

HOLIDAY EGGNOG

Makes about 25 servings

6 eggs, separated	2 teaspoons vanilla
½ cup sugar	nutmeg
½ cup Jamaica rum	3 cups heavy cream
1 pint brandy, rye, or bourbon	1 pint milk

1. Beat egg yolks well, adding sugar gradually.
2. Add rum while beating, then brandy, rye, or bourbon.
3. Add vanilla and a pinch of nutmeg. Chill several hours, adding cream and milk from time to time and stirring.
4. Beat egg whites until stiff. Fold half into mixture. Add 3 tablespoons more sugar to remaining egg whites and beat until very stiff. Spread on top of eggnog and swirl. Sprinkle with nutmeg.

The New York Times Magazine
RUTH P. CASA-EMELLOS

BOERENJONGENS COCKTAIL

This is a traditional Dutch drink served during the Christmas season.

Makes 1¾ quarts

1 pound raisins	2 cups sugar
2 cups water	2 cups brandy or whiskey
1 cinnamon stick	

1. Cook raisins, water, and cinnamon sticks for about 20 minutes. Add sugar and brandy and cook until dissolved.
2. Fill sterilized container with the mixture.
3. Seal tightly and let stand for at least 3 months for the best results.

HETE BISSCHOP
(HOT CLARET CUP)

In the Netherlands, this drink is designed especially for New Year's Eve.

15 cloves	1 cup sugar
1 orange	1 stick cinnamon
1 lemon	2 bottles red wine

1. Stick the cloves in the orange and the lemon. Dissolve the sugar in 2 cups hot water and add all these ingredients, with the cinnamon, to the wine.
2. Put over a very slow fire for about ½ hour and strain.

GLÖGG
(TRADITIONAL SWEDISH CHRISTMAS DRINK)

Makes about 6 servings

2 cups red wine (Burgundy or claret)	1 cinnamon stock (or 2 teaspoons powdered cinnamon)
2 cups port wine	5 cloves
1 tablespoon orange or lemon peel, finely chopped	¼ pound blanched almonds
	¼ pound seedless raisins
5 cardamom seeds	¼ pound cube sugar
	2 cups brandy

1. A large copper kettle is the proper utensil for preparing *Glögg*, but a large enamel or glass saucepan may be used. Combine the red wine and port in the saucepan over low heat.
2. Take piece of cheesecloth about 4 inches square and place in the center the orange peel, cardamom seeds, cinnamon, and cloves. Tie or sew the cheesecloth together securely and place it in the wine mixture. Simmer for 20 minutes.

3. Add the almonds and raisins and simmer for 10 minutes. Remove from the heat and discard the cheesecloth.
4. Place the cubes of sugar in a metal strainer and rest it on top of the saucepan if possible. Set the brandy aflame and pour it very gradually over the sugar. If there is any difficulty in lighting the brandy, warm it briefly. As the lighted brandy is poured over the sugar, it will caramelize. (As an alternative, ½ cup granulated sugar may be dissolved in the wine, and the brandy set aflame and poured into the wine.)
5. Serve hot in mugs.

The Complete Round-The-World Cookbook
MYRA WALDO

ACKNOWLEDGMENTS

This book, the first wide-scale recipe anthology, is made possible by the cooperation of many highly skilled culinary specialists. We thank the authors and publishers of the following books for permission to use original copyrighted recipes and other material, identified on this and the succeeding pages:

ABELARD-SCHUMAN, INC..
  The Hamburger Cook Book, by Esther K. Schwartz and Ruth Kooperman
ARLINGTON BOOKS (LONDON)
  The I Hate to Cook Book, by Peg Bracken
BANTAM BOOKS (LONDON)
  The Art of Jewish Cooking, by Jennie Grossinger
M. BARROWS & CO., INC.
  The California Cook Book, by Genevieve Callahan
  Cooking With a Foreign Flavor, by Florence La Ganke Harris
  Cook It in a Casserole, by Florence Brobeck
  Egg Cookery, by Lily Haxworth Wallace
  500 Recipes by Request, by Jeanne M. Hall and Belle Anderson Ebner
  I Wanted to Write, by Kenneth Roberts, copyright 1949
  Kitchens Near and Far, by Herman Smith
  Martha Deane's Cooking for Compliments, by Marion Young Taylor
  Secrets of New England Cooking, by Ella Shannon Bowles and Dorothy S. Towle
  Trending Into Maine, by Kenneth Roberts, copyright 1938
ANN BATCHELDER
  Ann Batchelder's Cookbook
THE BOBBS-MERRILL COMPANY, INC.
  The New Joy of Cooking, by Irma S. Rombauer and Marion Rombauer Becker, copyright 1931, 1953
CURTIS BROWN, LTD. (LONDON)
  A Cookbook for Poor Poets, by Ann Rogers
CIMA PUBLISHING COMPANY, INC.
  The State Fair Cook Book, by Lois J. Hurley and Isabelle J. Groetzinger
COLLINS-KNOWLTON-WING, INC. (LONDON)
  The Art of Fruit Cookery, by Stella Standard
  The German Cookbook, by Mimi Sheraton
WILLIAM COLLINS SONS & CO., LTD. (LONDON)
  Michael Field's Cooking School, by Michael Field
CONSOLIDATED BOOK PUBLISHERS
  United States Regional Cook Book, by Ruth Berolzheimer

COWLES MAGAZINES, INC.
Look Magazine, copyright 1952

THOMAS Y. CROWELL COMPANY
Delicious Seafood Recipes, by Louis Garrison, copyright 1953, by Louis Garrison, reprinted by permission of the publisher
The Electric Epicure's Cookbook, by Poppy Cannon, copyright © 1961, by Poppy Cannon, reprinted by permission of the publisher
100 Summer and Winter Soups, by Ann Roe Robbins, copyright 1943, by Ann Roe Robbins, reprinted by permission of the publisher

ANDRÉ DEUTSCH, LIMITED, PUBLISHERS (LONDON)
The Seducer's Cookbook, by Mimi Sheraton

CROWN PUBLISHERS, INC.
The Escoffier Cook Book, by A. Escoffier, copyright 1941
Jewish Cookery, by Leah W. Leonard, copyright 1949
The South American Gentleman's Companion, by Charles H. Baker, Jr., copyright 1951
The Talisman Italian Cook Book, by Ada Boni, copyright 1950
Viennese Cooking, by O. and A. Hess, copyright 1952

CURTIS PUBLISHING COMPANY
Holiday Magazine, "See You at Dave's," copyright 1951

THE JOHN DAY COMPANY, INC.
How to Cook and Eat in Chinese, by Buwei Yang Chao
Whole Grain Cookery, by Stella Standard

D. C. DIVRY, INC.
Greek Cookery, by Nicholas Tselementes

DODD, MEAD & CO.
Stars in Your Kitchen, by Marta Michel, copyright 1953

DOUBLEDAY & CO., INC.
Amy Vanderbilt's Complete Cookbook, by Amy Vanderbilt, copyright © 1961, by Amy Vanderbilt
The Art of Fish Cookery, by Milo Miloradovich, copyright 1949
The Art of Fruit Cookery, by Stella Standard, copyright © 1964, by Stella Standard
The Art of Hungarian Cooking, by Paula Pogany Bennett and Velma R. Clark, copyright 1954
The Art of Italian Cooking, by Maria Lo Pinto, copyright 1948
The Art of Making Italian Desserts, by Maria Lo Pinto, copyright 1952
The Art of Making Soufflés, by Frederica L. Beinert, copyright © 1967, by Frederica L. Beinert
The Coffee Cookbook, by William I. Kaufman, copyright © 1964, by William I. Kaufman
The Complete Book of Desserts, by Ann Seranne, copyright 1952, © 1963, by Ann Seranne
The Complete Round-The-World Cookbook, by Myra Waldo, copyright 1954
Good Maine Food, by Marjorie Mosser, copyright 1939, 1947
The Home Book of French Cookery, by Germaine Carter, copyright 1950

Luchow's German Cookbook, by Leonard Jan Mitchell, copyright 1952
DUELL, SLOAN & PEARCE, INC.
How to Cook a Wolf, by M. F. K. Fisher, copyright 1942, 1951
E. P. DUTTON & CO., INC.
When We Were Very Young, by A. A. Milne, copyright 1924
Winnie-the-Pooh, by A. A. Milne, copyright 1926
ESQUIRE, INC.
Esquire Party Book, copyright © 1965, by Esquire, Inc., reprinted by permission of the publisher
FABER AND FABER, LTD. (LONDON)
The Art of Making Soufflés, by Frederica L. Beinert
The Complete Book of Desserts, by Ann Seranne
The Home Book of French Cookery, by Germaine Carter
LESLIE FREWIN PUBLISHERS, LIMITED (LONDON)
The Cheese Book, by Vivienne Marquis and Patricia Haskell
FUNK & WAGNALLS CO.
The Emily Post Cookbook, by Emily Post, copyright 1951
BERNARD GEIS ASSOCIATES
Cooking with Love and Paprika, by Joseph Pasternak, copyright © 1966, by Joseph Pasternak, reprinted by permission of the publisher
VICTOR GOLLANCZ, LTD. (LONDON)
Blue Trout and Black Truffles, by Joseph Wechsberg
GOURMET BOOKS, INC.
The Gourmet Cookbook, copyright © 1957, reprinted by permission of the publisher
GREENBERG: PUBLISHERS
The Gold Cook Book, by Louis P. de Gouy
GROSSMAN PUBLISHERS, INC.
La Cuisine de France, by Mapie, Countess de Toulouse-Lautrec, copyright © 1964, by the Orion Press, Inc., reprinted by permission of the publisher
HAMMOND, HAMMOND & COMPANY, LTD. (LONDON)
Cross Creek Cookery, by Marjorie Kinnan Rawlings
French Cooking for the Home, by Louis Diat, published in America under the title *French Cooking for Americans*
Luchow's German Cookbook, by Leonard Jan Mitchell
HARCOURT, BRACE & WORLD, INC.
The I Hate to Cook Book, by Peg Bracken, copyright © 1960, by Peg Bracken, reprinted by permission of the publisher
HARPER & ROW, PUBLISHERS
The Alice B. Toklas Cook Book, by Alice B. Toklas, copyright 1954, by Alice B. Toklas, reprinted by permission of the publisher
The New York Times Cook Book, by Craig Claiborne, copyright © 1961, by Craig Claiborne, reprinted by permission of the publisher
The New York Times Menu Cook Book, by Craig Claiborne, copyright © 1966, by Craig Claiborne, reprinted by permission of the publisher

HASTINGS HOUSE, PUBLISHERS, INC.
Clementine in the Kitchen, by Phineas Beck (Samuel Chamberlain)

HAWTHORN BOOKS, INC.
A Salute to Cheese, by Betty Wason, copyright © 1966, by Betty Wason, reprinted by permission of the publisher
The Beer Cookbook, by Berneita Tolson and Edith McCaig, copyright © 1968, by Berneita Tolson and Edith McCaig, reprinted by permission of the publisher
The Complete Book of Pickles and Relishes, by Leonard L. Levinson, copyright © 1965, by Leonard L. Levinson, reprinted by permission of the publisher
The Outdoor Picture Cookbook, by Bob Jones
Peter Hunt's Cape Cod Cookbook

THE HEARST CORPORATION
The Good Housekeeping Cook Book, copyright © 1963, by The Hearst Corporation, reprinted by permission of the publisher

HERMITAGE PRESS
Holiday Book of Food and Drink

DUNCAN HINES
Adventures in Good Cooking, by Duncan Hines

HOLT, RINEHART AND WINSTON, INC.
Cooking in a Castle, by William I. Kaufman, copyright © 1965, by William I. Kaufman, reprinted by permission of the publisher

HORIZON PRESS, INC.
The Book of Mediterranean Food, by Elizabeth David
French Country Cooking, by Elizabeth David

HOUGHTON MIFFLIN CO.
Helen Corbitt's Cookbook, by Helen L. Corbitt, copyright © 1957, by Helen L. Corbitt, reprinted by permission of the publisher
The New Orleans Cook Book, by Lena Richard

ALFRED A. KNOPF, INC.
A Romantic in Spain, by Theophile Gautier, translated from the French by Catherine Alison Phillips, copyright 1926, by Alfred A. Knopf, Inc., reprinted by permission of the publisher
Blue Trout and Black Truffles, by Joseph Wechsberg, copyright 1953, by Joseph Wechsberg, reprinted by permission of the publisher
The Perfect Hostess Cook Book, by Mildred O. Knopf, copyright 1950, by Mildred O. Knopf, reprinted by permission of the publisher

CHARLES PARNELL LEAHY
The Spanish-Mexican Cook Book, by Don Carlos

JOHN LEHMANN LIMITED (LONDON)
The Book of Mediterranean Food, by Elizabeth David
French Country Cooking, by Elizabeth David
The New York Cookbook, by Maria Lo Pinto
The Viennese Cookbook, by Irma Rhode

J. B. LIPPINCOTT CO.
French Cooking for Americans, by Louis Diat, copyright 1946, by Louis Diat

LITTLE, BROWN & CO.

André L. Simon's French Cook Book, revised by Crosby Gaige, copyright 1938, 1948

The Cordon Bleu Cook Book, by Dione Lucas, copyright 1947

Delectable Desserts, by Ann Seranne, copyright 1952

400 Salads, by Florence A. Cowles and Florence La Ganke Harris, copyright 1944

Herbs for the Kitchen, by Irma Goodrich Mazza, copyright 1939

James Beard's Fish Cookery, by James A. Beard, copyright 1954

The New Fannie Farmer Boston Cooking-School Cook Book, 9th Edition, revised by Wilma Lord Perkins, copyright 1951

The Toll House Cook Book, by Ruth Wakefield, copyright 1930, 1936, 1937, 1938, 1940, 1948, 1953

THE MACMILLAN COMPANY

Antoinette Pope School Cookbook, by Antoinette and François Pope, copyright © 1960

Cook at Home in Chinese, by Henry Low

International Encyclopedia of Cookery, by Myra Waldo, copyright © 1967, by Myra Waldo, reprinted by permission of the publisher

MCGRAW-HILL BOOK CO.

Country Flavor, by Haydn Pearson

MCINTOSH AND OTIS, INC. (LONDON)

The Electric Epicure's Cookbook, by Poppy Cannon

WILLIAM MORROW & COMPANY, INC., PUBLISHERS

Michael Field's Cooking School, by Michael Field, copyright © 1965, by Michael Field, reprinted by permission of the publisher

THE NEW YORK TIMES

Recipes by Ruth P. Casa-Emellos and others

NORWEGIAN NEWS COMPANY

Cook Book of Norwegian Recipes

OXFORD UNIVERSITY PRESS, INC.

Tante Marie's French Pastry, by Charlotte Turgeon

PETER PAUPER PRESS

Recipes Mother Used to Make, by Edna Beilenson

POCKET BOOKS, INC.

Martha Logan's Meat Cook Book, by Beth Bailey McLean and Thora Hegstad Campbell

POLANIE PUBLISHING CO.

Treasured Polish Recipes for Americans

PRENTICE-HALL, INC.

The Casserole Cookbook, by John and Marie Roberson

The Chafing Dish Cookbook, by John and Marie Roberson

The Complete Barbecue Book, by John and Marie Roberson

G. P. PUTNAM'S SONS

The Continental Cook Book, by Josephine Bonne

RAND MCNALLY & CO.

Oriental Cookbook, by Alice Miller Mitchell

RANDOM HOUSE, INC.
The Art of Jewish Cooking, by Jennie Grossinger, copyright ©
1958
The Food of France, by Waverley Root, copyright © 1958, by
Waverley Root, reprinted by permission of Alfred A. Knopf,
Inc.
The German Cookbook, by Mimi Sheraton, copyright © 1965,
by Mimi Sheraton
McCall's Cookbook, copyright © 1963, by The McCall Corpo-
ration
The Seducer's Cookbook, by Mimi Sheraton, copyright © 1963,
by Mimi Sheraton
HENRY REGNERY CO.
The Dorn Cookbook, by General Frank Dorn
ST. JOHANNES CONGREGATION (SEATTLE, WASH.)
From Danish Kitchens
JOHN SCHAFFNER, LITERARY AGENT (LONDON)
The Art of Fine Baking, by Paula Peck
The Art of Good Cooking, by Paula Peck
The New York Times Cookbook, by Craig Claiborne
RHINEHART & COMPANY, INC.
The Best I Ever Ate, by Sophie Kerr and June Platt
The Rural New Yorker Magazine
CHARLES SCRIBNER'S SONS
A Cookbook for Poor Poets, by Ann Rogers, copyright © 1966,
by Ann Rogers
Cross Creek Cookery, by Marjorie Kinnan Rawlings, copyright
1942, by Marjorie Kinnan Rawlings, reprinted by permission of
the publisher
SIMON & SCHUSTER, INC.
The Art of Fine Baking, by Paula Peck, copyright © 1961, by
Paula Peck, reprinted by permission of the publisher
The Art of Good Cooking, by Paula Peck, copyright © 1961,
1966, by Paula Peck, reprinted by permission of the publisher
The Betty Furness Westinghouse Cook Book, by Betty Furness
and Julia Kiene
The Cheese Book, by Vivienne Marquis and Patricia Haskell,
copyright © 1964, 1965, by Vivienne Marquis and Patricia
Haskell, reprinted by permission of the publisher
The Fireside Cook Book, by James A. Beard
The Maxwell House Coffee Cookbook, copyright © 1964, re-
printed by permission of Pocket Books, a division of Simon
& Schuster, Inc.
The Natural Foods Cookbook, by Beatrice Trum Hunter, copy-
right © 1961, by Beatrice Trum Hunter, reprinted by per-
mission of the publisher
The Settlement Cook Book, by Mrs. Simon Kander
Soup!, by Evelyn Gendel, copyright © 1967, by Evelyn Gendel,
reprinted by permission of the publisher
A Treasury of Fine Desserts, by Margaret and John Storm
THE SOCIETY OF AUTHORS (LONDON)
Trending Into Maine, by Kenneth Roberts

462 ACKNOWLEDGMENTS

HELENA STRASSOVA (LONDON)
 La Cuisine de France, by Mapie, Countess de Toulouse-Lautrec
LYLE STUART, INC.
 10 Minute Gourmet Cookbook, by Yvonne Tarr, copyright ©
 1965, by Yvonne Tarr, reprinted by permission of the pub-
 lisher
THE UNIVERSITY OF NORTH CAROLINA PRESS
 The Southern Cook Book, by Marion Brown
THE VIKING PRESS, INC.
 Casserole Cookery, by Marian and Nino Tracy, copyright 1941,
 by Marian and Nino Tracy, reprinted by permission of the
 publisher
 The Christmas Cookbook, by Zella Boutell, copyright 1953, by
 Zella Boutell, reprinted by permission of the publisher
 Stella Standard's Menus and Recipes for All Occasions, copy-
 right 1953, by Stella Standard, reprinted by permission of
 the publisher
 You Can Cook if You Can Read, by Muriel and Cortland Fitz-
 simmons, copyright 1946, by Muriel and Cortland Fitzsimmons,
 reprinted by permission of the publisher
WARD LOCK & CO., LTD. (LONDON)
 The Art of Italian Cooking, by Maria Lo Pinto
WATER GATE INN, WASHINGTON, D.C.
 New Hobby Horse Cookery, by Flora G. Orr, copyright 1953
FRANKLIN WATTS, INC.
 Out of Kentucky Kitchens, by Marion W. Flexner
THE JOHN C. WINSTON CO.
 The Mennonite Community Cookbook, by Mary Emma Showalter
WILLIAM H. WISE & SON
 Recipes of All Nations, by Countess Morphy, copyright 1935
THE WOMEN'S REPUBLICAN CLUB
 Massachusetts Cooking Rules Old and New
THE WORLD PUBLISHING CO.
 Cocktails and Snacks, by Robert and Ann London
A. A. WYN, INC.
 The Cheese Cook Book, by Marye Dahnke
 The New York Cookbook, by Maria Lo Pinto
 The Smörgåsbord Cookbook, by Anna Olsson Coombs
 Sultan's Pleasure, by Robin Howe and Pauline Espir
 The Texas Cookbook, by Arthur and Bobbie Coleman
 The Viennese Cookbook, by Irma Rhode
To Irma S. Hyams, thanks for valuable assistance

INDEX